BY JONATHAN DANIELS

Clash of Angels
A Southerner Discovers the South
A Southerner Discovers New England
Tar Heels: A Portrait of North Carolina
Frontier on the Potomac
The Man of Independence
The End of Innocence
The Forest Is the Future
Prince of Carpetbaggers
Stonewall Jackson
Mosby—The Gray Ghost of the Confederacy
Robert E. Lee
October Recollections
The Devil's Backbone: The Story of the Natchez Trace
They Will Be Heard
The Time Between the Wars
Washington Quadrille

Washington Quadrille

JONATHAN DANIELS

Washington Quadrille

THE DANCE BESIDE

THE DOCUMENTS

Doubleday & Company, Inc.

Garden City, New York

1968

Excerpts from *Affectionately, F. D. R.* by James Roosevelt and Sidney Shalett. Reprinted by permission of Harcourt, Brace & World, Inc.

Excerpts from *This Is My Story* by Eleanor Roosevelt. Copyright, 1937, by Anna Eleanor Roosevelt; renewed 1965 by Franklin Roosevelt, Jr. and John Roosevelt. Reprinted by permission of Harper & Row, Publishers.

Excerpts from *Letters of Henry Adams* edited by Worthington Chauncey Ford. Reprinted by permission of Houghton Mifflin Company.

Excerpts from *FDR: His Personal Letters*, Vols. I & II, edited by Elliott Roosevelt. Vol. I copyright, 1947 by Elliott Roosevelt; Vol. II copyright, 1948, by Elliott Roosevelt. Reprinted by permission of Duell, Sloan & Pearce.

Excerpts from *Crowded Hours* by Alice R. Longworth. Reprinted by permission of Charles Scribner's Sons.

FOR

CONTENTS

Washington
Quadrille

APPARITION AS PROLOGUE

Alone or with those who were always eager for her company Sallie Carroll, a golden-haired horsewoman, cantered along the old roads of the District of Columbia. Those tree-lined lanes would in her lifetime become avenues extended from the national city design of Pierre Charles L'Enfant who had resigned in a quarrel with her landholding great-grandfather. She was a beauty who in grim Civil War times brought gleams to the eyes of soldiers, statesmen, even a President. She waltzed in Vienna as the wife of a count. She lived long enough in opulent charm not only to become one of the first women cigarette smokers in Washington ("My dear, it's my only vice!"), but also she survived to see her world, which ran—or danced—from the Potomac to the Danube, engulfed in world war.

Yet save for dazzling, once anger-brightened, glimpses she is forgotten in the story of the women who behind politicians, statesmen, journalists, diplomats made the drama of the national city of the Republic. Certainly she could never be included in the barbed description of the city given to Theodore Roosevelt by the witty wife of Justice Oliver Wendell Holmes: Washington is a city of famous men and the women they married when they were young.[1]

As a person of nothing more than high lineage, great beauty and much charm, she is, of course, less well remembered than Dolley Todd, the widowed daughter of a Philadelphia boarding-house keeper, who was introduced to the thin-faced James Madison by Aaron Burr. Naturally her folk looked down on the inn-keeper's daughter, Peggy, who married Mr. Eaton, Andrew Jackson's Secretary of War, and nearly disrupted that administration. Sarah Virginia Carroll, born in 1840, was still one of those ladies who is generally less noticed by the historians than are the orators and politicians. Despite the historians, Washington is not merely a monumented seat of government but a place of life, of loves and jealousies, disappointments and delights. It has been too much written about by solemn men sitting in the galleries of history unwilling or unable to join the company by whom history in heartbreak or hilarity, sometimes both close together, has been made.

Sallie Carroll may be taken either as a symbol or as a delicious figure in a succession. She was tall, young, lovely and twenty-one on December 10, 1861. To her wedding at this time in the splendid house of her father, William T. Carroll, then urbane clerk of the U. S. Supreme Court, came a company including Abraham Lincoln and his plump, brunette, often authoritarian wife. Though the disastrous Battle of Bull Run had been fought five months before, it was a gay occasion. The *New York Herald* declared the wedding was "one of the most brilliant assemblages ever witnessed in Washington." There were fourteen groomsmen and bridesmaids. Lincoln's secretary John George Nicolay wrote his own fiancée that more people had been invited than the house could possibly hold: "You may imagine that there was a great jam and that hoops suffered."

Sallie's groom, Charles Griffin, a West Point graduate from Ohio, had been promoted to captain for his own creditable role in the Bull Run rout. His commander, General George Brinton McClellan, came for the ceremony along with others in brilliant uniforms. The nuptial festivities went on for two nights after the wedding. Said Nicolay, "The lady evidently intends that her wedding shall be pleasurably remembered by herself and friends."[2] Love in wartime involved partings. While the war went on and Griffin fought ably but sometimes with irascible criticism of his superiors, Sallie for the most part remained a decorative bride in Washington.

Two months after her marriage she was so described in all her charms by Frank Leslie's *Illustrated Weekly*.[3] The occasion had been intended to be a ball at the White House on February 5, 1862. *Leslie's* gave to the event the attention its roving artists and reporters were giving to military movements. Rebellion across the river was one story. Some continuing revelry in Washington was another. But in the White House this night festivity was only a staircase distance from mourning.[4]

Lincoln had wanted to call off the ball. His boy, Willie Lincoln, had come down with a cold and fever after a ride in a chilly rain on his pony. Evidently he was desperately ill. But five hundred "distinguished, beautiful and brilliant" people representing "intellect, attainment, position and elegance" had, as *Leslie's* reported, been invited. Lincoln ordered that there be no dancing. But as one observer wrote, "the Marine band at the foot of the steps filled the house with music while the boy lay dying above."

Still, if the ball was "a ghastly failure," as one guest wrote, the music was loud and lively. It went on. Yet, another person remembered that "a sadder face than that of the President I have rarely seen." Lincoln spoke his fears about his boy to General John C. Frémont, whose vivid wife Jessie Benton Frémont had confronted him in her bitterness over the military treatment of her husband not many weeks before. But ceremony, White House grandeur, the presence of the powerful was what people generally saw.[5]

Leslie's in an issue soon afterwards provided sketches and descriptions of the costumes of Mrs. Lincoln and nine other ladies. Mary Todd Lincoln was often extravagant about her clothes. Gossips found much to criticize about her display in wartime. That and other charges must have been combined when she was strangely accompanied on a hat-shopping expedition to Washington stores by the elder Theodore Roosevelt.[6] Nothing in history suggests this Roosevelt was an expert on ladies' hats. But in this wartime his brother-in-law was the naval agent of the Confederate Government in Europe. Many defenders of the Union could not dismiss the fact that Mrs. Lincoln's brother-in-law was a Confederate general. Like the ball, this shopping couple only indicated the strange combinations which occur in Washington in war and peace. The picture drawn so sharply could actually have been out of focus. Mrs. Lincoln arrayed for her levee may have been a woman distraught and not merely elegantly displayed. Evidently in her forties with a sick child upstairs she did not shine as some others present did. *Leslie's* paid her deference but saw with delight some other women at the ball.

Sallie Griffin was, of course, among them. Another included was also a Carroll beauty. *Leslie's* raved: "Miss Carroll, a charming blonde of the purest type, wore a dress of white illusion, with a succession of puffs almost reaching the waist. The effect was very fine, and harmonized admirably with her delicate aerial style of beauty." The weekly magazine saved its place in prestige for Sallie: "Mrs. Griffin was simply but tastefully attired in a corn-colored silk; headdress of bright crimson flowers. She was observed of all, as she leaned on the arm of the President."

Though she was possibly as harassed as the President, Mrs. Lincoln was observing. Her watching was a constant, disturbed, incomprehensible matter. It was marked on other occasions, but not so pointedly by both music and the difficult breathing of a dying boy. Elizabeth Keckley, Mrs. Lincoln's mulatto seamstress and trusted companion, wrote of her feminine surveillance of the President. Once as Lincoln was pulling his white gloves on his big hands just before escorting his wife to a reception downstairs, he teased her about the handsome ladies to whom he might show attention. She flared in fury. He must not talk with "Miss C."[7]

But Sallie Carroll Griffin communicated with him, sometimes in great distress, seeking his favor. From her residence at the corner of F and 18th Streets she wrote the President in the dark month of July 1863, soon after her father had died and when her baby was dying, begging that he telegraph General McClellan to grant Griffin "an *immediate leave* of absence of fifteen days." She had learned, she said, "from various & most direct sources that no movements of importance are to occur for the next month in the army before Richmond." Shortly afterward she wrote him in "utter distress," importuning Lincoln to give Griffin "a station out of the field at least for a few months."

"You have been my friend in my happy days," she wrote, "may I not expect it in this hour of gloom & sadness? . . . Please don't let my request be fruitless, it is one of charity, & mercy."[8]

General Griffin himself, whose health Sallie said at the time was "greatly impaired," turned for aid to Fannie Eames as a power in Washington society.[9] Wife of Charles Eames, international lawyer and diplomat, Mrs. Eames dispensed a hospitality which in Nicolay's opinion brought together "the most interesting class of people that come to Washington." Mrs. Lincoln was her friend. Julia Ward Howe was her houseguest. Journalists wrote of her drawing rooms, "celebrated for their brilliant gatherings."[10] She wrote directly to Lincoln urging the leave as "almost a *necessity*" and stating that she knew "that when it is *possible* you are always ready to do an act of kindness."[11]

Sallie recovered from her depression. But it was a supposed act of kindness to her by the President which at the close of the war brought Mrs. Lincoln's jealousy about her and other ladies, too, to public explosion. Colonel Adam Badeau, General Grant's military secretary, described this outburst which occurred at a time when no tragedy seemed near but triumph evidently was at hand.[12] Badeau had been assigned to escort Mrs. Lincoln and Mrs. Grant on an excursion to the front in Virginia in March 1865. This was an incident on a trip which had begun with some evidence of marital unease in the White House.[13]

Lincoln was burdened then with concerns about swift military victory and the also less certain possibility of a peace of "malice toward none; with charity for all" which he had outlined in his recent second inaugural address. Furthermore, not only duty but a desire to get away from the tensions and pressures of Washington shaped his plans. He proposed to go down the Potomac, to meet Grant at his headquarters at City Point, on a small speedy dispatch boat, the *Bat*.

Orders, however, were changed. The President met the officer summoned about the change with cordiality but, as that young man put it, "with a kind of embarrassment, and a look of sadness which rather embarrassed me." He got his orders from Mrs. Lincoln: "I am going with the President to City Point, and I want you to arrange your ship to take me, my maid and my officer, as well as the President." A larger vessel was required. And, while the generals gathered in council, including Sherman from farther south, Mrs. Lincoln in her tragic fashion made history at City Point, too.

Two days after they arrived on March 24, it was deemed safe for the party to make a trip to the front of the Army of the Potomac, about ten miles away. On the last part of the journey, while others rode horseback, Mrs. Lincoln and Mrs. Grant were escorted by Colonel Badeau in an "ambulance" like a half-open carriage. Making conversation as they rode, the colonel wrote that he "chanced to mention" that a sure sign of impending operations was that all the wives of officers at the front had been ordered to the rear. Not a lady was to remain, he said, except the wife of General Charles Griffin, "who had obtained a special permit from the President."

Mrs. Lincoln stiffened.

"What do you mean by that, sir?"

Furious, she did not wait for an answer: "Do you mean to say that she saw the President alone? Do you know that I never allow the President to see any woman alone?"

Poor Badeau smiled to conceal his shock.

"That's a very equivocal smile, sir," Mary Todd Lincoln exclaimed. "Let me out of this carriage at once. I will ask the President if he saw that woman alone."

Much distressed, Mrs. Grant, who knew Sallie Carroll, finally persuaded Mrs. Lincoln to wait until the whole party assembled. Then General George Gordon Meade, whose strategy had prevailed at Gettysburg, calmed the President's lady. He told her that Mrs. Griffin's permit had been granted, not by the President, but by the Secretary of War. Though quieted, Mrs. Lincoln's bitterness was not ended. At a dinner for Grant and all assembled leaders on the President's steamer, she loudly insulted another general's wife. On the score of visiting ladies, Badeau wrote, she attacked Lincoln "like a tigress." All present were distressed. Lincoln was gentle, soothing but hurt. He stayed with his commanders, visited Richmond. Only on Palm Sunday, April 9, the day of Lee's surrender, did the party return to Washington.

There seemed no room in the city for anything but "gladness of heart" as the President put it. And on April 11, at the climax of celebration, to a crowd before the White House, the President gave his victory speech by candlelight. It was more an intellectual argument for his high purposes than an oration to meet the excitement of his audience. The speech, said the *New York Tribune*, "fell dead, wholly without effect on the audience." The crowd dispersed. Lights went out in the White House windows. The portico stood in darkness. It was a façade which solemnly concealed something less than complete "gladness of heart" within.

Three nights later Mrs. Lincoln planned a theater party. She invited General and Mrs. Grant to join the President and herself at Ford's Theater to see Laura Keene in *Our American Cousin*. But Julia Grant, according to Badeau, was still so distressed by the spectacle Mrs. Lincoln had made in Virginia that she made excuses for her husband and herself. They were far away when assassination occurred.

Sallie Carroll and her general were naturally invited to no Presidential parties now, including this fateful one on Good Friday, April 14. In the fine Carroll house near the theater where the Lincolns had attended her marriage, she may have been still resentful of Mrs. Lincoln's anger. War and glory were lost in angers and dispersal. General Griffin, with his war rank down to colonel, was ordered to the command of the military district of Texas. There when yellow fever broke out in Galveston, he refused to leave his post and died of the disease in September 1867.[14]

Sallie was a decorative widow of twenty-seven no longer described at receptions on the arm of the President. But she met and married Austrian Count Maximilian Ernest Maria Esterhazy, "of the first branch of the second line" as compendiums of

European aristocracy said. Evidently as a result of her marriage came also the wedding on April 13, 1887, of Agnes Carroll of Carrollton and Doughoregan Manor in Maryland to Count Anton Alexander Otto Heussenstamm of a well-known *gräfliche haus* in Austria. Sallie had already become a widow again at that time, though only forty-three.[15] Yet she kept both her Austrian and her Washington ties.

Edith Benham Helm, who was to become the social secretary to the wives of two Presidents, as a girl of the 1890s remembered the Countess Esterhazy at an exclusive ladies' club at 1710 Eye Street. This club and its cotillions, she said, constituted "the last stand of the Aborigines"—or the "cave dwellers" of old Washington society who regarded even many of the most famous of the recurring officials and their families as little more than transients. Mrs. Helm, after her service to Edith Wilson and Eleanor Roosevelt, wrote of those earlier times: "I can see now the row of ladies forming at the reception committee, most of them in dresses of daring décolletage showing as far as the collarbone. One exception to this list was the Countess Esterhazy, née Carroll. She was a very charming person with a lovely voice and must have been a great beauty when young."[16] These Austrian Carrolls remembered their American cousins. The two pretty daughters of the Countess Sallie's nephew Carroll Mercer, after he came on hard times, were educated at a convent in the picturesquely beautiful town of Melk on the Danube near their estates.[17]

Apparently age could not wither nor custom stale the Countess Sallie. In 1912 when she was seventy-two, an American gossip wrote that Carroll Mercer "in all probability will inherit something from his Aunt Sallie, the Countess Esterhazy, provided she does not lavish everything she possesses on her young admirers."[18] She was safe from gossip and jealousies only after she died on October 16, 1917, at Belgrave Mansions, Grosvenor Gardens S.W., in London. A Requiem Mass for her was held in Westminster Cathedral.

Mrs. Lincoln then was long dead. Her jealousies in history

might be better directed at the legend of Ann Rutledge than at the lively Sallie Carroll. Certainly the irrationality of all her furies was suggested by the mental instability which became more apparent after the assassination. After wandering through clouded years in America and abroad she died in the summer of 1882 in Springfield whence she and her husband had come to greatness and stress. Not Mary Todd Lincoln but Ann Rutledge received the poet's epitaph, "Beloved in life of Abraham Lincoln, / Wedded to him, not through union, / But through separation."[19]

Sallie Carroll now is only a wraith who once had looked like an angel.

ONE

"Where Society Amuses"

(1)

Henry Adams settled in Washington as an exuberant optimist in 1877. Then the old overgrown village was just escaping from the vulgarities of the gilded age under Grant and the shoddiness which made it a caricature of L'Enfant's dream. Still in his physical prime, possessed of plenty of the world's goods, a charming wife and a mounting reputation as a historian, there was no sign then that the diminutive Bostonian (five feet four inches tall) would become the capital's sardonic chronicler. He had escaped the Harvard environs where he had unhappily taught and which he described as "a social desert that would have starved a polar bear." Now he was certain that in Washington he had discovered "the only place in America where society amuses me."[1]

Almost ecstatically he wrote from his house at 1501 H Street to an English friend, "One of these days this will be a very great city if nothing happens to it. Even now it is a beautiful one, and its situation is superb. As I belong to the class of people who have great faith in this country and who believe that in another century it will be saying in its turn the last word of civilisation, I enjoy the expectation of the coming day, and try to imagine that I am myself, with my fellow *gelehrte* here, the first faint rays of that great light which is to dazzle and set the world on fire here-after."

He retreated a little from such almost apocalyptic enthusiasm: "Our duties are perhaps only those of twinkling, and many people here, like little Alice, wonder what we're at. But twinkle for twinkle, I prefer our kind to that of the small politician. . . ."[2]

His wife, Marian Hooper, called Clover, who John Hay said was to preside over an unequaled salon, put the matter more simply after they had been in Washington longer.

"Life is like a prolonged circus here—I grudge my night's rest."[3]

They had hardly arrived in the big house they took before Mrs. Rutherford B. Hayes sent cut flowers to them from the White House across Lafayette Square. They went to call on the President and Mrs. Hayes and sat in Hadley rocking chairs before a blazing wood fire which, Clover felt, almost made pleasant the upholstered barracks which the nation provided as executive mansion. But they quickly found a livelier and more crowded social life than that in the cold water, temperance-keeping White House of Lucy Hayes. Clover wrote on a February day: "This coming week is pretty full, a dinner at L. P. Morton's Wednesday, at the Bancrofts' Thursday, at the Schurzes' Saturday, despite evening toots if one is energetic. Lunches I despise and I lie myself out of. Fine sleighing, brilliant sun, clear cold. History goes on quietly. We barricade our doors till near sunset and are envied by our harnessed friends."[4]

They found other hosts and guests besides "Money Bags" Morton, then a Congressman from a Fifth Avenue district; the brilliant German-born Secretary of the Interior, Carl Schurz; and the venerable historian and diplomat, George Bancroft, whose lively daughter Suzanne was to marry another of the ubiquitous Carrolls and become mistress of Doughoregan Manor in Maryland. Henry and Clover twinkled in their own house which became a luminous center frequented by a witty, distinguished company. Its tight core was composed of the Adamses, the John Hays, and Clarence King. Someone named them "the Five of Hearts." Already famous and married to a Cleveland heiress, Hay had not yet written in collaboration with Nicolay the first, great life of Abraham Lincoln. Still poet and journalist, he was far away from the fatal fatigue which was to overcome him as diplomat and Secretary of State. King, a supposed bachelor, was prodigal with his great gifts as geologist, explorer, mountain climber, writer. Perhaps coming and going to and from the Adams house between exciting and sometimes frustrating excursions, he was most of all insatiable wanderer. But laughter remained for his prodigious puns when he was far away.

The Adams house was a place to be discovered with delight; welcome to it was a mark of distinction. Young Cecil Spring-Rice, as a secretary in the British legation, so described it in an American society which he generally found too often marked by "the whisky, the poker, the stock market conversation, the opulent wives and the drunken sons."[5] None accepted in it minded the undersized chairs which Adams had had made to fit his own small figure. Society at the Adams house twinkled and flashed.

Clover Adams had known Washington almost as long as her husband. As a boy he had first visited the sprawling and cluttered capital where his grandfather and great-grandfather had been Presidents. Then to his New England nose its Southern atmosphere was both repellent and intoxicating.[6] Clover brought bright perceptive eyes to the city. In letters before and after her marriage she described exciting moments with a vividness unsurpassed in her husband's historical and philosophical prose. She rushed to Washington on irresistible impulse in 1865 to see in both elation and tears the Grand Parade of the Union armies on the Avenue filled with sunshine, flags, roaring crowds and the tramp of soldiers' feet. She wrote home also of Ford's Theater where Lincoln had been shot and of the blood-marked pillow on which he died in the house across the street. She attended and reported the trial of those charged with conspiracy in the assassination. Only the eyes of Mary E. Surratt could be seen above her fan. Another of the accused was "handsome but utterly brutal." Clover's mood was to convict and hang.[7]

After she and Adams began to twinkle on H Street she wrote

similar descriptions of the trial of the murderer of Garfield: an "accursed beast" arrogant even in the midst of the trial that would send him to the gallows. But she wrote of less dramatic events, some merry, some sad. Occasionally she was sharp. Of Levi P. Morton, leaving to become Minister to France, she said, we will "not miss him nor his liveried flunkies, he's such a snob." And again: "I have asked Henry James *not* to bring his friend Oscar Wilde when he comes." But her heart was free if her standards were stern.[8]

The Adamses were very fond of and much amused by the popular, young Turkish Minister, Grégoire Aristarchi Bey, whose conversation was delightful, perhaps most so when his English was quaint. When anything appealed to him as a real hit he cried, "That's wealthy!" They were saddened—and Adams tried to find a place for him—when he was recalled by his country and had come to love Washington so much he did not want to go home. Clover wrote tenderly about the young illegitimate daughter of British Minister Lionel Sackville-West by a lovely Spanish dancer. Despite some lifted eyebrows, the girl had come to preside as hostess for her father at Queen Victoria's big brick legation. Clover wrote of many others: of Emily Beale who in Adams' later view, was to become as Mrs. John R. McLean the "reigning empress" of Washington society; of a Miss Mercer who dropped out before one of the picnics she and Adams enjoyed.

Most sympathetically she wrote of Elizabeth Sherman Cameron, niece of Statesman John Sherman and General William Tecumseh Sherman. In 1878, when hardly twenty, she became the second wife of Senator James Donald Cameron, rich, powerful, Pennsylvania politician twice her age. Such a social historian as Mrs. Burton Harrison, watching Mrs. Cameron serve tea at the Hays', called her "a lovely creature."[9] In 1882, Clover as the young woman's neighbor on Lafayette Square wrote of her with concern: "Mrs. Don Cameron came home yesterday from a six weeks' illness in New York. I'm going to see the poor little woman now; she's drawn a blank on Don, I fear, and for all his money and fine house, and she's not over twenty-three—a mere baby."[10]

There was more in Mrs. Adams' letters about Mrs. Cameron: "She is very young, pretty and, I fear, bored, and her middle aged Senator is fighting a boss fight in Harrisburg; so she came in Friday, wailed about Harrisburg; and was quite frank in her remarks about men and things. Poor 'Don' will think she has fallen among thieves when he comes back."[11] Some larceny did seem possible.

Yet few things seemed sad then around the Adams and Cameron houses on the square. There was no slightest question about Washington as the place of their preference. In 1880, the Adamses moved a little way to 1607 H Street, the famous old Corcoran House, which had been occupied by Daniel Webster who gave it up because it was too expensive. William W. Corcoran, who bought it and whose name it bore, was the son of a shoe merchant in Georgetown. Far from reticent about his father's trade, Corcoran liked to remember a witticism about him by his friend William T. Carroll, Carroll Mercer's grandfather. Asked whether he knew the elder Mr. Corcoran, Carroll replied, "I have known him from first to *last* and from *last* to first."[12] William Corcoran, whose philanthropies extended from art to the care of genteel old ladies and the education of young women in the Convent of the Visitation, could enjoy such a reference to his shoe merchant background. As a banker, who almost lost the house because of Confederate sympathies, he always wore gloves, carried a gold-headed cane and kept a fresh red rose in his buttonhole to the end of his days. Later when the house became the home of W. W. Corcoran's aristocratic, country gentleman grandson William Corcoran Eustis it was a favorite visiting place of Franklin Roosevelt. "Willie" Eustis, as he was called, had married Edith, one of Levi P. Morton's pretty daughters, who grew up at her father's estate near the Hyde Park residence of the James Roosevelts.

Corcoran elaborately remodeled the house in 1880 for the Adamses. While they waited for its completion, they collected furnishings for it in London and Paris. Meantime they made their residence at Wormley's Hotel at the corner of H and 15th Streets.

Though it was owned and operated by a Negro, William Worm-ley, historians report that for more than two decades it was "the temporary home of nationally and internationally famous men and its parlors were the scene of many distinguished social gather-ings."[13] Afterward Mrs. Adams borrowed servants from Worm-ley's when her own were ailing.

The house more than twinkled when it was furnished. Clover wrote her father of the admiration it had received. "Mrs. Bancroft said the other day, 'My dear, I dislike auctions very much, but I mean to go to yours after you die.'"[14] That was a merry compli-ment. The wife of the venerable historian had been married be-fore Clover was born. Still this rented house did not suffice. Adams, using a word which seemed stranger in his vocabulary than *gelehrte*, wrote in May 1884 that he and Hay had bought a "swell piece of land" at the corner of H and 16th Streets on which, with the square and the White House before their windows, they would build their twin houses.

They chose as architect Henry Hobson Richardson, whose work set an architectural fashion between 1880 and the Chicago World's Fair of 1893. Richardson had recently built a house in Washington for an Adams friend, General Nicholas Longworth Anderson. Clover and other Washingtonians were of divided opinions about it. "It is emphatically a gentleman's house," she wrote, "and the lines are very fine; it is very stern and severe as a whole."[15] She took a photograph of it and General Anderson was aware of the "fun" she and her husband had with his archi-tect troubles. Among other things the chimney of Anderson's big house did not draw properly.

Still Hay and Adams also turned to Richardson. Anderson felt revenged for the Adamses' fun at his expense. Their houses, he wrote, "do not meet public expectation and are ranked after ours" but "their exteriors will be of unusual magnificence and beauty, and corresponding costs. . . ."[16] Yet Adams wrote to Hay that in comparison with houses being built in Boston "ours look like cottages." And to this letter he added a final paragraph about Clover's father: "Poor Dr. Hooper died a week ago of heart disease, and we buried him on Thursday. My wife was with him for the last month."[17]

The joint house grew as the summer and autumn passed. Richardson's dark red brick house of Romanesque residential design, as Hay's biographer, Tyler Dennett, suggested, carried the intimation of a well-guarded and discriminating hospitality. But its windows, he said, let in too little light and provided a line of vision over the heads of passersby and even above the White House across the square. In contrast to the other houses around the park there was about it "less openness, and just a trace of scorn for Southern, or Western traditions."[18] It was apparent that the houses were for "people who were not accustomed to unpack their troubles, or their hearts, in public."

Impatiently Adams watched the double house grow. In November 1885 he wrote to the absent Hay that it was "calm as the Pyramids." Evidently he went to see it again a month later on Sunday, December 6, 1885, on one of his regular small-man-strutting constitutionals. The hour he left home is variously reported. Writing in the *New England Quarterly* long afterward, Katharine Simonds said that he took his stroll in the morning "when all believers were safe in church."[19] But Adams' neighbor, General Anderson, stated that Henry and Clover had breakfasted at noon, after which she went to her room.[20]

He went on in a letter to his son, Larz Anderson, at Harvard: "At two a lady called to see her, and Henry went to her room and found her, as he supposed, in a swoon before the fire. He placed her on a lounge and summoned a physician who said she had been dead an hour. I called as soon as I heard it, and offered to do all that I could, but Henry refused to see anyone. I appreciate his state of mind, but I am sorry he would not let me show my sympathy by my acts. Until his family arrived he saw, as far as I can learn, no one whatever, and I can imagine nothing more ghastly than that lonely vigil in the house with his dead wife. Poor fellow! I do not know what he can do."

Adams, indeed, moved into such a withdrawal that he did not even summon his closest friend, Hay, who was out-of-town but not too far away to come. Hay seemed bewildered by the failure to call him.[21] Other close friends were shut out. The little historian destroyed most of his diaries. Soon he went almost in flight from his new house to Japan with his friend John La Farge, painter, worker in stained glass, and writer. But before they departed La Farge helped him plan a monument to Clover which seemed almost to put a mark of mystery above her body. Augustus St. Gaudens was commissioned to do the inscrutable, hooded figure which, on a stone platform by Stanford White, stands in Rock Creek Cemetery. Adams devoted space in his autobiographical *The Education of Henry Adams* to a proud passage about the monument. But in the *Education* he put not one word about the woman who had loved him.

His grief seemed as hooded as the figure. He rarely mentioned her in the many long letters he wrote about everything else. He carried reticence to the point of a design as mysterious as the monument. Friends and relatives, even historians with docility accommodated themselves to his role of silence which seemed almost like one of concealment. His insistent silence before the fact of Clover's death gave the impression of a sense of fault if not of guilt. Such inarticulateness in loss was not generally characteristic of Henry Adams. In his *Education* he wrote an almost clinical study of Hay's decline and death. When a young man whom he dearly loved, George Cabot ("Bay") Lodge, poet son of his friend Senator Henry Cabot Lodge, died suddenly in promise and youth, Adams tenderly wrote the story of his life.

But for Clover and her death he seemed to will an eternal closed door. Her own sparkling letters were not published until half a century after her burial and the circumstances of her death were not mentioned in that volume. Allen Johnson, editor of *The Dictionary of American Biography*, wrote in that authoritative work only and blandly that she "had suffered ill health" and "died suddenly under peculiarly tragic circumstances." James Truslow Adams, not a member of the famous family, in his book about it wrote at least in euphemism that she had "been in poor health. . . . There was an over-dose of a drug."[22] History seemed much obscured around Lafayette Square. Thirty years after Clarence King, that other of the Five of Hearts, died, *The Dictionary of American Biography* stated flatly, "He never married." Actually he was married to a Negro woman who presumably was never in the Adamses' salon.[23] No wonder that fifty years after Clover died Katharine Simonds should write of the necessity "to prevent the mole-hill of fact from becoming a mountain of myth."[24] The truth is that reticence always cries for revelation.

The physical facts are not hard to find. Clover's death certificate, filled out by Dr. Charles E. Haynes and Coroner D. C. Patterson, stated that she died of "heart paralysis" induced by an "over-dose of cyanide of potassium" which was "self-administered." That was not, as James Truslow Adams suggested, a drug for "poor health." It is, of course, a deadly poison. It was available to her in connection with her hobby of amateur photography in which Adams had encouraged her. Cyanide was readily available then for use in "fixing" photographs to prevent their darkening or disappearance. Some had warned of its dangers. Said the magazine *Philadelphia Photographer* in 1882, "to be sure it is a virulent poison . . ." but "because a careless operator is killed by it occasionally is no better reason for excluding it from the studio than it would be to condemn the use of fire because people are sometimes burned to death."[25]

The causes of Clover's desperate act are not so clear. Mental and emotional post-mortems came quickly. She had been, it was said, worn out nursing her father and was broken by his loss. Actually she had been with him only the last month of his life. She shared the watching at his bedside with three others of the family. And during that time she arranged a dancing class for younger members of the family in the house of her sister next door.[26] Dr. Hooper's death at seventy-five, nearly eight months before her own, could not have been unexpected. Undoubtedly she shared some of Adams' concerns about the cost and slow completion of the new house. They had plenty of money and time. Undoubtedly at forty-two, childlessly facing change of life, her anxieties could have become psychiatric.

Some pious probers of the mystery suggested that her lack of religious faith preyed on her mind: her death was "a lesson of what a little way intellect and cultivation and the best things of this life go when you come to the heart of life and death." Moreover, one who remembered her generous youth said balefully after her death that as she grew older she acquired "a reputation for saying bitter things and of unsparingly using her powers of sarcasm whenever an opportunity presented itself. She was feared rather than loved."[27]

Whatever drove Clover to her wish to die was in her own heart and mind. Adams seemed almost her victim. The steady suggestion of her insanity carried with it the implication that he had been warned. General Anderson had written a month before her suicide that "Mrs. Adams is suffering from nervous prostration."[28] But in the context of his letter that could clearly have meant no more than the more colloquial expression that Mrs. Adams is "going crazy" over architectural troubles. Her death, he wrote, was "a great shock" to him. If there had been warning possibly it had grown thin in familiarity. A "confidential source" gave Harold Dean Cater, in preparing the 1947 collection of then still unpublished Adams letters, information about early warnings. Even when the Adamses were in Egypt on their year-long honeymoon in 1872, while Adams was taking photographs of antiquities Clover suffered a kind of nervous collapse. This was brought on, it was said, "by boredom from the sun, the flat landscape and the unpredictable winds."[29]

No man was ever more tenderly protected in his grief than Adams. Sometimes he appeared in his house to his towering fellow Bostonian, Justice Oliver Wendell Holmes, like a man "posing as an old Cardinal and turning everything to dust and ashes."[30] Far more people were awed by him. He made his costly monument to Clover a place where he liked to go and enjoy the speculations of gaping American tourists, who, of course, he wrote in his *Education*, could not possibly understand its meaning which would be clear to an Asian boy.[31] He did the work for which he was best remembered after her death. He obviously enjoyed the life he so sardonically mocked. He played with the chaos of worlds which he predicted like a juggler sure of his skill and his audience's credulity.

Nothing is so clear as this zest for life and ideas in his many letters to the lovely Elizabeth Cameron which, in publication, he directed should "precede all else."[32] In the thirty years of his life after Clover's death Adams gave Mrs. Cameron his first affection. Also he found room in his *Education* for a fulsome tribute to her husband who could not have been more different from Adams if he had been designed by God for that purpose. As Adams' niece, Abigail Adams Homan, wrote, the taciturn, hard-riding Cameron, if he read such a tribute, would have suspected it: he "mistrusted profoundly . . . Uncle Henry's philosophical whimsical musings."[33]

Mrs. Cameron was steadily showered with such whimsies, often ironic, in a lifelong correspondence. To her he wrote with unadorned candor. He spoke best for Clover, for himself, and for history when, in a rare outburst more than a quarter of a century after the suicide, he cried, "Those years 1880–85, were my last of life, when I loved and hated, and the world was real."[34]

(2)

Not all found ominous portents or nervous tensions in Egypt. Some brought home only the memory of a camel ride. Larz Anderson, the son of Adams' watchful neighbor, declared himself to be at first unimpressed by the pryamids.[35] Others, who were to be popular in the rich variety of Washington society, came to the end of a passionate procession across Europe to the flat, sunburned land of unpredictable winds. Like the Adamses they had had what amounted to a year-long—or almost a year-long—honeymoon. But Minnie (or Minna as she preferred later) and Carroll

Mercer were disturbed by no such introspection or New England rigidities as marked the Adamses even when they seemed most gay in a salon twinkling with wit. Possibly the only similarities between them was that both were patrician couples who recognized Washington as the American place where society amused them. Certainly Minnie and Carroll Mercer were little concerned with such profundities as the power and fate of nations about which Henry and John Hay were as usual corresponding not quite two years after Clover Adams died.

Hay in gossipy fashion told Adams, in 1887, that he had just escaped from "that jubilating and tiresome town" of London where he had attended Victoria's first jubilee. The pomp and power displayed and particularly the British self-esteem had been hard for him to bear.[36]

Beyond marching men of every kind and tribe, experts in Her Majesty's Kingdom were parading English superiority particularly, it seemed to Hay, over the United States. They proclaimed that the United States possessed not a single modern battleship. Americans were hardly in a position to deny that. Indeed, two years earlier in 1885, Cleveland's rich and vigorous Secretary of the Navy, William C. Whitney, had stated in his official report that "the United States has no vessel of war which could have kept the seas for one week as against any first-rate naval power."[37]

Hay was relieved in the country-estate hospitality of Andrew Carnegie who was in a position to decline any British condescension. That creative steel magnate, though Scotch-born, had in a book the year before, impertinently as it seemed to some, ridiculed Britain's imperial pretensions, made some sharp remarks about the British Royal Family, and given a glowing account of American progress. The book opened even the eyes of some in the United States which in two years would surpass the United Kingdom in steel production.

Carnegie's arguments were not fortified by any mounting power America was showing in the world's ports. Its strength, indeed, was almost made ridiculous by the arrival in England in 1886, the year the steel man wrote, of the U. S. Corvette *Quinnebaugh*

(216 feet long, 1900 tons displacement). This wooden, twin-screw gunboat had been commissioned twenty years before, just too late to participate in the far-flung naval operations of the Union in the Civil War. Apparently she had been built so badly that extensive and costly repairs were required four years later. She was practically rebuilt, with her white oak frame changed to live oak. A pair of Isherwood engines were added. The changes gave her greater beam, displacement, and speed. Still, in the picture of her preserved by the Navy Department, she carried three masts for auxiliary sailing power above her single stack.[38] Lying off Gravesend she was, said the American *Army and Navy Journal*, "the first American man-of-war that has anchored in the Thames for about eight years." The service paper added:

"The rarity of visits from American and European men-of-war to British ports is explained by a member of the American Legation to be owing to the number of desertions which occur from the Service, our treaties with Great Britain not allowing us to reclaim deserters as we can on the Continent."[39]

This first visit of a U.S. man-of-war to England in eight years was not to be the *Quinnebaugh's* last. She may not have given an awesome impression of American sea power but sailing in European waters from London to Constantinople and Alexandria she was to become a romantic vessel for Carroll Mercer as ardent Marine and for Minnie as decorative ship follower.

By all accounts Mercer, in Washington, had been a gay blade with an old name. Minnie became later a best witness of his charm. When she first met him in Washington in 1883, she wrote he was "a man a fraction of an inch over six feet in height, of fair complexion, with blond hair and greyish eyes and approximately 200 pounds in weight."[40] Obviously her report was not merely for purposes of identification. He had other attractions beyond his physical appearance.

Both a Carroll and a Mercer had been members of the Continental Congress. Carroll Mercer's mother, Violetta Lansdale Carroll, had married Dr. Thomas Swann Mercer of Cedar Park, "a noble estate built in Colonial times"[41] near West River, Maryland. A tribute paid to Dr. Mercer after his death declared he was "no ordinary character. Beginning life in luxurious ease and elegance, and closing it by years of toil in uncongenial work, the contrast brought out the full nobility of his nature, reflecting the character of the old Scotch nobles from whom he was descended."[42] Dr. Mercer died suddenly and obviously in declined fortunes even if, as the tribute said, his virtues as a Christian gentleman matched the family motto: Non Nobis Solum. So Carroll Mercer, born in Washington in 1857, faced no life of luxurious ease. His membership in the Society of the Cincinnati was not assurance of subsistence. But he had relatives and friends in the small but socially close-knit armed services of the time. So at twenty-three, six years before he arrived in the Thames on the Quinnebaugh, he got his commission in the Marines. He served ashore and at sea. His service was not entirely serene. On June 24, 1885, by sentence of a general court-martial he had been suspended on half pay for two years. On an expedition to the Isthmus of Panama he had been too drunk for duty on his ship en route from "Matachin to Aspinwall." Then after pledging himself to "abstain from the use etc., did dishonorably violate said pledge and become drunk and unfit for duty."[43] In a charitable Navy, however the suspension was lifted on July 28, 1886. A year later he was assigned to the Quinnebaugh on the European station. Before he sailed, however, he had met in Washington and become engaged to Minnie.

She was a young woman whose beauty attracted attention even on the Washington scene when Carroll met her in 1883,[44] during the administration of the widower President Chester A. Arthur. Born in Norfolk, Virginia, on June 18, 1863, she took wealth from her father, John Tunis, who had amassed a fortune in real estate, and an aristocratic heritage from her mother, Caroline Elizabeth —or Earl—Henderson, member of one of the most distinguished families in North Carolina.[45] She was remembered long afterward in Norfolk as a vision of dark beauty moving in a victoria about the town from her family's red brick house with iron filigree balconies at the corner of Freemason and Granby Streets. From many beaux she chose, not wisely as it turned out, a young Englishman, Percy Norcop. With her father's death, apparently when she was twenty, she came into her fortune, an estate which required the attention of lawyers in Norfolk, Boston, and North Carolina. Her life was tangled, too. In June 1886, she secured a divorce on the grounds of Norcop's adultery.[46] She had already met Mercer then.

It seems doubtful that Minnie ever wore any weeds for her marital misfortune. She went, however, for sanctuary to North Carolina. Later she was a resident of Lincolnton, North Carolina, where her relatives the Hokes lived. The head of that family was Robert F. Hoke, Confederate Major General whom North Carolinians liked to think was "Lee's best general."[47] His son, William A. Hoke, later Chief Justice of the North Carolina Supreme Court, became her lawyer and the chief manager of her estate. His plain, good, naïve sister, Sallie, became her companion and the chief historian of her romantic peregrinations.[48] Lincolnton, obviously, was inadequate to her exuberance. By the time Minnie was twenty-five she had a house in Washington at 1744 P Street near Dupont Circle. Hokes and Hendersons visited her there and reported on the high style in which she lived as a gay grass widow.

"Minnie's house is so rich and beautiful that it strikes everyone who comes in," her guest and house companion Nan Hoke wrote home. Its rooms were often filled with prominent people, most of them Southerners: a Hoke cousin, huge, war-crippled Congressman W. H. Forney of Alabama; a Henderson cousin, Congressman John Steele Henderson of North Carolina; Samuel Phillips, a brilliant North Carolinian who had not lost his home social position when he abandoned state political chances by turning Republican and became Solicitor General in Grant's administration; Senator Zebulon B. Vance of North Carolina. Mrs. Vance arranged a visit for Minnie and friends with young Mrs. Grover Cleveland. One visitor at Minnie's house, "Mr. Stevenson of the P.O. Dept. Nan's boss" was Adlai Ewing Stevenson of Illinois, who was to become Cleveland's Vice-President in his second term. Then he was engaged in firing thousands of Republican 4th class postmasters to make room for Democrats.

More important in Minnie's story, however, was a bit of information sent back to Lincolnton by one of the Hoke visitors who wrote that he was taken by Minnie "to see her Carroll Mercer kin, Mrs. Carroll and the Countess Esterhazy." That kinship had not yet been established by marriage. However, he wrote: "They are elegant people and Mrs. Carroll is an elegant old lady. Minnie wanted them to see me, and wished that I should see them. The Countess . . . could talk one to death in 15 minutes by the watch, unless he could take his share, which I did . . ."⁴⁹ Apparently Carroll Mercer's grandmother and aunt welcomed Minnie as rich and pretty wife who might settle down that not always dependable but much-loved young man. Minnie was determined to have him, wild as he might be.

Taking with her plain Sallie Hoke, who wanted to study music in Europe, Minnie sailed on the White Star Liner *Germanic* on June 20, 1888, to meet Carroll in England. Just before they sailed Minnie declared her independence even of the calendar.

"This is my birthday," she wrote, "my last one for I am twenty-five years old! Pray for us at church."⁵⁰

On the crowded liner they were in some sense chaperoned by an Episcopal bishop. He was Theodore Benedict Lyman of the Diocese of North Carolina, of which Minnie's cousin John Steele Henderson, as a prominent layman, became historiographer. Bishop Lyman, then on his way to the third Lambeth Conference, in the palace of the Archbishop of Canterbury, was also the bishop in charge of American Churches in Europe.⁵¹ Minnie wrote gaily of this eminent, bushy-bearded cleric. She told her "Uncle John" Hoke: "We have met the bishop and he is ours, or we are 'his'n' as the case may develop itself!!" Which was never quite clear. The bishop, she wrote demurely, did not like some of the passengers: "Some of them are fast—stylish—drink champagne and cocktails from morning to night."⁵²

Under the bishop's care they reached Carroll and London. There they moved from quarters in the Brickland Hotel to the Westminster Hotel to 36 Half Moon Street. They saw by accident "old Mrs. Norcop," Minnie's ex-mother-in-law. "There was no greeting of course," Sallie wrote. "She certainly does look hateful." But the Norcop marriage still caused trouble in Minnie's and Carroll's matrimonial plans. There could be no marriage without a certified copy of the divorce.

"Of course, Minnie has left it home and doesn't know where," Sallie wrote on July 9. "I think it is in the wooden box in the garret."

Though Minnie did not seem troubled about it, there was also a matter of money which disturbed one of the lawyers involved in her affairs, John Lowell, Jr., of Pemberton Square, Boston. That gentleman who was both a Cabot and a Lowell wrote W. A. Hoke in Lincolnton that she had drawn so much on her letter of credit that her funds were running out. Minnie had other things on her mind. Trusting Sallie wrote of a friend of Carroll's, Harry Kerr Coffey, who was taking Sallie sight-seeing: "Minnie and Carroll so fond of staying at home that it was well to have somebody to go around with, especially somebody who knows London thoroughly."

However, at last the copy of the divorce decree arrived. On July 30, 1888, with Sallie and Coffey as witnesses, the lovers were married at St. Martin in the Fields by the vicar, Reverend John Fenwick Kitto.[53] The wedding was duly reported in the *Army and Navy Journal* which gave the bride's name as "Miss Minnie Leigh Tunis of Lincolnton, N.C."[54] Apparently St. Martin in the Fields was a romantic center for Uncle Sam's seagoing officers then. Shortly before, according to the *Journal*, Assistant Surgeon Frank Anderson, U.S.N., was married there to "Miss Coffin, daughter of Commander G. W. Coffin, U. S. Navy."

Brides or not, sailors must go to sea. How much leave Carroll could get is not clear. It is clear that Minnie and Sallie set out with or without him to Paris and to Italy. Apparently he was with them—or her—in Liverno: "Carroll will start on a cruise in a day or two. *Quinnebaugh* already at Naples." The young officer had many friends here. One was "charming young Mr. Eames," who may have been the son of Mrs. Eames who appealed to Lincoln for Sallie Carroll Griffin. In Siena, solemn Sallie reported that

Minnie had "a one-horse carriage which she hires at $32 a month, including coachman." That certainly does not today seem extravagant, particularly for a lady who must have known then that she was pregnant.

Minnie may or may not have been with Carroll when he wrote, on October 28, to W. A. Hoke from the Club de Constantinople. In elegant, precise handwriting he addressed Hoke in a manner so formal as to seem insulting: "Mrs. Mercer desires you to send her a full and complete history of her estate and [how] it now stands. What is total value of estate."[55]

Hoke's answer appears to have been lost. Boston lawyer Lowell, however, must have received a similar inquiry. On January 25, 1889, he told Minnie: "The total income of your estate is $12,138." The total expenses, he said, amounted to $5169.79, making a net income of $6968.21. He thought the value of the estate was more than $300,000.[56]

By this time Carroll and Minnie apparently were in Alexandria since the *Quinnebaugh* was moored there from November 28, 1888, to April 10, 1889. Minnie, whose relationships seemed to be world-wide, had more cousins in the elastic Southern definition of kinship there. Americans in Alexandria were pleasantly situated in a serenity only assured by British soldiers and sailors. Some of those whose national flag flew from the *Quinnebaugh*'s mast were veterans or relicts of a group of U.S. civilians and soldiers recruited by Ismail Pasha. That extravagant and unscrupulous but expansive Khedive had brought them to train his army and to sit on an international court set up to deal with foreigners who had flocked to Egypt in the hope of fortune.

Two of the American judges deserve recollection for younger lovely ladies in their families. One who had departed before the *Quinnebaugh* arrived was Philip Hicky Morgan. His granddaughters were to be the twin beauties, Gloria Morgan Vanderbilt and Thelma Lady Furness. The other gentleman, of Minnie's North Carolina relationships, was Victor Clay Barringer.[57] Though now a gray-bearded man, concerned chiefly with study of Roman and Mussulman law, lively tales were related of his redheaded youth.

Years before he had been secretary to his brother David Moreau Barringer, Minister to Spain, who was concerned about possible peaceful American acquisition of Cuba. Then Victor, as a red-headed young man, was said to have created diplomatic tensions by his too intimate relations with a lady of the court who bore a redheaded child.[58]

Barringer and his wife welcomed the young Mercers. Minnie wrote to Sallie Hoke that the Barringers "have been so kind. Carroll likes Mrs. Barringer so much."[59] In the circle of their friendship the young couple enjoyed themselves. They shared the "really charming" little garden of the judge and his wife. The European-American colony was hospitable to the dashing Marine and his dark-haired wife. If Ismail Pasha had been deposed, the theaters and palaces he built remained. Visitors to Alexandria then wrote of breakfasts of tiny eggs and equally small fresh ba-nanas served on high verandas. Minnie's pregnancy did not pre-vent sight-seeing. She and Carroll drove in the desert to see the pyramids and the sphinx. They were more gay than archaeological. No flat land, steady sun, and unpredictable winds depressed them. Before the great figure of the inscrutable sphinx Minnie laughed aloud. She saw not a mystery but a reminder. Apparently like Car-roll she had been impatient with the prudent efforts of her lawyer-cousin Hoke in North Carolina. She remembered her traveling companion, his plain sister.

"It looks just like Sallie Hoke!" she shouted to the desert.

She did not mean to be bothered by riddles of income and outgo. Carroll was the company she required for the gaiety she demanded and Washington was the place in America where so-ciety would amuse them. Their first child, Violetta, was born on March 31, 1889.[60] The *Quinnebaugh* sailed on April 10. On June 12, Judge Barringer wrote Sallie that he saw Minnie and her child off on the steamer on the first lap of their voyage to the United States. The baby was "a beauty," he said.[61]

(3)

The old *Quinnebaugh* went out of commission and into scrap on July 3, 1889. In the following June, Carroll, without much necessary persuasion from Minnie, resigned his commission. Minnie had her P Street house in Washington and her husband's place there was as clear as that of one of the Cave Dwellers. Marietta Minnegerode Andrews, one of the company, later wrote: "This term, which is a little too suggestive of a limited horizon, is one highly relished by those to whom it properly belongs, and much coveted by such as aspire to be classed with the blue blooded and considered inheritors of old traditions."[62] Some of the tribe, as the *Philadelphia Record* said, "like their caves electric lighted and steam heated."[63] The Mercers did. This company had opened its doors to the Yankee Adamses and had room in its variety for Minnie. Certainly a hereditary aborigine was born on April 26, 1891, when Lucy Page Mercer entered the world. Minnie was delivered by Dr. Henry D. Fry, a dapper, fashionable physician listed in both the *Social Register* and *Who's Who in America*. Later he built an imposing structure (complete with private sanitarium) at the northeast corner of Connecticut Avenue and Q Street close to the Dupont Circle palaces. On the birth certificate Dr. Fry set down Carroll's occupation specifically and exclusively as "gentleman."

The Mercers cut, as a contemporary said, "quite a swathe in *fin de siècle society*."[64] In addition to Carroll's kin, Minnie's relative, John Steele Henderson, was a respected member of Congress from North Carolina. His was no dull Congressional household. His son was to become both a noted mathematician and the authorized biographer of George Bernard Shaw. His daughters, Mary and Elizabeth, were to gain prominence later in woman suffrage activities and historical research. Although Congressman Henderson strongly disapproved of divorce, Minnie had visited in his household in Salisbury, North Carolina, between her divorce and her trip abroad. All the Hendersons, though sometimes disapproving, found Minnie fascinating. Through them she and Carroll met such another Southerner as young Dr. Sterling Ruffin of North Carolina, a cousin of the Hendersons. He introduced them to Norman Galt, the jeweler, and his pretty wife, Edith, who had been a Bolling of Virginia. The Galts, being in trade, were less active in top rank society but established old Washingtonians.

This was, of course, the period of the Gay Nineties or the *Mauve Decade* in America, as Thomas Beer called it. Sometimes it was a grim decade in the United States. Washington on occasion was the target of hopes and angers as when Jacob S. Coxey led his ragged "Coxey's Army" of the unemployed to the city, in 1894, asking for relief and only getting arrests for walking on the grass. (It was, of course, only an irrelevant coincidence that Coxey and the commander who sailed the *Quinnebaugh* to Alexandria both came from industrial Massillon, Ohio.)

Also in Washington then thousands of Negroes lived in its disease-infested alley slums "developed" by real estate men who saw chance of an easy profit in converting to such use the deep gardens which L'Enfant had provided behind big houses. Certainly, however, no faults denied the city a glittering decade. Its prestige as a social center, attended by the diplomats of the world, was advanced by Act of Congress in 1893. Some politicians in residence like many people behind them were distrustful of ambassadors. They suggested kings and royal families. Ministers sufficed in a simple republic. But in 1893 the three great powers, England, Germany, and France, notified Washington that they would be happy to exchange ambassadors with the United States. The change required Congressional legislation. Washington felt relieved of a sense of inferiority. It was ready to waltz in power as statesmen had done in Vienna long before.

Millionaires from Chicago and other such crude "pork packing" places were moving in. With no Presidents behind them, they did not exactly follow in the footsteps of Henry Adams. They came, however, able to match memories with money. Adams quickly counted among his friends the Chicago Leiters. Levi and his wife Mary Theresa, who, though she had been a schoolteacher, was noted for her malapropisms. Levi was self-made, but sufficiently self-made in Chicago merchandising and real estate in these nineties to pay out his son Joe. Joseph lost something like $9,750,000 in trying to corner wheat in a pit battle with rich packer Philip Armour who knew wheat as well as pigs. The elder Leiter sometimes wondered in Washington what you did with eleven footmen in livery between the front door and the dining room of his house on Dupont Circle, which, according to General Anderson, they had built in 1891 as the most costly house in Washington. Leiter's losses in the wheat pit only dented the Leiter fortune. Years later Joseph Leiter, the big loser, still had enough inherited money to sail sumptuously around the world taking with him a young physician, William B. Marbury, licensed in Virginia in 1909, who married Violetta Mercer in 1919.

Levi's and Mary Theresa's triumph in Washington society and probably the biggest social event of the decade there came on April 22, 1895. Then their daughter Mary Victoria (already a favorite at Henry Adams' breakfast table) married a young Englishman, George Curzon, who was to become Lord Curzon and Viceroy of India. Other Leiter daughters married titled Englishmen. In Chicago, which was still trying to claim them, their pictures were sold in stores as the current equivalents of movie stars. Mary's marriage was a glittering affair though held in small historic St. John's Church across 16th Street from the Hay-Adams house. Young Mrs. Cleveland, effectually denying in her appearance the wild gossip that old Grover beat her while in his cups, was there in a perky hat. The remembered incident of the wedding was that Levi Leiter, having gotten on the wrong side of his daughter, startled the spectators by jumping across her long train.[65] Society swarmed at the reception afterward in the Dupont Circle Leiter palace.

Of course, Washington had not yet reached the point where

this wedding could secure the attention given a little later that year to the New York marriage in St. Thomas' Church on Fifth Avenue of the tall, lovely, eighteen-year-old Consuelo Vanderbilt to the short Duke of Marlborough. But Mary Leiter's wedding turned out to be a love match; Consuelo's then and later was a tragedy. The Duke had been forced on her by her ambitious mother though she was in love with a handsome and aristocratic young American named Winthrop Rutherfurd. A wit said at the time: "Winty was outclassed. Six feet two in his golf stockings, he was no match for five feet six in a coronet."[66] Consuelo, Rutherfurd, and the Duke could have served as the three models for Charles Dana Gibson's beautiful and handsome "Gibson Girl" and "Gibson Man" and his monocled titled mannikin after an American girl and her money.

Not all Americans, including some in Washington, approved such marriages. One was a young special friend of Henry Adams, who had come to town as President Benjamin Harrison's highly literate and volcanic civil service commissioner and was to return in other capacities. Theodore Roosevelt, who considered himself nobly sacrificing for essential economy by not serving champagne at his dinners in a small house on Jefferson Place, later spoke out sharply against these unions. He wrote that Marlborough was a cad and added: "I thoroly dislike . . . these international marriages . . . which are not . . . even matches of esteem and liking, but which are based upon the sale of the girl for her money and the purchase of the man for his title."[67] As a young man with vigorous notions about everything, including a sense of the destiny of America like that Henry Adams had had when he first came to town, he had similarly strong objections to divorce.

If Minnie and Carroll Mercer could not compete in spending with the Leiters, they did not give up champagne for economy's sake as TR did. Neither apparently did the fact that Minnie had been divorced before she married Carroll interfere with her entrance into society. She moved in it, one who knew her then remembered, in an elaborate brougham, complete with sleek horses in polished harness and with a liveried coachman and cockaded footman on the box. Also her friends were naturally those at the Cave Dwellers Club at 1710 Eye Street where young Edith Benham looked with admiration at the décolleté Countess Esterhazy who had returned to Washington as a still gay widow in her fifties. A social historian in *The Clubfellow and Washington Mirror* wrote of Minnie at this time as "easily the most beautiful woman in Washington society . . . to be invited to one of her dinners was in itself a social distinction that qualified one for admission to any home."[68]

Carroll, of course, was a member of the exclusive Metropolitan Club. Sometimes he played cards there, among others, with Horace Wylie. This gentleman was later to represent the Metropolitan when it accepted an invitation from the Racquet and Tennis Club of New York to a conference on standardized rules for the relatively new game of bridge-whist.[69] Mercer and Wylie were among those elected, in March 1893, to the first board of governors of the new Chevy Chase Club way out in Maryland. Carroll and Minnie were given first place in the *Washington Star*'s report of the club's Pink Coat Ball in December 1892 "in the beautifully decorated parlors at Wormley's."

Certainly it must have been a charming scene at the time of the Pink Coat Ball. Bowers of holly transformed one end of the ballroom into a hunter's woodland scene. The pink coats which Carroll and the other gentlemen wore indicated the current emphasis on riding and hunting in country clubs—not golf. Indeed, though there had been early golf clubs in Charleston and Savannah, the first golf club in the modern sense had been established in Yonkers only as recently as 1888. The Chevy Chase company was composed of cavaliers and their ladies. Minnie, at the club's ball, was one of those who, the *Star* said, "affected the glowing scarlet in their gowns or brightened up entirely white ones with scarlet waists or sashes." The ball was not over until nearly five o'clock. Among those present were: diplomats, admirals, cave dwellers, the Misses Patten and the Misses Boardman of the Dupont Circle company, Langhornes of Virginia, the daughters of senators and ambassadors, old and young and all gay. Not everything about the Chevy Chase society was on a grand scale, however. At a later ball given at the new clubhouse beyond Chevy Chase Circle and beyond easy carriage distance, the club paid $39.08 to the Capital Traction Company for running extra streetcars to accommodate the celebrants.[70]

Such aspects of the Nineties were gay. And society, by the standards of the time, was costly. It is not clear how long the Mercer splurge lasted. Carroll had enough money or pretended to have enough in June 1893 to draft a will leaving his everything to Minnie and naming her and Arthur D. Addison, banker and clubfellow, as executors. In 1879 they were still living in a fine house just off Connecticut on Rhode Island Avenue (opposite which St. Matthew's Cathedral was being erected).[71] One old Washingtonian seemed to recall that Minnie lost her money in the "Venezuelan panic" of 1895. There was panic enough to go around in those years. It may have been sharpened when President Cleveland, with a reviving Navy behind him, brought the United States and England to the verge of war in a message to Congress on December 17, 1895. Then, in effect, he bluntly told Victoria's government that the United States under the Monroe Doctrine was ready to insist, with force if necessary, that Britain submit to arbitration its dispute over the boundary between Venezuela and British Guiana. Britain bowed to the demand. The crisis, if not panic in the United States, passed. But Minnie's cousin, Elizabeth Henderson Cotten, later laughed at the notion that she lost her money in any economic quake caused by the international incident.

"Pooh," she said. "They just spent it!"[72]

Whatever the cause of pinch in the Mercer household, a greater international incident provided the way to graceful escape. Assistant Secretary of the Navy Theodore Roosevelt, the Pulitzer and Hearst press, and other jingoes got their war to save little Cuba from tyrannical Spain. Former Marine Lieutenant Mercer became Army Captain and Commissary of Subsistence U. S. Volunteers on June 9, 1899. He served, Minnie said later, under General Nelson Appleton Miles, spectacularly gallant soldier who had married the sister of Henry Adams' friend, Elizabeth Cameron. Adams regarded Miles as indiscreet, vain, and naïve. He was still a commander worth recalling as Minnie did in relating that Carroll served under him in Cuba, Puerto Rico, and the Philippines. For Miles, she wrote, her husband was "in command of needs at San Juan Hill—where Col. Theodore Roosevelt received cargoes & the companies of officers & soldiers." For his services he was promoted to major. He served to honorable discharge on June 30, 1901, after the war was over and Philippine insurrection was being put down.[73]

Though Minnie later said that he came out of the war with service-connected disabilities, she would have liked to have had him stay in the Regular Army at a rank reduced in peace from major to captain. From 1730 H Street she wrote about the matter to President William McKinley and Secretary of War Elihu Root. She got Maryland's Republican Senator Louis E. McComas and Martin Augustine Knapp, the five-foot-tall chairman of the Interstate Commerce Commission, to write urging Carroll's retention.[74] But the nation was eager to demobilize the big force of 144,252 men it had quickly created. There was no continuing commission for Carroll. In 1903 the family was reunited, though already evidently precariously, in a house at 1761 N Street, Northwest. That residence did not suggest poverty. The house stood in the same respectable row as that at 1733 N Street of Admiral William Sheffield Cowles who had married Theodore Roosevelt's sister Anna.

Perhaps, as John Hay said, the conflict with Spain was "a splendid little war." That war and the Philippine insurrection which followed it did not always seem so splendid to its participants. Ensign Lyman A. Cotten, who married Minnie's cousin Elizabeth Henderson, put the Philippine fighting into resounding military remembrance. The Mercers and their young daughters listened to and joined in the singing of the lively songs he wrote. They did not always please solemn statesmen troubled about American imperialism. They did serve the sentiments of people who enjoyed the new American militancy but were unimpressed, perhaps as Southerners, with mawkish talk about taking on the White Man's

Burden. One of his songs became the anthem of a convivial veterans organization called the Military Order of the Carabao. It ran:

> In the land of dopey dreams—Happy, peaceful Philippines,
> Where the bolo man is hiding night and day
> Insurrectos steal and lie where Americanos die;
> There you hear the soldiers sing this evening lay:
>
> CHORUS:
> Damn, Damn, Damn, the insurrectos [Filipinos],
> Cross-eyed, kakiack ladrones!
> Underneath the starry flag civilize them with a krag
> And return us to our own beloved homes.

Another verse loudly and lyrically reported:

> Social customs there are few—
> All the ladies smoke and chew
> All the men do things the padres say are wrong
> But the padres cut no ice for they live on fish and rice
> When you hear the soldiers sing this evening song.[75]

The chorus roared up again. If the Mercers were less rich in a new booming time, gaiety was around them. Some people, of course, were more serious. Hay was, as Secretary of State, having troubles, as other administrations were to have, with treaties in the Senate. That body seemed to keep parochial ideas of its powers in the new world power of America. Hay seemed increasingly fatigued to Adams who had just returned from Europe and the Paris Exposition of 1900. There among the U.S. commissioners were such opulent American social figures as Chicago's bejeweled queen, Mrs. Potter Palmer, and Thomas J. Walsh, Western miner who had struck it rich and was preparing to build in Washington an $835,000 house requiring the care of twenty-three servants.

Such Americans took Paris as a backdrop for their opulence. Adams, however, had spent much of his time in the Gallery of Machines watching the dynamos which to him expressed a mysterious force for the century ahead, almost like that of the force of the Virgin in the twelfth century which built the cathedrals and stained the glass in them. His "historical neck was broken," he said, "by the eruption of forces totally new."[76] And at home, not quite as he had expected it and much more quickly, America seemed ready to be "saying in its turn the last word of civilisation." What that was was not clear.

Whatever the irritations of the Senate or the crack in Adams' neck, the two small gentlemen, Hay and Adams, continued the constitutional promenades they had begun years before—up now solidly lined Connecticut Avenue, by Dupont Circle, past the big house called because of its remoteness "Stewart's Folly" when Senator William M. Stewart of Nevada had built it about the time Adams came to town. Now on Massachusetts Avenue bigger houses were rising. Adams wrote Elizabeth Cameron:

> Hay and I walked out to inspect the outside of the new Townsend and Wadsworth houses which look huge to our modest old eyes. The old Stewart Castle has the air of a dilapidated cottage. The last century is already dwarfed. The way we are swinging new rocks is a terror. Our people have forgotten that any world exists outside of America and their heads are excessively swelled. To me, fresh from Europe, the atmosphere gives vertigo. It is no use to preach caution. One might as well talk about Babylon and Nineveh as about England and France.[77]

Involved in politics and patronage which irked him, Hay could not be quite so flippantly pessimistic as Adams. The walk left him bone tired. Then in June at a Yale commencement his beloved son fell from a window and was killed. Hay assumed that his boy had sat in an open window to escape the intense heat, had gone to sleep and fallen. To his grief was added a sense of foreboding. It was almost like prophecy. On September 6, at a reception in Buffalo, an anarchist, hiding a pistol in a bandaged hand, shot President McKinley. Eight days later he died. Theodore Roosevelt, just before his forty-third birthday, became President of the United States.

In his sister's N Street house, which a small-town Middle Western observer described as a typical middle class urban house at the turn of the century,[78] Roosevelt waited for the sick and stricken Mrs. McKinley to vacate the White House. He was full of ideas and talk to his half-crippled sister, Mrs. Cowles, whom the family called variously Bamie, Bysie, or Bye (derived from bambino). Others eagerly came to listen. Old Admiral Cowles, who had heard Theodore much before, dozed as his brother-in-law talked. A visitor remembered that one thing that worried the animated and articulate man with the big teeth about becoming President so young was that he would be a young ex-President, too. He did not, he said, want to be an old cannon loose on the deck in a storm.[79]

Admiral Cowles snored. But Bamie regarded her younger brother with the wonder and affection she had always given him. In Washington as the new century began, while some were disturbed at the prospect, the name Roosevelt seemed a label for a force in history and society like the dynamos.

TWO

The Ugly Ducklings

(1)

"I am not quick at catching on the social tram," Henry Adams wrote to Elizabeth Cameron in January 1904, "and this time the tram seemed to be very crowded and much in a hurry."[1]

Still as a gentleman of sixty-six he was persuaded to attend in white tie and tails the President's diplomatic reception in the White House recently renovated along true palatial lines. He battled for an hour "down cellar" with two thousand people, he reported, then was rescued by an usher and run up the back stairs. There he was greeted with war-whoops by the President and bidden to supper. Adams was "a good deal bewildered by this style of royalty." Yet, in a room packed with a hundred of the favored, he was made to feel that his "social vogue was boundless."

The Chinese Minister, Sir Chentung Liang-Cheng, in marvelous dragons and jewels, embraced him tenderly. He was allowed to do homage to Mrs. Whitelaw Reid who wore a harness of diamonds and rubies. Mrs. Elinor Medill Patterson, collared with solitaires, received him as a member of the family. Other ladies beamed on him. Bamie Cowles, he wrote, "expanded."

As the President's oldest sister, Anna Roosevelt Cowles at forty-nine was in her heyday. So also seemed the Washington society about her, still free of the income tax even if, for those who depended on it, the government pay was low. Theodore set a swift pace for the government over which he presided. Something of his strenuous course was indicated to bramble-scratched ambassadors and other dignified personages whom he led on hikes through wooded areas where suburbs would soon spread. The world, of course, was in trouble. Old torn Russia and new truculent Japan were already moving toward their collision less than a month later in the Russo-Japanese War. In this Japan would lance old Muscovy, as Adams put it, "as if she were a sick whale."[2] Some Old Guard Republicans were feeling that TR was similarly attacking whale-like Trusts which seemed far from ailing. Some, including young Franklin Roosevelt at Harvard, had felt that the President was making a "serious mistake in interfering"[3] in a coal strike. But in the White House a new style of royalty prevailed which the historian reported made "the town hot and smoking with tales of the imperial court" of Roosevelt I.[4]

Adams approved of the redecorated White House that the Roosevelts had found not much changed from the days when it had seemed to Clover Adams an upholstered barracks. It was, as pert young Alice Roosevelt wrote later, furnished in the fashion of "the late Grant and early Pullman" period.[5] Now Adams found it "quite a gentleman's place." Slyly he remarked that in its transformation Mrs. Roosevelt had in that matter "rolled Bamie quite out of the house, and very properly."[6] But if Bamie's ideas of house furnishing seemed ugly to many of those who loved her best, she was not in other things often disregarded by her family or anybody else.

She held a sort of matriarchal position in the family, though if there had ever been an ugly duckling she was it. Only in spirit did she ever seem a swan. She had been born in 1856 the half-crippled child of the elder Theodore Roosevelt and his beautiful Georgia wife, Martha Bulloch. In her *Recollections Grave and Gay*, the novelist and social favorite, Mrs. Burton Harrison (a Cary from Virginia), wrote of old New York society in the 1870s presided over in queenly equality by Mrs. Hamilton Fish, Mrs. Lewis Morris Rutherfurd, Mrs. Belmont, two Mrs. Astors, and Mrs. Roosevelt. The last, she said, was by all odds the loveliest of them all.

Then almost as an aside she wrote a passage which seemed to refer to Martha Roosevelt's young twisted Bamie.

"One asks oneself," Mrs. Harrison wrote, "why such loveliness of line and tinting . . . cannot be passed down the years instead of dying upon the stem like a perfect flower! Why nature, having found such a combination, should not be content with repeating it!"[7]

Bamie was definitely no such repetition. Her parents presented her to society, Mrs. Harrison wrote, at a great ball to which 1100 invitations were issued. But no parental love could make her a belle. She was, her niece Eleanor wrote later, "not exactly a hunchback." But her "deformity" gave her a curious figure, "very thick through the shoulders; this was evidently caused by a curvature of the spine." Only her wavy hair and shining eyes made you "forget the rest of her face, which was not beautiful."[8] Her niece Alice was almost surprised to realize that, as one of her aunt's friends said, Auntie Bye was "very nearly ugly—she is almost a cripple."[9] Both of her nieces saw her in the reflection of the love their aunt had given them.

Left an old maid as her brothers and sisters married, she was the one upon whom all depended. She had been in her late twenties when both her mother and Theodore's young wife, Alice Lee, died on the same day in the same house. Her overwhelmed brother Elliott then cried, "There is a curse on this house!"[10] But Bamie assumed responsibility for the infant Alice who had survived her mother's death in childbirth. More than ordinary love for a niece marked her love for this child. She might have been an ugly duckling too. In her childhood, as Alice described it later, she became "an orthopedic case." As she grew a little older every night before she went to bed her feet had to be stretched "in a steel contraption that rather resembled a medieval instrument of torture."[11] For several years she wore braces on each leg from "ankle to knee." She was nearly three years old when Bamie went with Theodore to London in 1886 where he married Edith Carow and so found a new mother for Alice.

The stalwart sister's heart turned with special tenderness also to her niece Eleanor when she was left an orphan. She had in reality been left without parents two years before when her beautiful, scornful mother, Anna Hall Roosevelt, had died of diphtheria and her father, Elliott, was an alcoholic kept in exile by his family. Eleanor and her two brothers were left in the care of the Hall family but she remained close to Bamie's heart. There was a certain irony, not noticed, when Alice's new, good mother, Edith Carow, wrote to her bent sister-in-law after shy, awkward little Eleanor had visited the exuberant Roosevelts at Oyster Bay.

"Poor little soul," she wrote of Eleanor, "she is very plain. Her mouth and teeth seem to have no future. But the ugly duckling may turn out to be a swan."[12]

Bamie brought the child to bright afternoons at her house on Madison Avenue where she also welcomed Alice, only a few months older. They were very different children. Eleanor remembered a dark childhood marked by the derisive remarks of her pretty mother about her plainness and the mystery maintained about her errant father whom she adored. Alice, who escaped from her braces, said that she, too, was "a shy, uncomfortable child."[13] If so, she looked back unshaken by the experience.

"How miserable a child can be, and how remarkably soon it can get over that misery—until the next time. But there is a danger it may become a habit of misery and turn into chronic self-pity."[14]

Bamie found other children who needed her love and care. Her distant cousin, James Roosevelt Roosevelt (much older half-brother of Franklin), had married an Astor. Democratic campaign contributions had secured for him the socially pleasant post of first secretary in the American legation in London. There his wife died leaving him with two motherless children. The still unwed Bamie moved into his house despite, members of the family remembered, some lifting of eyebrows.[15] Such social disapproval never bothered Bamie. One piece of advice she gave to Eleanor later was: "No matter what you do some people will criticize you. But if you would not be ashamed to explain your action to someone you loved, then you need never worry about criticism, nor need you ever explain what you do."[16]

In this case her kindness carried her to her own happy marriage. In London she met and married Lieutenant Commander William Sheffield Cowles of an old Farmington, Connecticut, family. Though many feared for dangers due to her deformity, she produced a straight-backed son of her own. She moved to Washington not following her brother's political career but because of her husband's assignment there. Her place in society did not depend upon her brother's position or luck. With her own household, she still had room in her heart for others.

She had a special concern for those who despite heritage were disadvantaged. One such, a lovely young woman of old naval family, Edith Benham then (she married an admiral later), remembered Bamie's aid in her memoirs, *The Captains and the Kings.*[17] Her social position had entitled her to welcome in the 1701 Eye Street Club of the "Cave Dwellers" in which she had admired the opulent charms of the Countess Esterhazy. But she needed money. Washington was not then the city of thousands of young women swarming in independence to many jobs. But one special field was opening in the capital's expanding society.

Edith Benham remembered Nellie Hunt as the pioneer of the social secretaries of Washington. She was the daughter of William Henry Hunt, Secretary of the Navy under Garfield and Minister to Russia under Arthur. Perhaps more significant in terms of Nellie's craft was the fact that her brother Gaillard Hunt had edited *The First Forty Years of Washington Society.* This book was based upon the letters of Mrs. Samuel Harrison (Margaret Bayard) Smith, who came to Washington with the Jefferson administration. Others, like Belle Hagner, Helen Squire, and Laura Harlan, all of impeccable social position and thin purses, followed in the business of aiding and guiding other ladies able to pay. Bamie Cowles found a place for Edith Benham. Young Edith went to work for the wife of the British Ambassador, James Bryce, in the huge red brick Victorian embassy on Connecticut Avenue at N Street.[18]

In this Rooseveltian regime in Washington young Alice had advanced beyond the need of Bamie's helping hand. Sometimes as the Princess Alice she seemed to need a restraining one. She was certainly no longer any orthopedic case. One observer noted that she "always strides."[19] Without waiting for the gate to the House Gallery to be opened she stepped over it. With no deformity to hide, she wore flesh-colored stockings and when the band played at a party she held her very scant skirt quite high and "kicked about and moved her body sinuously like a shining leopard cat."[20] The diarist, Ellen Slayden, who left such reports, also said, "She has a way of throwing back her head and showing all her teeth just like her father, but hers are very white and handsome."[21]

Alice herself wrote that her major preoccupation was to "have a good time."[22] She did much as she pleased and pleased a watching press in doing it. Once her father after reading chronicles of her behavior wrote her a letter "that scorched the paper on which it was written." She answered promptly and presumed in remembrance that she promised to mend her ways but also: "in a temper at being interfered with, I burnt his letter."[23] Her ways were her own. She refused to be confirmed, but found the Bible so fascinating that she read some of it every day.[24] She declined to go off to school[25] but was educated by a governess, curiosity, and osmosis. She would not stop smoking. TR, who adored her as she adored him, is reported to have said, "I can try to run the country or control Alice. I cannot possibly do both."[26] Alice then and afterward managed very well for herself. In her life and loyalties she never lost a sort of elegant gamin spirit. The collected letters of her father's popular military aide, Captain Archie Butt, are replete with her mischievous escapades. But her marriage in the White House to the able, aristocratic Congressman, Nicholas Longworth of Cincinnati, was a royal event never to be equaled in the century.

Bamie's other niece, Eleanor, still desperately needed her when she came awkwardly and without self-confidence, as she herself reported it, into young womanhood. She had gone dutifully to a school in England chosen for her by Bamie. There the headmistress called her "Ma chère petite,"[27] and on her report card wrote "Excellent élève." Her behavior was impeccable to the point of boredom. Awkwardly, bashfully she entered the American society to which she was born. She danced dutifully in New York. She felt less lost in Washington where she visited Bamie early in 1903. There, though she was asked to stay for a night at the White House, she was awed by it—and evidently by her cousin, Alice, in it. Auntie Bye, however, introduced her to others of her age including Eleanor Medill Patterson, called Cissy, later to be the explosive publisher of the *Washington Times-Herald*. Cissy then was in tempestuous love with a dashing Polish count, Josef Gizycki. Such a black-eyed gentleman with a Guardsman's mustache held no appeal for Eleanor. He gave Alice a silver cigarette case when she joined Cissy's wedding party. Eleanor was pleased with others to whom Auntie Bye introduced her composed, as she wrote later, of "people of importance, with charm and wit and *savoir faire*."[28] She was aghast, however, at the rounds of calls that Bamie dutifully made each afternoon. It was back in New York that her life was illuminated by the declared love of her handsome, distant cousin, Franklin Roosevelt. Her delight was turned almost to despair at the thought that she might not be permitted to marry him.

Angry, hurt, and resentful she came again to Bamie's house in the winter of 1904. On the Thanksgiving before, Franklin Roosevelt had told his mother, the decorative and dominant Sara Delano, that they were engaged. The dowager wrote in her diary at the time: "Franklin gave me quite a startling announcement."[29] Obviously she was more than startled; she was stubbornly opposed to the engagement. Though Sara Roosevelt generally spoke with a soft, cultured voice, Eleanor wrote later that she could whisper louder than any woman she ever knew. Now her feelings seemed to call for an elevated voice. Franklin in a letter to her described her reaction as one of "pain."[30] Eleanor wrote her "Dear Aunt Sallie" that she realized "how hard it must be" for her.[31]

Aunt Sallie was not relenting. In February 1904 she took Franklin and his wealthy Harvard roommate, Lathrop Brown, off on a Caribbean cruise in evident hope that separation might cool her son's ardor. So Eleanor, in resentment, had come again to

Auntie Bye in Washington. That lady not only knew Eleanor but also the redoubtable Sara. Indeed Bye had been one of those present at her father's house when young Sara met her husband-to-be, James Roosevelt, a widower twice her age. Now in 1904 she understood how tenaciously Sara as a still handsome widow wanted to keep for herself the companionship of her son. Many others have since regarded this as her only reason for opposition to the match. Sara had, indeed, taken a house in Boston to be near Franklin at Harvard. Also Bamie and others could not disregard Sara's contention that Franklin and Eleanor were too young. Sara's happiness had been with a man who was fifty-two when at twenty-six she married him. Franklin at twenty-one had not yet graduated from Harvard. Eleanor was only nineteen. In her wisdom, however, Bamie must have understood that Sara in any selfishness might have fears as well.

Eleanor's uncle might be President of the United States but Bamie understood congenital defects in the family, though she overcame her own. Even the strenuous Theodore had been born a sickly asthmatic child and as President he was so nearsighted that he mistook a statue of Diana for one of Apollo.[32] She understood how well Sara knew the story of her brother Elliott who had been in his charming days made the godfather of this boy Franklin. People had not begun in Sara's society to talk about genes but they had a firm feeling about blood. Elliott had been in many ways irresponsible before he became an alcoholic. He was also, in another term not yet common, accident prone. Twice he had been seriously injured in events of bold horsemanship. He died following an accident in which he was thrown from the carriage he drove with skill and speed. On the occasion of one accident at Sagamore Hill in 1886 Theodore wrote his friend Henry Cabot Lodge:

"Yesterday I took Sagamore out after the hounds, and he kept me right in the first flight till the death; I have never been on as good a horse. Poor old Elliott broke his collar bone the third time he was out with the hounds; so did Winty Rutherfurd. . . ."[33]

"Poor old Elliott" was not the only sad item in Eleanor's heritage. Sara's home at Hyde Park was only twenty miles down the Hudson below Tivoli and the country home there of Eleanor's mother's family the Halls. That old house of big rooms with high ceilings, lit only by lamps, marked Eleanor's descent from the great Colonial landowner, Robert Livingston. But in her childhood there the household had, as Frank Freidel said, some of the decadent undertones of a Poe story.[34] Some might say this of a Faulkner novel. Eleanor's Grandfather Hall, as she wrote, never engaged in business but lived on what his mother and father gave him. It was sufficient for him to live very well as a sort of amateur and perhaps fanatic in theology able to retain a clergyman in residence with whom he could talk on equal terms. But he treated his wife, born Mary Livingston Ludlow, like a child.

When he died without a will she had never written a check. And when his stern discipline relaxed at his death she was incapable—almost incompetent—in the rearing of her children. The younger children quickly became problems. Her sons, Vallie and Eddie, were heavy drinkers. Pussie was often and tempestuously in love, sometimes accompanied or followed by prolonged hysterics. All were improvident. Some gambled disastrously. Yet even Vallie sang and decorated Christmas trees for the poor. It was a home of eccentricity. "No one," Eleanor wrote, "was ever invited to come for a meal or to stay with us who was not so intimate that he knew the entire situation."[35]

Sara Roosevelt knew the situation and saw it as one of those Delanos who, young Eleanor wrote later, "watched their pennies which I had always seen squandered."[36] Certainly Sara was not without better reasons for her opposition to the marriage than her unwillingness to cut the umbilical cord or loose her apron strings. Franklin, visiting at Tivoli in May 1904 as one of those so intimate that he understood "the entire situation," wrote in evident reassurance to his mother, "Vallie has been exemplary— I seem to have a good effect on him."[37]

Whatever were Sara's fears, she was inept in her plans to prevent the engagement. And Bamie provided both refuge for Eleanor and the scene for Sara's defeat in Washington. Eleanor could

not have been there long. Franklin sailed away on the cruise at
the beginning of February. But Eleanor was certainly present in
New York at the marriage on the 16th of the month of the amor-
ously unstable Pussie to W. Forbes Morgan, Jr. It was an occasion
on which Eleanor herself expressed matrimonial doubts: "Forbes
was a number of years younger than Pussie, and we knew she was
temperamental and wondered how they would adjust themselves
to the complicated business of married life."[38]

She had no doubts about her own ability in that regard. With
Bamie behind her she was confident when at the end of the cruise
Franklin and his mother came to Washington. There Sara made
one more almost desperate move. She took Franklin to see her
old friend, Ambassador Joseph Choate, and asked him to take
her boy to England as his secretary. Old Choate demurred. He
already had a secretary. Franklin was too young.[39] And he must
have been made to seem younger than he was with his handsome
mother doing the job-seeking for her beautiful boy while he stood
apparently docile beside her.

He was not docile. Sara won over a year's delay but Franklin
and Eleanor were married on March 17, 1905, in the double old
brownstone house of Eleanor's godmother-cousin, Mrs. Henry
Parish, Jr., and her mother, Mrs. E. Livingston Ludlow, at Numbers 6 and 8 East 66th Street. The wedding was held on St. Patrick's Day so that TR could both give away his niece and review
New York's many wearers of the green as they paraded up Fifth
Avenue. The Princess Alice was Eleanor's maid of honor. The
couple was young but their world was secure. Franklin had an
annual income left him by his father of $5000. Eleanor had her
own income which varied from $5000 to $8000 a year.[40] (Cabinet
officers in Washington then received only $10,000, an Assistant
Secretary of the Navy, $4500.)

Whatever she may have suggested about her awkward appearance, on a long European honeymoon a little later she was a lovely
long-limbed young woman in a photograph taken in a gondola in
Venice. She may have caught there some of the charm of her

father before he threw it away. She kept a memory of him singing lustily in Venice with the gondoliers.

It seemed not only to them but to many other Americans the best of possible times. There were no threats to American democracy from abroad. To such an exuberant reporter as Irvin S. Cobb it was "the jubilee age of this earth."[41] Henry Adams this year was finding Washington even in the turbulence TR stirred "socially pleasant and simple, like thirty years ago. I rather like these late autumns of life."[42] He watched the Roosevelts across the square with as much pleasure as he had observed other presidential families but with more affection. When TR readied himself for voluntary retirement, Adams regarded his departure as "another great loss to me." He gave him the accolade: "He kept us amused."[43]

But the succeeding Taft seemed to Adams a "fat mush . . . a hippopotamus . . . too ripe for a stroke."[44] The new President, walking with his aide Archie Butt, had hailed Adams in Lafayette Square. Adams saw Taft, not Butt, as doomed. And in January 1912 he blurted his disgust at the society around Taft. "The longer I live under this Cincinnati regime, the cheaper and commoner and fatter I find it. John McLean is about its measure."[45] Many found McLean less than attractive though he had come from Cincinnati long before Taft and had acquired a bank, traction lines, newspapers. Also he had married Emily Beale whom at about this time Adams regarded as "the reigning empress." She had as a dainty sister-in-law Mrs. George Dewey. And her sister Mary was back in Washington with her Russian husband, George Bakhmeteff. As a result of some international string pulling, it was suggested, he came as the Czar's Ambassador. John McLean's daughter-in-law, Evalyn Walsh, who had married young, strange Edward Beale McLean, described her father-in-law as odd hybrid "of gentle friend and fierce monster"[46] who practiced a smooth kind of blackmail with his newspapers. Her Aunt Mamie Bakhmeteff was, she said, an ugly little sharp-nosed woman whose dyed red hair was pink in spots. His Excellency the ambassador was a pock-marked, sharp-tongued gentleman who always wore a monocle.[47]

From such a regime Adams planned flight. His square, he wrote, is "being converted into a hole."[48] Adams was not merely speaking figuratively. The old and famous Arlington Hotel at Vermont Avenue and Lafayette Square had been torn down by its owner, Willie Eustis, but no replacing building had been erected. The country seemed in such a hole. TR, back from African big game hunting, was on the home hunt again heavily armed with what seemed a new radicalism including the promise of a "welfare state." Eustis's wife reported to Adams that the only way to wake up her old father, Levi P. Morton, was to say "Roosevelt" whereupon he would rouse in querulous indignation.[49] TR, roaring at Taft whom he had hand-picked for the White House, seemed to the old historian to have nothing ahead of him but the lunatic asylum.[50] So beset, Adams engaged himself an "extravagant apartment" on the new magnificent ship the *Titanic* for its first eastward voyage to Europe on April 20.[51]

The news suddenly came of the sinking of this unsinkable British liner on its first gala westward passage on April 14. Adams was more than ordinarily shocked. Neighbors, including Edith Eustis, came to share shock and exchange views about the catastrophe in which 1513 persons out of 2224 aboard had been drowned. She had dined the night before with admirals who had derided the possibility of any disaster for the great vessel.[52] The old historian saw the event as only one item in the collapse he had long predicted of the society around him.

He wrote his old friend Elizabeth Cameron, "In half an hour, just in a summer sea, were wrecked the *Titanic*; President Taft; the Republican Party, Boise Penrose, and I. We all foundered and disappeared."[53]

That was quite a diverse collection even for Adams. He saw more than a maritime disaster in the swift sinking of this vessel, "the sum and triumph of civilization,"[54] after its collision at full speed with an iceberg hidden by smooth waters in clear weather. Like others he was shaken by the reports of gallantry, heroism, sacrifice as the great and the obscure, artists and Astors, million-aires and immigrants went down into the sea while bands alter-nately played hymns and ragtime. Washington was particularly saddened by the loss in the sinking of popular Archie Butt and his companion, the much loved artist Frank Millet. More than a coincidence, Adams saw symbolic connections in the great ship's helpless death at approximately the same time—though hardly limited to half an hour—in which TR, ready to split his party to regrasp the presidency, was moralistically impaling not only Re-publican Boss Penrose but also dismayed old party friends. He certainly seemed ready with the lance for a sick whale. More clearly he was in his own metaphor the old cannon loose on the deck in a storm. To Adams, in advance of his most pessimistic predictions of the past, the two catastrophes seemed to mark the end of an era of blind felicity.

Not all who were shocked by the *Titanic* tragedy found in it any omen of the end of an era—even of the collapse of civilization—as Adams did. In expansive mood at the time, young Franklin Roose-velt did not. He was off on another cruise in the Caribbean and the Gulf, unaccompanied by Eleanor who among other things feared seasickness. He had sailed with her Harvard undergraduate brother, Hall Roosevelt, and a friend during a recess of the New York legislature in which, as an insurgent and some felt upstart Democrat, he had won both attention and enmity. He had led an insurgent Democratic revolt which thwarted the candidacy for the United States Senate of William P. Sheehan. Sheehan was no crude, pugugly politician. He belonged to the very best clubs. His residence at 16 East 65th Street was in impeccable precincts. Roosevelt found him "delightful personally."[55] He was a business-man, *Social Register* citizen. But he had been picked by Tammany Hall. He was licked. But the legislature named another Irish Catholic who was far more of a Tammany man than Sheehan. Still somehow Franklin seemed the shining knight standing vic-torious above the dragon—or the Tiger.

The *Titanic* disaster did not disturb Franklin's self-confident serenity in the legislative recess. To his ever-attentive mother he wrote of the disaster at sea as "too horrible"[56] but he saw no ominous symbolism in the event. Certainly he was not prepared to share Adams' opinion that "Our dear Theodore is not a bird of happy omen. He loves to destroy."[57]

In New York Democrats felt that way about Franklin. In the Canal Zone, the younger Roosevelts regarded Uncle Ted's tremendous ditch as a wonder greater than the Pyramids or the Tower of Babel. Babel evidently suggested to him no confusion of tongues. It did not occur to him in his own young exuberance that an age of confidence went down with the *Titanic*. Yet, certainly in the same year Roosevelt's scuttling of the Republican Party made inevitable the election of Democratic Woodrow Wilson. There was room in his administration for a young Democrat wearing the exciting, if explosive, Roosevelt name in the same post of Assistant Secretary of the Navy from which TR had begun his catapulting advance to the presidency. No era seemed at an end for him.

(2)

Appalled by the prospect of her duties as wife of the Assistant Secretary of the Navy, Eleanor "dashed" for advice to Auntie Bye then in the old Cowles house in Farmington. But Franklin pranced to Washington.

The capital itself was both appalled and prancing. It had been sixteen years since the last Democratic administration. And the eager incoming Democrats seemed "odd beings" to Alice Longworth and other established residents. Ellen Slayden of Texas, whose Congressman husband had had some vague hopes of a Cabinet post, recorded such feelings. She wrote, perhaps more tartly because he hadn't gotten it, of the "ultra smart who profess to scorn the Presbyterian Wilsons and anticipate a Wednesday-night-prayer-meeting social atmosphere."[58] Another gentler chronicler, Marietta Minnegerode Andrews, aristocrat and artist who watched the changing scene from her studio on Scott Circle as Adams did from his house on Lafayette Square, noted that Wilson had assembled the first Cabinet in which the hostesses "were not women of wealth."[59]

Possibly lack of such opulence among top Democrats led to the selection of such a nominal party member as Willie Eustis as chairman of the committee to stage the customary Inaugural Ball. There was no question about his affluence or social position. He was rich enough not to have to appear so. Some spoke critically of the run-down appearance of his ancient Corcoran House in the Lafayette Square neighborhood. Despite such distinguished background, professional gossip reporters were amused by the prospect that, with Willie, the ball would be led by his wife Edith, daughter of so rich and prominent a Republican as former Vice-President Morton. There was consternation among gossips and others when Mrs. Wilson insisted that there be no ball on the solemn occasion of her husband's inauguration.

Eleanor Roosevelt was less concerned about the change in Washington than that in her own life. She needed Bye's wisdom. Her beloved aunt was now older, deaf, and more bent than ever. Washington, which she knew so well, was less important in her life since the retirement of her husband and what appeared to be the final disappearance of her brother from the political scene. She still had great warmth and strength. She welcomed Eleanor to the old Cowles house "Oldgate." It was no urban middle class row house, as the Washington Cowles residence had been described. There were at this time five Cowles houses in old Farmington regarded as monuments to its quiet, elegant past. And of these, "Oldgate," sometimes referred to as the Samuel Cowles House, was the most notable and elaborate. Alice Longworth thought it got its name from a design by Sir Christopher Wren for a Thames River watergate. Architectural historians spoke of its gate to Farmington's tree-shaded streets as one of modified Chinese design.[60]

Certainly, behind its gate of whatever origin, it was impressive. Its façade focused upon a beautiful projecting pediment supported by four Ionic columns. Built in 1780, supposedly designed by a British Army officer, an architect named William Spratt who was imprisoned in Farmington for two years, it was the first house in Connecticut which brought into provincial architecture the influence of the classical renaissance as developed in the English Georgian. Other British prisoners were said to have carved its woodwork. The greater house had been built in front of a smaller, older residence. Among many legends about it, Alice had heard that the original kitchen had been built by Jonathan Edwards. This room Auntie Bye, before Eleanor came, had converted into a library-sitting room with the big fireplace unchanged.

Certainly the house was a place of family continuity which inspired confidence. In it Auntie Bye was an accepted fairy godmother to her nieces and others even if she looked more and more like a witch. By the great fireplace she had wisdom and kindness, both readily shared. Eleanor, who had been the plain child for whom she had provided cookies, now sought some of her confidence, not so easily given. Bamie had memories; Eleanor, fear. The younger woman had found herself queasy at boating, a duffer at golf, awkward in all the sports to which her husband was addicted. Now she felt appalled at the official life to which all his ambitions pointed.

The older woman warmed and encouraged her niece. But Eleanor was not reassured by her aunt's firm insistence that she dutifully make the endless rounds of calls which Washington custom then required. But she took to heart and remembered well Bye's ultimate and less formalized advice.

"You will find that many of the young officers' wives have a hard time," the older woman said, "because they must keep up their position on very small pay. You can do a great deal to make life pleasant for them when they are in Washington, and that is what you should do."[61]

Franklin, more cocksure than concerned, was getting advice and encouragement, too. He was pleased by a letter from "Uncle Ted" who had held the same post: "I am sure you will enjoy yourself to the full as Assistant Secretary of the Navy, and that you will do capital work."[62] And his mother, not fearing separation this time, still wrote him as if somehow he was still the boy she had taken to old Ambassador Choate in quest of a job. "Try not to write your signature too small. . . . So many public men have such awful signatures, and so unreadable. . . ."[63]

Others thought of him as a boy. He was, indeed, one of the youngest men who had held the office. A naval officer's wife was shocked to find that this new civilian superior of her husband was one whom she had recently chided at a dinner party as a naughty boy for making some irreverent remark.[64] Franklin certainly had no sense of his immaturity. He meant to write his name big. And he came as no odd stranger to the capital's society. More through Eleanor's ties than his own he was not only in office as a Democrat but also welcomed by some who resented the Democratic invasion. He went immediately to dinner, the theater and afterward back to their house for midnight eggs with Alice and Nick Longworth. Apparently all had a fine time though Alice then was appalled by the prospect of exile to Cincinnati caused by her husband's defeat in the three-party brawl of the year before. Edith Eustis welcomed him to Corcoran House. Franklin found in Washington, too, his wealthy classmates, Edward Bell in the diplomatic corps, and Lathrop Brown who had just been elected to Congress from a New York City district. Brown definitely could not be counted among the poor Democrats. As a freshman Democratic Congressman, destined for only one term in office, he leased the great Doughoregan Manor which Charles Carroll of Carrollton had built about 1827. It was about forty miles from the capital but would provide escape from the heat of Washington in a quietness broken only by the katydids.

Apparently the Roosevelts' own housing was arranged in Farmington when Eleanor went for advice and received the offer of the Cowles house, too. Some of that house's appeal to Franklin was connected with his assiduous cultivation then of the idea that he was another Roosevelt "on the job." Still, even in 1913, this

Cowles house on N Street must have been crowded with family as well as memories. As in all things the dominant Sara helped in their move from the house she had given them adjoining and joining hers on East 65th Street in New York. This, Eleanor wrote, was "as usual."[65] Aid was needed in what amounted to a migration. There were three children, the oldest of whom was seven. Also they brought a car and a young chauffeur with them from Hyde Park. In addition Eleanor came to the house, in which two Negro servants had sufficed for the Cowles, with the "four servants whom I had had for sometime in New York, and a nurse and a governess."[66]

Apparently she only joined Franklin on a permanent basis after the end of the summer, spent as usual at Campobello where Sara had also bought them a house close to hers. Then in the autumn she went with Franklin in a large official party which his chief, Secretary Josephus Daniels, had assembled to watch the target practice of the fleet off Hampton Roads. She was afraid she would disgrace Franklin by being seasick. "Somehow or other I lived through that trip," she said later, "but it took me many years before I ceased to dread dinner or luncheon on board a battleship."[67] There were more tests ahead. Other aspects of his duties called for her company. Off they went, accompanied by his well-loved first cousin, Laura Delano, a maiden lady then and later, to inspect deactivated Navy Yards in the South.

Laura was a companion Roosevelt enjoyed on this trip and later ones. This journey, of course, was not quite a holiday. There is some reason to suspect that Secretary Daniels, who had already visited these bases in the summer before, as a Southerner wanted his New York assistant to recommend the reopening of the yards in the South. After sixteen years in exile not only were deserving Democrats eager for offices but also Southern ports were eager for naval attention. Righteously they believed that appropriations had been spent on cold and isolated New England stations while Southern yards were closed or neglected. With his ladies Franklin set out on his mission in exuberant spirit.

Daniels, in the May before, had been pleased with the eager

hospitality of New Orleans. But though native to the flowering South, he was captivated by the Pensacola base which, long closed, had been allowed to go wild in an almost jungle of lilies and oleanders, flowering trees and shrubs. Eleanor, as this autumn trip's historian, naturally made no mention of the spring flowering. Her concern was the conscientious learning of her duties. She regarded this and other journeys on official errands as "feats of endurance"[68] which prepared her for the future. Laura Delano had no such sense of her duties in democracy. Indeed, as FDR's son wrote later, she had "something of the same patrician approach toward life" as Sara Roosevelt did.[69] FDR himself loved to tell an undoubtedly much decorated story about Laura. Once in the midst of a total eclipse of the sun, he too much teased her with the suggestion that it might portend some approaching final natural disaster. Laura, he said, hurried to her room and returned shortly with the one possession with which she was determined to face the possible end of the world—her jewel box.[70]

Though Roosevelt was much amused by the story, it was not necessarily a strange one. Laura was not only a provident Delano, she was also granddaughter of William T. Walters, Baltimore philanthropist who was not only a great art collector but had a special fondness for trinkets of gold and enamel of which he gathered a large number. Her uncle, Henry Walters, who became known as the richest man in the South, had a notable fondness for finger rings which he changed daily. In both these gentlemen the acquisitive and the artistic hand were combined. Ironically if irrelevantly, Laura was the child of a marriage which a father had tried to prevent as Sara had tried to prevent Franklin's. A widower the elder Walters wanted the companionship of his daughter Jennie. He resented the courting Delano. When they married nevertheless, he disinherited Jennie. Fortunately for her, her brother Harry divided the inheritance with her. Also a legend grew in Baltimore that in his last days, though he didn't change his will, the elder Walters kept a light always burning at his door to welcome the errant daughter home. Laura showed no marks of this romantic episode. But she was early and late a woman bent on her own ways. In the pressures of this inspection trip she declined to be pushed or disturbed.

The young Assistant Secretary led his ladies at a rapid pace. He and his two companions arrived in New Orleans early on the morning of November 15. *The Daily Picayune* gave their visit equal front page news play with the convention of the United Daughters of the Confederacy then being held there. In a *Picayune* photograph Laura looked diminutive by the tall Roosevelts. As became almost standard in the description of Rooseveltian relatives later, she was described in the same edition as both FDR's sister-in-law and his niece. Both ladies' skirts almost reached the ground. Franklin looked ready for action in a dark suit, tall stiff collar, and a black derby. They were off immediately to inspect a more or less deserted navy yard. There the Assistant Secretary declined a car provided to take him about the grounds: "He preferred to walk." He went from building to building, "climbed the narrow iron stairs with a familiarity and ease that must have been acquired on naval vessels. He wanted to see everything and overlooked nothing. . . . He went upstairs and downstairs, through shops and storerooms, and as one of the party jokingly remarked, if there had been any cellars handy he would have investigated them, too."[71]

Then in a crowded day they were carried off, as tourists the city much wished to please, to see the old cemeteries where because of the sogginess of the soil the dead were buried in tombs above the ground, the old slave block in the Cabildo, the Vieux Carré and its old French houses with wrought-iron balconies. Franklin was called to speak and listen at an official dinner. But Laura and Eleanor were taken by a "delightful retired naval gentleman"[72] to a restaurant where after a delicious dinner they drank café brûlé in a room illuminated only by the burning brandy. Still the night was young. They went first to the opera and afterward to a supper party. The feats of endurance were already begun.

They got to bed at two and were aroused at five to leave for Biloxi on the yacht of Ernest Jahncke, maritime magnate who himself was to become Assistant Secretary of the Navy under President Hoover. Eleanor did not enjoy the trip. With no breakfast and only warm champagne served them, she began to feel queasy even in completely landlocked waters. At Biloxi, while Franklin was shown the harbor which local patriots hoped might become scene of a naval base, the ladies were given another sightseeing tour. Tired and sleepy they faced a banquet at which the "horrified but fascinated" Laura was taken in to dinner by a gentleman who had on patent-leather shoes of the high, buttoned variety but with the buttons left loose so that the uppers flapped as he walked.[73]

Their train to Pensacola was an hour late but Franklin assured them that though the train arrived at five their car would be dropped off there and they could sleep later. Instead, at 4:45, as Eleanor remembered, while she and Laura were sound asleep "in our stateroom" he knocked on the door to say that they had to be off at five. He had to come in and help dress Laura who was accustomed to take her leisurely time. And when that lady heard that they were supposed to go to both a preliminary breakfast and a later more formal one, she balked. She was going to bed. Docilely Eleanor went down to her duty "as pleasantly as possible."

There was a picnic on an island "with no shade and a blazing sun." Still it was a pleasant occasion. Franklin studiously visited the naval properties which could be used as a base for Marines. In mid-November the wild flowering of the lilies, the oleanders and the larkspur which had so much impressed Secretary Daniels the May before were not evident. There was still beauty about the place. The naval properties had first been acquired for their great trees in the day of wooden ships and iron men. Nobody, including its sharp-eyed young Assistant Secretary, dreamed then that the Navy, which had bought its first two airplanes just two years before, would build here the greatest of its air training centers. Certainly the day in mid-November 1913 when Roosevelt and his ladies were there they were sleepy in a sleepy town. On they went to Brunswick, Georgia, which apparently was also eager for naval attention. This time as a tired little troupe, they traveled with a mediocre theater group making one-night stands like themselves. In Brunswick, Eleanor was taken to see these acting traveling companions perform. Then they were homeward bound.

"I learned," said Eleanor, "that I could be tired and it did me no harm. Some time or other I had to catch up on sleep, but I learned that if I kept myself well, when I had an exhausting strain to endure, it could be borne."[74]

But Laura said, "I have had all I want of official travel."

Eleanor came back to the round of endless calls which she dreaded. Moreover, despite the rush, crowding and chaperonage of the trip, she came back pregnant with her fifth child to be born (just nine months after their weary day in Pensacola) on August 17, 1914. Eleanor had not had to worry about the children in her absence. In addition to the nurse and governess, she wrote, "My mother-in-law always had an eye to the children when we were away."[75] The other four servants kept the household in order. Still there were the calls which her sense of duty would not let her neglect after the fashion of Alice Longworth. That vivid young woman had calmly announced that she was too much interested in other things to "waste her time calling on women who were, after all, not important in her scheme of life." Eleanor was appalled by such "independence and courage."[76] There were luncheons, dinners, and receptions. And every afternoon she went from door to door, as Bye had directed she must, carrying her cards and repeating her formula, "I am Mrs. Franklin D. Roosevelt. My husband has just come as Assistant Secretary of the Navy."[77] She stopped at great houses, climbed stairs in rooming houses, searched large and small hotels. She wondered why New York Congressmen moved so often from place to place.

Society had not changed its pace though new personages moved in it. Henry Adams had noted an item in change at the beginning of the Wilson years with a note soon after the inauguration to Mrs. Cameron: "Mrs. Leiter died, as you must have seen. She was lucky in getting away so easily, but she carries off one of our landmarks. With her has gone the whole bunch of Taft people and nearly all the old politicians."[78] But not all who remained were pleased with the change.

Some for whom *The Clubfellow and Washington Mirror* spoke, took a "decided distaste" to the President after he had called off the Inaugural Ball even though they snorted that of course such a ball was "only a stranger's revel, partaking of the nature of a stampede."[79] And Mrs. Wilson's statement that she had put a limit of a thousand dollars a year on her wardrobe brought some derision. *The Clubfellow* saw her concern for the city's alley warrens, containing so many of the Negroes who made a third of the city's population, as slumming. It conceded disdainfully that if visits to these alleys were to consume her time she might well stay within her thousand dollar budget. It declared defiantly, however, that society would go on wearing gowns some of which "will cost more than her entire wardrobe."[80]

Even such a Democrat as Ellen Maury Slayden made some disdainful entries in her journal about the new administration. Actually Ellen, daughter of the famous Maury family of Virginia with its seat at Charlottesville, had known Wilson as a student at the University of Virginia and did not like him then. As wife of a Kentuckian who had become a Congressman from Texas in 1897 she had made a socially secure place for herself before the Wilsonians arrived. But she kept Texas prejudices against what she considered to be the comic pretentiousness of Wilson's great friend Colonel E. M. House and the Texans of his own choice for whom he found jobs in the Wilson administration.

She was ready with more than impish power to conduct a feminine vendetta with Wilson's Cabinet wives who, supposedly at the lead of Mrs. Franklin K. Lane, had announced that they could not be bothered with social obligation to mere members of the House of Representatives. Her victory may have contributed later to the President's political purge of her husband. She wrote both ruefully and ruthlessly of personages on the Washington scene, not all of them Wilsonians.

She had none of the pretensions of Henry Adams as an "old cardinal" commentator. She lacked his money and his philosophy.

But she was a pretty charming woman who brought a relentlessly feminine eye to an often feminine scene. Devoted to arts and causes she could see the ridiculous aspects of both. She supported woman suffrage but was irritated by the bad manners of the suffragettes. She was for peace but irked by some of the shrill pacifists. She was deeply religious but offended by a belligerent clergy. On occasion she could even see herself as a snob.

She found Ellen Axson Wilson "short, round-faced, round pompadoured, red-cheeked and not becomingly dressed." She wrote in her diary: "I don't question the Wilson breeding, but they certainly lack manner and cordiality."[81]

Few understood the strain which her place as First Lady put on Ellen Wilson. At her husband's inauguration she felt inadequate. Then, as her daughter Eleanor wrote later, Ellen "so white and helpless and so tiny"[82] had burst into tears as she prepared to make the formal pre-inaugural call on the very kind and helpful Tafts. After she was gone Eleanor threw herself down weeping and pounding the floor crying, "It will kill them—it will kill them both."[83] Soon, however, forgetting her fears, she was at a party in a "divine dress" doing the foxtrot and feeling that the world was "a rosy place, particularly designed so that I might have a good time."[84] But Taft, looking like a man more released than defeated, told his successor in the White House, "I'm glad to be going—this is the loneliest place in the world."[85]

Ellen Wilson was lonely. She could not count on much social sympathy. In January 1914, *Town Topics*, a journal which provided protections to those who lent money to its publisher mustachioed Colonel William d'Alton Mann and "never tried to get it back," described the Wilson version of the diplomatic reception which under Theodore Roosevelt had seemed a little too regal to Henry Adams. Now this organ of gossip reported: "Never were the glooms more ably represented than at the President's recent diplomatic reception; never was frugality more perfectly observed, and never were the arrangements for a White House entertainment more abominable. The guests were herded within silken ropes after the fashion of immigrants on Ellis Island, or common steers awaiting slaughter. . . .

"The diplomats did not linger long in the dining room, or anywhere else, for that matter. As soon as etiquette permitted they fled, Madame Bakhmeteff leading the rout. I saw her as she approached the private elevator, wonderfully bejeweled, her diadem of enormous aquamarines nodding with every step as she pulled the ambassador along and expressed palpable anger in fluent Russian."[86]

Still the new democratic society did not seem unsophisticated to Eleanor Roosevelt, who had not had quiet Ellen Wilson's social experience as wife of the president of Princeton and the Governor of New Jersey. In any perplexity Mrs. Wilson had the guidance and aid of Belle Hagner who had taken the post of social secretary under Mrs. Theodore Roosevelt and kept it under the Tafts. Even *The Clubfellow* had to admit that Belle was "smart even if she is proportioned on mammoth lines."[87] Under pressure and pregnant, Eleanor needed some such help.

"I tried at first to do without a secretary," she wrote, "but found that it took me such endless hours to arrange my calling list, and answer and send invitations, that I finally engaged one for three mornings a week."[88]

She did not give the secretary's name in her memoirs. But she was Lucy Page Mercer. She was not modeled on the mammoth lines of Belle Hagner. But she was the kind of girl of assured social position but very insecure finances whom Auntie Bye had delighted to help. It would not be too great an assumption in this case also that in seeking a secretary Eleanor turned again to Auntie Bye for advice and recommendation. Certainly Lucy Mercer, then twenty-three, pretty and poor, was the kind of girl old Bye always saw with a sympathetic eye.

THREE

Sinister Street

(1)

Blond, slim, young Lucy Mercer moved a familiar way to the Roosevelt house at 1733 N Street. When she was in her first teens she had lived in the same block of row houses behind almost postage-stamp lawns. She had run in and out of many of the decorous houses then. More recently she had come calling as welcome and decorative guest of old friends behind prim doors. This row of respectability contained much of her story and the city's, too. It ran from Connecticut Avenue where then the British Embassy stood—or reared—as an enormous, ornate red brick monument of Victorianism long after Victoria was dead. The building, in which many of Franklin Roosevelt's friends were to live and work, often invited amazed description.

Its exterior, wrote Nathalie Colby, whose husband Bainbridge was later and briefly to be Wilson's Secretary of State, was "disarming, it was so ugly." It had been built, she said, "in the wrong period one knew, without looking up American architecture. Its cracks were so sooty it might have been steeped in a London fog. Outside on the pavement a guard in a red jacket who wore an opossum muff on his head was the only bright spot."[1] But Edith Benham, who worked as social secretary there, found great warmth within it. She remembered always the "Victorian solidity of the

Embassy staircase of the 'black walnut period.' It climbed solidly from the entrance hallway, dividing at the landing midway to the second floor, and over the landing hung a charming portrait of Queen Victoria in her youth." Once she spoke of the staircase to Sir William Tyrrell, diplomatic agent who often seemed a more continuous presence in Washington than changing ambassadors.

"Do not regret that example of the Victorian period, Miss Benham," Sir William told her. "It was a period in British history which will never return."[2]

Still, when Lucy Mercer passed it in 1914, change seemed imperceptible not only in the embassy but on the street which ran eastward from it. Beyond Connecticut Avenue, shaded N Street itself unostentatiously monumented a period. Many of its residents were period persons who definitely had no regrets about Victorian examples in architecture or anything else. A number of them were listed within the black, purple-titled and still very thin Washington *Social Register*.

Some were retired civil servants and members of Congress who lingered in Washington after their service was over. Here resided retired generals who had fought the Confederates and the Sioux Indians. Here lived an admiral who had explored New Guinea and succeeded to the command of the Asiatic Fleet after Dewey's victory at Manila. A house undistinguishable from others was the home of a gentleman who had helped erect the uniquely ugly State, War and Navy Building on Pennsylvania Avenue beside the White House. At 1748 the widow of Edward Everett Hale kept sacred the memory of that author-clergyman who had spent his last years as chaplain of the Senate. The house in which Lucy had lived as a child was at 1761. Helen (Nellie) Hunt, whom Edith Benham regarded as the pioneer social secretary, lived at 1710.

Just across from it, at 1707, was the impeccable-appearing house which seemed to some to mark the collapse of Victorian values. Here lived, as if behind closed curtains, Mrs. Philip Hichborn, widow of an admiral said to be a descendant of Paul Revere who had risen from shipwright apprentice to the flag rank. The balanced turrets he had invented had helped make possible modern battleships. He had been, of course, an honored member of professional and patriotic societies. But in 1914 the Hichborn house was chiefly noted because of the scandal and tragedy which had engulfed it, sending waves of shock to society in Washington and Philadelphia.

In 1905, Admiral Hichborn's son, Philip, fisherman and sportsman, had married "luminous and radiant" Elinor Morton Hoyt when she was twenty. Her father, son of a governor of Pennsylvania who married a Philadelphia banker's daughter, came to Washington in 1903 to be Solicitor-General of the United States. Her older sister, Constance, had married a popular German diplomat. Perhaps as an aspiring poet Elinor felt at first an affinity for Hichborn as a young writer of stories about horses. Their marriage seemed as uneventful as it was fashionable. A son was born to them in 1907. But Elinor, as her younger sister Nancy afterward wrote, disliked days spent in burning sun on Philip's small, smelly motorboat. She seemed imprisoned in the "stiffly starched collars and strangely cut garments" which he insisted that she wear.[3] She was, wrote Nancy in her biography subtitled *Portrait of an Unknown Lady*, "a winged arrow, bound to be released at some sudden impulse from the bow of this world."[4] The form of that release "crashed the mirror"[5] of the society which ran along N Street from the portrait of Victoria in the ugly brick embassy.

In December 1910, Elinor eloped with the much older Horace Wylie, able lawyer, clubman, and the skilled card player of the Metropolitan. Wylie left a family, too, and a wife who declined to agree to a divorce. But on his side the deserted Hichborn marked the scandal with his blood in 1912 when he killed himself. This was the same year in which his stories were published in a volume called *Hoof Beats* and in which Elinor's mother, declining to abandon her errant daughter, had printed for her in London, as a gift, a thin volume of Elinor's verses called *Incidental Numbers*. Literary critics found in the book little of the felicity which marked her later work. With stony faces, social critics in Washington passed the places she had known.

Lucy Mercer, as she came along N Street in 1914, was only a little younger than Elinor Wylie had been when she had fled from such proprieties as marked it. The street seemed not wounded by her behavior. All its houses kept their bland faces. Gentlemen took their constitutionals. Ladies made their calls. And the Roosevelt house, with Bye's ugly walnut furniture and the tiled fireplaces with carved mantels, seemed the epitome of durable domesticity. Its rooms set like cubes in a box, with sliding double doors between the salons on the main floor, seemed crowded with children and servants. Eleanor's pregnancy was advancing. One visitor to the house at this time observed that it appeared to be already full of babies and got the impression also "that the young Roosevelts had not been taught to blow their noses or just did not care to blow them."[6]

Ugly as even Eleanor sometimes thought it, the house was comfortable. The meeting of Eleanor and Lucy, both products of similar well-bred backgrounds, was comfortable too. Eleanor needed Lucy's aid as Lucy needed Eleanor's pay. No sharing of their experiences was required. Yet Eleanor found in Lucy a girl who had been listed in society in both New York and Washington. Also she had been an eighteen-year-old girl sharing aristocratic company in Austria which Eleanor had only visited as a tourist in the Tyrol. Perhaps, even more startling, she was familiar with the not entirely parochial society in North Carolina from which Roosevelt's chief, Secretary Daniels, came.

Whatever may have been their first impressions of each other, they were similar in gentility. Also, though imperceptible, both had had troubled girlhoods. Eleanor, as she could afford to do, wrote her seemingly realistic book about herself as a poor little rich girl. Lucy as less affluent had perhaps greater reasons for reticence—or less inclination to recite remembered woes. Actually when her world was least secure, it had been gay—sometimes improvidently so. There had never been anything of the ugly duckling about Lucy, yet in such fairy story metaphor both she and Eleanor were Cinderellas, though Eleanor then had found the Prince Charming. Eleanor was still acutely conscious of inadequacies which she tried to hide before she described them in detail and possible exaggeration. There was no secret about Lucy's need. It had brought her to the house. A social secretary was not a scullery maid; neither did it quite carry regal rank. She had definitely then lost the perquisites required of a princess. So lacking a fairy godmother she needed a job.

Since her family had left N Street a decade before, hers had been what a later day would call a broken home. Perhaps then gossip was more safely directed at the male. The day of physical resentment at any slur at a lady had not quite passed. At any rate gossip chroniclers had reported that Carroll Mercer, after the century began, had "descended to obscurity and want, having dissipated fortune and alienated his wife and nearly all his friends."[7] Actually many old friends stood by him across his lean years. Also, later Minnie reported that in 1901 an examination showed he had chronic diabetes and Bright's disease. Whatever may have been the cause, family tensions were created. Early in the decade Minnie moved with her girls to New York to engage in what was then called the "inside decorating" business.

Evidently, however, she was in no real want. Her address, listed in both the *Social Register* and *Dau's New York Social Blue Book* of New York City, suggested comfortable circumstances. Other tenants in the Holland Apartments at 66 West 46th Street where they lived included several listed in the *Social Register* and one gentleman who had helped build the House and Senate Office Buildings in Washington. Minnie was still a tall, very handsome, dark-haired woman. She was said to have had rich patrons including Grant Barney Schley, wealthy New York stock broker and banker. In 1909, Minnie was apparently alone in the apartment as that year's *Social Register* noted: "Mr. absent—Juniors Miss Violetta C. and Lucy P. care Ctss. Heussenstamm, Melk, Austria."[8]

The Countess, of course, had been Agnes Carroll of Carrollton and Doughoregan Manor. Some suggestion of her place in society was indicated in a Parisian vignette of the time when the Mercer girls were in her care in Austria. Her relative, the current Charles Carroll of Carrollton, had married Marie-Louise Suzanne Ban-

croft, daughter of Adams' famous neighbor. Adams wrote of seeing this Suzanne as a "resplendent figure in full diamonds" who
stopped to speak to him in a corridor of the Ritz in Paris while
on her way to a ball given by the Grand Duchess Cyril and Grand
Duke and Grand Duchess Vladimir in June 1909.[9]

The Vladimir name suggests the Russian country where then
cherry orchards spread wide on the slopes of hills. In each orchard
was a small watchtower with cords drawn in all directions to be
shaken by the watcher when birds came. The watchers and their
masters were not warned of greater dangers than that to the red
cherries when, in 1904, the Moscow Art Theater produced *The
Cherry Orchard* by Anton Chekhov. Everybody at the Ritz, Adams wrote of the ball in Paris, was "pleased or furious at being
asked or neglected."[10] Among the furious and neglected, Adams
noted with happy malice, was Harry Lehr, who then presumed to
have taken Ward McAllister's place in American society.[11]

Evidently the Countess Heussenstamm kept up, as the Countess Esterhazy did, with Maryland-Washington cousins and old
friends. The Countess Heussenstamm was in her mid-forties when
the Mercer girls came to her husband's family seat at Matzleins-
dorf near Melk. This country by the Danube was not only picturesquely beautiful but was also marked by such monuments as
the splendid Benedictine monastery of Melk and the ruins of Dur-
renstein, the prison of Richard Coeur de Lion. The girls were not
children in 1909. Violetta was twenty, Lucy eighteen. On the same
Austrian scene they had attended a convent patronized by patrician Austrian and some American girls. In the Catholic school to
which the Mercer girls were sent was also Marguerita Pennington
of Maryland, who would come into their story again later. Evidently Carroll kin helped with the Mercer girls' education. Apparently, however, Minnie sent her girls well equipped. Their cousins,
the Cottens, remembered an amusing incident of their convent
days. Their nightgowns were so dainty and lovely that the nuns
were shocked by them. One austere sister opined that only
prostitutes wore such garments. She was abashed when the girls
asked her to tell them what prostitutes were.[12]

No record exists of their education abroad such as Eleanor wrote of her troubles and triumphs during her schooling in England. The Mercers were not given to self-documentation. The Austrian nuns provided the kind of education deemed required by a young lady of the time with emphasis on prayer as well as pedagogy. Certainly in the years after her convent days Lucy was unostentatiously devout. Also she was a woman involved in the mock morality of gossips. Washington, which was so shocked by such scandal as the elopement of Elinor Wylie, enjoyed chewing on old morsels of gossip. It was reminded in 1912 of the Mercer separation in an elaborate rehash. *Town Topics* reported that the Mercers were reuniting in the capital.[13] It stated that Carroll had returned to the city as one of the managers of the Riding Club of which he had once been a leading member. While Minnie had supported herself as a decorator in New York, it said, Carroll had lived "any old way."[14] But now he was "a bit stouter, a bit grayer and much more serious."[15] Mercer fortunes were looking up again: "Mrs. Mercer has forgiven Carroll, they have gone back to Washington, and all goes merry as a marriage bell."[16]

That does not seem to have quite been the case. It was a gossip's irrelevant statement in 1912 that "the Mercers have two lovely daughters, Violetta and Lucy, both old enough to come out."[17] They were older than that. Both were past twenty-one. In her old age Edith Benham Helm thought she remembered seeing Lucy as a very pretty girl at her debutant party "as her family were old friends of mine."[18] Actually both girls needed jobs and *The Clubfellow and Washington Mirror* in 1912 reported, "Mrs. Mercer has placed both her daughters in self-supporting positions; one a trained nurse; and the other an inside decorator."[19] Minnie herself, as reported later, found a position in "an art establishment in the Northwest"[20] section of the city.

Lucy was the inside decorator. In 1914 when she took the place as Eleanor Roosevelt's social secretary she and her mother and sister were living at the Decatur at 2131 Florida Avenue, N.W. Carroll was boarding at 1307 K Street. Obviously no reunion of Carroll and Minnie had occurred. None was in prospect.

Like their residence in New York, the Decatur address of Minnie and her girls indicated no dire poverty. Many of the genteel, though none of the opulent, lived in its apartments. The Cave Dwellers do not quickly abandon their own. Hard times and hard luck do not erase a patrician heritage. Some insecure snobs undertook to condescend to the established poor. Some even tried to draw a line between themselves and the better born who had happened to be "in trade." With less money the Mercers were still the aborigines. The place of the Mercer girls in Washington society was secure even if their finances were precarious. They were pretty. They had charm. Eleanor Roosevelt could hardly have found a young woman who understood the society of the old capital city better than Lucy. If its social system sometimes seemed to oppressed and pregnant Eleanor like a demanding maze of customs and duties, she could not have found a better or more decorative aide.

Possibly Lucy could not have found a better job. Still, as Edith Benham Helm described the craft of social secretary in her memoirs, it could be both pleasant and sometimes demanding. It required attendance to much detail, ability to share and sometimes assume the duties of a hostess with poise and charm. Sometimes the secretary who presided at the tea table was, as Edith said, expected to "air the dog and wash the baby."[21] With so many servants in the Roosevelt house such duties were rare. But the pay by general standards was not opulent. For two hours a day on her first job Edith got $50 a month. When in 1915 she took on the greater duties required of the social secretary at the White House for full time her pay, as she remembered it, was between $1200 and $1800 a year. This seems approximately correct. When Belle Hagner went to the White House as Mrs. Theodore Roosevelt's social secretary, the New York World reported, she received $1400 and was carried on the White House payroll as a clerk. But generally affection for social secretaries went along with the pay. After Edith Carow Roosevelt left the White House she wrote Belle, "you have been my eldest child for so many years." Soon after Edith Benham became social secretary to the second Mrs. Wilson,

Secretary Daniels made a note in his diary about her, the naval officer James M. Helm, whom she later married, and the Wilsons: "Cabinet—One of the few times that the President asked about assignments. Helm had been ordered to Mare Island, & Pres. thought he was being shelved. I think due to Miss Benham." To whatever due, Helm was not sent to the West Coast station, he remained in Washington until 1918, when he was named Commandant of the Fourth Naval District with his station at Philadelphia.

In lesser ménages than the White House a social secretary's work could be by turns elegant and menial. Soon after Eleanor hired Lucy in 1914, she was away on one of her many absences with the children. Franklin came back to Washington where his presence was required at a reception for Latin American diplomats. He also had a luncheon date with the long-time friend of all Roosevelts, Ambassador Spring-Rice, to meet a very nice young professor from Calcutta to whom he gave a letter of introduction to "Uncle Ted." A preoccupied young man in a hurry, he wrote Eleanor: "Arrived safely and came to the house and Albert [the chauffeur] telephoned Miss Mercer who came later and cleaned up."[22]

(2)

Arranging the calling lists for Eleanor Roosevelt and checking off the innumerable calls already made was a dull chore for Lucy Mercer. Still she liked the job and the Roosevelts found her "well acquainted with the social obligations of an Assistant Secretary's wife."[23] It was not actually necessary for the wives of all officials to have secretaries, as Roosevelt's editor-son said later in the *Personal Letters* published with Eleanor Roosevelt's blessing. But in a household crowded with servants such a secretary was a natural addition to the staff of a lady who could afford one. Lucy was qualified to handle efficiently all invitations and correspondence of an official nature.

On the days when she came down windy Connecticut Avenue from the dull Decatur Apartments on Florida Avenue the world she worked with was different from that in which she lived. There was still gaiety as well as occasional tempestuousness in her mother. But as a fading beauty of fifty-one, Minnie Mercer did not like to be poor. Out of her past opulence she was coming to an age when she was eager even for small additions to her limited income. And undoubtedly she fretted about the lack of wealth to set off the beauty of her daughters. Her husbandless household needed Lucy's pay and Lucy enjoyed earning it in the Cowles house with its walnut furniture and back windows which looked out on a little garden with a rose arbor on one side.

In the fashion of social secretaries then, she appeared dutifully even when she was summoned by a chauffeur to come and clean up. From her desk and through the papers on it, she had a window also on the rich society which, despite her gentility, she could not quite enter. Washington, regardless of the reports of some carping critics, had not lost its glittering social life around a White House presided over by an intense professor and his timidly aloof and fragile wife. Some invitations to the Roosevelts indicated that not all of the *ancien régime* of the long Republican establishment had become émigrés. Knowledge of the kind of parties they still gave warmed the rough winter of 1914 even for the uninvited. One special party early in the year had about it some of the fair-lady-and brave-man glamour of continental society—even of Vienna where Lucy's aunts—maybe she and Violetta—had waltzed by an undisturbed Danube.

On the Potomac the Roosevelts were among those bidden to a gathering of Washington's new fencing club.[24] This group of the agile and the elite had been organized by Colonel Robert Means Thompson, rich president of the Navy League. Colonel Thompson was noted for his generous support of his two chief interests: a bigger American Navy and United States participation in the

Olympic Games. He was a little miffed at this time since the new administration had decided the colonel did not merit a uniformed naval officer as aide when he attended the international games. Still he was unsubdued by a government composed, as it seemed to him, of pedestrian Puritans.[25] The fencing club he organized, it was reported,[26] exceeded in numbers and élan even that one once activated by a former Russian Ambassador Count Cassini, whom Henry Adams described as sometimes almost apoplectic in his arrogance.[27] All the new club's members, said a much impressed society reporter, were "a bona fide collection of both sexes, all having won their spurs in European cities."[28] Its party brought together a company "as smart as Washington has seen gathered under one roof in many a moon."[29] Also it brought together some who would soon not be happily together under any roof: "Lady Spring-Rice was present and danced a few numbers, as did her intime, Madame Dumba," the wife of the Austro-Hungarian ambassador. The reporter noted that "a touch of officialdom"[30] was added in the charming person of Mrs. Franklin Roosevelt. It is safe to assume, however, that as a lady who could not manage a golf club, she did not wield a blade.

There were other pleasant parties, large and small. Ellen Slayden, as an eager diner-out and astringent reporter, found the company of those around Washington tables that winter concerned like the fencers with smaller problems than the reform of the currency, the revision of the tariff, even troubles in torn Mexico. Then topics included: shorter skirts, cigarette smoking by women, the tango. One Senator said to her, "For generations women have been showing off their clothes, now the clothes are reciprocating."[31] Other dinner partners were less frivolous. In a discussion of women smoking, Mrs. Slayden said to a more austere figure in the forces of the New Freedom that Austrian ladies did it so very prettily and naturally. This personage replied, "I never saw an Austrian lady." And, wrote Mrs. Slayden, he made it clear that he did not think "an Austrian could be a lady."[32]

Old Henry Adams, who wrote that in this long continuing winter he could only look out on a snow-covered square,[33] was not

involved in the debate of the outraged and the delighted about
the tango. Sourly, in a land by no means all rich, he contemplated
other American gyrations, social and political: "All are sad and
very much ruined. . . . As for New York, . . . everyone there is
begging for soup and dancing like grasshoppers."[34] But the most
militant of the admirals, Bradley A. Fiske, a small man with a
wide mustache, took the dancing very seriously. The turkey trot
seemed to him to go beyond the tango as an ominous portent.

"There have been several dancing crazes in recorded history,"
he wrote. "One dancing craze preceded the Crusades, another
dancing craze preceded the Reign of Terror. Every dancing craze
has been followed in about a year by an awful war."[35]

Sometimes in his wish to display his powers that prospect did
not seem entirely unpleasing to Fiske. Others, even of the less
prophetic, did not quite share a happier backward view expressed
by Herbert Hoover that the year marked the end of "the happiest
period of all humanity in the Western World in ten centuries."[36]
In the White House, across the square from Adams' icy prison,
many improvements on such possible perfection seemed required
even for Americans. Wilson believed he was making them. Others
in this "happiest period" doubted that. They had considered Wilson as not merely aloof but even supercilious in his early rejection
of membership in the Chevy Chase Club where Roosevelt spent
much time on the links. Others now insisted that a President
could not be merely solemn who so often appeared enjoying himself so much in his box at Keith's Theater. Obviously he delighted
in the girls and clowns of vaudeville with its swift, sometimes
abrupt, change of scene.

Outside his group in the box and in the Cabinet which met
around his table, little sympathy in March attended the report
that Ellen Wilson had been injured in a "fall" in the big mansion.
And not much attention was paid to a gossip magazine's revelation soon after that "the accident" was "far more serious than at
first suspected. The true condition of affairs has been guarded from
the public, but two well-known specialists from Philadelphia went
to Washington at the President's suggestion."[37] Whispers were

quieted when the little First Lady appeared in the gallery on April 20 when Wilson addressed Congress on troubles in Mexico. Certainly all seemed quietly festive in the White House when, on May 7, Mrs. Wilson played her role as mother of the bride at the marriage of her daughter Eleanor to the much older William G. McAdoo, Secretary of the Treasury and a widower with nearly grown children. Of course, it was said that the episode was received generally "with a sigh of weariness . . . McAdoo's picture doesn't exactly present a subject for love's young dream."[38] There was speculation about costly wedding presents. Actually McAdoo at fifty, riding on the Mall with the White House physician, Dr. Cary Grayson, USN, looked like a man on horseback or a rider in romance. He seemed almost as charming as the galloping doctor beside him who had been baffling matchmakers under three administrations. Eleanor, the bride, wrote that Grayson, generally described as a Virginia Apollo, had a chuckle like the sound of tearing silk.[39] Both men were friends of young Roosevelt who did not rate an invitation to the Wilson-McAdoo wedding. It was a small and simple affair compared to the last such White House event he had attended—the nuptial extravaganza of the Princess Alice Longworth.

In this same May, however, before the heat descended upon such places as the Decatur Apartments and even the White House, Franklin and Eleanor were guests at the more pictorial, if less publicized wedding in Hyde Park of Anne Pendleton Rogers and J. Griswold Webb. This one at the *Die Schöne Rosenzeit* estate of the Archibald Rogers family, in whose house Franklin had gone to a select kindergarten, arrayed many of the numerous company of the Dutchess County rich. Not all, of course; no one event could hope to include all the wealthy persons associated by residence or marriage with this one Hudson River county: Astor, Vanderbilt, Morton, Rutherfurd, Eustis, Delano, Mills, Livingston, others. On this occasion Mrs. Rogers continued a custom she had initiated two years before at the wedding of another daughter to Kenneth Schley, son of the banker Grant Barney Schley. In addition to the adult guests, in a manorial manner, Mrs.

Rogers, as a society writer related, arrayed "all the little village maidens, in their Sunday best, and squeaky shoes." It was a gala occasion and among the many guests present, said a reporter who had a bad eye for altitude, was Franklin's "sensible little wife."[40]

Tall Eleanor was about to head for Campobello with her staff and children to escape the Washington heat and await the arrival of her new baby. It seemed to her, she wrote, that "for ten years I was always just getting over having a baby or about to have one."[41] This would be her fifth. As evidence of their wealth and position, the Roosevelts had arranged for Dr. Albert Ely of New York, one of the leading gynecologists of the country, to come to Campobello to deliver her.

Others were getting away from the muggy heat of Washington. Not all could escape. One bored wife of a Congressman said of this time in 1914, "this is the dullest place on earth in summer. No gardens, theaters, or music, and no driving except for the opulent."[42] It was not quite that dull for the young and gay like Lucy Mercer and her friends. Others later, when duty bound them to the capital, were also to discover the fun of picnicking on the Potomac, walks in the Virginia woods and dancing in pleasant inns and amusement parks. Even Alice Longworth and her Nick were later to avail themselves of the public pools of a so-called bathing beach. Then Alice was noted in a bathing suit "which is a vision and delight. It is sea-green with broad bands of white. With this she wears apple-green hose and a beautiful head covering topped off with a big bow."[43] Even in 1914 there were such facilities for fun and figures to enhance it. This year, however, the richest departed, many on annual visits to Europe. People only vaguely wondered why the Wilsons did not leave the White House for Cornish, New Hampshire, where the year before and the year after the Summer White House was the leased Harlakenden estate of the romantic American novelist Winston Churchill.

Many departed. Henry Adams sailed in April, joining an American invasion of Europe which he pretended to scorn. The year before he had written Mrs. Cameron, "Every château in the Verein seems to be occupied by Americans. . . . Some Jew is of course the swellest."[44] English country houses were filled with more Americans. Few of them were unable, as was the bluff Don Cameron, to "fit himself into the lazy alien life of an English country house existence."[45] Among visitors and travelers were Adams' brother Brooks and his wife, Senator and Mrs. Lodge and their daughter and son-in-law, Congressman Augustus Peabody Gardner. The Willie Eustises were living the life of country gentlefolk on an Irish estate. In a village in Surrey, Elinor and Horace Wylie had been letting time flow through their fingers in their flight or escape in terms of all for love and the world well lost.

Most dramatic figures in the American throng abroad in the felicitous summer of 1914 were the father and daughter, Theodore Roosevelt and Alice. While her husband, Nick Longworth, was mending the political fences TR had smashed for him in 1912, Alice went to Madrid with her imperial parent. There in June, Kermit Roosevelt married Belle Willard, daughter of Wilson's Ambassador to Spain, Joseph Edward Willard, who earlier had been described as the richest man in Virginia. The combination of Willard wealth and Rooseveltian prestige made the event an international spectacle in which even the Royal Family played a hospitable role. Spain apparently neither remembered nor cared that it had been Roosevelt who mightily helped in the deflation of the fiction of Spanish power sixteen years before.[46]

From the wedding Alice and her father moved to hospitable France, then to England where entertaining for the ex-President was at the peak of protocol. Roosevelt went on home but Alice "managed to miss two or three boats." For her those June and July days seemed almost the tango time of the age of felicity. She had the feeling in England that, while the ladies and gentlemen she met ardently debated such questions as Irish home rule and the reduction of the House of Lords to impotency, "a political novel . . . was in process of writing itself day by day before one's very eyes."[47]

One of its scenes was at Cliveden, beautifully situated on the banks of the Thames in Buckinghamshire. Already then the great house, which was to become a name for debate about a war in history later, was presided over by thirty-five-year-old Nancy Langhorne of Virginia. Her sister Irene had married Charles Dana Gibson and become his model in his pictorial satire of international marriages. But only five years before, following her divorce from the Bostonian Robert Gould Shaw, Nancy had married William Waldorf Astor, Jr., son of the expatriate Lord Astor who many felt had purchased his peerage. Cliveden was as serene as its swans. But there Alice met "a particularly pretty, attractive gentle lady" who the week before had violently defied police in a suffrage demonstration.

The placid English countryside did not suffice. In London, Alice stayed "on my own" at a hotel, evidently a rather daring thing then even for a matron of thirty. Then she was off on a weekend jaunt to Paris for the running of the Grand Prix at Longchamps. Very hospitable to her in Paris was Neil Primrose, son of former British Prime Minister Lord Rosebery, whose horses had won the Derby three times. Primrose, then a rising Liberal politician in his early thirties, took Alice and friends to the great houses of his Rothschild kin on a scarcely interrupted round of "gay, carefree parties of pre-war Paris."[48]

At the race track the news came of the assassination of Francis Ferdinand, Archduke of Austria, and his morganatic wife in Sarajevo, Bosnia-Herzegovina, on June 28. This seemed a matter of little importance to the box holders at Longchamps. An American woman who had married a German said to Alice that due to the Archduke's morganatic marriage this might prevent troubles in the succession to the Austro-Hungarian throne. Violence and Hapsburgs were not a surprising combination. Archduke Rudolf, who before Francis Ferdinand had been heir to the throne, had killed himself at Mayerling years before in a suicide pact with a pretty seventeen-year-old baroness. That had only been followed by the fumbling efforts of the emperor to disguise the facts. The almost standard effect of that had been to arouse curiosity and produce the most sensational reports.

Certainly the incident at Sarajevo did not interrupt Alice's gay summer. Back in London, after only six hours' sleep in thirty-six, she went—and stayed late—with the Raymond Asquiths to "White City," a restaurant in a brightly illuminated amusement park. This Asquith was the son of the then Prime Minister Herbert Henry Asquith. The lights seemed turned up all over the world. On the night before she sailed on an unthreatened sea, Alice played bridge with Primrose, "Jimmie" Rothschild, and F. E. Smith— not yet Lord Birkenhead—until just in time to get a bath and breakfast and make the boat train. She missed the outbreak of war by two weeks. And, of course, as she sailed there was no thought that Primrose would die as a soldier leading a charge in Palestine, or that young Asquith had a *rendez-vous* with death in France as a lieutenant in the Grenadier Guards.[49]

Alone in the N Street house in this somnolent summer, Franklin reported unexciting activities to Eleanor in letters addressed to "dearest," the same term he used to his mother. As often as he could he got away to Campobello. He was able to put his official duties and personal predelictions together by inspecting New England Naval stations and attending the launching of the battleship *Nevada* in Quincy, Massachusetts. En route, on one trip in July, he got in twenty-two holes of golf with his old and lively Harvard mate Livingston (Livy) Davis at the Essex Country Club in the Massachusetts North Shore neighborhood of Roosevelt's Republican friend, Congressman Gardner.

Then from Washington, on Sunday, July 19, three weeks after the assassination,[50] he wrote Eleanor his most significant news. He was so full of energy that that day he had gone by trolley to Chevy Chase and played forty-five holes of golf. He was almost dead, he told her. But he went out to dinner and afterward wrote this long letter. In it he indicated ambition or discontent, perhaps both. He had been in the post of Assistant Secretary of the Navy longer than TR had been when he left it as an already used stepping stone toward the presidency.

"They" (anti-Tammany Democrats, including McAdoo) wanted him to run for the Democratic nomination for the United States Senate. He got little encouragement from his politically more realistic chief, Secretary Daniels. The older politician doubted that he could win in the primary; and if he did, indications were that the Republicans would carry the state in the general election.[51]

Franklin went off, still undecided, to see Eleanor again. He took along two English friends, the Archer-Shee brothers, one of whom had married a Dutchess County girl. As lithe and skillful sailor, Roosevelt took his friends sailing in his *Half Moon* on the high tides and swift currents of the Bay of Fundy. While they sailed ominous tides were rising in the belligerent and almost unbelievable antagonisms of the European powers following the assassination of the Archduke whom most Americans had never heard of in the town the name of which few could pronounce.

Even at Campobello the news clearly indicated general war. The Archer-Shee brothers departed to join their regiments, the younger of them to die within the next month. Franklin headed southward to play a subordinate but official role in the ceremonial opening of the Cape Cod Canal on July 29. He seemed a little surprised by a wire from his friend Livy Davis that he could not join him "because of the business crisis." But Roosevelt himself, he said, was less surprised when he reached Washington on August 2, the day after Germany declared war on Russia.

He went straight to the Navy Department, he wrote Eleanor, "where, as I expected, I found everything asleep and apparently utterly oblivious to the fact that the most terrible drama in history was about to be enacted."[52]

He went on in greater impatience and what would have seemed impertinence to the point of insubordination to any other eyes but Eleanor's. He wrote: "To my astonishment on reaching the Dept. nobody seemed the least bit excited about the European crisis—Mr. Daniels feeling chiefly very sad that his faith in human nature and civilization and similar idealistic nonsense was receiving such a rude shock. So I started in alone to get things done and prepare plans for what *ought* to be done by the Navy end of things. . . .

"These good dear people like W.J.B. and J.D. have as much conception of what a general war means as Elliott has of higher mathematics."[53]

His boy Elliott was then a bowlegged child of four. And Roosevelt not only put William Jennings Bryan and Daniels in the category of his mental age. He had already, ten days before, registered his impatience with Wilson's whole administration in matters of foreign affairs: "We drift on from day to day as usual. . . ."[54]

Roosevelt's Elliott (at an age when he may have understood higher mathematics) later depreciated these remarks as "youthful and impetuous."[55] Actually, however, though possibly boastful, Franklin's report was probably accurate. Compared to the society in which he moved Bryan and Daniels, even Wilson, were insular men. Franklin's friends and associates were more familiar with Europe—or at least its hotels, cafes, galleries, and country houses —than with North Carolina or Nebraska. His friend Livy Davis had made nine trips to Europe before he entered Harvard. Before he became Assistant Secretary, Franklin had made twenty such crossings.

Wilson, Bryan, and Daniels were primarily concerned with domestic reform. Daniels, who had issued an order banning intoxicants for naval officers as they had long before been outlawed for enlisted men, seemed as Navy chief more concerned with democracy and morality than militancy. Sometimes he seemed to regard armament makers—and armament promoters like the fencing Colonel Thompson—as the chief enemies with which the Navy had to contend. Bryan, who had recently had some old sabers melted down to make paperweights shaped like plowshares, was negotiating a whole series of treaties designed to substitute negotiation for war. In July, Wilson sent the Senate twenty more of these Bryan peace treaties. All three men apparently regarded the Navy as a necessary evil in a world in which peace should prevail. At best they regarded it as a sort of police instrument in a hemisphere in which such delinquent nations as Mexico, Haiti and Santo Domingo had to be kept in order. What Roosevelt, with some of the easy maneuverability of a small boat man, confronted was a sort of stunned inertia of older men who had been reckoning on reform not explosion. Roosevelt's report, if not his behavior, was correct enough.

But Roosevelt had come into the long, dark, parqueted corridors of the ugly old State, War and Navy Building at a time when, apart from war in Europe, there was a sense of foreboding. The summer weather had been hot and enervating. In the heat, the city, which always takes much of its mood from the White House, began to feel that something like the end of a time of felicity was symbolized by a tiny woman dying there. Little was said about it, hardly anything printed. Then some felt that a "rather meaningless secretiveness"[56] about her illness was suddenly dispelled when on the morning of August 6, the papers announced that she was at the point of death from Bright's disease. She died the same day. The next day Roosevelt wrote, "It is too horrible about Mrs. Wilson. We knew on Wednesday that there was little hope and the end came last night. The President has been truly wonderful, but I dread a breakdown. The funeral is Monday at the White House, I don't yet know whether Assistant Secretaries will be expected to go or not."[57]

They were not expected. But he was not too much cast down. In the same letter he exulted, "Gee! But these are strenuous days." He added, "Most of the reports of foreign cruisers off the coast have really been of *my* destroyers."[58]

There seemed little time for his or the nation's mourning. Before Ellen Wilson died the Senate, almost as an offering of flowers to a sick room, passed a bill she had urged to clean up the alley slums of the city. She was not told of the war. There was, said Ellen Slayden, "much less effusion and gush"[59] than normally attended such events. So far as the public could see, all things connected with the death and funeral were of a "cold, perfunctory nature." Ellen Wilson was such a little woman to die at so tremendous a time.

Franklin was to be in Washington steadily less than two weeks in the next two months. But he had an exciting sense of his importance. He wrote, "Alive and well and keen about everything. I am running the real work, although Josephus is here. He is bewildered by it all, very sweet but very sad."[60] He cited an instance of his exasperation: "To my horror, *just for example*, J.D. told the newspapermen he thought favorably of sending our fleet to Europe to bring back marooned Americans."[61]

"Naturally," he wrote Eleanor, "I am worried about Coz, Susie and Henry and Aunt Jennie and Laura and Sara."[62] Those Parish and Delano relatives were more of the throng in Europe. Also at sea on the *Kronprinzessin Cecilie* headed for England as the war began was his half-brother, Rosy, who was convalescing from recent surgery on a honeymoon with a new wife. More of Franklin's friends were caught helpless in Paris, London, Berlin. They lined up at shipping offices which had no transatlantic bookings to offer, queued up at banks which declined to honor their credit, milled about overwhelmed American embassies and consulates.

Old Adams, caught on the Avenue du Trocadero, rather liked the situation at first: "to me the crumbling of worlds is always fun." But by the time he managed escape to England his philosophy was battered by experiences which "verged on hell, and no slouch of a bad one." The Cabot Lodges, he wrote, were, "not strictly happy, mais a la guerre!"[63] Adams himself found temporary refuge at the estate of Mrs. Ronald Lindsay, the daughter of Elizabeth Cameron, in Dorset. In London Gardner and Eustis volunteered as extra members of the embassy staff and mightily helped with "American refugees" who were clamoring for ship space. If the refugees' credit did not extend to the war zone, their clamor was negotiable in the United States. Roosevelt, however, was disgusted with Daniels' battleship plan to relieve them.

"Aside from the fact that tourists (female etc.) couldn't sleep in hammocks and that battleships haven't got passenger accommodations, he totally fails to grasp the fact that this war between the other powers is going inevitably to give rise to a hundred different complications in which we shall have a direct interest."[64] He dodged assignment to go along with the *North Carolina* and the *Tennessee* when they sailed with public and private funds to relieve the refugees. Then almost simultaneously, "through a stern sense of duty," he announced for the United States Senate and set out again for Campobello.[65] Eleanor was delivered safely on

August 17, though by a local doctor in the absence of the famous gynecologist who didn't turn up.

Franklin's labors were more difficult. There was some genteel liberal applause for his candidacy. But in his own Dutchess County he had aroused antagonisms in his party by trying to dictate the appointment of his choice for postmaster in Poughkeepsie. His pince-nez independence in the State Senate still riled Tammany. The mildest attack upon him was that he was too immature for a Senate seat. More angrily, it was charged that he was undemocratic, condescending and that his hostility to Tammany was based on racial and religious prejudices, notably against the Irish. A story was revived that when he first sought a seat in the State Senate, he walked into a local political meeting wearing riding boots and breeches. A county leader, who understood that not all the rural voters in Dutchess County were the gentry or particularly cared for them, told him to go home and put on a regular pair of pants. Many years later when he was running for governor he understood the danger of the charge that he was a squire and a snob.[66]

The real blow came when Tammany presented as its candidate James W. Gerard, a man of culture, integrity and ability who was Wilson's Ambassador to Germany. Roosevelt turned for help to Bryan of whom he had recently been so contemptuous. Bryan urged the President to advise Gerard not to run.[67] Wilson declined to intervene. He had no intention of jeopardizing support of his program by New York regulars who had recently complained to him that Roosevelt had been one of those characterizing them as "representatives of crooks, grafters and political buccaneers."[68] Gerard did not come home from his critical post to campaign but he overwhelmed Roosevelt, upstate as well as in the city, by a vote of nearly three to one. After "six weeks of campaigning," as his son reported,[69] Franklin came back to Washington. On the surface at least he was unsubdued. "We paved the way," he said in a statement minimizing the proportions of his rejection. But, said Secretary Daniels, he was "hurt."[70]

He turned, for more congenial company than New York Democrats, to many of those who had recently been "refugees" abroad, and with whom he was comfortable as members of his class. He found good and elite friends in the Metropolitan and Chevy Chase Clubs. He visited the Eustises who had no prejudices against elegantly accoutered horsemen. Indeed, Willie, after his sojourn abroad, seemed more than ever as was noted, "a typical English country squire."[71] Edith, like other Morton girls, was much attracted to horse-and-dog men. Her sister Alice, who was often in town visiting at her father's place on Scott Circle, was the wife of Winthrop Rutherfurd, well-known as one of the nation's leading breeders of fox terriers.

Roosevelt found particularly more exciting company in two other of the recent "refugees." Uncle Ted's friend Senator Lodge and his son-in-law Congressman Gardner. Gardner, Nick Longworth's "intimate friend,"[72] was soon to become Secretary Daniels' "most vehement foe in congress."[73] They had come home not only with relief but in a fervor. Both were impatient with the pacific attitude of the administration. Quietly, Franklin as Democratic official passed to the Republican Gardner information about weaknesses in the Navy. He dined with General Leonard Wood, Uncle Ted's comrade in Cuba, now most belligerent of the generals. Franklin found his ideas, including military training for businessmen, "most interesting."[74] He confided to Eleanor that the country "needs the truth about the Army and Navy instead of a lot of soft mush about everlasting peace which so many statesmen are handing out to a gullible public."[75] He was bold and careful by turns, however, in dissenting from the "statesmen" who were his superiors. He was having difficulty not speaking out despite Wilson's proclamation of neutrality. There was no neutrality in his choice of friends. He was honored by the company of British Ambassador Spring-Rice and shared that delicate diplomat's resentment when at the Metropolitan Club the German Ambassador, Count Johann Heinrich von Bernstorff, at a next table seemed to be trying to overhear their conversation.

Later events drew von Bernstorff's portrait in resentment. Before this time he was drawn in terms of both admiration and revulsion. In effect he had been brought to his Washington post by Theodore Roosevelt's friend Henry White, admirable American diplomat who had married one of the beautiful Rutherfurd girls. In London, White had known and admired von Bernstorff who was councilor of the German Embassy there. When von Bernstorff's name was suggested with others to Roosevelt, White had warmly recommended him.[76] On the other hand, Archie Butt reported that President Taft considered the German Ambassador "very much of a prig." In addition, "He had never thought the same of him since he saw him playing golf with a lady in his shirt sleeves. He did not so much object (to the lack of coat) as he did to the fact that he wore a pink shirt and red suspenders."[77] But the ladies liked him. Several American universities gave him honorary degrees. Newspapermen found him accessible and amiable.

Franklin on the basis of more than the color of suspenders preferred Spring-Rice and his embassy associates. More and more he turned to the increasing number of Englishmen in Washington. He saw much of Sir Arthur Willert, chief U.S. correspondent of the London *Times*. Another Englishman who was to be a special friend arrived in America on the *Lusitania* in November 1914. He was dining with the Roosevelts in January.

His name was Nigel Law. He was a bachelor only twenty-four years old, eight years younger than Franklin. Son of Sir Algernon Law, long connected with the Foreign Office, Nigel, a Cambridge graduate, had only entered the diplomatic service the year before in Vienna. Now among those who had been handed their papers in Austria at the outset of hostilities, he was joining the staff in Washington expanded to take care of vast war supply purchases in America. Society papers excitedly noted Law's presence as a man belonging to "the House of Ellenborough, and, although the present head of that family is childless, there are many standing between it and Nigel."[78] His maternal grandfather was the late Reverend Walter Bagot, rector of Castle Riding. More intriguing it was discovered that he was also the great-grandnephew of "one of Washington's earliest financiers, Thomas Law, who was associated with Warren Hastings in India."[79] That earlier Law, a talented but eccentric land speculator, married a lively daughter of George Washington's stepson.

This Elizabeth Custis Law set tongues wagging. A British travel writer published the tales that she was "particularly attached to the military, at the marine barracks, in Washington; nay, that she had been dressed *à la militaire* in company with the officers."[80] Another such visiting writer quoted a minister in Washington as saying that Elizabeth, "the most beautiful lady in Virginia," while Law was absent "eloped with a young dashing officer in the army."[81] Law, however, spoke up gallantly for his lady: "No elopement took place."[82] Though there was a divorce, it only originated "in a disagreement in disposition." He always paid, he wrote, "the tribute correctly due to Mrs. Law's purity of conduct, which I never did impeach." Gossips insisted, however, that after the divorce she still lived "in high style, and her house is the resort of the most fashionable parties."[83]

Whatever were the circumstances under which Law lost his lady, apparently he lost more money than the $15,000 a year he was reported to have settled on the gay Elizabeth.[84] His greater losses were in land dealings, some with the large landowning Carrolls of Lucy Mercer's tribe. One of them once owned all the land now embraced within the Capitol grounds and much other property as well.[85] This Daniel Carroll (aging when Law arrived before 1796) regarded himself as the most favorably situated of all the land proprietors or real estate operators in the District. Not much was left when young Nigel Law arrived. Still, as Lucy's ancient ties became clear, it was evident that she was not a young woman born to be summoned by a chauffeur to clean up a house. Young Nigel evidently was attracted to her as he was to the Roosevelts. Also, long afterward he wrote of the young Assistant Secretary, then politically battered but bounding, whom he had met in Washington.

"I found him the most attractive man whom it was my good fortune to meet during my four years in America," he said. "One was first struck by his gaiety and kindliness. He always seemed to be considering the feelings of others and doing all he could to make those in his company happy and cheerful. He was intensely interested in other people, not I think as a mere study in diverse humanity, but because he liked all people. He was intensely patriotic, but next to his own compatriots I think he preferred the English to other nationalities and during the period of American 'neutrality' he never disguised his strong pro-Ally sympathies."

Law added a passage which, though their fortunes were to be greatly different, described his own ideals as well as Roosevelt as he saw him.

"He was a fine physical specimen in the days I knew him, delighting in all sorts of outdoor activity. But he was not just a gay athlete, for he had a deep understanding of politics and a sound knowledge of history and foreign affairs, strong convictions and ideals and a deep desire to serve his country with all his powers. In my own mind I gave him the highest praise an Englishman can give a man, that he was a perfect example of the English Country Gentleman, and by that I mean (a type which is fast passing away) the landowner, whether large or small—with roots in his family estate who nevertheless disinterestedly devotes all his talents to his country, in local affairs, in Parliament, in the Army and if need be a great Minister of State, Viceroy or Ambassador and who, when the need of his service is past, returns once more to his fields and his library with relief."[86]

At the time of Law's arrival such an Anglicized eulogy might not have gone well with many Americans who regarded both England and Germany with equally dubious eyes. It would have made Roosevelt seem more and more like the young man who appeared in riding boots and breeches at the political meeting of the yeomanry of Dutchess County. Still in Washington even a democratic President sometimes rode so dressed in Rock Creek Park at the urging of Dr. Grayson, one of whose dictums for a too sedentary executive was that the outside of the horse is good for the inside of the man. Roosevelt needed no prod to physical activity. Still in society there a man—or a lady—might well need to be booted and spurred to escape the darts and arrows of merry malice. Not even a widowered President could be guarded from it. A handsome minor official like an Assistant Secretary on prim N Street could expect it.

FOUR

Tower of Jewels

Early in 1915 Franklin Roosevelt took a holiday from militancy. In the congenial company of Secretary of the Interior and Mrs. Franklin Lane and Assistant Secretary of State and Mrs. William Phillips, Franklin with Eleanor set off for decorative duty at the Panama-Pacific Exposition in San Francisco. Lane, a debonair, bald-headed man who loved the good things of life and often resented his inability to afford them, was the orator. He addressed himself to the plain figure of legend "that slender, dauntless, plodding modest figure, the American pioneer." Though war had reduced the participation of involved nations in the Exposition to 50,000 people who could hear him—and more beyond the range of his voice—he cried that the pioneer's "long journey . . . beside the oxen is at an end."[1]

Certainly many hoped that the hard ways were passed. In 1915 more Americans preferred the tame pyrotechnics of the fair to the grim gunfire across the Atlantic, an ocean itself three thousand miles away. Many came in plush Pullman cars. A bold— perhaps pioneer few—came in the cars of Henry Ford. The jokes about his Tin Lizzies were more amiable than those about his pacifistic views. Still in peace the fair created a mood of undisturbed affluence. Roosevelt and Phillips had largely formal duties as federal commissioners to the fair. They were not plodding personages. They were carriage gentlemen, not ox-cart drivers. Both had seen more of Europe than this West. At the fair each day they went in top hats and tail coats to one national pavilion after another, taking turns as brief speakers and adding to the exuberant mood of the exposition. As a sparkling team they seemed perfectly in the pattern of the fair which was symbolized by the glitter of its soaring Tower of Jewels.

Many saw the tower above the eloquent Lane and the elegant Roosevelt-Phillips combination. Few forgot it. R. L. Duffus, as obscure young San Francisco newspaperman then, wrote later that in its time and place it was a thing of magic. The jewels, he reported factually, consisted of fifty thousand bits of glass, each backed by a mirror surface, each made to twinkle at night by the blaze of powerful searchlights. The tower was 435 feet high. Such structural details were the inconsequential ones. Duffus sang: "The winds came in from the sea, and the bits of glass were hardly ever still; and the crowds stared and exclaimed, and nobody worried too much about the future on those days and in that place . . . many thousands of us saw it at various times of the day, and loved it at sundown, and marvelled at it after dark; and sometimes it seemed that this Exposition and its Tower would stand forever, or at least until the whole earth had been converted to justice, freedom and peace."[2] Certainly there seemed about it no remote resemblance to Babel in a country where the feeling was widespread that it could get rich from war and be secure from it. It was monument to the pioneer whose journeyings were to be remembered but whose sacrifices need not be shared.

The Roosevelts came home leisurely, stopping to visit old friends in New Mexico. But back in Washington the clamor between those intent upon keeping the peace and those demanding "preparedness" for war had mounted since the German announcement just before Roosevelt set out for the fair, that, in retaliation against unlawful British blockade, it was beginning submarine warfare. New detonation was given to debate when the great British liner, *Lusitania*, was torpedoed on May 7, with the loss of 1200 persons, 124 of them Americans. Even more shocking to many of Roosevelt's friends was a remark by the President, in a speech three days later, that "there is such a thing as a man being too proud to fight."³ Franklin was a man much torn in his loyalties when he attended the fleet review in New York in the middle of the month. There, while the Secretary in a speech at a Navy League banquet praised the Congress, Roosevelt boldly spoke his concern about a Congress which failed to carry out the recommendations of "the real experts, the naval officers."⁴ He was rather surprised at the friendliness of Secretary Daniels a few days later in Washington. But when the President, on July 21, 1915, ordered the Secretary to draw up a naval program adequate to the situation, Roosevelt was not on hand to participate in the preparation.

On July 1, he suffered a sudden acute attack of appendicitis and was rushed to the Naval Hospital. An appendectomy under such circumstances was no simple operation then. A year later the Roosevelts were saddened by the death after a similar operation of the small son of their French Embassy friends, Lefebvre and Marie de Laboulaye. When Franklin was stricken his mother from Hyde Park outraced Eleanor from Campobello to his bedside. Impatient and irritable as he was in the hospital, his illness took him off the scene when some of his friends who were Wilson's critics were adding mounting gossip to their arsenal of antagonism. Roosevelt had no part in that though it marked the advent on the scene of a great lady whom inadvertently he later offended.

Years before when politicians had sniffed at rumors about Wilson and a pretty lady, Mrs. Mary Allen Peck, whom he had met in Bermuda, Theodore Roosevelt had dismissed the reports: "You can't cast a man as Romeo who looks and acts so much like an apothecary's clerk."⁵ Militant TR was not altering that view now. But in the summer others, particularly women, were relishing and reporting scandalous or comic stories about the President, who had been widowed less than a year, and the handsome widow Edith Bolling Galt. Actually she was the last of a list of ladies in talk which ranged from sentimental sympathy to smirks about middle-aged lechery.

Less than six weeks after Ellen Wilson died Mrs. Slayden, at an intimate little luncheon in the garden of Mrs. Robert Lansing,

shocked her hostess by "casually," as she put it, predicting that
the President would soon remarry: there was reason to believe
he "rather leans to the ladies."[6] Mrs. Lansing armed her indignant
dissent with a bet of a five-pound box of Huyler's candy—"the
usual stake these days." Witness to the bet—to get some candy
whoever won—was Mrs. James Brown Scott, seldom considered
in relation to gossip or gambling. Her husband was a famous international lawyer who was to become secretary of the Carnegie
Endowment for International Peace.

Gossip about the possibility of the President's remarriage was
not restricted to a quiet garden. Quickly came the names of possible ladies. The sheets which purveyed gossip only dared to print
little of what its listeners heard at parties, many of which were
still in a prim administration euphemistically called "teas." In addition to casual whispers here and there, Washington had its special
sources of communication. One was staffed, if that word can be
used, by highly auditory and articulate ladies, the three wealthy
spinster sisters Patten: Mary, Josephine, and Nellie. They were
devout ladies who entertained a Cardinal. As a nighttime prank
Alice Longworth had once placed a placard on their residence
labeling it as the Irish Embassy. No national or sectarian lines
were drawn in their hospitality. They entertained everybody and
went everywhere. Mary, who was the senior sister and chief com-
municator, was already known as a source of titillating reports
before the Wilsonians came to town. Archie Butt described Mary
as one "who sees in every closet and behind every sham."[7] Not
all were so charitable. Often the sisters seemed more concerned
with closets than shams. For those who wanted to speed the
spread of scandal, a wit prescribed, "Don't telegraph. Don't telephone. Tell-a-Patten."[8]

First lady on all tongues naturally was Mrs. Peck. (At this point,
after losing one husband by death and the other by divorce, she
called herself Mary Allen Hulbert. Everybody else still called her
by the name she bore when Wilson met her.) She was the blythe
lady Wilson had found delightful on a rest trip to Bermuda in
1906, after his first warning of hardening of the arteries. She

visited the Wilsons at Princeton, later at the White House. The Wilsons occupied her Bermuda house after the election in 1912. During the years of their friendship the scholar politician had written her a series of amazingly self-revealing but non-incriminating letters. Apparently Wilson felt a need to pour out his ideas and ideals, aims and struggles, in epistles to ladies. Others went to the entirely non-suspect Nancy Toy, wife of an elderly professor of Romance languages at Harvard.

But in 1915, Mrs. Peck apparently was ready and willing for his courtship. As a recently divorced woman, her friends said later, she had already purchased yards of beautiful lace, to which she clung ever after, to be made into a dress for her wedding in the White House.[9] As the world did not know then, Wilson's daughters disapproved of her, as their mother had, as a silly, fading coquette. As came out later, Wilson had recently "lent" her $7500 when she suffered financial reverses. Possibly this was an act of kindness to an old friend or a salve to his conscience about a lady whose expectations he had not meant to raise. It was made the basis for ridiculous charges later of a $75,000-blackmail pay-off.[10] Gossips in 1915 only knew somehow that she was out of the running.

Apparently only in wild search, they turned to Mrs. Borden Harriman as "the mooted future sharer of his joys and sorrows."[11] Some Washingtonians referred to Daisy Harriman as "the suffragist, Civic Federation, all pervading"[12] Mrs. Harriman. Distinctly a member of society by birth, in the mounting social fashion of good works she had been manager of the New York State Reformatory for Women. As a lady interested in labor disputes, Wilson had brought her to Washington as public representative on the Federal Industrial Relations Commission. At the other end of the spectrum, in a day when it was not considered nice for lone ladies to stop at hotels, she had been a founder and the long-time president of the exclusive Colony Club in New York for which Stanford White designed the building and which, before many years, had a waiting list of a thousand ladies aspiring to membership.[13]

Later she was to become organizer of a wartime woman's motor corps in Washington and abroad, then as the years passed and her eminence grew, both a member of the Democratic National Committee and (under FDR) an envoy to Norway. But in 1915, when the gossips plucked her as a possible presidential bride, her husband had been dead only as recently as December 1, 1914. Perhaps she, like some of the White House entourage, resented this gossip though Colonel House noted a few years later in his diary that she telephoned him and "gave much gossip . . . some of it hardly fit to print."[14]

As the year advanced the perceptive should have needed no Patten or other aid in determining the presidential choice. By the time of the naval review in May, even small boys on the Secretary of the Navy's yacht *Dolphin* knew that Edith Bolling Galt was *the* lady. As the President's guest on his yacht the *Mayflower*, she moved grandly to a luncheon in her honor on the *Dolphin*. She seemed majestic, as the chief of the Secret Service detail wrote later, though she was "somewhat plump by modern American standards."[15]

The sentimental and the slanderous watched eagerly but only after more than two decades did the lady in *My Memoir* tell her whole story of the romance.[16] In it she wrote as if she were first brought to Wilson as a sort of doctor's prescription for Wilson's loneliness which was complicating the tendency toward arterio-sclerosis about which the doctor, White House physician Dr. Cary Grayson, was worried that year.[17] She described an almost clinical scene when Wilson took to his bed for fear that he might have to give her up. Grayson had been worried about both political and physical complications. His turn to Colonel House, who tried to prevent the marriage by inventing a tale that Mrs. Peck was threatening scandal, had only made matters worse.[18] Evidently the doctor turned also for consultation to Mrs. Galt's physician and friend, Dr. Sterling Ruffin, who conducted his fashionable practice from his house on Connecticut Avenue across from the British Embassy. Also, he was a North Carolinian kin to the Hendersons and so related to Minnie Mercer. Ruffin may not have been the "master hand" in the Wilson-Galt wedding as *Town Topics* reported.[19] Still outside of family, top officials and the intimate White House entourage, Ruffin was the only guest Edith Galt mentioned as present at her wedding in her small house bulging with caterers and a section of the Marine Band.[20]

One item she mentioned in the story of her courtship, which she passed over lightly, seems mysterious. At the time, rising feelings about the contesting European powers were symbolized in cartoons by the British bulldog and the German dachshund. One gift which came to her quickly was a tiny black dachshund to which a red, white and blue ribbon attached a big card bearing the legend, *My name is America*. She only sent it back, she said, with "a courteous note" because the dog was "too young to keep."[21]

Edith had shown her temperament in the restriction of her list of wedding guests. Against Wilson's gentler judgment she had dispensed with the services of a bishop who was to have married them. Though he had been told when asked to perform the ceremony that there would not be room for his wife, he tried, evidently at his wife's demand, to push her in. So Edith pushed him out. She was imperiously not to be imposed upon. She had shown herself as a woman of quick stubborn decision when during their courtship Wilson had told her he was troubled about the threat of resignation by William Jennings Bryan in the stiffening crisis with Germany. Taking her text from a romantic play she had seen, Edith gave him her advice.

"Take it, sir, and thank God for the chance."[22]

She looked majestic and she was prepared to be. She had been the first woman in Washington to own and drive an "electric" which became almost as much the standard equipment of the elegant as furs. In her smart clothes on its high seat she was like a noble lady on a rolling throne. Not only did pedestrians admire her, policemen gallantly waved her on her way. One particular officer, whom she long remembered with appreciation, at his busy post at Pennsylvania Avenue and 15th Street always held up traffic for her, allowed her to cross and gave her a salute as she rolled on, oftcn in the direction of the long-established jewelry store which she had inherited from her husband.[23]

There were those, especially after she was enthroned as First Lady at the White House, who felt that, as a Bolling of Virginia, she stepped down when she married Norman Galt in 1895.[24] He was nine years older than she was. The only earlier beau she remembered in *My Memoir* as the figure in "my first serious love affair,"[25] a New Yorker with money, had been thirty-eight when she was sixteen. Perhaps the significant thing was that she had been by Virginia belle standards an old maid of twenty-three when she married Galt. Possibly more serious, he was "in trade." A supercilious reporter noted that she and two of her sisters "chose their husbands from Washington merchants"[26]—the two others, a leather man and a flour man. But Edith knew what she was doing. As she wrote later, "The name of Galt on a piece of paper had always been as good as a bond."[27] That was important to a girl from a family which had raised nine children on the slenderest of means, however genteel it was regarded in Wytheville, Virginia. Also it was important that Mr. Galt had jobs in his jewelry business for three of her brothers.

Left a childless widow of thirty-six, in 1908, she continued to live alone in the house in which her husband had died at 1308 20th Street, N.W., declining the offer of her mother, brothers and sisters to come and live with her. Also with the advice of an old employee at Galt's (not of any of the three Bolling brothers Galt had given jobs there), and a lawyer friend, she continued the jewelry business. She cultivated the friendship of such older men as this lawyer, Nathaniel Wilson, dean of the Washington bar and president of the Metropolitan Club. He was a "loveable old man" and "a good deal of a dictator." One of his abominations was the telephone and he repeatedly lectured her as to "how unworthy of my dignity it was to allow young men to telephone me instead of writing a proper note."[28] So delicately but definitely she indicated that she was not always left a lonely widow.

Another such older friend was a widower, James Gordon, a picturesque Scotch mining engineer, who had made and lost several fortunes. Moreover, as a virtue worth mentioning, he "had married a Virginian." He had managed to keep his last fortune and before he died in 1911 he asked Edith to look out for his heiress and only child, seventeen-year-old Alice Gertrude Gordon, always called Altrude. Evidently the jewelry business was not confining. Edith and Altrude traveled to Europe ending their journey in Paris where they "invested almost our last penny in dresses and hats."²⁹ Perhaps it was on this occasion that she first dealt with Worth, the couturier, whose dresses for her she so lovingly described later.

In the fateful summer of 1914, the two women remained in the United States, in Maine, in order to be near the Summer White House near Cornish, New Hampshire, to be close to Altrude's beau, Dr. Grayson. Grayson never came. The house, leased by Wilson, was not occupied this year. He had been, of course, in Washington at the bedside of Ellen Wilson in the illness which brought her death on August 6 as war was beginning in the world. No one, least of all herself, conceived that sixteen months later the decorative and dominant Edith would take Ellen's place as First Lady.

Edith's story, in a generation freshly nostalgic about a Southern society, lovely and lost, was almost a rerun of the romantic Virginia stories of Thomas Nelson Page whom the President had sent as his Ambassador to Italy. Like Ellen, of course, Edith was a lady in the Southern tradition, only more so. As a preacher's child, the first Mrs. Wilson had been reared in fewer memories of the sumptuous South "before the war." Edith began her memoir with those times when her mother had had her own maid, her father his man, when there were slaves and abundance. She wrote of the old Negroes who didn't want to be free and of the unreconstructed ladies of her family who preferred to go hungry rather than choke on Yankee bounty.

Southern ladies in Washington were diverse and similar. Long afterward it would seem irrelevant to think of Edith Galt and Minnie Mercer, though acquaintances, as parts of the same world. And they were different. Edith came with nothing to fortune and lasting position. Minnie had come with much to become poor. But in 1915, Minnie was listed in the *Social Register*. Edith was not. She insistently told Dr. Grayson, "I am not a society person."[30] Minnie clung to her social position which was about all she had left.

There were, of course, other differences. Minnie, as a slightly faded beauty of fifty-two, steadily smoked her cigarettes in a society which still had serious doubts about ladies who did. At forty-two, Edith, in her clothes and everything else, had almost an addiction for appearances. Her two trim maids kept her impeccable house; with the help of her daughters, Minnie tended to her apartment alone. In any parade of pride, however, save for the luster the word "Virginia" carried in ancestry, Minnie could regard her antecedents as superior. Then, as later when Edith moved with royalty, she traced a sort of royal ancestry of her own to the Indian Princess Pocahontas. But behind Minnie as a Colonial Dame, the Henderson kin of her mother included the aristocratic land speculator who dispatched Daniel Boone to Kentucky. Furthermore for any notable figure in lineage Edith had to go all the way back to Pocahontas. In Minnie's North Carolina relationship were judges, Congressmen, bankers, a Confederate major general. As recently as 1911 her cousin, Archibald Henderson, had written a first and authorized life of George Bernard Shaw.[31]

The obvious differences all the same in 1915 were that the rich widow Galt married the 28th President of the United States. Minnie, in effect neither maid, wife nor widow, lived in genteel poverty with her daughters apart from her once romantic Carroll, now fifty-seven. The "any old way" in which he was said to be living indicated the society to which he belonged and from which he would never be lost. In his separation from Minnie he moved about. He lived at the Benedict, a bachelor apartment across the street from the Metropolitan Club and occupied by many of its members. He "boarded," a directory said,[32] in 1914 at 1307 K Street, which was the residence of an investment banker who had no need to take in boarders. Another of his listed residences was at 1833 M Street, not in a boardinghouse district, and oc-

cupied at the time of his stay there by either the widow of
Supreme Court Justice John Marshall Harlan (whose daughter
Laura, like Lucy Mercer, was a social secretary and later served as
such for Mrs. Warren G. Harding) or by Captain Philip H. Sheridan, a Metropolitan Club man.[33]

His position in 1915 was indicated by those who remained his
friends throughout his life. Perhaps as *Town Topics*, gently kick-
ing him in misfortune, said, these gentlemen were friends who
"stood between the wolf and the sadly changed gallant."[34] They
could well afford to. They were a decorative and elite lot:

Truxton Beale, of the distinguished Washington family whose
sister, Mrs. John R. McLean, had been described by Henry
Adams as "the reigning empress" of Washington society.[35] Beale,
whose home was the historic Stephen Decatur house at 28 Lafayette Square, served as U. S. Minister to Persia and Greece. He
belonged to so many clubs that after listing a number he added,
"etc."

General Charles L. McCawley's stepdaugher had married Henry
Cabot Lodge's son. McCawley's dress uniform sword had been
used to cut the wedding cake at Alice Longworth's wedding.

George Howard came from the family of Governor George
Howard of Maryland, whose estate Waverly was near Doughoregan Manor. Legend listed this governor as a frustrated man who
wanted to own a thousand slaves but, due to deaths among them,
never got beyond 999. His father, John Eager Howard, Revolu-
tionary soldier, was immortalized, along with a Carroll, in his
reputation for chivalry and valor in the lines:

> *Remember Carroll's sacred trust,*
> *Remember Howard's warlike thrust,*
> *And all thy slumb'rers with the just,*
> *Maryland! My Maryland!*[36]

Henry Randall Webb, whose middle name was the same as
that of the author of the song, was president of the Maryland
Society of the Cincinnati.

There were other similar gentlemen, sportsmen, aristocrats,

hereditary patriots. All of them were members of the Chevy Chase Club which Carroll had helped to establish.[37]

However impossible it was for Carroll and Minnie to live together, she did not give up her claim to him then, certainly not later. He was corresponding with Lucy in the years in which she served as social secretary to Eleanor Roosevelt.[38] It seems certain that she and Violetta visited him, mindful of his needs for care and affection. Certainly his relationships in the city in which they all lived emphasized the position of his daughters in it. Out of old ties perhaps, they were welcomed into the houses of his friends and welcomed the more because they were young and lovely and gay. They were the same houses into which the young Roosevelts were glad to go.

A fully recovered Franklin returned from Campobello in August. In hot Washington he saw old friends and picked up his mounting duties. He was glad to get away for a weekend with his friends the Willie Eustises at their estate near Leesburg.[39] But, in addition to his duties in connection with stepped-up Navy preparations, he had a special preparations project of his own on his mind. Interested in a similar project for the Navy, he planned to go to Plattsburgh, New York, where, under the direction of General Leonard Wood and with the blessing of Theodore Roosevelt, gentlemen were drilling in preparation for war. The training camp there got its real impetus when Wood addressed a meeting at the Harvard Club in New York in June. As Francis Russell wrote, the Plattsburgh trainees, who paid for their own training, "were a well advertised elite." There were four Roosevelts in the group, Ted, Jr., Quentin, Archie, and their cousin Philip. Richard Harding Davis, fresh from war reporting in Europe, wrote that in his squad were "two fox-hunting squires from Maryland, a master of fox hounds, a gentleman jockey from Boston, and two steeple chase riders who divided between them all the cups the country offers."[40]

Roosevelt wanted a similar Navy group composed of the yachtsmen of the country. He planned to go to Plattsburgh on a weekend early in September but gave it up "as they practically close there on Saturday."[41] But at about the same time he "sprang an announcement of the National Naval Reserve," and hoped the Secretary would like it.[42] The Secretary, who was suspicious of the elite whom Wood had mobilized at Plattsburgh, did require reassurances from Roosevelt that a training cruise he wanted would appeal to more than just "college boys, rich young men, well-to-do-yachtsmen, etc."[43] He irked Roosevelt by delays in approval and especially later when he named it the "John Paul Jones Cruise." Roosevelt commented, "It is an awful mistake to leave the Department for more than five and a half minutes at a time!"[44]

Despite the Secretary's efforts to put the emphasis on skilled craftsmen, the trainees whom Roosevelt sought and found were, as Frank Freidel discovered, largely well-to-do young men with a leaning toward yachts.[45] Many of them were not sympathetic with the direction of Wilson's Navy Department by Daniels. They rather shared the views of such of its critics at the time as J. Pierpont Morgan; elderly General Horace Porter, soldier, diplomat and railroad executive; Beekman Winthrop, Roosevelt's Republican predecessor as Assistant Secretary of the Navy; and Colonel Thompson, president of the Navy League.[46]

Franklin was a man in a hurry. Though more and more work piled up on his desk, he was in the months after he "sprang" his announcement much preoccupied with wealthy men's speedboats. This, Freidel concluded, was a "reflection of his own background" and "even after the United States entered the war, he rode his small-boat hobby to the limit."[47] He demonstrated his own prowess and delight in this preference on a social holiday with Nigel Law in the summer of 1916 shortly before the "John Paul Jones Cruise" of the Reservists sailed from several ports on nine battleships.

In June 1916, he invited Nigel Law to go with him to the wedding of their mutual friend, Ruth Wales, niece of Elihu Root, to Henry F. du Pont, son of Senator Henry A. du Pont of Delaware.[48] Miss Wales' father, Edward H. Wales, had been commodore of the New York Yacht Club and belonged to the other best clubs in New York and Washington where, in addition to Hyde Park, he maintained residences. His wife naturally was a member of the Colony Club. They were rich and Republicans but old friends and neighbors of Franklin. Harry, the groom, had been his schoolmate at Groton. Roosevelt also knew the du Ponts. He visited at the Senator's place, Winterthur, a little later in the year.

He and Nigel had been seeing a good deal of each other. They had dined in May, Law remembered, "at Dover House" (possibly Dower House which was then a smart restaurant near Upper Marlboro, Maryland, and later the home of Cissy Patterson). Law and several other members of the British Embassy staff were to have dined with Roosevelt on June 7, but word came just before that Field Marshal Kitchener had been lost at sea when his ship carrying him to Russia for discussions with the Tsar's forces had struck a mine off the Orkneys. Roosevelt phoned that in view of such terrible news he knew they would prefer not to come. But mourning even for the great did not last forever.

On June 23, Roosevelt and Law set out for the Wales-du Pont wedding. That night Roosevelt took the young Britisher to the Harvard Club where the gentlemen of the Crimson were celebrating their victory in the annual boat races at New London.

"It was," said Law, "naturally a gay evening."

Someone suggested that the Harvard men go over to the Yale Club and give them a "friendly cheer." All linked arms, every other man carrying a bottle of champagne. Also, as Law recalled, they had with them a rudimentary brass band. After such preparations the serenade might have been disappointing. All the Yale men had gone to bed except two who from a balcony had heard the tumultuous approach of the Harvard celebrants. They, however, demonstrated the Ivy League aplomb of young gentlemen like those who drilled at Plattsburgh and soon would be fighting together. Two against many, they invited the Harvard company in for a drink which invitation, "needless to say," wrote Law later, "was gratefully accepted." Afterward, he and Franklin spent the night "or what was left of it" at a hotel. Indeed, the night was cut as short at its end as at its beginning.

"The following morning we were called at 5 A.M. and set out for the Hudson River where we embarked on the U. S. Torpedo Boat Destroyer No. 59. Franklin as Assistant Secretary of the Navy then took charge and we proceeded up the Hudson at such speed that our wash nearly sank some barges moored to the bank."[49]

The Dowager Sara welcomed them. Law remembered that a Mr. and Mrs. DeRau were also staying at her house. Possibly he was mistaken when he recalled the name years later. More likely they were the Henry DeRhams. DeRham, who had married Frances A. Dana of Boston, granddaughter of both Henry Wadsworth Longfellow and Richard H. Dana, had been like Franklin at Harvard with the du Pont groom.

At night, after the wedding, Franklin showed Law a room which had been added for him when Sara put north and south wings on the house and made alterations on its front the year before. There were a dozen tables in the room. Franklin explained to him that the tables were so arranged that, "as each table got littered up with papers, he could move to another where there was room to write."[50] The tables seemed symbolic of the man in a hurry in a country cluttered with contentions about peace and war, reform and the rescue of the world.

The Washington to which he returned was surging in change. Henry Adams had been myopic in November 1914 when he wrote Elizabeth Cameron that "the social tide seems violently set one way, and we are all allies."[51] There were many who were unwilling to see America ally itself with the cause of any of the warring nations. Two months after he gave that opinion, the peace advocates had already begun to mobilize even—or especially—in Washington.

Yet, perhaps justifying Adams about the pro-Allied "social tide," the advocates of peace often seemed very dowdy and the women among them most shrill as 1915 began. Even Ellen Slayden as one of those who had set her soft chin most firmly in opposition to

American involvement in war then saw that with rueful humor. She had joined a group which in January 1915 had come through the coldest rain to a peace meeting in the auditorium of the Carnegie Library. The company, she wrote in her journal at the time, came straggling in, "eminently peaceful looking spinsters in out-of-date black and brown silks; shaggy old men with large, wet umbrellas, and pallid youths of a Jewish type with big eyes which seem to look beyond the stars."[52]

The room, she said, rang with clichés: "If half the power that fills the world with terror" . . . "our old friends the plowshares and the pruning hooks" . . . [the] "Parliament of Man, the Federation of the World." There was some restless shuffling of feet. Then the hall hushed when a perfect model of the woman of good will and good causes then and later, spoke. She was the then famous Belva Lockwood, a first lady of women's rights, temperance, peace, arbitration. A few present remembered when she had first come to Washington, a stout, confident Amazon with short hair riding a tricycle to the scandal of the city. Now at eighty-five, she was a tottering, wheezy old woman wearing a wretchedly bad hat. Still she spoke with more authority than fluent young women who had preceded her. She referred to a Congressional Committee which had found American coast defenses weak and reported that it would cost millions to make them adequate. She quoted with approval the *Detroit Free Press* as saying that no doubt it would, but it wouldn't cost ten cents to mind our own business and keep out of war. The audience applauded and poured out into the rain.

Now, in 1916, the same diarist wrote about a very different company of ladies who were encamped beyond the Chevy Chase Club where Franklin went for the golf which not even the approach of war interrupted. There the Women's Service Camp, promoted by the Navy League, was a popular resort. The women in smart uniforms they had purchased left the parade ground to drink tea and darn their silk stockings. The "hardening" was being done, she said, gradually so as not to shock the systems of the fair trainees. In other ways they were not suffering. On the day of her visit the dinner menu was chicken and fresh asparagus, peas, strawberries. And "to prevent real suffering" Rauscher, the city's most expensive caterer, had put up a pavilion at the gate where ice cream, pastries, and cold drinks could be had at any hour. Still the serious campers, paying for their training, permitted only one bit of levity about their activities. To both distinguish their camp from Plattsburgh and associate it with that gentlemen's camp in New York State the ladies, smiling, called theirs Catsburg.[53]

The country was in no joking mood, however, as fall came on. Theodore Roosevelt, once more back in the Republican Party, seemed in his militancy more its voice than the bearded candidate, Charles Evans Hughes. And running for re-election Wilson, tagged with the slogan "He Kept Us Out of War," seemed almost embarrassingly captured by the peace forces led by Bryan whom he had let depart. Franklin Roosevelt, if he had seemed to stray, was back in the Wilson company. That seemed a routed group on Election Night. Hughes appeared to be elected until the news came in from California. That state's returns seemed to Democrats as bright and beautiful as the Tower of Jewels there at the fair by the Golden Gate.

The morning after the close election brought what Franklin described as "the most extraordinary day of my life." Of course, politics was not all. Around him in Washington was a new political and personal sense of elation. Franklin expressed it in domestic detail in a letter to Eleanor: the curtains were up and a new servant, named Jenny, had arrived. But he added almost as if he had just escaped a danger, "I hope to God I don't grow reactionary with advancing years."[54]

He was thirty-four. Reaction in advancing years did not seem to be his danger.

FIVE

Dust on a Windy Street

"It is a curious thing," Franklin Roosevelt once wrote almost plaintively, "that as soon as I go away we seem to land Marines somewhere."[1]

He hated to miss action. On the occasion of this letter he was at Campobello in 1915 during the last days of the six weeks it took him to recover from his appendectomy. The Marines then were dispatched to chaotic, bankrupt Haiti which, near the Panama Canal, some feared might fall like a rotten plum into German hands. In January 1917, however, he was with the Marines who had landed two years before on the Caribbean island and, in rough Marine terms, had the situation well in hand.

Despite some fears by his mother that he wouldn't wear a pith helmet and dark glasses in the tropical sun of which she reminded him he was sensitive,[2] the trip was delightful and instructive. With top Marine officers, he took along his frequent golf partner, John A. McIlhenny; his Harvard classmate and close friend, Livingston Davis; and a former Groton master, George Marvin. In Haiti he found another Harvard classmate, Preston Davie, who had been living on the island trying to grow cotton. Davie's cotton had been ruined by tropical rains. He feared being stranded on the island as a result of reports that the Germans would attempt to make a war zone of the waters about it. He was anxious to get home. He hailed Roosevelt as one who could—and did—help him.

On horseback the Roosevelt party traversed the beautiful island. They studied conditions and played, too. It was on this trip that Roosevelt learned to make a special cocktail which he always afterward called "my Haitian libation." His sons violently differed as to its potableness. James, who regarded it as "a deplorable invention," disclosed only that it involved a mixture of a strong, dark Haitian rum, very dark brown sugar and orange juice.[3] Even the sun seemed intoxicating. They swam before an attentive audience of Negro women who had never seen a nude white man—an incident more embarrassing to Livy Davis than the rest; he wouldn't get out of the water until someone brought him his bathing suit. Roosevelt felt that the Marines were doing a fine job despite some native complaints about tyrannical Marine methods. And the Marines, who had rounded up Haitian weapons, provided a cache of them for Franklin as inveterate collector. Then on February 3, while he was dining in the flower-filled courtyard of an old palace, he received a code message from Secretary Daniels calling him home because of the "political situation." The "political situation" was that Washington had just learned that Germany was embarking upon unrestricted submarine warfare.[4]

Roosevelt sailed on the collier *Neptune* on which he had time to sort his souvenirs. But in Washington, as when he had arrived at the beginning of war in Europe, he found, he wrote later, a somnolent Navy Department: "no excitement, no preparations, no orders to the fleet."[5] All that Washington in general knew was that Ambassador von Bernstorff had been handed his papers in a gesture which sternly suggested war. The declaration came early in April. It was accompanied by patriotic applause but also attended before and after by a confusion of loyalties in which Roosevelt was involved as a restive, ardent, highly self-confident young man.

In the Navy Department he got into a contention which amounted to a row over his great interest in small motor patrol boats with some of the chief admirals who regarded them as toys. These boats were to be engined by the company of a very attentive promoter, Arthur P. Homer, whom years later Roosevelt had to publicly repudiate.[6] On Inauguration Day he had a conference with Colonel House and gave him "some guarded views" about conditions of Navy.[7] House at about this time, almost as a conspirator for favor, was noting in his diary that "the little circle close to the President seems to have dwindled down to the two of us, Mrs. Wilson and myself." He assumed the duties of an extra bodyguard. As a very mild-appearing man on Inauguration Day, the colonel wrote, "I sat with my automatic in my hand ready to act if the occasion rose." He was ready to "prod" the President along the lines of the Roosevelt views.[8]

More remarkable in terms of Franklin's loyalties was a dinner meeting he attended at the Metropolitan Club in New York six days after Wilson's second inauguration.[9] The small group included almost the Sanhedrin of President Wilson's critics and opponents. In addition to Theodore Roosevelt and General Wood others were significant figures. The wealthy Cornelius Bliss had been treasurer of the Republican National Committee in the campaign the year before. Other prominent Republicans included Elihu Root, Governor Walter E. Edge of New Jersey, and Mayor John Purroy Mitchel. The greatest wealth and power was represented by J. P. Morgan, whose great banking house was handling British war spending in America. Morgan had lost a bet the year before to Franklin's close Hudson Valley friend, Mrs. Charles Sumner Hamlin, wife of a member of Wilson's Federal Reserve Board.

"Here is a promise," the big banker had told her on his yacht the *Corsair*. "If by any ill chance Wilson is elected, I promise to keep a picture on my desk in plain sight of Secretary Josephus Daniels, the man I hate most. If Mr. Hughes is elected then your husband must grow pink whiskers. After the election Mrs. Hamlin gaily bought and sent Morgan a picture of Daniels in an impressive package. The great banker, she said in her diary, kept his promise but had a noose painted on the picture around Daniels' neck.[10]

"T.R.," Franklin wrote of the Metropolitan Club meeting in a briefly kept diary, "wanted more vigorous demand about future course—less endorsement of past. I backed T.R.'s theory."[11]

But what may well be described as Rooseveltianism was under wraps when, on April 9, the elder Roosevelt came to Washington to ask the President to let him recruit and lead in France a division somewhat like the regiment of Rough Riders which, with Wood, TR had led in Cuba nearly a score of years before. His chances were limited by more than any administration resentment of past antagonisms, though Wilson may have noted that TR's first visitor in Washington was Senator Lodge whom he already hated. The pattern of war had changed since 1898 when the Rough Riders, composed mainly of cowboys and college boys, had won the Battle of San Juan Hill scarcely three months after that war was declared. Roosevelt, at fifty-nine, was no longer the man he had been when he fought before. He was blind in one eye and had not recovered from the tropical infections of his last exploration. Already the decision had been made that such an American army as would be required would have to be raised by the draft. But Roosevelt was eager, almost plaintive.

"Mr. President," he told Wilson in his plea for a dramatic commander's role, "all that has gone before is as dust on a windy street."[12]

There was appeal in the old President's ardor. However combat-fit or not his volunteers might have been, TR's arrival in France would have been dramatic evidence that the United States was charging to war. Franklin worked for his cause. He arranged an interview for Uncle Ted with Secretary of War Newton D. Baker. He and Eleanor were prominent among the many callers in the crowded Longworth house where the old Rough Rider stayed.[13] Eleanor wrote that "Uncle Ted returned in a very unhappy mood" from the White House: "I hated to see him disappointed and yet I was loyal to President Wilson." She was relieved when it was decided that "it would be a grave mistake to allow one division to attract so many men who would be needed as officers in so many divisions."[14] Franklin's opinion was not so clear. Later that year when the Bolshevik revolution in

Russia permitted the Germans to take Riga with comparative ease, he blurted, "We ought to have sent TR over to Russia with 100,000 men. This would not have happened."[15]

One thing old Theodore felt very strongly about then and later was that Franklin should resign and go into uniformed service. He was "always urging Franklin to resign," Eleanor remembered.[16] Franklin was thirty-five, and had five children. TR had been forty and the father of six children when he resigned the same post to go to the Spanish-American War.

Others were going. Franklin's opposite number in the War Department, Henry Breckinridge, left the Assistant Secretary's post and became a major in the Army. Eleanor's brother, Hall, and her cousin, Quentin, had apparently rigged the eye test to get into aviation. Young Sheffield Cowles went into the Marines. Congressman Gardner, to whom Franklin had slipped ammunition in his criticism of the Navy Department, resigned from Congress to join the Army, saying that he had advocated preparedness so strenuously that he could not stay out. But George Marvin, old Groton master and Franklin's companion in Haiti, sent him word that General Wood had said, "Franklin Roosevelt should under no circumstances think of leaving the Navy Department. It would be a public calamity to have him leave at this time."[17] In agreement with Wood for once, Daniels shared the same view.[18]

In the Department and out of it, the young Assistant Secretary was equally active. He pushed production and participated in ceremony. Foreign missions, led by such figures as Marshal Joffre of France and Balfour of England poured into Washington seeking speedy aid to their forces. Elaborate entertainments were given for them. Suddenly, as Alice Longworth wrote, everyone who had any possible excuse turned up in Washington.[19] Some with no excuse arrived—or lingered. Ambassador and Mrs. George Bakhmeteff had been giving one of their dinners, served by servants in the costumes of Cossacks, on the evening when the first phase of the Russian Revolution began in March. The elegant, monocled ambassador was quickly out and another, a professor amazingly also named Bakhmeteff, came from the Kerensky government.

Asked if they were any kin, the original Bakhmeteff replied: "The same as George Washington and Booker T." His pink-haired wife spread the word that the new ambassador had been a plumber and emphasized her contempt with a gesture of her jeweled arm like the pulling of the chain on the water closet. Washington had little time for their rueful wit. Not even madame's native status as a cave dweller stemmed the tide of change. One ex-ambassador counted for little in a city which grew by 60,000 in the first year of war.

Some who came were as resplendent as the first Bakhmeteffs. Dollar-a-year men arrived, headed by Bernard M. Baruch, whom Colonel House had disparaged as "a Hebrew Wall Street speculator."[20] They took large houses, brought wives and daughters eager to join in the society which suddenly flowered with a variety of Allied uniforms. Not only the rich came to the exciting city. Young women war workers poured in from Vassar and Wellesley as well as a feminine multitude from obscure back country towns. They were both elated and cheated. Some, who regarded them as overpaid at $1200 a year, said that they spent their new riches in an orgy of extravagance. Scornfully they were described as tottering on high "hourglass" shoe heels, their ears elaborately concealed under round, snail-shell coils of hair, displaying their flesh-colored silk stockings to the knee. Others saw that many of them were crowded in horrible lodging houses where grasping landlords took a big share of the bounty before it could go for filmy silk and lace underwear.[21]

The demands of the expanding departments for stenographic and similar feminine help increased. The bulging Navy Department needed girls as well as gunners. As early as March 1917, women were enlisted in the Navy as yeomen, the Secretary having discovered that there was nothing in the law requiring these enlisted clerks to be male. The "yeomanette" uniform had its patriotic appeal, though one girl who wore it later declared that it was certainly not designed by Mainbocher: "The skirts were straight, tight and of the most awkward length possible. The jackets were shapeless affairs, loosely belted in a sort of 'Norfolk' attempt. . . . The hats were flat, blue sailor models, just the wrong size and shape for any girl who ever wore a hat, except when taking a comic part on the stage."[22] Their garb seemed particularly unattractive in comparison with the uniforms some organizations designed for their lady volunteers. The variety of their dress seemed infinite. Before the war ended Mrs. Isabel Anderson, who served at home and abroad, had a whole wardrobe of different uniforms to choose from.[23]

Not all the ladies ardently engaged were uniformed. Before the war began, Franklin's friend Edith Eustis, in February, gathered in her historic house a group of matrons who called themselves "The Patriotic Economy League." They signed a pledge that they would dress simply and save food. Eleanor Roosevelt was one who signed it. She was relieved because Washington ladies had no longer time for incessant rounds of calls. She went to an organizational meeting of the woman's motor corps of the Red Cross, called by Mrs. J. Borden Harriman, but since she could not drive a car looked for other war work. She joined the Red Cross canteen operating in the railroad yards where troop trains passed. She began early to distribute free wool for the Comforts Committee of the Navy League. In this work, Lucy Mercer, relieved of arranging calling lists, helped also. Violetta Mercer was going to France as a Red Cross nurse[24] and Lucy was destined, if briefly, for a job in the armed service.

Still there was time for diversion as the year turned into the hot Washington summer. On Saturday afternoon, June 16, Franklin led a company of friends to the Washington Navy Yard where they boarded the Navy Yacht *Sylph*. The guests packed the accommodations of the small yacht. There were two Marine officers, one of them his cousin, Major H. L. Roosevelt. Along also were McIlhenny and his wife. Two other passengers were Nigel Law and Lucy Mercer. Down the Potomac at the Indian Head naval facility they sent a boat ashore to pick up Eleanor who apparently had not been able to make the sailing time at the Navy

Yard. The next day they sailed, sight-seeing, to Stratford Cliffs and went ashore to see the old house in which Robert E. Lee was born. They dropped farther down the river to go ashore at Wakefield, Virginia, to see the restored birthplace of George Washington. The whole trip was not devoted to patriotic pilgrimages. They swam and played on the river shore. This was the voyage which Law remembered with some pain. Lucy, whose partner on this and other outings Law appeared to be, watched the young Englishman as he undertook a feat at Franklin's direction.

"I was stung by poison ivy for the first and last time because I climbed a wild cherry tree in bathing trunks to pick the fruit for Franklin. Probably George Washington had overlooked that particular tree."[25]

No sting or other incident of the trip appears to have shaped Lucy's decision a week later. Then she went back to the Navy Yard again, this time on the serious mission of enlisting in the Navy as a yeoman (F). The induction experience may not have been so disturbing to her as it seemed to some other young women who found themselves lined up for examination as "poor, stripped feminine patriots." One who recalled the experience in the nude also remembered that the examiner was "a weary, over-aged M.D." who was not a bit interested in anything but getting through his work and home to supper.[26] An examiner did note that Lucy was 5 feet, 9 inches tall; eyes, blue; hair, brown; complexion ruddy (perhaps from the *Sylph* trip the week before). Also he noted: "small vac. scar on left arm, scar on right leg caused by an injury." She was given Serial No. 1160. Oddly the Navy's record of her birth made her one year younger than the twenty-six she actually was. She was assigned to duty in the Navy Department.[27]

Eleanor stayed later than usual in sweltering Washington that summer. The three oldest children had the whooping cough. So, to protect the younger two, they were shipped off with a governess to stay with Sara at Hyde Park. With danger of contagion past in mid-July, she set out, knitting in hand which had become a habit with war work, to take all her children and staff to Campobello. Behind her Franklin wrote about his loneliness in the N Street house. Also he referred to a fear she had evidently expressed that he didn't want her there. He indicated apologetically that he had been irritable before she left.

But, he wrote her from his office, "I really can't stand that house all alone without you, and you were a goosy girl to think or even pretend to think that I don't want you here *all* the summer, because you know I do! But honestly *you* ought to have six weeks straight at Campo, just as *I* ought to, only you can and I can't! I *know* what a whole summer here does to people's nerves and at the end of this summer I will be like a bear with a sore head until I get a change or some cold weather—in fact as you know I am unreasonable and touchy now—but I shall try to improve."[28]

A day later on Tuesday he told her, "It seems years since you left and I miss you horribly and hate the thought of the empty house. Last night I thought I heard a burglar and sat at the head of the stairs with the gun for half an hour, but it turned out to be the cat."[29]

On this same day *The New York Times* printed under a bold headline a war savings story:

HOW TO SAVE IN BIG HOMES

Food Administration Adopts
Mrs. F. D. Roosevelt's Plan as Model

Washington, July 16.–The food saving program adopted at the home of Franklin D. Roosevelt, Assistant Secretary of the Navy, has been selected by the conservation section of the Food Administration as a model for other large households. Mrs. Roosevelt on her pledge card said that there were seven in the family, and that ten servants were employed. Each servant has signed a pledge card, and there are daily conferences.

Mrs. Roosevelt does the buying, the cooks see that there is no food wasted, the laundress is sparing in her use of soap; each servant has a watchful eye for evidences of shortcomings in others, and all are encouraged to make suggestions in the use of "left overs."

No bacon is used in the Roosevelt home; cornbread is served
once a day. The consumption of laundry soap has been cut in
half. Meat is served but once daily, and all "left overs" are
utilized. Menu rules allow for two courses for luncheon and
three for dinner. Everybody eats fish at least once a week.

"Making the ten servants help me do my saving has not only
been possible, but highly profitable," said Mrs. Roosevelt today.
"Since I have started following the home-card instruction prices
have risen, but my bills are no larger."

Mrs. Harry Payne Whitney came here today to talk about
food conservation plans and announced that about August 1 she
would open her home in Newport for the first of a series of meetings to be held in the fashionable summer resorts. Mrs. Willard
D. Straight, formerly Miss Dorothy Whitney, has promised to
interest the Summer colony at Southampton, L.I., and arrange
the classes on food conservation there.[30]

Franklin read and wrote. Perhaps his comment was, as his
son and editor said thirty years later, "a jesting letter." There
was sharp sarcasm in it.

"All I can say," he told his lady in Campobello, "is that your
latest newspaper campaign is a corker and I am proud to be the
husband of the Originator, Discoverer, and Inventor of the New
Household Economy for Millionaires! Please have a photo taken
showing the family, the ten cooperating servants, the scraps saved
from the table and the hand book. I will have it published in the
Sunday *Times*.

"Honestly you have leaped into public fame, all Washington is
talking of the Roosevelt plan and I begin to get telegrams of
congratulation and requests for further details from Pittsburgh,
New Orleans, San Francisco and other neighboring cities."[31]

Only the final paragraphs of news about their friends, his cold
and the weather kept this epistle from being a blast. Eleanor was
aghast at what she had done.

"I do think it was horrid of that woman to use my name in
that way and I feel dreadfully about it because so much is not
true and yet some of it I did say. I will never be caught again that's
sure and I'd like to crawl away for shame."[32]

Apparently the incident was quickly forgotten in Washington where Roosevelt was working hard and having time in which to play, too. On the day after his "jesting letter," Franklin and friends happily boarded the *Sylph* again. Chief among his guests were Rear Admiral and Mrs. Cary Grayson. Mrs. Wilson's ward, Altrude Gordon Grayson, had married the handsome doctor sixteen years older than herself on May 24, 1916. Mrs. Wilson had acted as her chief attendant. Almost a year before that, while Mrs. Galt was visiting the attentive Wilson and his daughters at Cornish, New Hampshire, the President had written a letter to Secretary Daniels. The President asked the Secretary if there was anything "I can properly and legitimately do to set forward Cary T. Grayson's chances of promotion." Grayson knew nothing about the letter, the President wrote. "Anything irregular" would embarrass the doctor. Wilson only hoped that he might "legitimately increase his opportunities in some way that would be above criticism."[33]

"Above criticism" was suggesting much in a sharp-tongued capital. The jump to rear admiral which the President proposed meant hurrying the doctor past 127 older, senior officers. His nomination brought forth the witticism that Farragut had become an Admiral through the Civil War, Dewey through the Spanish-American War, and Grayson "through the boudoir." The promotion took some doing in the Senate. When Grayson called on the Secretary of the Navy to give his thanks upon his confirmation, Daniels noted in his diary that it had taken a "good navigator" to get it through the rough weather in the Senate. Now, in the summer following, Grayson was a good friend for Franklin to cultivate.

One of the other guests on the *Sylph* this July day was Charles A. Munn of the Harvard class of 1910, yachtsman, greyhound racer, and an old friend of Franklin's who had come to Washington as a reserve officer. As an enthusiastic horseman, he had become a frequent riding companion of Grayson's. Even in wartime Washington these two naval officers in uniform were sailors on horseback who attracted much attention in the parks.[34]

Munn's wife, who also came along, was the former Mary Astor Paul of Philadelphia. She worked with Eleanor and Lucy Mercer in wartime activities.

The other two members of the party were Lucy and Nigel Law, presumably cured of his poison ivy and possibly warned by it of the danger of picking fruit for Franklin. Lucy evidently did not wear her awkward yeomanette uniform. The whole group made, Franklin wrote to Eleanor, "a funny party, but it worked out *wonderfully!*" It was, he said, "a bully trip."[35]

". . . and they all got on splendidly," he told his wife in Campobello. "We swam about four times and Sunday afternoon went up the James to Richmond. We stopped at Lower and Upper Brandon, Westover and Shirley and went all over them, getting drenched to the skin by several severe thunder storms. Those old houses are really wonderful but *not* comfy!

"I found much food for thought in the fleet—things not right and due to old lady officers and lack of decision in the Department."[36]

Evidently wartime security was responsible for this brief reference to the fleet. The log of the *Sylph* did not mention the concealed American armada. Years later, however, in lively remembance Nigel Law described their visit to the big ships sheltered in the York River. He remembered that they visited the battlefield at Yorktown where his countryman Cornwallis had surrendered. They lunched on the *U.S.S. Kansas* with the admiral and his staff.

"After lunch the ships passed in review, with bands playing. Most of them managed the *Star-Spangled Banner* successfully, but some auxiliary ships at the end of the line, presumably not trusting their newly formed bands to play the national air went past to the tune of *Alexander's Ragtime Band* and other popular ditties. Franklin laughed heartily at this episode and the Admiral joined in after some hesitation."[37]

Next day they continued their cruise up the James River to Upper and Lower Brandon and Westover. An incident at Westover added to the amusement of the gay party.

"Franklin and I and some of the party landed at the bottom of the garden and rang the bell," the Englishman recalled. "A darkie servant came out and he was told to say that the Under Secretary of the U. S. Navy would be glad to be allowed to visit the house and garden. The servant looked doubtful and soon came back with a curt 'No.' For the moment we were nonplussed for we particularly wanted to visit this famous old place. Then Franklin had an idea. He said to me, 'Maybe they don't like Yankees in these parts. You send in your card.' So as a joke I told the man to take my card on which I was described as 3rd Secretary of His Britannic Majesty's Embassy. To my surprise he came running back to say, 'The Master wants you all to come right in.' Franklin was much tickled by this Southern rebuff to Federal authority and kept laughing over it all afternoon."³⁸

Franklin got back to find the N Street house filled with "plumbers, paperers, etc.,"³⁹ working under the direction of Auntie Bye. She had come to prepare the house for new tenants since the Roosevelts with five children and the ten-servant staff Eleanor had described were finding her house too small. Bye went to dine one evening with Senator Lodge, whose wife and Bamie's dear friend Anna Cabot Davis Lodge had died the summer before. The next night she went to dinner with the Longworths. Franklin saw little of her.⁴⁰ He was in the midst of appearances before a House Committee "trying to get 147 millions!" But it was on this occasion that Bye received the impression which her husband passed on to Franklin later in the year.

"She speaks of you as her debonair young cousin, so brave and so charming, but the girls will spoil you soon enough, Franklin, and I leave you to them."⁴¹

He did seem charming to young ladies and old ones alike. On the night Bye dined with Alice he went to an elaborate dinner and garden party which the Commandant of the Marines and Mrs. George Barnett gave "in honor of the Daniels!"⁴² (Sometimes it is difficult to sense the meaning of Franklin's many exclamation points.) On this evening, however, he seemed trapped with dowagers: Mrs. Townsend, whose great Massachusetts Avenue

mansion had been hospitably open to von Bernstorff until he departed; and Mrs. McCawley, wife of one of Carroll Mercer's gay
friends. They were two ladies whom the elegant Larz Anderson
described as among the dwindling few who still entertained
beautifully.[43]

Then almost on a regular summer schedule Franklin was ill
again, this time with a recurrent throat infection. His chief, Secretary Daniels, believed that this sickness of Roosevelt and the
coincident sickness of other top officials was at least contributed
to by strenuous exercises they took in the early morning under
the direction of the famous football coach Walter Camp. Daniels
preferred his rest and kept his health. If the morning exercises
on top of strenuous desk duties took its toll with Franklin, it
brought him a tribute from Camp.

"Mr. Roosevelt," Camp wrote admiringly, "is a beautifully built
man, with the long muscles of the athlete. Even his hard and
confining work has not caused much deterioration as yet, but
his heart and lungs cry for more exercise already."[44]

Still the athlete was laid low early in August. Sara wired that
she was preparing to rush down from Lake Placid.[45] But Eleanor
hurried first to Washington to be with him during the four days
he spent in the hospital. His recovery was such that he was soon
back on the golf course. He was off on another relaxing excursion
on August 19. After golf and a quick lunch at the Chevy Chase
Club he set off at 2:30 in the afternoon on a motor trip to "the
Horsey's place near Harpers Ferry," about seventy miles away over
dusty and crowded roads.

"Lucy Mercer went and the Graysons," he wrote Eleanor "and
we got there at 5:30, walked over the farm—a very rich one and
run by the two sisters—had supper with them and several neighbors, left at nine and got home at midnight!"[46]

The two sisters, Elizabeth and Anna Horsey, lived much of the
time in Washington and had known Altrude and Lucy there. Apparently Anna Horsey had a somewhat similar relationship to
Altrude as older friend that Mrs. Wilson had. In 1914 she had been
living with Altrude on 16th Street and was present among a glit-

tering array of guests at her wedding to Grayson in May 1916.[47]
Possibly the richness of the farm of which Franklin wrote related
to the nearby Horsey Distillery. In 1850 this family-owned distillery began the ingenious process of shipping its whiskey in slow
sailing vessels around Cape Horn to California. This was supposed
to age it in a voyage. Certainly in California it must have sated
the thirst of the '49ers.[48] Like other distilleries in 1917, it was
involved in wartime prohibition which a little later explained
Franklin's report to Eleanor that after another round of golf
with McCawley—thirty-six holes—they dined at "a very dry Metropolitan Club."[49]

In the same letter about the excursion to Harpers Ferry, he
told Eleanor incidentally that "they," presumably Altrude and
Lucy, "handed in a record amount of sweaters and other wooleys
on Saturday and all wanted to know how the Daniels-Thompson
row would affect the work. I told them to sit tight, keep on knitting
and not rock the boat!"[50]

The Daniels-Thompson row marked the final collision of
Colonel Thompson of the Navy League and Secretary Daniels.
The League, largely supported by steelmakers and shipbuilders,
had been increasingly critical of Daniels. He had a baleful eye
for armor profits and profiteers, as he regarded them. Now
Thompson, as president of this organization, charged that investigation of an explosion at the Mare Island Navy Yard in California had been blocked at the demand of labor leaders.

The charges were proved to be untrue. Daniels called the
League's statement "a gross slander of the patriotic worker" and
called upon Thompson and other officers of the League to resign
"from what had come to be an unpatriotic organization."[51]
Thompson minimized the League's mistake and replied pertly
that he would resign if Daniels would. Unamused, the Secretary
issued an order barring all representatives of the League from all
ships and stations. The Navy League had already been complaining that the Red Cross did not cooperate in its efforts. Franklin
did not mean to get involved in this row. His position had not
been made more secure by praise for him by Colonel Thompson.

Moreover he recognized the implacability of Daniels backed by the President.

On Tuesday, September 11, he wrote Eleanor, "No news, except that Daniels has chucked the Comforts Committee entirely and is trying to organize a rival set under the Red Cross and to be directed by Mrs. Stotesbury. The end is not yet as the League (or at least the Comfort Com.) is I think going to fight back."[52] In this battle, however, the contestants were unequal. The Navy controlled access to its men. And in Mrs. Stotesbury, Daniels had a decorative and determined agent. Her riches and her famous pearls, which a detective carried back and forth from Philadelphia to Washington, did not suffice for her ambitions. She had been Mrs. Oliver Cromwell, of 1808 New Hampshire Avenue, in Washington, in 1912 when she became the second wife of the sixty-three-year-old Edward Townsend Stotesbury, Philadelphia member of the firm of J. P. Morgan & Co., and breeder of thoroughbred horses. Only the name of her first husband suggested congeniality with such a Puritan as Daniels. He needed her; she needed him.

Gossips had not been kind to Lucretia Roberts Cromwell Stotesbury. In the year of her marriage to Stotesbury *The Clubfellow and Washington Mirror* had noted, "Prosperity certainly agrees with her, but I fear she is a trifle more buxom than before."[53] That sheet went on to sharper comment in January 1913. With little charity for the lady whose parties and jewels had dazzled the Quaker City, Philadelphia felt sorry for Mrs. Stotesbury, it said. "She went up like a skyrocket and came down like the stick. The root of the whole thing is jealousy. The millionaire's wife made the mistake of her life in the way she burst into Philadelphia society."[54] Yet now in Washington in spacious quarters at the Shoreham Hotel, she was both decorative and formidable.

Off the scene of battle Eleanor declared, "What a mess about the Navy League but I think Mr. D. has made a mistake to refuse all garments from them. People will be discouraged and the volume of work will take forever to pick up if it does at all."[55]

Franklin, however, had no intention of being caught now on the

League side against the amply armed Mrs. Stotesbury and the angry Daniels.

"*You,*" he wrote Eleanor underlining the pronoun, "are entirely disconnected and Lucy Mercer and Mrs. Munn are closing up the loose ends."[56]

Evidently Lucy was still available for chores. Yet there was a greater trouble than her clean-up role in the League fight in her life at this time. No mention of it is made in any of the available Roosevelt records. But on September 11, her father, long-ailing Carroll Mercer, was taken dying to Sibley Hospital by Dr. Norman R. Jenner. Dr. Jenner reported that Mercer had suffered from chronic nephritis and valvular disease of the heart for twenty-five years, which seems unlikely since that period included his Spanish War service. He died on Thursday, September 13. The immediate cause of death was "cardiac decompensation—exhaustion."[57]

In his obituary the *Washington Post* described him as "one of the most widely known of the old residents of the District."[58] *Town Topics*[59] added its loquaciousness to the bare details of news. "Poor Carroll Mercer," it said, "was laid away with some semblance of his former state, attended by old cronies who served as pall-bearers. . . . A sparse company gathered in old St. John's, and it was a dreary day in keeping with the mournful purpose." It listed his pallbearers with evident social familiarity: Truxton Beale, George Howard, Tony Addison, Barry Bulkley, Randall Webb, Dick Harlow, Charlie McCawley.

"At the church," the magazine went on, "they may have reflected on what the primrose path had brought to their associate, but the same afternoon as they talked things over at the Metropolitan Club, they did not look very grave."

Mrs. Mercer, it added almost like a smirk at the obsequies, "Naturally, . . . did not appear at the funeral." This might have been the sort of cruel conjecture of which the paper was often guilty. Yet the fact was that neither the *Post* nor the *Washington Star*[60] in their reports made any mention of Minnie, Lucy, or Violetta at the funeral or as survivors. Other items in the paper then reflected times too hurried to take much note of Mercer's death. The *Post* noted patriotically that the day of the funeral was the anniversary of the birth of the *Star-Spangled Banner*. Six more women were arrested for picketing the White House for woman suffrage; their banner was torn down by two sailors. Mrs. Larz Anderson would sail shortly for France to work in refreshment booths near the front.

Lucy was working then in the Navy Department. She had been quickly promoted from yeoman 3rd class to yeoman 2nd class. But on October 5, 1917, after less than four months' service, she was discharged. Her record for conduct was given top rating. She was qualified for re-enlistment. But severance from the service was "by Special Order of Secretary of the Navy."[61] This was, of course, a small incident in a great war. Possibly the death of her father seemed to create a hardship case for her family. Actually, of course, she and her mother were no worse off after Carroll's death than before. No reason for the Special Order was given in the record or noted in Daniels' diary or recollections. The Secretary at the time was concerned with larger matters. He had been to New York the day before to review the Red Cross parade. He had dinner with Mrs. Stotesbury. In Washington, on the 5th, he devoted his diary to his resentment of Theodore Roosevelt's activities: "T.R. at large, writing and speaking in disparagement of America's preparation for war, is helping Germany more than little fellows who are being arrested for giving aid and comfort to the enemy." Still he always had time for concern about individuals, particularly his yeomen (F), possibly especially for such a girl who, as a part of his assistant's household, he must have known. In the case of a more obscure girl he wrote in his diary: "Woman Yeoman court-martialled & reduced because she left when sick & Pratt did not like it. She was jerked up without time for advice. I overruled the action. Cannot deal with women as with men."[62]

The Franklin Roosevelts were very busy at this time. After conferring with Lord Northcliffe and one of his aides, Arthur Pollen, the British naval expert who had accompanied him to America, Franklin sent what he described as a "stinging memorandum"[63] to the Secretary and dispatched a copy to the President. He wanted an end of delays in the effort to bottle up the U-boats by a mine barrage. The job, he said, should be "placed in the hands of one man on our part and one man on the part of the British." Someone with "imagination and authority to make the try"[64] was needed. Evidently Franklin regarded himself as that man. But other things were on his mind and on Eleanor's. They were moving into the new house at 2131 R Street which had been recently occupied by Illinois Congressman Ira C. Copley, who was already then building the big Copley chain of newspapers. The house was big enough for the Roosevelt household. Yet servant problems developed. In exaggeration Franklin reported that all the servants had not "left in a body." Also at about this time he triumphantly noted the acquisition of a "K.M."—or kitchen maid.[65]

Evidently, however, there was no outside evidence of difficulties in logistics in the Roosevelt move from N to R Street. The agents of *Town Topics* reported this October that "in a crisis which threatened Washington's 'little season'" Eleanor had come to the rescue and had taken charge of the preparations for a Hallowe'en dance at Rauscher's for the benefit of the American ward in the hospital "at Neuilly, France."[66] She was also busy at the Red Cross canteen in a little tin building in the Washington railroad yards where they prepared sandwiches and coffee for the trainloads of soldiers passing through. They were very fortunate, she thought in the "wonderful women" working there. The one such she listed in her memoirs[67] was Mary Patten who "worked on a number of shifts with me." Eleanor often had her chauffeur stop for her on the way to the canteen. "So," she said, "I came to know her very well, and I grew to have great affection and respect for her character and willingness to work." Apparently she had no fear of her tongue or hoped to direct its wagging.

It was as of this time that her son Elliott inserted, in part, into the *Personal Letters* of her husband her statement of her developing philosophy.

"I think I learned then," she wrote later, "that practically no one in the world is entirely bad or entirely good, and that motives are often more important than actions. I had spent most of my life in an atmosphere where everyone was sure of what was right and what was wrong, and as life progressed I have gradually come to believe that human beings who try to judge other human beings are undertaking a somewhat difficult job. When your duty does not thrust ultimate judgments upon you, perhaps it is well to keep an open and charitable mind, and try to understand why people do things instead of condemning the acts themselves.

"Out of these contacts with human beings during the war I became a more tolerant person, far less sure of my own beliefs and methods of action, but I think more determined to try for certain ultimate objectives. I had gained a certain assurance of my ability to run things, and the knowledge that there is joy in accomplishing a good job. I knew more about the human heart, which had been somewhat veiled in mystery up to now."[68]

Other things were—and still are—veiled in mystery. One is a letter which Sara wrote to Franklin and Eleanor at this time, on October 14, 1917. The "particular issue which guided Sara's pen is unknown" her grandson Elliott wrote in 1948. Also, he placed the letter "chronologically out of order," two years before its proper 1917 place into the correspondence of 1915. Eleven years later grandson James said that, "as Mother remembers it," the letter related to Sara's wish that FDR promise her "that the Hyde Park estate would be kept in the family 'forever.'"[69] That seemed an odd basis for Lady Sara's outburst. Obviously in the changing mores of America at war, the highly emotional letter was an old lady's and an old order's lament.

Sara began blaming herself and placating Eleanor. "I feel *too* badly that I let you go without your pearl collar, *too* stupid of me! Do wear the velvet one Aunt Doe gave you!"

She went on in a pain equal to that she had shown when she disapproved of their marriage.

"I am sorry to feel that Franklin *is* tired and that my views are not his, but perhaps dear Franklin you may on second thoughts or *third* thoughts see that I am not so far from wrong.

The foolish old saying 'noblesse oblige' is good and 'honneur oblige' possibly expresses it better for most of us. One can be democratic as one likes, but if we love our own, and if we love our neighbor, we owe a great example, and my constant feeling is that through neglect or laziness I am not doing my part toward those around me."

Sara was evidently deeply disturbed.

"After I got home, I sat in the library for nearly an hour reading, and as I put down my book and left the delightful room and the two fine portraits, I thought: after all, would it not be better just to spend all one has at once in this time of suffering and need, and not think of the future; for with the *trend* to 'shirt sleeves,' and the ideas of what men should do in always being all things to all men and striving to give up the old fashioned traditions of family life, simple home pleasures and refinements, and the traditions some of us love best, of what use is it to *keep up* things, to hold on to dignity and all I stood for this evening. Do not say that I *misunderstood*, I understand perfectly, but I cannot believe that my precious Franklin really feels as he expressed himself. Well, I hope that while I live I may keep my 'old fashioned' theories and that *at least* in my own family I may continue to feel that *home* is the best and happiest place and that my son and daughter and their children will live in peace and keep from the tarnish which seems to affect so many."

Throughout the letter it was clear that Sara's indignation was directed at Franklin, not Eleanor. And she felt frustrated in arguing with her son.

"When I talk I find I usually arouse opposition, which seems odd, but is perhaps my own fault, and it tends to lower my opinion of myself, which is doubtless salutary. I doubt if you will have time dear Franklin to read this, and if you do, it may not please you."[70]

There was no evidence on R Street that the young Roosevelts were disturbed. Eleanor had undertaken the ambitious task of making the arrangements for the ball for the Ambulance Corps on Thanksgiving eve.[71] It was unique in that every debutante of

any social pretensions was to be in attendance—and their number was increased by the daughters of dollar-a-year men who had
moved swiftly into Washington society. The word "recruit-
ment" was applied to beaux for the buds in the capital which was
gay but could not be sure that the dancing partner tonight might
not be gone mysteriously on security guarded movements to
France tomorrow.

Soon after this dance TR, at the urging of Republican leaders, came back to the capital. Alice, as always, serving as his advance guard, had conferred with many, notably Franklin and
Eleanor, before her belligerent father arrived. In the Longworth
house the elder Roosevelt, now ready to stir the dust on a stormy
street, presided as plans were made "to concentrate on Father to
lead the Republicans."[72]

"The President," Alice wrote, "may have been, as we thought
darkly, trying to run the war in the interest of the Democratic
Party, but the Republicans were far from being politically
idle."[73]

Blood ties then were at least as strong as political ones. At about
this time vigorous-seeming old Theodore wrote Franklin, "I
continually hear how well you are doing."[74]

Lines were being drawn at home as men and armaments
moved in volume now to the war zones. Great convoys moved on
secret sailing dates from guarded harbors. Nigel Law was one of
those who sailed on darkened vessels late in the year. He went to
England to find additional staff, he said later, "for our overworked
Embassy."[75] His departure coincided with one of those items
compounded of perhaps some truth and certainly much conjecture for which *Town Topics* was famed. On December 13, it
tantalized its readers as follows:

"The gossip in Washington concerning a charming young girl
highly placed in the official world, and an equally delightful young
man, close akin to the loftiest of British nobility, may or may not
be true. I merely repeat it as it came to me, but if anyone may
judge by propinquity, then it seems that Cupid has scored again
and another international alliance will be an event of the near

future. The young diplomatist is more highly regarded in Washington than subalterns usually are. He has undertaken some campaigns of usefulness and carried them through successfully, and recently he was sent to London on an errand requiring both resource and delicacy in handling. It would be an ideal match, as the young couple's ideas entirely harmonize. As the girl has recently gone into retirement because of family bereavement, the affair may reach a culmination sooner than expected."[76]

The clues in the piece pointed pretty clearly to Nigel. But no one save a society writer reaching for prominence for her characters then could have described Lucy as "highly placed in the official world." Only the fact of recent bereavement suggested her. The whole piece may have been fiction given credence later merely by the long remembrance of each other by these two. Already then some gossips, without benefit of printing, were saying that Nigel's role with Lucy Mercer was largely that of a shield for Franklin Roosevelt. If he needed protection from tale bearers, it was to be provided by the amazed attention given taller, better authenticated tales involving another Englishman. Afterward this Briton seemed not so much one to ease the burdens of the "overworked Embassy" but a man who increased them in fantastic fashion. He was a gentleman of many talents, adventures, and devices. He was Major Charles Kennedy-Craufurd-Stuart, D.S.O. Socially exciting report had it that he was a descendant of the Stuart Kings. He seemed more like John Bull in an American china shop.

SIX

Accompaniment to War

Social registers and scholarly reference books have variously spelled the first name of Huybertie (or Huberje) Pruyn Hamlin, but in the long years of her husband's services in Washington everybody who was anybody knew Bertie Hamlin—and vice versa. Sometimes her readily expressed opinions, even to such a personage as J. P. Morgan, disturbed her cautious husband, Charles Sumner Hamlin. He was a *cum laude* Harvard law graduate, member of the best Boston and Washington clubs, and was put on guard on the Federal Reserve Board by Wilson to watch American finances and financiers. Sometimes he also felt he had to watch Bertie's tongue. He need not have worried.

Mrs. Hamlin was gay with her debutante daughter, Anna, and observant in the society of her own contemporaries. She was qualified as witness of it. Her Flemish ancestry ran back in America to 1665, but a Gallic quality came down to her undiminished by American centuries. In those years the Pruyns had acquired wealth and prestige. Long before she was born her father, John Van Schaick Lansing Pruyn, Albany lawyer, had drawn up the agreement consolidating ten railroad companies into the New York Central. One of his relatives, Robert Hewson Pruyn, had in the 1860s, as U.S. minister resident in Japan, helped force the revocation of the Mikado's order expelling foreigners from the islands.

Bertie's own life touched history. She had known young Franklin Roosevelt in her Hudson Valley childhood. She knew him later when as student at Harvard he took a course under her husband on "Administration of the Government of the United States." She saw much of him and Eleanor in Washington in the Wilson years. Later he would casually visit her summer house at Mattapoisett on Buzzard's Bay. Finally, she was visiting at the White House, sleeping in the Lincoln bed, when the day of Pearl Harbor dawned. Importantly she kept a diary and shared memories. The testimony of Bertie Hamlin can be regarded as dependable. She recalled the fact of the whispers about Franklin and Lucy and the amazing story of Major Kennedy-Craufurd-Stuart which mounted from gossip to communications between chancellories.

Of Franklin and Lucy she wrote: "There was a heavy blast of gossip and a lot came from the Patten sisters though Mary Patten worked at the R. R. canteen in E. R.'s group & E. R. was always fond of her and counted her in for particular occasions. The worst talkers were Mrs. T. R. Marshall—Justice McReynolds etc."[1]

But this was a whisper about a gentle matter compared with the scandal stirred by the British officer. Possibly the only explanation of his behavior was that he was intoxicated by the exciting temper of wartime Washington society. It was a time of pressures and fears, of a race between German armies released from the Russian front driving into France as submarine losses mounted at sea, and American efforts to provide the muscle necessary to Allied victory. Much real bad news came and many wild spy scares were spread. In the old city of politicians, bureaucrats and cave dwellers, parties were sprinkled with the new glittering figures of crisp speaking dollar-a-year men and others with the uniforms and accents of expanding Allied commissions.

The physical and mental strain on the participants was intense. But, as Alice Longworth wrote, "during the day members of the commissions were hard at work. After working hours they were equally hard at play. Everyone had parties for them, and they gave many parties themselves. I think it pleased the Washington

that went to and gave dinners to feel that entertaining the representatives of the Allies had a recognized part in 'winning the war'!
Anyway it was a far pleasanter form of 'war work' than can-
teens, Red Cross classes, and Liberty Loan drives. One, of course,
did that sort of thing too—washed dishes, scooped ice cream, cut
pies, peddled Liberty Loan bonds, and made clumsy attempts at
first aid."[2]

As a subordinate in the British staff, Franklin's friend Nigel
Law remembered the gaiety as well as the work of those days, "We
had little time for diversion," he said of his associations with
Roosevelt. "You can guess how busy he was, and my own hours of
work began at 9:30 A.M. and seldom ended until 2 or 3 A.M., with
a break of a couple of hours or so at supper time." Yet he recalled
the dinners and luncheons, some at such places as Dower House
and the Lock Tavern Club on the Potomac, canoeing, picnicking,
walks in the Virginia woods.[3]

Franklin himself in another world war recalled the lively society
of the first one. In World War I, he said, the tired official looking
for recreation after labor could take his choice in the Dupont
Circle neighborhood. There was the house where, despite wartime prohibition, every kind of drink was served. In another
residence artists and writers and intellectuals served high
talk around an artistic hostess. Finally in a pleasant dwelling the
music was soft, the conversation was light and gay, and the ladies
were very pretty. They listened with admiration to the recitals
of the war-winning exploits of their guests.

"The Saloon, the Salon, and the Salome," Roosevelt facetiously
called them in remembrance of a wit's phrase of the time.[4] Mrs.
Longworth in effect and detail identified "the Saloon" as the
home of Percy Rivington Pyne II, rich New York businessman and
clubman, now serving with the War Industries Board. She said
he kept "open house" every afternoon.[5] Mrs. Hamlin joined Alice
in identifying "the Saloon." "The Salon" was the residence of
the John Saltonstalls, she thought. Wealthy yachtsman and one
time diplomat, Saltonstall had been one of those Franklin early

interested in his small boat campaign. Now in Washington his house and Franklin's were in the same block on R Street.

Any number of houses, however, could have fitted the merry malice of the alliterative terms. Certainly there was more than any one place the bibulous could slake their thirst. Tall talk went on in more rooms than the salon of one residence. And Washington in wartime became a mecca not only for the patriots at desks but for socially elite ladies, too. Many of the rich and patrician gathered in an exciting society which, even as war changed it, contained along with other elements a sort of last coterie of the society which Edith Wharton gently satirized. Many in the elegant old houses, on which rents were steeply rising, not only offered hospitality but attracted hostility.

Alice Longworth, whose ties were political, patrician and plutocratic, enjoyed the hospitality which she both dispensed and received. She was aware, too, of the hostility which both personal pique and overwrought patriotism sometimes created. In her *Crowded Hours* she wrote of the humorous aspects of "spy fever" in wartime Washington: "Listening devices, I have been told, were put in the houses of individuals whose sole claim to being suspect lay in the fact that they were not unnaturally interested in meeting and talking with the people who were doing the big jobs—the 'important people' who were so much in demand at dinner tables in war Washington."[6]

Others, including her relative by marriage, Mrs. Larz Anderson, were not entirely pleased by the swift, decorative changes in the wartime capital. Isabel Anderson saw bogeys. In her *Presidents and Pies*[7] she remembered not only her multiuniformed war activities at the time but some distaste in the alterations of officialdom. "Looking over the list of political people," she wrote, "one notices more than ever before men of Jewish extraction. Faint rumors of a great Hebraic world movement headed by some very prominent Jews have been heard, but the movement is still kept very quiet."

Like some of the "spy scares" the movement was non-existent. She did not name her Jews. Clearly and prominently in the com-

pany, however, was Bernard M. Baruch, head of the War Industries Board, whom even Colonel House had called a Hebrew from
Wall Street.[8] Baruch led to the city a throng of other such officials
for wartime only, by no means all or many of them Jews. Some
were as genteelly gentile as Pyne and Saltonstall. But Baruch was
the tall shepherd of the flock.

He had not only made a great fortune on the basis of great
ability, he also enjoyed it with great zest. He had only played on
the edges of government and politics before as a lavish contributor
to Democratic politicians, many of whom he liked to entertain
at his vast plantation and hunting preserve, Hobcaw Barony, in
South Carolina. Shortly before Wilson called him to Washington
to head industrial production for war, there had been charges
that he had made huge sums on the stock market as a result
of a leak to him of government information. Before a Congressional Committee he debonairly refuted them. He didn't need
leaks to get rich. A society magazine commented with a little
awe on his branching out into race horse breeding on a scale
which only a princely income could sustain.[9]

Though he had nothing to hide about his operations in Wall
Street when he began service in Washington, the "leak" inquiry in
Congress brought him into confrontation with the sometimes
more awesome whispers and whisperers in Washington. As a
novice in government his innocence did not prevent his nervous-
ness when he took the stand to refute the charges. He was "fright-
ened half to death," he wrote later, and saw Alice—the least lost
in the Washington wonderland—sitting in the committee room
audience as a lady symbol of the merciless observer. He did not
then know, he said, "the vivacious daughter of T.R." Still, "although she was an exceptionally charming woman, there flashed
in my mind a picture of the women of Paris seated about the
guillotine, knitting as the heads rolled into the baskets. Mrs. Longworth was there to see my head roll."[10]

Perhaps to her disappointment Baruch's head did not fall. Instead he rose in prestige and power. He leased a big house near
Dupont Circle and also a country place where he might escape

the capital's heat. Both were hospitable houses. Such a guest as
Cary Grayson, who played tennis with him, indicated his proximity to presidential power. His already white head towered
over the company at receptions. His biographer, Margaret Coit,
wrote that he still loved dancing. But she said, as Mrs. Baruch was
often absent, "his springy, graceful figure would have cut too conspicuous a figure on a Washington dance floor, so this was one
pleasure he gave up when she was not in town."[11] As one who
delighted in the society of lovely ladies, however, he found pleasant the company at several such mansions as matched the image
of the legendary "Salome."

Any talk like Mrs. Anderson's was, of course, the vapors of
small minds. Yet, such a writer as John Dos Passos concluded in
Mr. Wilson's War that in Britain wily Prime Minister Lloyd
George believed that in order to be most persuasive for Britain's war needs it would be well to send his own ablest Jew to deal
with the powerful Baruch in America.[12] He turned to Britain's
Lord Chief Justice. Certainly as British emissary who came first
briefly as commissioner in the fall of 1917, then as ambassador
early in 1918, the first Marquess of Reading, born Rufus Daniel
Isaacs, son of a fruit importer, was a remarkable man and adequate
counterpart to Baruch. He came, however, with something like a
weasel or a monkey in his bosom.

One of his aides was Kennedy-Craufurd-Stuart (a name often
abbreviated and misspelled in written reference to him). His
career seemed to entitle him to warm welcome in hero-worshiping
Washington. Badly wounded in the jaw at Gallipoli, he was at
this time at the summit of a remarkable career. He made some
mystery of his age, leaving his birthdate out of *Who's Who*, but
he was old enough to have been decorated for his service in the
Boer War sixteen years before. He had served in the Punjab
Cavalry and the Burma Military Police. Recently his gallantry in
Gallipoli had brought him the D.S.O. But he was by no means soldier only. He was a skilled polo player. As amateur photographer,
he had exhibited his work in the London Salon of Photography.
A musician also, he had written at least two popular songs, *At*

Gloaming Tide and *Make-Believe Land*.[13] Apparently his only defect was a slight impediment in his speech resulting from a recent war wound.

Many of his duties, Mrs. Hamlin wrote in her diary, were social: "He was most useful to Lady Reading—practically ran the Embassy for her and stood about with her coat at receptions. He was in fact a 'Handy Man.' . . . Lord Reading is High Commissioner —he has everything he wants—and I must say he is an unusually interesting man. The atmosphere at the old Embassy is very different—Lady Reading is very fine looking but quite deaf."[14]

Not all of Kennedy-Craufurd-Stuart's social activities were as Lady Reading's attendant. He joined in other wartime festivities. Naturally there was welcome for him in "the Saloon." His various interests qualified him for "the Salon." But he came to a rendezvous with the ridiculous in one cooing court which the joking might classify as "the Salome." There he spent a good deal of time with a young lady whom Bernard Baruch, among others, found fascinating.

Mrs. Hamlin wrote in her diary that "we are all very much excited"[15] about this young charmer and her many beaux. She noted: she "seems able to keep a string of admirers. One of the T.G.s (Temporary Gentlemen) at the British Embassy is mad about her—Crawford-Stewart [sic] but we hear she has had enough of him and that he is very angry with her."[16]

In his fury at rejection, so the Washington gossip ran, the Major was ready to destroy the girl. Mrs. Hamlin wrote of his operation in revenge in her diary and later amplified the story in recollection. Craufurd-Stuart learned that the young lady and her family had gone out of town: he went to the "house and the maid knew him and he got in on some excuse and managed to install a dictograph to register conversation."[17]

The supposed results made resounding gossip. When the Englishman later retrieved his device, it was said, a voice recorded on it along with the girl's was that of Baruch. Mrs. Hamlin's information was that he was "indiscreet." In his exuberant talk, she said, he told the young lady and the Dictaphone "some quite important information . . . and as it came from the head of the War Industries—Crawford-Stewart made the most of it and the State Dept. took it up. . . ."

There are no records that the State Department took it up. Still the report spread and, as Bertie reported, the young lady "was in quite a jam" as Craufurd-Stuart insisted she was a figure in a new and dangerous leak not *to* but *from* Baruch about security matters. The number of callers at the once happy house declined. The young lady was not welcomed in other houses as before.

"The story got about in all kinds of shapes," Bertie wrote, "but it was some time after the war before her family and friends got her out of trouble. Many people dropped her and when the 'Ball of Nations'—I think that was the name—chose her to represent Liberty as she looked the part there was quite a riot."[18]

"Riot" seems an excessive word for a matter which never became more than the rumbling of social suspicions. Under any circumstances the British major's attention to security matters in the American capital would have seemed presumptuous. The English still had a notion that Americans, coming late into the war and into the sinister operations of espionage, were innocent—even naïve. Some Americans shared that view. Still it seems incredible now that, in striking a lady, Kennedy-Craufurd-Stuart would involve Baruch whom his chief, Lord Reading, had come to persuade. Any lapse on the part of Baruch also would have entangled the administration and President Wilson, who had chosen the tall financier and supported him in his important work. Baruch was not only doing a magnificent job; also inevitably in pressing industry as to price and production, he was making some enemies in this battle on the Potomac. Some welcomed any reflection on him to add to their prejudice against him as a Jew. Also he seemed more a speculator than a financier to some in the Establishment presided over by J. P. Morgan, most of whose members were Trinity Church type Episcopalians.

Years later John Chamberlain, referring to an incident in Wilson's first campaign for the Presidency in *Farewell to Reform*, echoed this attitude not limited to wartime when he wrote: "The

Morgan interests might have been rebuffed and affronted when Wilson broke with Colonel George Harvey, but the Morgan crowd merely gave way to Bernard Baruch and the Kuhn, Loeb crowd."[19] Chamberlain was referring to the supposed repudiation, in 1912, by Wilson of aid from Harvey as Morgan-backed editor which threatened his support by anti-Wall Street William Jennings Bryan. Some wondered even at the time if Harvey's friends had not welcomed the break with a candidate whose increasing liberalism disturbed them. Whatever may have been the facts about this incident, some important Democrats, notably Colonel House, resented Baruch's intimacy and influence with the President and Mrs. Wilson. Some, ready—even eager—to believe that Baruch had been involved in a leak for admiration rather than profit, emphasized his penchant for pleasing ladies. With their assistance, disturbing credulity was added to the story of this conversational indiscretion by the understanding that Baruch, who circumspectly did not dance in Washington, had a reputation as a ladies' man: he might enjoy talking expansively about himself and indiscreetly about his work to an admiring beauty.

Alice Longworth, who heard all gossip and evaluated it with precision, dismissed as ridiculous this item among others in the "spy fever." She wrote: "I personally know of not a single case in which anything was proved. In fact, when they were gone into I think it would take a pretty inveterate spy hunter to continue to feel suspicious."[20] Mrs. Hamlin dismissed Craufurd-Stuart in his role as vindictive vigilante in this matter and in his other qualities, too, as an "obnoxious" man and "a bounder."

Craufurd-Stuart took a giant step to prove the validity of such epithets. Certainly in view of the confidence placed by the President in Baruch, it is difficult to conceive of him as a blabber, even in the service of his vanity. The beauty may have been as foolish as she was young in the frenetic gaiety of the exciting capital. Perhaps in the bewildering Washington she was briefly and perilously similar to a character drawn by Mrs. Wharton's friend Henry James. In Washington a "Daisy Miller" might have found herself in a plight in a world of greater intricacy than she was accustomed to. She suffered only the temporary stings of malicious mischief.

Still it was fortunate for her that Craufurd-Stuart, as a man of devices, was blown up by his own booby trap in such a way as to discredit him as a witness against her or anybody else. While talk about the Dictaphone was raging, Mrs. Hamlin noted in her diary that he had said such dreadful things about President and Mrs. Wilson at a dinner that "he was reported by a guest" to Secretary of State Lansing. She went on, "Gossip says Mr. Lansing took the matter up with Lord Reading and that the man's name was dropped off the little Blue Book issued by the State Dept. every month. The Embassy omitted his name in their list but kept Crawford-Stewart there."[21]

Sir Arthur Willert, correspondent for the London *Times* then and a great friend of Franklin Roosevelt, recalled the episode later. Sir Arthur was aware of the case as both newspaperman and one who served in the British Foreign Office. His memories give Craufurd-Stuart, whom he knew well and liked, the most charitable characterization.

"He was good at managing dogs, horses and children," Sir Arthur said, "but bad at managing his tongue. An important Washington dowager asked him why he got on so well in Washington and he replied, 'I think because I am middle class myself.' "[22]

The report about Craufurd-Stuart's unguarded tongue which was relayed to the White House was that at a dinner party he made a remark "in the form of a riddle." It was a joke which was never very funny and became offensively stale as it went around. It ran:

"What did Mrs. Galt do when the President proposed to her? "Fell out of bed."[23]

He related no such riddle, Craufurd-Stuart insisted strenuously. He pled his innocence with solemn explanation in a document now in the archives of the State Department. All he had done, he affirmed, was to ask Mrs. George Thomas Marye, wife of Wilson's

first ambassador to Russia (an American who described himself in
Who's Who as a member of the Church of England), if she had
seen an article in the *New York Tribune*. As far as he could remember, the major said, it "criticized the President's power and
ability when compared with Mr. Balfour, Mr. Asquith, and Mr.
Lloyd-George. It was not my opinion nor was it given as mine. I
said nothing further. After dinner I did not join the ladies as I
played piano accompaniments for Mr. Constantinidi" (an Italian
diplomatic attaché who sang).[24]

"C-S is intolerable," Mrs. Hamlin wrote at the time. Apparently
that was the general American view. Certainly it became the opinion at the White House. Yet his actions or the rumors he aroused
so dominated gossip in the winter and spring of 1918 that any
other talk seemed hardly worth remembering, including even such
a "heavy blast of gossip" as Mrs. Hamlin remembered about Franklin Roosevelt and Lucy Mercer. Such vignettes of Franklin in the
social sphere as survive make him seem the devoted husband—
and son.

Whatever she may have heard Mrs. Hamlin saw him in such a
role at the end of the old year 1917 when on December 28, she
and her husband dined at the Roosevelt home on R Street. The
diners seemed almost to embody the firm defense of the " 'old
fashioned' theories" Sara Roosevelt had expounded in her explosive letter to Franklin and Eleanor the fall before. Then Sara
had expressed the hope that "*at least* in my own family I may
continue to feel that *home* is the best and happiest place and that
my son and daughter and their children will live in peace and
keep from the tarnish which seems to affect so many." This dominant lady was at the December dinner. So were the Hamlins and
a couple of inevitable but inconsequential English gentlemen
(certainly not including Craufurd-Stuart). Also present were Secretary and Mrs. Daniels. Daniels had been much ridiculed for his
concern about the moral protection of the young men called to
his Navy. Indeed, at the time there were charges that Franklin had
so responded to the Secretary's insistence that the areas about
naval bases be cleaned up that as Assistant Secretary he had ap-

proved the use of enlisted men in the entrapment of homosexuals at Newport. Franklin later violently resented and resisted the charge.

Daniels definitely held to "'old fashioned' theories" about the home. Plump Mrs. Daniels seemed to some even more moralistic. Sharp-penned Ellen Slayden wrote of her as "patriotico-pious," "hen minded." She noted, "Good, creamy Mrs. Daniels—one always thinks of dairy products where she is around. . . ."25

Not long before this time Daniels, with his wife's approval, had in effect, dismissed his own brother-in-law, Henry Bagley, as the business manager of his newspaper because Bagley had gone beyond philandering, which could be regretfully overlooked, to the final step of demanding a divorce from a sweet, forebearing little Catholic wife in order that he might marry another woman.26 The Danielses had as stern a feeling about divorce as did Eleanor's Uncle Ted who a few years before had given his support to a national movement for more rigid divorce laws.

Despite gaiety and gossip, Washington then was in a "patriotico-pious" mood. The winter was grimly cold. It seemed marked by cruel separations. All the Roosevelts of both the Hyde Park and Sagamore Hill branches were saddened by what seemed to them the abrupt and heartless way in which their old friend Ambassador Spring-Rice was dismissed to make room for Lord Reading. Springy died before he got home to England, "literally killed" Alice thought by the manner of his removal. And almost on the day they told Spring-Rice goodbye, Congressman Gussie Gardner, who had hurried into uniform, died of pneumonia at a camp in Georgia. Many, who had not shared his early belligerency, came to join in the last quiet rites for a brave man.

A resounding religion of wrath, however, was being preached in a great temporary tabernacle down near the Union Station where the Reverend Billy Sunday roared in equal terms at sin and the Germans. His "God damn the Germans" theology was given approval in prayer meetings in the houses of Cabinet members. Among those in prayer at the Daniels house was Franklin. Mrs. Hamlin, however, heard one gentleman at a Sunday prayer meeting at the home of Secretary Lansing say, "If he is going to under-take his reform—he will have to stay here forever."[27]

Some felt that the Presbyterian President was putting on the robes of a messiah when early in January he outlined his peace aims of 14 points in a message to the Congress and the world. One who felt so was Uncle Ted. Now asking no favors but girded for political battle, he returned to his Washington command post at the Longworth house on January 22. The house, said Alice, became a "rallying point for all those Republicans, and some Democrats, who were dissatisfied with Wilson's conduct of the war." While the storming TR attended a political dinner, Alice and her mother dined with the Franklin Roosevelts. Also on this visit the mother and daughter called on Henry Adams, who loved Roosevelts though he found them amusing. To Alice now he looked little and old.[28] Two months later, while armies abroad and politicians at home stiffened their lines, he slipped out of life like a withered leaf falling. There was only room for brief an-nouncement of his death in newspapers filled with casualty lists.

The intimacy of Roosevelt Republicans and Roosevelt Demo-crats seemed natural. Blood was thicker than politics. There were, however, those questioning Franklin's loyalties in his household. The loquacious Pattens, the Hoosier wife of the Vice-President, the reactionary Justice McReynolds, others were talking, as Bertie Hamlin had reported.[29] Their gossip was a whisper beside the wails about Craufurd-Stuart's tricks and tongue. They left no rec-ords in any archives. Indeed, apparently the first written reference to Franklin and Lucy came only in 1946. Then Olive Clapper, wife of the famous newspaperman Raymond Clapper, made a veiled reference to it in her book *Washington Tapestry*. She was more complimentary to Franklin than Eleanor. She described him in the earlier time as "handsome and gay." But Eleanor, she wrote, was "far from being a beautiful woman" and had a high-pitched voice which in excitement screamed into "shrill arpeggios."

There was, she said, "a persistent rumor" that their marriage was threatened by his affection for another woman. She wrote: "Mrs. Roosevelt was supposed to have called her husband and the enamored woman to a conference, at which she offered to give her husband a divorce if the woman wished to marry him. A Catholic, the woman could not marry a divorced man. When she expressed these sentiments, Mrs. Roosevelt issued an ultimatum that they must stop seeing each other—to which they promptly acquiesced."[30]

Only Lucy's Catholicism seems to identify her in this story. Some other historians have dismissed the whole matter out of hand. As family historian, James Roosevelt wrote that "the Washington gossip mill being as maliciously active then as it is now, there was the usual amount of talk, seeking to cast the handsome Assistant Secretary in the role of 'ladies' man,' particularly when he was a summer bachelor for the period when Mother would take 'the chicks' to Hyde Park or Campobello." He concluded flatly, "I think the record of their long and successful marital partnership is the best and most dignified answer to such rumors."[31]

As objective historian, Frank Freidel, in his detailed volumes about these Roosevelt years, gave the story only a footnote. "There were rumors," he said, "apparently emanating from a prominent society figure who had the sharpest tongue in Washington that FDR during this period was enamored of another woman, who, being a Catholic, would not marry him even if he got a divorce. In view of the consistently endearing fashion in which he always wrote Eleanor, and the lighthearted way in which she has described how he dazzled the 'lovely ladies' during the campaign of 1920, these rumors seem preposterous. They reflect more on the teller than FDR."[32] Freidel, whose book remains the best biography of Roosevelt, was clearly more concerned with his public career than his private life and social relationships.

Others were not quite so sure. Arthur Schlesinger, Jr., who did much research for his series of books on *The Age of Roosevelt* summed up his views in *The Ladies Home Journal* of November 1966. He wrote that he had "thought a long time about Franklin Roosevelt and Lucy Mercer." He had "talked to people who knew them both." The story had been overblown, he thought. But he added:

"There can be little question, I believe, that in the summer of 1917 Franklin Roosevelt was emotionally involved with Lucy Mercer. By that time he had been married a dozen years. His wife, as we all know, was the most admirable woman of her time. But she was not in 1917 the poised and lovely lady that we remember from the United Nations after the Second World War. She was still gawky and insecure, tied down by five children and harassed by a dominating and possessive mother-in-law. She was, in addition, a woman sternly devoted to plain living, invincibly 'sensible' in her taste and dress, oblivious—and to some like her brilliant cousin Alice Longworth, it seemed humorlessly, even self-righteously so—to the gaieties of existence. Her husband loved her. But he liked the pleasantness of life a good deal more than she did; and, in the summer of 1917, burdened with the responsibility of mobilizing the American Navy for war, he must have felt more acutely than ever the need for moments of surcease and relaxation."

Lucy, Schlesinger went on, was "from all accounts, a girl of enchanting charm—as tall as Eleanor Roosevelt—graceful and lively; she was also a girl from patrician background having to earn her own way in life, and this must have enlisted sympathy. No doubt Franklin began to show a delight in Lucy; no doubt this worried Eleanor, as it would any wife."[33]

Lucy might be, as she sometimes does seem in the determined reticence with which her story has been surrounded, a lost lady in history if it were not for the forthright testimony of her Henderson cousins, the late Miss Mary Henderson and Mrs. Lyman Cotten of Chapel Hill, North Carolina.[34] They regarded the long attachment of Franklin and Lucy as "a beautiful story."

"She and Franklin," Elizabeth Cotten wrote simply, "were very much in love with each other."

Mrs. Cotten added: "I know that a marriage would have taken place but as Lucy said to us, 'Eleanor was not willing to step aside.' I am also sure that she thought that the religious opinions of the two could have been arranged. Nothing is easier in the Roman Catholic Church than annulment, especially among those occupying high places. At least I was given to understand this.

There was never anything secret or clandestine about their love for each other as far as Mrs. Roosevelt was concerned. They were frank and honorable. I think we both know that it was real love for each other and that it lasted through the years."[35]

It does seem "preposterous" that such a long affection should have been so long hidden. In the Wilson years both were shining marks for any who wished to bear tales. Men and women, too, looked at Lucy with admiration and delight both when she was a girl and in her later days. Freidel wrote an almost lyrical passage about the tall Roosevelt in the First World War days. He quoted Walter Camp about his physical perfection. Government girls, the historian said, "used to watch with admiration as he strode past on his way to work." He reprinted a description from the *New York Tribune* at the time:[36] "His face is long, firmly shaped and set with marks of confidence. There are faint wrinkles on a high, straight forehead. Intensely blue eyes rest in light shadow. A firm, thin mouth breaks quickly to laugh, openly and freely. His voice is pitched well, goes forward without tripping. He doesn't disdain shedding his coat on a hot afternoon; shows an active quality in the way he jumps from his chair to reach the cigarettes in his coat. He is a young man, a young man with energy and definite ideas."

The gossips did not quite pass him by. But neither he nor Lucy gave them any materials. They moved in a company which did not quarrel in public. There was no dirty linen in their story for anybody to wash. Still there were those who noticed and knew. There were others who shared the motto Alice Longworth displayed later: "If you can't say something good about someone, sit right here by me."[37] That does Mrs. Longworth injustice. But she is a woman who declines to be awed by reticences. Also she is a woman who will never forget that another Roosevelt matched her father in fame. Possibly she was one of those who talked earlier, possibly not. But on September 8, 1966, when there was renewed talk about FDR and Lucy, she inscribed a copy of her book *Crowded Hours* for a dinner guest: ". . . after an evening of revelry from the fifth cousin-once-removed of the impeccably virtuous friend of Lucy Mercer. HA!"[38]

Not long afterward she was less cryptic and less facetious. She recalled: "Lucy Mercer was very attractive, very charming, very well-bred. She and Franklin became devoted to each other.

"I remember one day I was having fun with Auntie Corinne [Mrs. Douglas Robinson, TR's youngest sister] . . . I was doing imitations of Eleanor, and Auntie Corinne looked at me and said, 'Never forget, Alice, Eleanor offered Franklin his freedom.' And I said, 'But, darling, that's what I've wanted to know about all these years. Tell.' And so she said, 'Yes, there was a family conclave and they talked it over and finally they decided it affected the children and there was Lucy Mercer, a Catholic, and so it was called off.' "[39]

This was not the story as Lucy's friends and family remembered it. Even Eleanor's Aunt Corinne in this statement indicated that the plans for separation and divorce had advanced so far that they had to be "called off." Mrs. Cotten quoted Lucy as saying definitely that "Eleanor was not willing to step aside." Lucy and Franklin and those who sympathized with them must have held a "conclave" too. Lucy by all reports was no mere placid figure in this situation. She was not given like Eleanor to Griselda moods. Decorous as she always appeared she was the child of Minnie and Carroll who, not counting future costs, took headlong the life they enjoyed even though briefly. Her beauty was not merely pictorial; the warmth in her eyes indicated fire in her spirit. The grace with which she stood aside does not prove relinquishment without resentment. Certainly the manner in which Eleanor dismissed her as nameless in her name-crowded memoirs suggested a triumph over one whose name she could not even bear to confront. Clearly Lucy Mercer was not one to be serenely set aside by a conclave of Roosevelts. Such a conclave could make a barrier of children and Catholicism. It could not dismiss a lasting devotion.

The chief known fact is that when the conclave was most concerned and the gossip might have grown, or greater basis given to it, Roosevelt sailed to Europe. Held out of uniform, though in an essential position, he had long wanted to go to the war zone to inspect the naval operations he was helping to direct from Washington. "By the spring of 1918," Elliott Roosevelt wrote, "the strain on the Navy Department had eased sufficiently to enable J.D. or himself to leave Washington long enough to make a thorough inspection of the U.S. naval forces in European waters. Wilson preferred to have Daniels remain in the capital, thus F.D.R. was designated for the trip. . . ."[40]

There is nothing to suggest that Daniels, who was always concerned about the moral welfare of the young men under him in service, had any such ideas in mind about FDR when he sent him abroad. He was a man who never let it be known that he knew what he did not want to know. Certainly he did not indicate in his diary or by word of mouth that he had heard of Lucy Mercer. In his diary there were passages indicating that he knew well of Franklin's lapses in loyalty to him and of his communications with the enemies of the administration he served. But he loved Roosevelt to the end of his days. He held Eleanor in high respect and deep affection. He would have regarded a divorce by Franklin as a political suicide and a personal tragedy. Impatient as he sometimes was with Franklin's impetuosity, he would have taken almost any step to save him from what in terms of his " 'old fashioned' theories" would have been unpardonable folly.

Certainly Franklin's assignment to go abroad was reported with enthusiasm by Livy Davis. In his diary on Saturday July 1, 1918, the gay aide to the Assistant Secretary wrote: "About 4:30 was changing combination of safe when FD came in and told me to pack up my old kit bag. Hand slipped and drove screw driver into index finger of left hand. Too excited to get combine straight and after much fussing abandoned all attempts."[41]

Franklin preferred to go abroad not on one of the convoyed ships but on a destroyer in the group guarding them, the U.S.S. *Dyer* which had just been commissioned after swift construction. He designed himself a destroyer uniform—"my own invention— khaki riding trousers, golf stockings, flannel shirt and leather coat."[42] The destroyer had had no shake-down cruise. Stormy weather smashed its crockery. An engine broke down. There was a false U-boat alarm and a very real danger of a collision with another convoy. Under an Assistant Secretary of the Navy's flag which he had designed, he shared sea dangers. It was a rough voyage to a useful, exciting and convivial tour.

Livy Davis, coming over on a transport, met him in Paris. Roosevelt was irritated by the efforts of a naval officer assigned to him to keep him safely behind the fighting lines. He moved about the front while touched with fever. He saw the great naval guns mounted on flatcars on which he hoped soon to serve in uniform as a lieutenant commander. He made a splendid impression on British, French, and Italian authorities, though in Italy he got a little tangled in some problems of inter-Allied jealousies. He talked with admirals and the Astors at Cliveden. He was given a long private audience with the King of England. David Lloyd George gave a luncheon for him. At a dinner at Gray's Inn in honor of the War Ministers, he met Winston Churchill, though neither he nor Churchill apparently made much impression on each other then.[43]

It was a very serious trip but one which also emphasized the proximity of war work and war fun even in the war zone, about which Alice wrote in Washington. Possibly that was overemphasized by Livy Davis who turned out to be a sort of historian of the journey. Under the pressure of events Franklin's own diary of the trip broke off on Friday, August 16. Livy's diary became more and more enlivened as the inspection tour drew toward its end.

Nobody ever enjoyed a war more than Livy. Eleanor Roosevelt never quite trusted him. Toward the conclusion of his war service she wrote Sara that he was "lazy, selfish, and self-seeking to an extraordinary degree with the outward appearance of being quite different."[44] Only much later did she write that he was an "excellent executive and I am told that he proved an extremely efficient administrator."[45] Freidel, in his biography, concluded that though Davis provided Roosevelt with delightful companionship and was well liked by the officers, he "did little to lighten the Assistant Secretary's load."[46]

Of the companionship there can be no doubt. In Washington Livy's frank and staccato diary recorded that he lunched or dined or had cocktails with Franklin almost every day. He began his journal early in the grim winter of 1918 and filled it with the details of a Washington at war which was having a wonderful time. His was certainly no Billy Sunday recital. He and his friend and boss saw a variety of lively and interesting people. In many ways the mobilization on the Potomac shore seemed a sort of re-union of old friends. Their Harvard classmate Dick Crane had a house on 21st Street big enough for a dinner dance for eighty people. At it Livy danced until 2:30 and then took home the band.

At one of a variety of other dinners he recorded that he "sat between Princess Ihika, a Britisher who married a Roumanian, and Countess Polignac who was Mrs. Jimmy Eustis—a screamer." Mrs. Barnett, the wife of the Commandant of the Marines, he noted, "appeared bewitching in her daughter's bathing suit." It was a bewitching time for the thirty-four-year-old Bostonian: ". . . dined at Montgomery's . . . Bully time. Danced till 3 o'clock. Champagne flowing like water." Occasionally after such a night he made the entry, "Broke out feeling like wrath." There were daytime parties, too: "All motored out to the Canal and had fine swim. After which we picnicked on huge rock where I got the sillies and had a huge time." But there were not a few nights when he reported that he and Franklin "worked until 1:30 A.M."[47]

It was on the European inspection trip, however, that Davis really made his playboy footnotes on the solemn record of history. His record mounted in gaiety as the trip moved toward its end in Scotland with an inspection of the work on the mine barrage against the submarines about which Franklin had an almost pos-sessive feeling.

Roosevelt had had a fever a week before as they drove about the front in France. Health certainly was not guarded by the pace the party set in Scotland where Admiral Joseph Strauss was supervising the laying of the net of mines to catch the submarines. They got little sleep. They were drenched by rain. And they plentifully fortified themselves with the liquor of the land. The Davis diary entry for August 31, 1918, is cryptic, abbreviated, and as to some names obscure. It is illuminating as to austerity in wartime:

> *August 31*–Up at 5:30. Breakfast at 6:00 consisted of oatmeal, cream, sugar, butter, fish, eggs, ham, marmalade and mushrooms. Brann, FD, Jack and I with Wallace drove out to Black Water in a dos-a-dos. Gillis late in coming so all had some Scotch and a fine sing-song. All in regular clothes, low shoes. I in my new brown suit for first time. Lovely stream, falls, pools, etc, but no one got a strike. Weather was so dour all had to keep it out with copious draughts of sublime Scotch, so all sang all the way home. While clothes were drying Wallace concocted a brew of hot Scotch, honey and oatmeal served in beakers. All had at least two, and on descending found all guests and servants assembled so all hands to parlor, formed circle and sang Auld Lang Syne. Left Shatteffeffer at 12. FD, McC. took long way round and got a puncture. Rest arrived at Inverness with glorious buns at 1:10 to find Admiral Strauss spitting mad as he had knocked his men off work at 10 AM and had had many false alarms of our arrival getting them out in pouring rain. FD and McC. finally arrived at 1:45 just time to beat it to Admiral's house for luncheon and beat it to train at 3:15. Brann buying some tweeds on way. Found our car again. Route very picturesque. More Scotch and all got out at Perth for delicious and extremely jolly dinner. Had sing-song in train till bed time at 10:30. One of jolliest days of my life![48]

But the jollity was not over. Livy made an entry in London:

> *Sept.* 6–All lunched upstairs. Worked at hotel then went to Coliseum to see Russian dancers in "The Good Humored Ladies." Thence to H-2. At 6 FD, Lt. Hayden and I went to American Officers Club in Lord Beaconfield's house on Curzon Street. Several rounds of delicious c.ts, and saw many friends. Returned to hotel where had very rough dinner with a man named Thomas

as guest . . . Lt. Com. Jack Garde, and John Roys brought in Prince Axel of Denmark and his staff consisting of Thicle, Korwin and Laube. . . . Everybody very drunk. All finally faded away except FD, Brann, Jackson and I. Stayed up until 4:30 pitching coins, playing golf, etc.[49]

Three days later he noted: "Franklin in bed with floo."[50] They sailed from Brest on the *Leviathan* on September 12. Apparently Livy was laid up too as he noted at the landing in New York: "Saw FD for first time. Looked rotten. Eleanor had not received wire so Brann telephoned her. He landed via ambulance."[51] Eleanor's version of Franklin's return differed from Livy's. She had, she wrote, received word from the Navy Department a day or two before the ship was due that Franklin was ill with pneumonia. She and her mother-in-law got a doctor to meet them at the dock with an ambulance.

"The flu had been raging in Brest and Franklin and his party had attended a funeral before leaving in the rain. . . . My husband did not seem so ill as the doctors implied."[52]

From a funeral or a frolic he was safely home. Eleanor and Sara hovered over him in the month before he could go back to Washington still looking to Livy only "fairly well." Family ties were strengthened. While he was still ill a letter came to him from Sagamore Hill:

Dear Franklin:
    We are deeply concerned about your sickness, and trust you will soon be well. We are *very* proud of you.

                                    With love,
                                    Aff. yours
                                    THEODORE ROOSEVELT.

Later, Eleanor will tell you of our talk about your plans.[53]

Three weeks after he got back to Washington the war was over and with it his own plans to get into uniform. As a sailor he was home from the perils of the sea and apparently other things as well. On December 23, Daniels made a cryptic entry in his diary. It was simply, "Mrs. James R———."[54] She evidently had called at his office. Unlike the voyage in the Caribbean she had planned in 1904 in the hope of cooling Franklin's ardor, this one had brought him home and perhaps back to his sense of the value of "'old fashioned' theories" which Sara and Josephus both upheld.

SEVEN

Lady in Waiting

(1)

Lucy faced her twenty-eighth birthday in April 1919 as young working woman in a city where, even after the Armistice, more and more young women every day poured in and out of the departments. She was able, as her mother recorded,[1] to pay the $35-a-month rent on the apartment which they shared in the Toronto. Also, her earnings went to their living expenses. Minnie, now fifty-six, described herself in terms of shabby genteel domesticity. She wrote that she "helped with the housework, kept the house, did the mending and did the things that mothers do." There was no requirement that she like such an existence in which only her cigarette smoking marked her as different from other aging home-bodies at the time. Perhaps one other thing did: Lucy saw her mother, who had let fortune run through her fingers, become as she grew older more than ordinarily eager for small sums.[2]

Carroll when he died in September 1917, as Minnie produced sworn testimony to prove later, left practically nothing.[3] However, as one who once could give his occupation simply as "gentleman," he left two wills. In connection with both he turned naturally to the American Security and Trust Company, one of whose directors was William Corcoran Eustis of the old Carroll-Corcoran ties. In one, dated June 6, 1893, he left everything to Minnie, the girls to take only if she predeceased him. In another dated June 20, 1906, drafted by the law firm of Wayne MacVeagh and Frederick D. McKenney, which handled the Washington affairs of the Pennsylvania Railroad, he gave all "to my children Violetta C. and Lucy P. Mercer. . . ."[4]

The change, while evidently emotional, was only an academic matter. All that he had at the last was the hope of getting, after the death of his aunt, the Countess Esterhazy, "a legacy in remainder bequeathed to me by my lamented grandmother Mrs. Sallie S. Carroll."[5] Mention of that "lamented grandmother" evoked nostalgic memories of social affluence in the Carroll house at 18th and F Streets. There long before, wrote a Washington witness, Marian Gouverneur, sister of Mrs. Eames, was "a continuous scene of hospitality." Old Mrs. Carroll, she said, "retained two sets of servants, one for the day time and the other for the night." To an advanced age she always remained standing while receiving her guests with her four beautiful daughters, Carrie, Alida, Carroll's mother Violetta, and Sallie the Countess.[6] Now the lights had gone out in the mansion. Carroll's hope that he would receive even a residue of its wealth seemed a remote one. The Countess Esterhazy was as durable as she was beautiful. Five years before Carroll died *Town Topics* had impertinently reported that in all probability he would "inherit something from his Aunt Sallie, the Countess Esterhazy, provided she does not lavish everything on her young admirers."[7]

Since the Countess was then seventy-two, such loss to young admirers did not seem likely. That lady, however, did survive her nephew Carroll. She died just a month after he did while she was situated in London at Belgrave Mansions, Grosvenor Gardens, S.W. A Requiem Mass was said for her at Westminster Cathedral. Also, probably there was a general thanksgiving in the Mercer apartment in Washington. Henry E. Davis, a lawyer member of the capital cave-dweller company and a long-time friend of both Minnie and Carroll, helped her get a thousand pounds from the estate of the Countess. Minnie needed and wanted more. She cabled her London lawyers, Soames, Edwards & Jones, Lennox

House, Norfolk Street, Strand W.C. 2. They wrote her rather sternly that there was "no possibility of you succeeding in an appeal against the decision with regard to your interest in the residue." What she got, Davis said, went quickly to meet old debts. She kept the house and did the mending. And on February 14, 1919, she filed a claim for a pension as Carroll's widow on the grounds of her need and the allegation that his death resulted from illness connected with service twenty years before.[8]

The date of her claim pointed great differences in fortune. Now Minnie, born rich, claimed destitution. The city and the world were, of course, and in terms of both popular acclaim and some social acidity, vastly more interested in her contemporary, Edith Wilson, born poor, who this same month seemed the dazzling first lady of the planet. With her husband bringing home his Covenant of the League of Nations, she had just returned from Europe on the *George Washington* on which Franklin and Eleanor had been fellow passengers. Boston had roared the Wilsons welcome. But in the high levels of society in Washington, in which Alice Longworth moved or strode, bitterness was feline. In the month before on January 6, while the Wilsons, attended by servants in royal scarlet, were rolling across Europe in a king's train, Theodore Roosevelt, who had been expected to put this pretentious professor in his place, had died in his sleep at Oyster Bay. Republican Senators who had been planning to put TR back in the White House "by acclamation"[9] the following year, now grimly awaited Wilson. But sharp tongues turned on Edith Wilson who had so recently been only a lady "in trade."

Reflecting such bitterness, on the day before Minnie filed her pension claim, *Town Topics* wondered how Mrs. Wilson could possibly settle down to her former life in Washington "after her extraordinary experiences in Europe—surely the most wonderful that have ever fallen to the lot of a daughter of Uncle Sam. . . . Everywhere she has been received as the consort of a reigning sovereign and been welcomed by queens on a footing of equality. In London her secretary, Miss Benham, has been officially described as her 'lady in waiting'."[10]

Edith Benham's reported role was far above any Lucy ever attained as social secretary. In a much more real sense, however, she was a lady in waiting at this time. Certainly she left Mrs. Roosevelt's employment when she enrolled as a Yeoman F on June 28, 1917. She was, however, available to "entirely disconnect" Eleanor from Navy League affairs on September 9, four days before her father's death. She was discharged from the Navy less than a month later but, according to her mother's pension file, she was apparently living at the Toronto throughout 1919. Violetta, Minnie said, was in this period "in France, being an Army nurse."[11] Lucy's employment was not listed after her name in Washington directories.

During this time Lucy and her mother saw much of her cousins, the Hendersons. Elizabeth Henderson Cotten had come to Washington to live when her husband, Captain Lyman A. Cotten had become a member of the General Board of the Navy in March 1919. They lived during the next two years in Sunderland Place, a block from Dupont Circle. The Mercers were often in their house. Young Lyman Cotten, Jr., then ten years old, later remembered not only the loveliness of Lucy but that his "Cousin Minnie" used to take him and his brother to the movies and afterward to tea at her apartment. The boys thought her cigarette smoking very daring.

"In the *Victor Book of the Opera* [dated 1912]," he wrote, "there is a full page picture of Emma Calvé as Carmen, smoking a cigarette; ever since I saw it as a child it has reminded me of Cousin Minnie. . . . Lucy was very different from her mother. She was tall and stately and quiet in manner. Her features were regular, her skin exquisitely fine, and her smile was the most beautiful and winning that I have ever seen."[12]

His mother added: "Don't get the idea that there was anything of the shrinking violet about Lucy. She had a vibrant personality, great strength of character. . . . She was with me in Salisbury when the affair was at its height, but they realized it was hopeless."[13]

Possibly that little North Carolina town provided sanctuary for

Lucy when her love was "hopeless" as it had for her mother following her divorce long before. She could not afford to languish,
however. The $35 for the rent of the Toronto apartment had to
come from somewhere. Bertie Hamlin had recollections about Lucy's work.

"Did not Miss M," she wrote, "go for a time to 'Tranquility' to
try to smooth out the household and affairs of Alice Morton
Rutherfurd? She had one girl and four boys all in a heap—one
boy died later at Edith Eustis's house of pneumonia."[14]

(2)

Certainly there was a lapse, if not a break, in the story of Lucy
and FDR during the war and immediately afterward, though possibly not so long or so continuous a one as it has been made to
seem. Franklin, along with his abbreviated Boswell, Livy Davis,
had sailed for France on July 9 in the last summer of the war.
This was the trip from which he returned so ill that he had to be
taken off the *Leviathan* on a stretcher on September 19. Only on
October 18 was he able to go back to Washington. Then, according to Eleanor, he was stricken again. Franklin, the five children,
and three servants, she wrote,[15] went down with the influenza
which to another Washington witness seemed like a repetition "of
the plague in the Middle Ages."[16]

With the help of one trained nurse she got from New York,
Eleanor wrote, she nursed and cooked for all and tended to her
Red Cross duties as well. These included providing food and cheer
to "poor girls lying in the long rows of beds" in improvised hospitals. This period of stress, she wrote, was "extremely good
training."[17] The period did not seem quite so austere to Davis.
According to his records, Franklin was certainly not much confined. Roosevelt beat Davis at nine holes of golf on October 20.

Livy lunched with the Roosevelts on October 24 and again on October 31. That same day Roosevelt saw President Wilson and learned that it was too late for him to get into uniform. The Assistant Secretary was on the golf course again on November 9. He was certainly at the Navy Department on November 14 and two days later he made a speech for the United War Work drive. On November 18 the Roosevelts had a large farewell luncheon for their friends, the French naval attaché and Madame de Blanpré. He was golfing again on November 30, December 3, December 8, December 14, December 15. During the time Davis recalled gay parties including among others Nigel Law. Despite Mrs. Roosevelt's grim remembrance, the two months from October 19 to Christmas when they set off for New York for a fleet review prior to their sailing to Europe together on January 1, could hardly have contained a week when FDR was seriously ill. He was up and striding.[18]

Franklin's job on this second trip to Europe, then celebrating a sort of springtime of peace, was the sale of Navy surpluses and the settlements of Navy obligations in its vast commitments overseas. It brought him and Eleanor to Paris when all the world seemed gathered there for the ceremonies of triumph and the shaping of the peace. It was a sort of mecca for those expecting the millennium and those only grasping for the pieces of a shattered world. It was an unprecedented world social center, too. Writing faithfully home to Sara, Eleanor described the beautiful city as "full beyond belief and one sees many celebrities and all one's friends!"[19] There were Delanos there, of course. There was almost a complete Roosevelt family reunion when the FDRs dined with Kermit Roosevelt who had first joined the British Army in order to get early into the war. His wife and her sister were there. So was Theodore Roosevelt, Jr., who had been wounded and much decorated. Archie Roosevelt was also in France then as captain in the 20th Infantry. All of this generation seemed present except Alice Longworth who, with saturnine eyes from Washington, was already watching the peace conference and the glorified Wilsons. This family gathering, Eleanor wrote, was a "delight" though it was, of course, saddened by the recent death of the great TR and the loss of young Quentin as an aviator in the summer before.

"All one's friends" included enough members of the Harvard Fly Club to hold a reunion dinner. This apparently was the only occasion on which any tension between Franklin and Eleanor was recorded. Livy wrote in his diary on February 9: "Found FD and E very cool as he had been to Fly Club dinner night before."[20] Eleanor's coolness could be chilling. Later she herself described her "Griselda moods," after the legendary medieval woman of intolerable meekness and patience. It constituted her habit, as she admitted, "when my feelings are hurt or when I am annoyed, of simply shutting up like a clam, not telling anyone what is the matter and being much too obviously humble and meek, feeling like a martyr and acting like one."[21]

Livy, who often seemed more an aid in gay companionship than in administration to Franklin, was evidently a target of the Griselda mood. Eleanor, suffering from pleurisy, was insistently brave on much of the trip when they went to the front, sightseeing and collecting souvenirs. She was definitely irritated with Livy when they returned to Paris.

"On arrival here," she wrote Sara from the Ritz, "he found that for 12 hrs. he must occupy a room without a bath and I thought the poor manager's head would be blown off! I have decided that trips of this kind either make very firm friendships or mar them. . . . Franklin is too loyal ever to change in his feelings but I am deciding more firmly every day that the estimate I've been making of him [Livy] for over a year is not far from right."[22]

Perhaps it was well that Livy did not come home with them. He did not, however, seem to be insisting on personal comfort when he joined the American Relief organization under Herbert Hoover and worked in the torn new republic of Czechoslovakia. Franklin's European job had been, as Eleanor reported to Sara, accomplished in triumph. On the same day she wrote about the Roosevelt reunion, she described a deal Franklin made with André Tardieu, who had been French High Commissioner to the United States: "F. saw Tardieu at 6 and his biggest deal is done, the Fr.

Gov. will take the big radio station and pay 22,000,000 frcs. This is a big success but don't mention it!"[23]

After his return with President and Mrs. Wilson on the *George Washington,* Franklin himself mentioned it with much pride. One to whom he described the negotiation was his young British friend Law. Law remembered: "He was having an argument with the French over the price at which he would sell them a radio aerial which the U. S. Navy had set up in France. The French were obstinate and offered a ridiculous sum counting on the fact that the cost of dismantling and removing it would be prohibitive. But just when a deadlock had been reached at the conference a messenger handed a telegram to FDR which read, 'Dismantle and ship aerial to America.' The French opposition at once collapsed and they agreed to buy it at the offered price. FDR had of course arranged for the telegram before he went to the meeting. He told me this story with much gusto."[24]

He came back to America full of gusto. A fortnight later the departure for France of Secretary Daniels left him Acting Secretary, a status in which he delighted. Eleanor, in a period of adjustment involving among other things the "servant problem," was, as she evidently felt, embarking upon the adventurous experiment of trying Negro servants emboldened by the stories of her Southern Grandmother Bulloch's family about "the old and much-loved colored people on the plantation."[25] She was still non-committal on the woman suffrage problem. As soon as school was out she took the children to Hyde Park, and then, instead of going to Campobello, she deposited them at the old Delano place at Fairhaven, Massachusetts, near which her friend Bertie Hamlin had a fine beach at Mattapoisett. She came back to Washington on July 28. She was there until mid-August when her Grandmother Hall, whose love of her children clouded her judgment about them and who had no life of her own, died at her home in Tivoli.[26] Eleanor was in and out of Washington and in her absences Franklin wrote her affectionate letters.

Washington was already torn with the fight in the Senate over Wilson's League. Cousin Alice Longworth, taking a fiercely feminine part in the fight, prided herself at being called the colonel of the Battalion of Death. Less vigorously than later Franklin spoke up for the League. Wilson had already been stricken on his Western tour in support of the League when Franklin went off to New Brunswick. Across Pennsylvania Avenue the White House gates were locked before the stricken Wilson. The great mansion, an observant journalist wrote, "seemed to the sensitive local intelligence to exhale a chill and icy disdain. . . . It all made for bleakness and bitterness and a general sense of frustration and unhappiness."[27]

There were other irritations around the old square. In July 1919, tattling *Town Topics* reported, ". . . a big difference has arisen between the dwellers in the mansions about old St. John's in H Street, over the action of William Corcoran Eustis in selling his historic dwelling known as Corcoran House. This splendid old mansion, built in the earliest days of the City of Washington's history for Governor Swann, of Maryland, and purchased from him by the admirers of Daniel Webster is to be demolished and a big apartment house is to be erected on the site."[28]

Town Topics was correct in its statement that the old house had been built by Carroll Mercer's ancestor Thomas Swann but, as was often the case, was wrong about the purchaser. Not an apartment house but the monumental headquarters of the U. S. Chamber of Commerce was to be built on the site. The gossip journal was probably correct about the irritation of John Hay's daughter, Alice, wife of Senator James Wadsworth of New York, at the "advance of trade" on ancient, gracious Lafayette Square. Alice Hay Wadsworth, then occupying the Hay portion of the joint houses her father had built with Henry Adams, was a woman of strong opinions as President of the National Association Opposed to Woman Suffrage. She had tried to impose her views on reticent and politically timid Eleanor Roosevelt. But landmarks as well as genteel traditions were shaken. Her neighbor Edith Eustis, who had often run into the joint Hay-Adams house to talk to the old historian, had ideas, too. Correctly or incorrectly, the New York gossip journal reported that she had never appreciated the house "and disliked the fact that former residents, especially Daniel Webster, overshadowed all successors." Edith's husband, William Corcoran Eustis, it added, preferred his Leesburg country place and "for the past five years Corcoran House has been closed ten months of each year."

"Its demolition will undoubtedly spell the end of the fine old Slidell Mansion adjoining and eventually of the Henry Adams House and John Hay's comfortable brick house at the corner of H and Sixteenth Streets."[29]

More than the Wadsworths were sad about the change. Cave dwellers were shaken. Some others were regretful. One undoubtedly was Franklin Roosevelt. The old house had been directly on the way he often walked to the Navy Department from his residences on N and R Streets. His associations with it were more intimate than that. It was of the old house doomed to demolition that Elliott Roosevelt noted in his collection of his father's personal letters that "during the war years F.D.R. frequently spent evenings with the Eustis family."[30]

(3)

The Corcoran House was a natural place for Franklin to visit, stretch out his long legs, and relax his spirit. Its mistress, Edith Morton Eustis, was one of his oldest friends. He was only four years old when her father, Levi P. Morton, whom Henry Adams called "a money bag,"[31] built with the aid of the fashionable architect, Richard Morris Hunt, his great country house on his Hudson River estate, Ellerslie, near the James Roosevelt place in Hyde Park. Young Franklin had gone with his parents on a winter sports trip to the Adirondacks with the Mortons. The Roosevelt and Morton families had made Atlantic crossings together. Edith, one of five handsome sisters, was older than Franklin and was a glamorous figure to him as a schoolboy. She was an admirer of the young Assistant Secretary of the Navy and a sympathetic, sensitive woman.

Her father, though Clover Adams had called him a snob, had risen to munificence from birth in his preacher father's parsonage in little Shoreham, Vermont. He began his career as a small merchant in Hanover, New Hampshire, but never entered Dartmouth College there. Before he was thirty, however, he was associated with Junius Spencer Morgan (founder of the great banking house) in a mercantile firm. He moved to New York where, in 1861, because of the then worthless Southern debts, his firm failed. This was a brief setback. He paid off his creditors, launched a banking business in Wall Street in 1863, and with the Morgans and the Drexels rose to a dominant position in post-Civil War American finance. His Morton Trust Company, set up when he was seventy-five, increased in wealth and prestige and was merged in munificence with the Guaranty Trust Company.

The Morton magnificence in politics and society began only after he married his second wife, Anna Livingston Read Street of Poughkeepsie, a match which some said was arranged by Mrs. August Belmont. He was elected to Congress, was appointed Minister to France, became Vice-President in 1889, and Governor of New York in 1895. There was some support for his nomination as Republican candidate for President in 1896, but Mark Hanna had that situation well in hand for McKinley. In addition to his great estate in Dutchess County, he also acquired an impressive residence near Scott Circle in Washington. His New York house provided the background for the entrance into society of Edith Newbold Jones who, as the novelist Edith Wharton, became its historian. This entrance emphasized the position of both Edith Wharton and the Mortons. Mrs. Wharton's mother had been Lucretia Stevens Rhinelander and her ancestors included such ancient and elegant folk as the Schermerhorns, Pendletons, Gallatins, and Ledyards. None, of course, supposed then that this Edith would write in irony of the society of such folk which Leon Edel described as a "tight little world, with its splendid decencies, its stratified codes, its tradition of elegance, and its brownstone mansions, soon to be fenced in by skyscrapers."[32]

The important thing was that the Mortons had a ballroom. Mrs. Wharton wrote, "Houses with ball-rooms were still few in New York: almost the only ones were those of the Astors, the Mortons, the Belmonts and my cousins the Schermerhorns." She recalled: "The New York mothers of that day usually gave a series of 'coming-out' entertainments for debutante daughters, leading off with a huge tea and an expensive ball." Her Rhinelander mother thought this was absurd: "I was therefore put into a low-necked bodice of pale green brocade, above a white muslin skirt ruffled with rows and rows of Valenciennes, my hair was piled up on top of my head, some friend of the family sent me a large bouquet of lilies-of-the-valley, and thus adorned I was taken by my parents to a ball at Mrs. Morton's, in Fifth Avenue."[33]

The several Morton daughters were more elaborately presented. The debutante position of Edith was demonstrated by her role as one of the bridesmaids in the nuptial extravaganza in St. Thomas' Church on Fifth Avenue when unwilling Consuelo Vanderbilt was pushed along with a marriage settlement of $2,500,000 into the arms of the diminutive Duke of Marlborough. The *New York Times* gave this wedding precedence over all other news. Some of the lady guests made it almost a mob scene in contention for places in the pews.

At least one other of the bridesmaids got a duke, too. So did Edith's sister Helen who, like Consuelo, did not keep her titled spouse. The Duc de Valençan to whom she went with a $6,000,000 fortune insulted her immediately after the wedding. Then he deserted her. The marriage was annulled.[34] She spent her later life as simply Mrs. Helen Stuyvesant Morton and during her lifetime and by her will became a great contributor to Catholic charities. She founded and built a Carmelite Monastery in Brooklyn. She gave Ellerslie, where the Morton girls had played as children, to the Roman Catholic Archbishop of New York for the establishment of a Catholic military academy.[35]

Edith was content with a member of the American gentry, William Corcoran Eustis. Apparently their romance flowered in France where Edith's father served as U. S. Minister and afterward spent much time there. Eustis's father, George Eustis of a distinguished Louisiana family, as an un-Reconstructed Confederate had become a fixed expatriate in the France of Napoleon III. With his wife, daughter of the rich Washingtonian W. W. Corcoran, he was living at his villa in Cannes when his son William was born. William's uncle, James Biddle Eustis, was a successor of Morton as U. S. Minister in Paris. Willie Eustis and Edith Morton were married in 1901.

They were a couple who had all the world's gifts of wealth and position. Furthermore Edith, when she came to Washington as a bride, was praised for simpler virtues as well. A publication of the time, *The Washington Capital*, reported that she and her sisters were not only raised as reigning belles but "were taught to wait upon themselves and take care of their clothes. Whenever they came in from a walk or drive they put away their own gloves and wraps and hats, not in the ordinary careless way of children, but carefully. There were maids to assist in this as well as other duties, but the little girls were taught to wait on themselves. As there are few things that play so important a part in the happiness pertaining to the lives of individuals and families as the art of good living, well learned and well carried out, it may be safe to assume that the happiness of this couple is assured."[36]

Such sententious reporting did not portend a life of opulent domesticity only. Vice-President Morton, according to Henry Adams, was pulling strings to put Eustis into diplomacy.

"Willy Eustis will go to London in young Choate's place if he chooses," the gossip Adams wrote, "but old Morton thinks that Vignaud is dying or dead, and wants his son-in-law to run Paris."[37]

Henry Vignaud, a Louisiana expatriate like the elder Eustis, had in effect been running the U. S. Legation in Paris for a quarter of a century. He was seventy in 1901 when Morton figured he was dying or dead. As diplomat, scholar, and historian, he was to survive not only Morton but young Eustis. Young Joseph Hodges Choate, Jr., did give up his post as third secretary in London to come home this year to practice law in New York. Eustis evidently was not pushing as hard for such posts as his father-in-law was pulling strings for them. Instead he devoted his life to handling his inherited wealth in Washington and living the life of a sporting gentleman.

He and Edith spent much of their time on his estate, Oatlands, in the country of the horsey set near Leesburg, Virginia. As a welcome visitor, Roosevelt often joined the select company in the lovely old house, with its yellow walls, a high portico supported by white Corinthian columns, and a balustraded terrace with a dark green magnolia tree in the center.[38] He described the place as "the old President Monroe house."[39] Apparently he was mistaken about that. *Virginia—A Guide to the Old Dominion*, prepared later by his Works Progress Administration, said that the Monroe house was nearby Oak Hill,[40] designed by James Hoban, architect of the White House. Certainly, however, there could be no question about his statement that they "keep it up excellently."[41] Certainly also, by one of those multiple coincidences of relationship, the Eustis house was near the old Mercer house, built by Charles Fenton Mercer, early American soldier and Congressman. The Eustises also intermittently occupied an estate in Meath County, Ireland. In relation to his residence there he was described as "one of the best men after the Meath over the big banks and ditches of Ireland."[42] This evidently referred to his winning the Meath Hunt Cup three times. It was proudly displayed at Oatlands when Franklin was there along with trophies for his marksmanship with the rifle.

Even better known in the fashionable horse and dog world was William's sister Louise. As a frail young woman she had been taken to the balmy climate of Aiken, South Carolina, by her aunt, Miss Celestine Eustis, born in New Orleans, who had spent much of her life like the other members of her family as an expatriate in Paris. She was chiefly remembered as author of a creole cook book. Miss Celestine and Lulie in a real sense, however, were the creators of Aiken as a resort for mounted millionaires. Great houses rose with stables close at hand. Its society was more muscular than ostentatious. Bridle paths marked it more than ball-rooms. Playboys spent their energies on the polo fields. By control of land and a certain austerity in welcome the colony was kept exclusive. Its hotel, Willcox's, seemed less than luxurious to some. It was, as a historian of the resort wrote, "not a club, but its guests are select and at dinner in the big dining room are found, in full evening dress, many leaders of the social, political and business life of the world with their families."[43] Its first guest, arriving in January 1898, was Reverend William Stephen Rainsford, exuberant and evangelical rector of St. George's Church in New York of which J. P. Morgan was senior warden.[44] The next was "Rosey" Roosevelt, Franklin's half brother. Early on the list also were Edith Eustis's sister Alice and her husband, Mr. and Mrs. Winthrop Rutherfurd.[45]

The frail Lulie Eustis did not remain fragile long. In the little South Carolina town, she became one of the first American women in society to ride astride. She married Thomas Hitchcock, banker and sportsman, and with him helped create winning American polo teams. Hitchcock had his foxhounds; Lulie bred beagles at Aiken and in kennels at Broad Hollow, Long Island. Hitchcock himself was a noted polo player and their son, Tommy Hitchcock, himself became perhaps the leading polo player of the world in his time. Father and son went to war with the zest of sportsmen. In 1917 they became the youngest and the oldest aviators in the service of any country.

Edith Eustis's relationship to this world of fashionable sport was, of course, marked too by the marriage of her sister Alice to Winthrop Rutherfurd, the equestrian companion of Theodore and Elliott Roosevelt in 1886, gentleman farmer, and noted breeder of fox terriers. He himself, as Mrs. Burton Harrison wrote, was the product of perfect breeding. Scientists honored his father for work in astronomy. His mother, who had been Margaret Stuyvesant Chandler was, Mrs. Harrison said, "an uncommonly beautiful woman married to an uncommonly handsome and distinguished man."[46] Edith Wharton, who grew up as the friend and neighbor of the Rutherfurd children, made them, as she wrote, "the prototype of my first novels."[47] She recalled a conversation of an Englishman and an American strolling down Piccadilly together discussing the good looks of their respective compatriots. The Englishman was prepared to grant that many American women were prettier and more graceful.

"But your men—yes, of course, I've seen very good-looking American men; but nothing—if you'll excuse my saying so—to compare with our young Englishmen of the Public School and University type, our splendid young athletes: There like those two who are just coming toward us—"

Then it turned out that the two approaching young gentlemen were Winthrop and his brother visiting in England. He was handsome enough to win the love of Consuelo Vanderbilt but not able to win her hand in the face of her imperious mother's determination to marry her to a duke. He was evidently not soon reconciled. Not until seven years later when he was forty did he marry Alice Morton. Then society reporters described her as the tallest and fairest of the Morton girls. Evidently in a life of unostentatious country living, much of it spent at the ancient Rutherfurd seat Tranquility, near Allamuchy, New Jersey, they were happy.

Edith Eustis seemed less serene. She was never merely a woman of the world of sport. As a serious young matron she wrote an article, "Why Should Girls Have Nothing to Do?", a plea for self improvement and good works in a journal called *Charities*.[48] In a time when society was disturbed, in what Edith Wharton called its "blind dread of innovation," Edith Eustis and her neighbor Henry Adams shared amusement. She told him about her aging father who with others of his wealth and class regarded Theodore Roosevelt as a destructive radical. The only way to wake him from his lengthening dozes, she told Adams, was to say "Roosevelt!" to him. Whereupon he would arouse crying, "To think that a daughter of mine etc. etc."[49]

In the year after her marriage to Eustis, however, she dedicated "To My Father" her novel, *Marian Manning*, a story of politics, love and infidelity on the Washington scene. It is not so well remembered as *Democracy*, the somewhat similar novel about the interlocking of society and politics which Adams had published anonymously in 1880. Critics and gossips differed about the quality of Mrs. Eustis's book. *Town Topics*, with acerbity and inconsistency, wrote both that it "fell flatter than the scenery of southern New Jersey"[50] and that it was "widely praised" and showed "some indications of genius."[51] The novel, it also said eighteen years after its appearance, "caused a row and the details seem about to creep out."[52] It was, this definitely non-literary publication said, an "enigmatical novel." Finally it declared, dragging in an irrelevant story, that the book "created a sensation, although the plot was no more sensational than the marriage of her sister, now known as Mrs. Helen Morton, to the Duc de Valençan, and the subsequent divorce."[53] Such chitchat criticism was more snide than significant. Far more important, *The Bookman*, in the year of the novel's publication, displayed Edith's picture in an issue carrying an article on "Washington in Fiction."[54]

Edith's book did not bring her the acclaim her family's friend Edith Wharton received. In the society to which both belonged literary success, as Mrs. Wharton reported, "puzzled and embarrassed" old friends. Some, she said, regarded it as "a kind of family disgrace."[55] Edith Eustis's work only added a trifle to the literary tradition of Corcoran House where Daniel Webster and Chauncey Depew had entertained literary figures as well as statesmen.

Read long afterward, the book seems as quaintly romantic as its picture of the Washington of gaslit streets, cable cars and the horse-drawn herdics which preceded the advent of taxis. Still it was a story which seemed to set almost a stereotype for romance later. Marian Manning was the lovely and loving wife of an ambitious, handsome, striding young political figure, Congressman John Manning. Suddenly the happy and brilliant pattern of their life on Farragut Square, a block from Corcoran House, was shattered by Marian's discovery that her husband was in love with another woman. In such times no divorce ensued. The surface—and only the surface—of their relationship was maintained. Then suddenly in the midst of Manning's political ascent he was stricken with typhoid fever.

"Marian at first," Edith wrote, "was staggered by the news of the serious character of his illness, but she soon recovered herself, and with great calmness reordered her household and her own life. She sent to Baltimore for the most efficient nurses; she gave the patient into the care of the best doctors in the city, and she did all that human effort could do to effect his early recovery. At the same time she refused to accept assistance from any one, and bore the whole burden of responsibility upon her own shoulders."[56]

Also: "With his illness, Marian's feelings toward John underwent another change. Pity and sympathy for his weakness and suffering took the place of harsh resentment, and as the days went on she knew that something that had been hard within her was softening and melting. . . . John had wronged her grievously —in many ways he had shattered her life; but he was now at death's door, and it was her duty and her desire to tend and care for him. She grudged no moment of those long tedious days, although the world pitied her for them. But she was now absolute mistress, and while she avoided the thought of what might happen, was happy in the work forced upon her. . . . For it is difficult to feel anger or resentment against a child for the blow which it has struck us, and many older people are weak, yea, as children, and cannot always help the wrong they do. For each one has his own light to guide him, and some lights may be pure and very high and others low and colored. Marian, watching him, prayed silently: 'Let God judge us, not short sighted humanity.' "[57]

Almost too neatly for the purposes of her story Edith Eustis let John Manning die. Not all such gentlemen in similar Washington stories did. Certainly death came less neatly into Edith's own story when her sister, Alice, died in June 1917, leaving the handsome Winthrop Rutherfurd a widower of fifty-five with six small children, none of them out of their teens. No one could have been more concerned than Edith for the motherless flock. As the mother of five children, her own household was temporarily fatherless then. Though in his middle fifties, Willie Eustis had quickly entered his country's service in the war. Armed with his impeccable French, he had sailed in the same month Alice died as a captain and aide to General John J. Pershing. Franklin, who saw him a year later in Paris, reported him in "fine form and doing really useful work."[58] At home Edith was active in patriotic activities.

In a world in which all seemed caught in crisis, the motherless Rutherfurd family may have seemed a small matter. It could not have seemed so to the dead Alice's family. Her sister, Helen, built a Carmelite monastery in Brooklyn in her memory. Monuments did not meet the needs of the family Alice left behind. More was required than nurses, governesses in a household of lively children. A family concerned with the welfare of the Rutherfurd household may well have found aid, as Mrs. Hamlin thought, in such an able and charming young woman in old Corcoran-Carroll ties as Lucy Mercer.[59] She was available. She had the graces, the manners, the gentleness which more than ordinary disciplines or schooling the young Rutherfurds needed at this time. As employee or friend she came into their lives. Certainly, she was the one to whom, when grief struck Winthrop Rutherfurd again, he turned for the solace, the companionship and the affection which he and his children required. A gentleman beyond the age of romantic fervor, wealthy, close in relationship to the society in which Lucy had moved as a sort of Cinderella, Rutherfurd offered the refuge which Lucy required, too. She was not getting any younger in the apartment where Minnie counted the pennies of her pension.

EIGHT

Blindman's Buff

Franklin came home from the lively fifteenth anniversary reunion of his Harvard class, late in June 1919, "more dead than alive." Yet the four-day celebration, during which he treated his classmates to a cruise on a destroyer was, he wrote Eleanor who was off with the children, "great fun and a grand success in every way." Concerning this convivial occasion, however, he added reassurance to his wife, who, according to their son James, was "almost fanatically against drinking."[1]

"I took very good care of myself in every way except sleep," he wrote. "Yesterday—no Friday—I lunched with Mary Miller and she said she never saw me looking better. That afternoon on my way home during a rain squall a piece of tree hit me in the right eye. It was a little cut but is almost well."[2]

At the time of this luncheon with their mutual friend, Mrs. Adolph Miller, Franklin was full of bounce not only from the "hectic" Harvard reunion but from the illnesses of the year before. Also, as the little incident of the tree and the rain squall indicated, he was, like all other mortals, subject to the unexpected hazard. He and Eleanor, however, had recently experienced luck in escape from greater danger.

On the night of June 2 they turned the corner into the block of their residence on R Street just minutes after a bomb exploded at the front of the house of Attorney General A. Mitchell Palmer across the street from their own. Palmer, who as patrio-politician had been super enthusiastic in rounding up "Reds" of all shades, was safely sleeping at the back of his house. Eleanor found her children safe, too, though in shock she sharply scolded one for being out of bed. Then back on the sidewalk they met Alice and Nick Longworth who so often turned up in their company in these days. They had come quickly as spectators. The street was a sight to see. The whole front of the Palmer house, Alice reported, looked "as if it might fetch loose at any moment." The street was plastered with debris, leaves, grass and bloody pieces of the body of the bomber who had been killed in his own terrorist act. The whole business, said Alice, "was curiously without horror."[3] The four of the Roosevelt clan went into Franklin's house for talk about the incident and probably, despite Eleanor's views, for a steadying drink.

Alice, who described herself as a sort of perambulatory night creature, seemed always in those days turning up at historic scenes, not all of them shared by Franklin and Eleanor. Certainly they were not with her when she drove to the Union Station on July 8, more as spy than spectator. She parked on the edge of the station plaza to witness the return from Paris of the Woodrow Wilsons. Her bitterness against them and his League had grown to obsession since her father's death six months before. On the margin of the crowd, she was delighted to find it sparse, feminine and shrill. Then she drove to see what welcome they would receive at the White House gate. And there, she reported, like a would-be witch she crossed her fingers and made the sign of the evil eye.

"A murrain on him, a murrain on him, a murrain on him!" she cried so loudly that a companion feared they might be picked up by the Secret Service.[4]

Before the President and his party had first sailed to the Peace Conference the December before, he already had been the target of less sorcerous maledictions. Some significant ones had come from Alice's father and their friend Henry Cabot Lodge. Also an almost feline bitterness about the Wilsons among some in Washington, even in the first flush of victory, was best expressed by Ellen Slayden. Her Democratic Congressman husband had just been forced out of Congress by Wilson as one who had not supported his administration. She wrote before the President first departed for Paris of "his amazing trip to Europe, preparations for which exceed in grandeur those for the Field of the Cloth of Gold or the Queen of Sheba's visit to King Solomon. The apes and the peacocks alone are lacking, and there are those people unkind enough to say that even they will go along in one form or another."[5]

In the months between the time she wrote that and Alice spoke her curse, Franklin in Paris and Washington had watched, largely as spectator, the fight over the League and the developing resistance to it in the United States Senate. There were apes and peacocks in that spectacle. He listened to the gossip which came back from Paris about Wilson's illness there, about Mrs. Wilson's peacock passage to the signing of the treaty in the Galeries des Glaces at Versailles, and her increasing feeling about House and Lansing as fox and jackal. Roosevelt, however, was certainly among those still cheering his chief, though not personally repelled by those who opposed him. He would have laughed loudly at Alice's childish curse. Also he would have understood the feeling of Edith Wilson less often wearing "the great pin with the diamonds and the doves of peace which had been given me by the City of Paris."[6] She rejoiced in return to American simplicity.

"How good to be surrounded, once more," she wrote, "by the simple dignity of the White House, spick and span with cool linen on the chairs and flowers everywhere."[7]

Only the linens were cool that summer in Washington. The weather matched the mood of city and nation. Tempers mounted in both the White House and the Senate. Franklin wrote of the swift succession of deluges of rain and burning sunlight: "all the doors and the windows won't move from the damp."[8] There were irreconcilables of every kind in the streets as well as the Senate. Soon after Wilson's return, as grisly sample of the angers released from the unity of war, bloody race riots brought havoc to Washington's green avenues. Luckily, Franklin wrote Eleanor, who this summer had taken the children to the Massachusetts shore where they bathed on Bertie Hamlin's beach, the trouble did not spread to R Street. Still "though I have troubled to keep out of harm's way I have heard occasional shots during the evening and night."[9]

He seemed out of harm's way in other respects. His position in the Wilson administration did not disturb his close relations with Alice who never troubled to hide from anyone her animosity toward it. He chatted easily as dinner partner with Senator Lodge's daughter Constance, widow of Gussie Gardner, though the Wilson-Lodge differences had advanced from political contest to personal hatred. Similarly at a time when British-American relations seemed at a low point he kept his close ties with his many friends at the British Embassy. Indeed, these ties seemed stronger than ever in the early fall of 1919 when tall, patrician Edward Grey, Viscount of Fallodon, long-time British Foreign Minister, came out of retirement to Washington as a very special ambassador. His eminence and his amiable qualities as a man made him seem especially suited to treat with Wilson about postwar British-American problems. He came with "great reluctance," said Colonel House who had helped arrange the mission, but with a high sense of duty and hope for lasting peace.[10]

"The lights are going out all over Europe," Grey had said on the August night in 1914 when war began; "we shall not see them lit again in our lifetime."[11]

Now the light was going out for Grey. As a man who had so much enjoyed watching birds and other aspects of nature his eyesight was failing and he could only dimly see. One thing beyond his duty which made him willing to assume the mission was the hope of benefit from the famous American ophthalmologist, Dr. William H. Wilmer, in Washington. He wore, Mrs. Hamlin noted, "dark blue glasses & has to have someone always with him . . . fine looking, very tall & unmistakably British."[12] So he came as a man going blind. And to some, who knew the background of bitterness in Washington, the British government which sent him seemed blind, too.

House's part in arranging the mission did not then greatly recommend Grey to the White House household. Mrs. Wilson particularly had resented what she and Admiral Grayson believed were self-inspired press reports paramounting House's role in Paris even above that of the President from whom the colonel took all the position he possessed. Also of this time Eleanor Roosevelt wrote that "on account of Sir Edward Grey's affection for Uncle Ted, the name of Roosevelt was a key to his affections and we saw a good deal of him."[13] The name of Theodore Roosevelt did not endear him to the White House. Wilson, in his telegram of condolence on TR's death early in the year, had carefully erased the word "grieved" and substituted "shocked."[14] These matters might have been overlooked both in London and Washington. A third aspect of the Grey mission, however, seemed not an irritation but an affront. Grey brought with him as aide the same Major Craufurd-Stuart whom the Wilsons had demanded be sent home when he served under Lord Reading the year before.

Franklin was not officially concerned with these matters but as a man with many intimate friends in the British Embassy, notably now Sir Arthur Willert, he must have been fully aware of the Craufurd-Stuart affair at the time. In addition his friends William Phillips and Frank Polk were involved in the diplomatic correspondence about it. Furthermore, perceptive and communicative Bertie Hamlin wrote in her diary on November 3, of meeting "General Crawford-Stewart" at a dinner party. He had "returned with Lord Grey to everyone's astonishment." She added: "Apparently Lord Grey is innocent in the matter and has no idea how obnoxious the man was last year. Lord Reading must think that the reported dressing down given him by the foreign office and the extraction of the bullet from his jaw has made matters satisfactory. Charlie was amused by him—he came over and told him 'in confidence' to reserve Thursday night for the British Embassy party for the Prince of Wales. He was never so polite before."[15]

Craufurd-Stuart had reasons to be ingratiating. In the furies which surrounded his presence, others needed to be wary, including Franklin. Earlier, in a way, the greater gossip about the British officer had sheltered him. Evidently he saw no reason to expect that the affair might involve him now in the spreading circles of

White House resentments like those of a stone thrown in a pond. Soon after Grey and his entourage arrived, Franklin went off on an enjoyable hunting expedition in New Brunswick with Livy Davis, who had come back from overseas, and Richard E. Byrd, not yet the famous aviator he became.

Certainly back in Washington as Assistant Secretary of the Navy he became aware, as all were, that the White House now held a household more emotional and implacable than before. Grey had arrived in New York on September 25, the same day on which the President was stricken in the midst of his continental crusade to array the people behind his League threatened in the Senate. When the ambassador reached Washington Wilson had suffered a second more serious stroke. Secretiveness about the President's condition aroused both fears and callous curiosity. Behind the great mansion's now "closed and chained and locked" gates, it seemed to one observer "to exhale a chill and icy disdain." Around it, he wrote, "the social-political atmosphere of Washington" became one of "bleak and chill austerity suffused and envenomed by hatred of a sick chief magistrate that seemed to poison and blight every ordinary human relationship. . . ."[16]

Yet Washington this autumn was receiving with much ceremony and social activity, in which Franklin and Eleanor participated, such glamorous visitors as young Edward, Prince of Wales, and the King and Queen of the Belgians. These royal figures were admitted to see the propped up, now white bearded President. Yet Grey, whose mission was more serious and whose interest in such an organization as the League had seemed almost as great as Wilson's, waited to be received—and waited and waited. His friends professed to be amazed. Yet from within the White House refusal to see him may have seemed only proper resentment to insult and impertinence.

The closed door at the White House, across a narrow street from Franklin's office, brought a flood of rumors about the President's illness, slanders that he was suffering from paresis as the result of venereal disease, and, most infuriating, that he was only sulking in defeat. These reports were fantastic, said even Alice

Longworth, then operating so energetically against Wilson's League that she was dubbed "Commander of the 'Battalion of Death'." They were, she said, "noticeably lacking in the Greek quality of Aidos—the quality that deters one from defiling the body of a dead enemy."[17]

Also, as even Cabinet officers in the most important matters communicated with the President as a vague figure behind a veil, reports grew that a sort of regency was in command. The President's emotional Irish secretary, Joseph P. Tumulty, was its agent and face. But in a situation in which access to the President was the basic constituent of power Mrs. Wilson seemed supreme. Associated with her was handsome Dr. Grayson whom someone had described as a "panoplied Apollo" when in Paris Wilson's illness had pushed him into some staff activities as well as medical attention. A variety of ties, including his wife who had in some sense been Mrs. Wilson's ward, bound him to the First Lady. Others, notably Colonel House and Senator Lodge, expanded this supposed "regency" to include Baruch. Lodge complained to Elihu Root that the Constitution did not contemplate "a regency of Tumulty and Barney Baruch." Baruch mentioned as an absurdity that a prominent lady "firmly believed that Grayson and I were running the Presidency with Mrs. Wilson's help."[18]

Mrs. Wilson wrote that she and her husband had "learned to count [Baruch] as a friend and counselor, and to regard [him] with personal affection."[19] Baruch recalled that Mrs. Wilson "always called me affectionately, 'my dear Baron,' after the name of my plantation, Hobcaw Barony."[20] Also in his biography, the great speculator and elder statesman said that Grayson was "a fine and gentle man whom I loved dearly."[21] The Craufurd-Stuart case illumined the legend or the fact of the triumvirate's power in some matters at least. At the same time this business brought Franklin into a socially and politically perilous position.

Just as wild rumors surrounded the White House, so reports seeped into it from the social front. There were many ready to bring information which sharpened the sense of injury and indignation in the sequestered mansion. Secretary Lansing, aware that Wilson now doubted his full loyalty in the League fight, was enthusiastic in supporting the demand that Craufurd-Stuart be sent home. Possibly the meticulous Secretary of State was not acting merely to provide himself with protective coloration. Still, Colonel House, who at the time was out of communication if not entirely out of favor with the Wilsons, reported that it was a time of rampant jealousy of which he feared he was the victim. In his diary (some of the entries of which are not in the published version), House reported that Grey and his first associate, Sir William Tyrrell, had "some corroborative evidence from Mrs. Wilson's secretary, Miss Benham,"[22] who was soon to suffer a nervous breakdown, that some of the insistent complaint about Craufurd-Stuart did not come from the President himself. The trouble, he wrote, "involves Baruch and a lady friend of his. Grayson has evidently taken Baruch's end of the controversy and has succeeded in persuading the President, or at least those acting for him and who speak in his name, to demand that Stuart go home. Grey had a meeting with Lansing and Grayson and refused to dismiss Stuart without at first investigating the charges."[23]

Then the colonel added: "Tyrrell lunched with the lady in question and she complained bitterly, among other things, that the British government, at Stuart's suggestion, had placed a Dictograph in her house in Washington and kept her under surveillance.

"It all shows the power of the Baruch-Grayson influence at this time when no one other than Grayson has access to the President. The lady told Tyrrell she intended to bring suit against the British government. Tyrrell advised doing so and said Lord Grey would throw no obstacle in her way and would rather help to secure her rights if she brought the case before the courts."[24]

While this controversy went on in secret, the Senate, on November 19, rejected the League both with and without Senator Lodge's reservations. Alice Longworth jubilated in the gallery. Then she brought other League foes, including Lodge, home with her for midnight celebration. "Mrs. Harding," she noted, "cooked the eggs."[25] Franklin and Eleanor were in less

1. Minnie Mercer

2. Statue: "The Kneeling Woman" by Ralph Stackpole.
Statue sent to FDR in 1943.

3. Model "The Kneeling Woman" by Ralph Stackpole.
Model of the original which FDR had seen and admired in San Francisco
around 1917.

4. Mrs. Winthrop Rutherfurd (nee Lucy Page Mercer)

5. Alice Roosevelt Longworth.

6. Laura Delano. Christmas 1939.

7. Sara Delano Roosevelt. 1907.

8. Following the casket into the White House. Basil O'Connor, Grace Tully, Margaret Suckley and "Fala," Laura Delano and "Sister," Mrs. Edwin Watson. FDR's funeral. Washington, April 4, 1945.

9. FDR in Washington May 22, 1941 with "Missy" LeHand.

10. Eleanor Roosevelt on honeymoon trip, in gondola in Venice. July 7, 1905.

11. Anna Roosevelt Cowles (Mrs. William Sheffield Cowles)

12. Edith Wilson wedding photo to Woodrow.

13. Adams monument over grave of Clover Adams,
Rock Creek Cemetery, Washington, D.C.

14. Marian Hooper, from a tintype taken at Beverly Farms in 1869.

FROM THE BOOKMAN, VOL. 15, JULY 1902

15. Edith Eustis

16. Mrs. William Corcoran Eustis and Mrs. J. W. Wadsworth. Prominent Washington women conduct sale for benefit of wounded.

jubilant company that evening. Secretary and Mrs. Daniels dined with them, along with Willert who had been working on the Craufurd-Stuart case. Daniels noted the defeat in his diary, "Lodge has one passion—hatred of Wilson."[26] The Wilsons, however, were good haters, too. They almost welcomed evidences to support their venom. David F. Houston, a member of the Cabinet especially trusted at the time, wrote later—and certainly did not keep secret then—that at a dinner party he had heard Grey speaking to Lodge in approval of his course in the League fight in the Senate.[27] Dinner parties seemed almost broadcasting mechanisms.

Certainly blythe Franklin and innocent Eleanor Roosevelt had no intention to provide materials for the whispering gallery in connection with their intimate family Christmas dinner this year. They expanded it only slightly. At this time Grey had already stubbornly declined to send Craufurd-Stuart home. He was preparing for departure himself from what his biographer called his "abortive visit to America."[28] Still Eleanor and Franklin had found Grey and his chief associate, Tyrrell, a "delightful pair."[29] They invited them to the holiday feast. Also invited was Alice. On the Sunday before, this commander of the "Battalion of Death" wrote, she had left the house of the Patten sisters, "whose Sunday afternoons are a Washington institution," to call on Senator Lodge. She was disturbed to find Lodge conferring with Senators who were less irreconcilable in opposition to the League than she demanded that he be.[30]

She came to the Roosevelt dinner. Also Grey and Tyrrell accepted "much to our joy," wrote Eleanor.[31] Others at the Christmas dinner included the matriarch Sara from Hyde Park and swarthy, gnome-like Louis Howe, Franklin's assistant who already believed he could put another Roosevelt, namely Franklin, in the White House. Eleanor rather vacuously commented that Howe "was of English descent and always got on well with our English cousins."[32] The party was a gay occasion, only marred by the discovery in the midst of it that young James Roosevelt had the German measles. When Eleanor telephoned Grey afterward, she wrote, "he remarked that he did not think he was subject to childish diseases."[33] Though they did not realize it the Roosevelts were not immune to other more malignant contagions prevalent in Washington at the time.

Apparently unscathed, though not cured of his blindness, Grey sailed home. He was in no wise embittered by his lack of welcome. He built bitterness behind him, however, when in England he sent to the London *Times* a letter suggesting that in practice the Lodge reservations to the League would have proved harmless and that Britain could have accepted them. Mrs. Wilson did speak then almost as a regent when she commented, "It may be safely assumed that had Lord Grey ventured upon any such utterance while in Washington as an ambassador . . . his government would have been promptly asked to withdraw him."[34] Perhaps he was lucky at this time not to be at hand to feel her wrath.

Actually he had enjoyed the trip. While in the United States he had spoken at Harvard on his lifelong interest (shared in companionship with Theodore Roosevelt) in birds and fishes. From Washington he had written a friend: "I get a nice walk occasionally and some good music, and sometimes bridge after dinner. I love the Americans. They seem to me more easy to get on with than English people, but they are very civilized and wear white waistcoats, and have not as a rule any passion for country life; and I, being at bottom primitive and uncivilized, would have to go and live in the backwoods if I stayed in the country. Nevertheless life in Washington if I was an Ambassador, would be far more tolerable than life in London."[35]

The controversial Craufurd-Stuart went serenely home at the mission's termination. Evidently he was not permanently troubled by the furore raised about him. He was a member of the ancient Royal Company of Archers. To the D.S.O. which he had been awarded for his fighting in Gallipoli other honors were added apparently for his services on the Washington front. He was made a Commander of the Order of the British Empire in 1920, and a Commander of the Victorian Order in 1922. He went, loaded with his medals, to become military secretary to the Viceroy of India,

Lord Reading who, as a perfect match for Baruch, had brought him to Washington in the first place.

In addition to its diplomatic documentation in State Department archives, other less austere records exist about this boudoir imbroglio in British-American relations at a crucial time. In its gleeful treatment of gossip, *Town Topics*, in an article signed by "The Widow," told the story, without using names, in a fashion remarkably in conformance with the letters and cables of U.S. diplomats on the subject. The straight story at the time, however, had been too hot to handle even by newspapermen working in the pattern later popularized by Drew Pearson in the *Washington Merry-Go-Round*. Such a journalist at the time was Fred C. Kelly, writer for the *New York Sun* and *The Saturday Evening Post*. He collected the facts about this great tragi-comedy though he could not get them printed. His information varied from that of others only in the possibility that Craufurd-Stuart may have been innocent so far as the planting of the Dictaphone in the lady's house was concerned. He "was not popular" with his embassy associates, Kelly wrote, and, when the lady came protesting against the invasion of her privacy, in impatience with her and as a trick on him they made a scapegoat out of her onetime suitor.

Kelly, however, was sure that the Dictaphone records were made. They indicated no treason but almost ludicrous indiscretion. He also reported, on the basis of information which he said was given him by Secretary of War Newton D. Baker, that in the last years of the Wilson administration a "dollar-a-year man was moving heaven and earth to gain possession of those Dictaphone records, to make sure they were destroyed. It is said he offered vast sums to anybody who would get them out of their secret hiding place in the War Department."[36]

Baruch later said flatly that he was not involved, despite Colonel House's diary entry. He had learned that some of the unpublished parts of the House diaries contained "incredibly mean and vindictive" statements about him. Baruch wrote: "The Craufurd-Stuart incident had nothing to do with any friend of mine but

had to do with a scurrilous remark that he, Stuart, made at a dinner to two most respected married women in Washington, regarding Mrs. Wilson. This was reported to Mr. Wilson and he
asked that Stuart, who was then Reading's assistant, go home. I
believe he was sent home (or went with Reading) but when Grey
came over, he brought Stuart which caused a great deal of tur-
moil. I believe the President did not see Grey because he had
brought back this man who had spoken so scurrilously of Mrs.
Wilson. With that I had nothing to do."[37]

In the notes Kelly made he did not identify the "dollar-a-year
man." Of the Dictaphone records, however, he said that Baker,
daring to trust nobody, had hidden them "in an old safe that
had not been used for years—a safe containing a lot of old Civil
War records. He hid the key behind a mirror in the washroom off
his private office."

He elaborated: "One day Cary Grayson came to Secretary of
War Baker's office (about six months before Wilson retired from
office) and said the President wanted him (Grayson) to fetch
the Dictaphone records the President and Baker had once discussed. Baker, suspecting Grayson might be acting for somebody
else and not for Wilson, said: 'Since this was a military matter,
I couldn't give these records to you on a verbal order from the
President. I couldn't even give them to you on a written order
from him *personally*. It would have to come from him as *commander-in-chief of the army and navy.*'

"Grayson went away and did not return—not for a long
time. But he did return on March 3, in the afternoon, the day
before the Wilson administration ended. And he had an order,
signed by Woodrow Wilson as commander-in-chief of the army
and navy."[38]

This denouement of the story, of course, runs far ahead of the
Roosevelt Christmas dinner in 1919. Franklin was remote from
any possible regency then. He was to become, as the years went
on, grateful for the aid and advice of both Grayson and Baruch.
He was to have the old and broken Wilson's appreciation for his
efforts in creating the Woodrow Wilson Foundation. He was to

invite the presence in the House Gallery and have the support of Mrs. Wilson when he led the nation into the Second World War which Wilson's League was designed to prevent. But when he joyfully welcomed into his most intimate circle, in 1919, the erect Englishman, who declined to bow to the evidently emotional demands of the White House, Roosevelt built no affection for himself there to cushion him if he should stumble. And, all unwittingly, the way ahead contained pitfalls as unpredictable as a summer storm.

NINE

The Children's Hour

(1)

In gaiety and sadness children have their places in history as actors and as witnesses, too. Certainly in terms of a man captured in all the troubles which may beset a father of five, Franklin Roosevelt appeared troubled, wan, and irritated to Bertie Hamlin in January 1920. Perhaps his situation then had been triggered by Eleanor's disovery two weeks before that young James had a fever at the merry family Christmas party attended by British statesmen. Certainly ills had intervened since that time and on January 10, Mrs. Hamlin noted in her diary:

"As I was walking along R Street . . . I met Franklin Roosevelt—he has had his tonsils out and has been ill too—he looks rather poorly for him. He had two of his boys and a dog with him and we walked along together. Several of the children have had or are having chicken-pox. James is to have his appendix out— Eleanor was getting out 2000 invitations for Navy teas. He said he did not expect to run for the Senate—that even if he wanted it or could get it—he thought it stupid."[1]

If James was then laid up with appendicitis, the oldest of the two boys with the tall man was not yet ten. The baby, John, not quite four, was probably not walking on R Street in January. The two boys were evidently Elliott and Franklin, Jr. Franklin

was a gay five-year-old. Elliott at nine was a child who attracted
most sympathy. He had been an infant of "unhappy disposition,"[2]
who had to wear braces because he was bowlegged. As a child of
three he had been badly burned when he fell into a bonfire on
the beach at Campobello.[3] Recently, however, he had been
able to join the older Anna and James in a children's dancing class
at the British Embassy. All were children of much appeal, especially to a very busy father who left discipline to his wife. Evidently with so much sickness in the house they were wan beside
their poorly looking, protective father.

Obviously Franklin was both "poorly" and irritated. But
troubles in his crowded household seemed only begun. On
February 4, the busy Eleanor received a telegram from New York.
Her Aunt Pussie and her two little girls had been killed in a fire
in "an old stable on Ninth Street, which had been done over into
a house."[4] She had reasons from her own childhood to resent this
beautiful and tempestuous aunt. In Pussie's tantrums, which
often attended her love affairs, she had hurt and shocked her
niece. Eleanor, her aunt had shouted at her then, was too homely
to ever find a husband. Venting her furies Pussie had in outbursts
revealed to Eleanor the full story of her beloved father's last
years as a drunk. Eleanor not only remembered these emotional
explosions directed at her. Also she recalled that in the same
year in which she did catch her very charming husband, there had
been fears about the marriage of the "temperamental" Pussie
to the much younger Forbes Morgan.[5]

Those fears had been justified. The Morgans had been living
much apart. Still the description of Pussie's residence in a converted old stable gave a false impression. In the advancing auto-
motive age such converted stables in the Greenwich Village area
had become popular with artists and such arty people as Pussie.
Eleanor wrote that "she made the house charming, as she always
did, but as usual she could not make life in it an easy matter."
Sometimes Pussie, who had no maid, left the house attended only
by her pretty youngest child, a girl of nine.

The erratic charm of the household made the family holocaust

more grim. Eleanor took the first train to New York and was the
first of Pussie's kin to arrive. When she arrived she found New
York overwhelmed by a blizzard. To cross town on necessary
errands from her mother-in-law's house on 65th Street, she had
to walk across Central Park several times. Some of those errands
involved trips to the undertaker. Years later she said that she
could not afterward "bear any funeral parlor." She went with a
"sad little group" of relatives to Tivoli. There they "placed the
three bodies in the vault where, the summer before, we had laid
my grandmother." Neighbors fed them and warmed them.
Eleanor was glad that her Grandmother Hall had not lived to
have this tragedy added to others in her life. She wondered if her
grandmother's "life had been a little less centered in her family
group, if that family group might not have been a great deal
better off."[6]

Certainly in this bleak winter her family group was not only
crowded with "childish diseases." Also at this point a recovering
Franklin added to its troubles an only presumably mature explosion. Freidel, in his biography of Roosevelt, wrote of this time:
"As always, he leaped before he looked."[7] Usually he landed on
his feet, but this time he engaged in some perilous plunges.
Three days before Eleanor received the news of Pussie's death, he
made a dramatic speech in Brooklyn. It received full press cover-
age.[8] Also it infuriated Secretary Daniels and the White House.
The Associated Press quoted the Assistant Secretary of the Navy
as saying that prior to the war Wilson had "opposed" his efforts
to prepare the Navy for war; it had been readied only because he,
bold Roosevelt, had committed enough illegal acts in purchasing
arms to justify his impeachment if he had guessed wrong.

His reception in the Navy Department next day was approximately as frigid as the weather Eleanor found in New York and
at Tivoli. Shocked at his own verbosity, he issued a statement
saying that his speech had been twisted to make a sensation.[9]
As usual the "correction" got much less news play. His explanation
did not satisfy Daniels especially at this time when Republicans
were busily investigating the war effort in the hope of finding

political munitions in this election year. Evidently Roosevelt's explanation did not satisfy Wilson either. The short limits on presidential patience with what he regarded as disloyalty was soon to be shown in his dismissal of Secretary Lansing for reasons, which, as stated, seemed to many a display of pique.

Franklin, as Daniels noted in his diary a few days later, came into the Secretary's office "as usual."[10] The situation surrounding him, however, was hardly normal.[11] He was involved in rows with regard to what some officers felt was the too lenient treatment of convicts at the Portsmouth naval prison and charges that he had approved of acts of perversion by naval agents at Newport in the effort to catch homosexuals. Republicans were to make the most of this last matter later, to the point of making it difficult for Roosevelt to get his indignant denials into the record. Some officers were suspicious of his support of a plan of his promoter friend, Arthur P. Homer, which was supposed to get cheaper oil for the Navy but certainly a big profit for Homer. Daniels, who did not like the oil deal, still regarded Franklin as "clean as a hound's tooth."[12] The Secretary was less certain of his judgment and sometimes of his loyalty. Apparently Daniels did not know at this time that Franklin had originally sided with Admiral William S. Sims in a furore he raised about the war decorations Daniels approved.

Amidst such matters it is unlikely that Roosevelt had time for more than casual sympathy about the death of another child. This was Lewis Morton Rutherfurd, the teen-aged son of the widowed Winthrop Rutherfurd. Franklin undoubtedly expressed his condolence to the boy's aunt, his friend Edith Eustis. The boy's death, despite his family's great wealth which could bring the best medical care to him, caused much sympathy for his father who had been bereaved two years before by the death of the mother of this son and five other children. Some of the saddened were surprised a few days later by Rutherfurd's marriage to Lucy Mercer.

It was a quiet event treated quietly. On Friday the thirteenth of February the *Washington Post* reported: "Mrs. Carroll Mercer announces the marriage of her daughter, Lucy Page, to Mr. Winthrop Rutherfurd of New York. The ceremony took place yesterday morning at the home of Dr. and Mrs. William B. Marbury, the latter a sister of the bride. On account of deep mourning only the immediate families were present."[13]

Minnie, of course, was there as the well-preserved mother of the bride—and, as a matter of fact, only a year younger than the groom. Her daughter, Violetta, had married Dr. Marbury, with whom she had served as a nurse in France. Marbury was a member of a distinguished Maryland family. Before the war he had gone as private physician to the rich Joseph Leiter on a trip around the world. No guest list was published to mention others present.

Certainly "the immediate families" would include the five surviving Rutherfurd children—Winthrop, Alice, Hugo, Guy, and John—none over eighteen. The term may well have included the children's Washington aunt, Mrs. Willie Eustis, and perhaps her children, their cousins. *The Journal of Society,* self-called, later said, however, that some members of the Morton family were resentful because "he failed to tell his first wife's family of his intended marriage, and he hastened to have the knot tied a very short time after the death of a son." This report also said that some of the family felt that "a marriage might have been arranged between him and his very charming sister-in-law, the former Duchesse de Valencay (sic)."[14] It is more than doubtful that another sister of his first wife, Edith Eustis, felt any resentment. Instead, her later friendship with Lucy suggests approval.

Present and approving was Elizabeth Henderson Cotten, and her son, Lyman Atkinson Cotten, Jr., was there in official capacity as a big-eyed, eleven-year-old ribbon boy. Years later as an English professor at the University of North Carolina, his two chief recollections were (1), his wonder why pretty Lucy was marrying this "old and ugly" man, and (2), the very big and delicious wedding cake.[15] His memories indicate that, despite mourning, the festal and decorative aspects of a wedding were not dispensed with.

Where there were ribbons and cake there must have been some festivity, too.

The event, of course, recalled the earlier gossip about Franklin and Lucy. Some wondered why Lucy had not married Nigel Law, who had now been transferred to Paris where he found sensational romance of his own. Mrs. Cotten, commenting on Law, said he hadn't any money. Yet she added vehemently of Lucy, "She married Mr. Rutherfurd, *not* for money but because she felt he needed her."[16] Mrs. Cotten did not share her son's view about his age and appearance. He was and remained, she thought, a handsome, ageless man.

Far from these nuptial festivities, however muted, Franklin Roosevelt this day was closer to danger than he knew. Divorce was not the only threat to his career which he faced in these years. Now Secretary Daniels was still resentful of what he regarded as Roosevelt's ridiculous boasting, in disloyalty to himself and to the President. A week after the Mercer-Rutherfurd marriage, he indicated in his diary that he was contemplating an open break with his assistant. Then on February 21, he made a cryptic entry which was clear nevertheless:

> "I hate him, said E. Wanted T to tell L that Major S must be sent back or would not receive. T refused. Must put it on other grounds.
>
> FDR persona non grata with W. Better let speech pass.[17]

The code of these capital letters is not difficult to decipher. Daniels had talked with Joe Tumulty. In post-mortem discussions of the circumstances surrounding the sudden removal of Lansing as Secretary of State on February 12, Tumulty had unburdened himself and at the same time unconsciously revealed his own isolation in his office as Secretary to the President. He told Daniels that Edith Wilson had hated Lansing and had wanted Tumulty to tell Lansing that Major Craufurd-Stuart must be sent back to England or the President would not receive Lord Grey. Tumulty apparently had insisted that they must put the re-call of Craufurd-Stuart or the refusal to see Grey on some other grounds than talk at a dinner party. The matter obviously had been taken out of Tumulty's hands. Evidently Tumulty had not known that Lansing was entirely sympathetic with the White House feeling in the Craufurd-Stuart affair.

Tumulty had better reason to be sure about Wilson's current antipathy to Roosevelt. There was nothing hush-hush about FDR's unfortunate Brooklyn blast. In the whispering gallery of Washington his close ties with British Embassy men and his hospitality to Grey were common knowledge. With a sick man's intensity, Wilson seemed to cling to the barbs and arrows. He expressed resentment against FDR again later that year.[18]

"Better let speech pass," is crystal clear.

Enough furore had followed the dismissal of Lansing on the grounds that he had presumed to convene the Cabinet in the President's absence and without his permission. Daniels had made a note about the Lansing dismissal, "Occasion unfortunate."[19] Now, however, that dismissal had already provided too much evidence of irritation within the administration. It was no time to add to it in the Navy Department by similar evidence of resentment. Also energetically back on the reservation, Roosevelt could be wisely forgiven.

Whether or not Franklin had any idea of the dimensions of the official irritations he had caused, he had plenty of personal problems. On the day before Lucy was married in a letter to his mother he described himself as a very domesticated man. He wrote about schools and stomach aches, of the absence of an English nurse which put the care of the younger children on Eleanor. Also he expressed much thanks.

> Dearest Mama—
> You are not only an angel which I always knew, but the kind which comes at the critical moment in life! For the question was not one of paying Dr. Mitchell for removing James' insides, the Dr. can wait, I know he is or must be rich, but of paying the gas man and the butcher lest the infants starve to death, and your check which is much too much of a Birthday present will do that. It is so dear of you.[20]

Roosevelt was undoubtedly under heavy expenses at the time. His salary was still under $5000 a year. Even though he and Eleanor still had their private incomes, like everyone else they were caught in the postwar high cost of living. He and Howe were both looking for ways to make money quickly. Later in the year he told Daniels that Howe had a "bona offer of $20,000." Daniels commented in his diary, "He believes it but I have a great big swallow but I cannot swallow that."[21] It turned out later that Daniels was right. Roosevelt with his big house, many children, many servants, many bills, was—or seemed to be—in financial straits. The December before he had confided to a friend, "I am honestly a fit candidate for a receiver. . . ."[22]

More startling in this February 1920 was a less facetious plea of poverty made by Minnie Mercer. On February 25, scarcely two weeks after her daughter had married the wealthy Rutherfurd, she filed with the Bureau of Pensions the affidavit of her long-time friend, the lawyer Henry E. Davis. He swore that Minnie was "now without resources of what kind soever." Minnie followed this up on March 1 with a sworn statement of her own that she was completely broke.[23] She was eager for her pension of something like $30 a month. There might be a new life for her with well-married daughters. She still wanted a dependable pittance of her own.

The Franklin Roosevelt-Lucy Mercer story now seemed only an episode completely and neatly ended. With Lucy as wife and mother the Rutherfurds, old Winthrop and his lively brood, made a beautiful picture of handsome sports-loving people in elegant residence in Washington, New York, or the ancient Rutherfurd estate at Allamuchy, New Jersey. As a family in the tradition of outdoor activity, they seemed even more rooted in Aiken, South Carolina, where Rutherfurd purchased the Ridgeley Hall property, just across the road from the Palmetto Golf Club, from the estate of Franklin's dead friend Gussie Gardner. The house had been designed by Julian Peabody, architect son-in-law of Louise Eustis Hitchcock, wife and mother of the two famous Hitchcock polo players, and sister of Willie Eustis, at whose Washington house Franklin frequently spent evenings during the war years.

Washington in the postwar doldrums was no such center of sport. Still its more athletic personages found time and place not only for golf but more strenuous sports. On a lovely spring Sunday of this year the ubiquitous Bertie Hamlin found Franklin in much better shape than when the year began. When she called at the British Embassy she came upon him just starting out for a game of hockey with his good friend Willert of the London Times.[24]

(2)

Alice was a creature in familiar environment at the Republican National Convention in Chicago in 1920. Politicians paid her deference. Indeed, perhaps her eminence in America was indicated by a conversation among Democrats at Wilson's Cabinet table. Palmer, whose bombed house had made a spectacle for her, told of a German doctor in Washington whose property had been taken over in wartime by the Alien Property Custodian. Now, since his wife was an American, under law it had been returned but he complained it lacked a priceless possession—"the appendix of Alice Roosevelt Longworth in alcohol."[25]

Not missing it, Alice strode among the gathered Republicans of the nation. Though she was quartered in the mansion of a millionaire, she moved among the delegates in the hot city. She breathed as accustomed air the cigar smoke in hotel rooms and corridors among politicians, many smelling of rye whiskey. She and many of the sweating politicos, however, had an orphaned sense. For the first time in two decades her father was absent. Before Theodore Roosevelt died, a year and a half earlier, his old friends and old enemies in the party were ready to renominate him by "acclamation." Now in processes, involving maneuver and money, which Alice watched with some scorn, the convention came to Warren G. Harding. His was not a name like a flag.

Eleanor did not go to the similar Democratic gathering in San Francisco. There the problem with an old name was different. The concern of Wilson's oldest and wisest friends was to prevent efforts, evidently emanating from the White House itself, to make the paralyzed President the Democratic candidate again. Franklin was involved in no such plan. He did make a dramatic show of his loyalty to Wilson and his own independent powers, however, when he grabbed the standard of the reluctant, Tammany-dominated, New York delegation and joined a Wilson demonstration.

Though he had irritated that organization's leaders in the past, Tammany was not too much disturbed by the vigorous, impulsive young man. Along with other city bosses, Murphy of Tammany got the candidate he wanted in Governor James M. Cox of Ohio. He acquiesced when Cox, after balancing political geography and balancing independence with the bosses, gave his ultimate reason why Franklin Roosevelt should be his Vice-Presidential running mate: "Roosevelt was a well-known name."

Franklin, who had lifted the banner for Wilson, now turned in affection to Daniels. His letter of resignation and Daniels' reply made an exchange which set a pattern for the future. In his letter Franklin wrote:

My dear Chief:
This is not goodbye—that will always be impossible after these years of the closest association—and no words I write will make you know better than you know now how much our association has meant. All my life I shall look back,—not only on the work of the place—but mostly on the wonderful way in which you and I have gone through these nearly eight years *together*. You have taught me so wisely and kept my feet on the ground when I was about to skyrocket—and in it all there has never been a real dispute or antagonism or distrust. . . .[26]

Daniels, who had praised Franklin at San Francisco, wrote in his diary of his departure. "He left in the afternoon, but before leaving wrote me a letter most friendly & almost loving wh. made me glad I had never acted upon my impulse when he seemed to take sides with my critics."[27]

Also in his loving reply he said:

> . . . My thought and feeling has been that of an older brother and your nomination to the great office of Vice-President by our party pleased me very much, and I shall always rejoice in your successes and victories and be glad if in any way I can contribute to them. More intimately I shall share with you the happiness that [comes] to you in your beautiful home life and we will be brothers in all things that make for the good of our country. . . .[28]

Franklin's home life was involved in inevitable change. Of his nomination, Eleanor reported that she was pleased for her husband but "it never occurred to me to be much excited."[29] Symbolically she spoke of the official notification ceremonies at Hyde Park. Then she was impressed by the sight of the impeccable lawns of old Sara, whom at this point she admired, "being trampled by hordes of people."[30] This was more than a Democratic Party occasion. The trampled lawns marked the end of the time when Franklin could keep his ties with his party and his class with impartial ease. The "class," largely Republican, which later he was said to have betrayed, abruptly discarded him.

Soon after their nominations Cox and Roosevelt called on the ailing President at the White House. Wilson was evidently decrepit. He could little more than gasp his gratitude for their pledge to campaign for his League. It was for the candidates a moving occasion, though not so reported by their opponents. Charles S. Groves, correspondent of the *Boston Globe*, was one of those who met them after they saw Wilson. He reported to Senator Lodge: "Young Roosevelt acted as a sort of master of ceremonies ushering Cox into Tumulty's office where the correspondents had assembled; the candidate for Vice-President was bright and boyish and a little silly in his exuberance—the thing has gone to his head."[31]

Senator Lodge, who, with his son-in-law the late Gussie Gardner and other elegant Republicans, had been so hospitable to
the young Roosevelts when they first came to Washington, figuratively shook his head as he pushed his pen.

"He talked well in the early days of the [Wilson] administration," he wrote in reply. "He is a pleasant fellow whom I personally liked, but now that the administration is coming to a close we
can see that when it came to the point, he did exactly what
Daniels wished him to do. He is a well-meaning, nice young fellow, but light."[32]

More sharply this new Roosevelt was described within the same
week by the *Chicago Tribune* of his one-time Groton schoolmate, Robert R. McCormick. That powerful journal called him,
"The One-half of One Per Cent Roosevelt," nominated only
in the hope of appealing to TR's Progressive following. It
added: "He is to put the honey of a name on the trap of a ticket.
Franklin is as much like Theodore as a clam is like a bear cat . . .
If he is Theodore Roosevelt, Elihu Root is Gene Debs, and
Bryan a brewer."[33] The repudiation came closer home. Theodore
Roosevelt, Jr., with whom Eleanor and Franklin had had such
happy reunion in Paris the year before, spoke for the Oyster Bay
Roosevelts.

"He is a maverick," he said in a speech in Sheridan, Wyoming.
"He does not have the brand of our family."[34]

As TR's niece, however, Eleanor came completely, though at
first shyly, to Franklin's support. At the beginning of the campaign she declined to provide a picture of herself: "I take such
bad photographs that I've not had any taken for years."[35]
Later she relented. Then in October, as a lone woman on a campaign car, she joined the whistle-stop political tour her husband
was conducting. She listened to his often repeated speeches, made
appearances herself, and was amused on occasion by "lovely ladies
who served luncheon for my husband and worshipped at his
shrine."[36] She was not jealous of such hit-and-run adoration and
wrote that she joined others in teasing him about it. This trip
she regarded as a part of her political education. The defeat at its

end did not cause—but definitely marked—a change in their marital relationship in which, without ever altering appearances, both went more and more their own separate ways.

That was not immediately apparent. Soon after the election Franklin rather emphasized their ties by going off on a hunting trip to Louisiana with Eleanor's brother Hall. Seven years younger than Eleanor, he had lived with her and Franklin almost as their child. Naturally he had gone to Groton. He had graduated from Harvard with Phi Beta Kappa honors. Then, not quite twenty-one but with money of his own, he had married Margaret Richardson of a prominent Boston family. By the time of this Louisiana trip, they had had three children. There seemed no suggestion at this time that their marriage might be in trouble or that the brilliant Hall might be headed down the fated alcoholic path of his father. Franklin reported: "Hall seems very fit and sends much love."[37]

Under forty Franklin was fit and more than ever free. More than death had cut the ties between him and "Uncle Ted" who had once talked with Eleanor about plans for him. He was under the supervision of no boss like Daniels. The demands of politics in the future were not immediately present. The children were growing older and to an increasing extent could be delegated to the care of others. Perhaps most important, financial problems were less pressing. Even after his profession of poverty early in 1920, he had been able to contribute $5000 to the Democratic campaign fund.

Now to his and Eleanor's private incomes, he added substantial earnings. Though bored with law and never giving it much attention, with old friends, Grenville T. Emmett and Langdon P. Marvin, he became the last named (an odd place for a Roosevelt) in the firm of Emmett, Marvin and Roosevelt. More important, Van Lear Black, wealthy Baltimorian who shared with Franklin an addiction to yachting, made him vice-president in charge of the New York office of the Fidelity and Deposit Company of Maryland, a large surety bonding house, at a salary of $25,000 a year. Black who, among other enterprises, had resuscitated the

Baltimore Sun papers, knew that he was getting in Franklin a go-getter with connections in state and federal governments and with figures in business, labor, and politics. Earnings from these sources in the years ahead did not seem to suffice for his needs. As said observant Rexford Tugwell, who long served him and studied him, "he always felt himself to be pinched." His own expenses as patient and collector, a wife, "whose homemaking virtues were not her most conspicuous ones," and five expensive children provided reasons, Tugwell thought, for "his many attempts to tap the springs of easy money during the boom." He embarked on a variety of enterprises "intended to make him rich."[38]

With the Washington years behind her Eleanor embarked upon what she described as "the budding of a life of my own."[39] Very seriously—though apparently to no gourmet qualifications—she learned to cook. She attended a business school to learn shorthand and typing. Through work with the League of Women Voters she moved toward increasing activity with the Democratic party organization. She found women friends with whom she spent pleasant evenings when Franklin, as was often the case, was otherwise engaged. As time went on she became a partner-teacher in a school and a partner in a craft industry making furniture. With the help of Howe she got over the inane giggles which had marred her public speaking.

The house which Sara had given them adjoining and connecting with her own on 65th Street was relinquished to them by their Washington-time tenant, T. W. Lamont, the Morgan partner, early in 1921. From it and from their diverse activities they moved on weekends to Hyde Park where some of the children stayed all the time. Their lives seemed the routine of the new, useful elite. As heat came with the summer Eleanor set out as usual for Campobello. She wrote, "My husband did not go with us, but came early in August, after we were settled. . . ."[40] It is part of the obscure chronology of this summer that there is evidence that he had been up earlier than August.

Still when left behind, Franklin was a gregarious, free gentleman in his prime. Since January 1920, when Mrs. Hamlin saw him ailing and looking "poorly," he had had, for him, an exceptionally long period free from ills and infections. He presented, wrote Freidel, an "appearance of vitality and excellent health."[41] His felicitous independence was seriously interrupted, however, early in July when he learned of the impending Republican purpose in the Senate to smear him by reviewing and publicizing his supposed responsibility for the use of repulsive methods to entrap homosexuals in wartime around the naval establishment at Newport. The *New York Times* ran a lurid story under the sanctimonious headline:

LAY NAVY SCANDAL

TO F.D. ROOSEVELT

Details are Unprintable[42]

Franklin, rushing to Washington in the "awful heat," wrote that he had "found all the cards stacked, only even worse than I thought."[43] The Republican majority on the investigating committee gave him little chance to be heard. He had trouble in getting his case before the public. Fortunately for him, the clearly partisan character of the Republican charges was evident. He came back to New York angry, but so sure that he was unsullied that he was in a "skylarking mood" a few days later at a conference of Boy Scout executives and supporters at a scout camp in Palisades Interstate Park.[44] Following this meeting, according to Howe's biographer, Alfred B. Rollins, Jr., he spent "a hasty week end" at Hyde Park.[45] The Roosevelt house was deserted at this time, his mother being off on one of her many trips abroad. He had, however, friends in the neighborhood. Nearby the Eustises still shared the great Morton estate Ellerslie at Rhinecliffe. Possibly he saw them then; certainly they were in residence there later in the year.

Franklin's movements in these last walking days are not easy to trace. The Franklin D. Roosevelt Library at Hyde Park reports that it has only the information provided by his early biographers, Ernest Lindley and Earle Looker.[46] They were casual about this

period. Indeed, Lindley, even in the revised edition of his book
in 1934, had Roosevelt still in New York "about the middle of
August."[47] If he went to Hyde Park on the day after the Boy
Scout conference on July 27, the "hasty week end" would have begun on a Thursday. The *New York Times* reported him partici-
pating in a Woodrow Wilson Foundation meeting in the city on
the following Thursday, August 5. Only after that did he join his
boss and friend, Van Lear Black, on his yacht the *Sabalo*.[48]

Black was a high-spirited as well as an acquisitive individual. He
entertained not only on his luxurious yacht but at his Folly Quarter Mansion, a great Maryland house built nearly a century before
by one of the expansive Carrolls of Carrollton. There Black staged
rodeos and other spectacular affairs for journalistic, governmental,
and diplomatic guests.[49] Later in this year, with the help of his
friend and *Baltimore Sun* associate, Henry L. Mencken (who was
to be no friend of Franklin), he gave on his estate a party "marked
by a flow of lively liquors beyond the dreams of thirst personified."
In addition, for this occasion, he imported a troupe of coon shout-
ers from Virginia and a band of Indians from the West.[50]

No such highjinks marked Franklin's brief cruise on the *Sabalo*,
though Eleanor wrote that there was "quite a party" aboard her.
Apparently, as Lindley reported, Black had sailed into New York
and asked Franklin to join him. He agreed to the suggestion that
they go to Campobello. On the way they ran into dirty weather.
In a fog, Franklin, who knew this coast like the palm of his hand,
took the wheel and finally brought the 140-foot power yacht
through the waters of the Bay of Fundy safely into Welchpool
Harbor. This must have been August 8, as Lindley, whose account
is taken as the standard one, related that "Black stopped a day,
and then, restless as always, moved on."[51] With guests gone,
Roosevelt joined in his usual rough sport with the children on
water and ashore. It was only afterward that accumulated fatigue
and this vigorous activity then seemed portentous. Undoubtedly
he demonstrated his "superabundant energy, a belief in his own
invulnerability" which his White House physician years later
regarded as a basis of danger then.[52] His vigorous play was routine

Roosevelt behavior, only emphasized in rueful retrospect after August 10, 1921, when the polio struck.

"For Eleanor Roosevelt," wrote Alfred B. Rollins, Jr., in his study of *Roosevelt and Howe*, "it was a moment of tragedy and triumph."[53]

Sometimes in terms of the woman who had earlier seemed to her own son "almost supine,"[54] this tragedy was the beginning of her stalwart time. Certainly the immediate aftermath of the illness was a story of shock, of medical fumbling, and of courage and devotion by all concerned. Of Eleanor's courage there can be no question. Certainly Howe, who was visiting at Campobello at the time, shared her concern and her labors. Considering the shock, the anxiety and the fatigue, it was only natural that she wrote in a little confusion about Howe. When Franklin was stricken, she wrote, Howe "was considering an offer to go into business on a rather lucrative salary and decided to take his holiday at Campobello before he actually made up his mind." But now, she said, Howe "made up his mind to give up all idea of taking the position which was open to him and to come back to his old boss, because he saw quite plainly that his help was going to be needed."[55] Actually, according to Rollins, Howe had made his decision by March 1921, five months before, to become Roosevelt's assistant in the Fidelity and Deposit Company.[56]

Franklin was dependent upon Howe and Eleanor. Their need for him was scarcely less. In every aspect of appearances the marriage of Franklin and Eleanor had been maintained on its old terms after it was threatened by his affection for Lucy. Now, however, he was wholly Eleanor's to serve and save. Like her, the small swarthy Howe lacked possibilities of fulfillment alone. He was later to show almost feminine jealousy when Franklin preferred an important speech written by others to one prepared by him. He was to stay on Franklin's payroll or payrolls provided by Franklin for the rest of his life. Both Eleanor and Howe made sacrifices and had aspirations. They collaborated in the familiar pattern of reticence to keep the public from knowing the true condition of the political and very personal figure for whom they devotedly cared. Actually interest in his condition seemed slight. The *New York Times* first mentioned his illness in a small item on August 26. Apparently its local correspondent was not aware that Howe was carefully maneuvering to prevent publicity when he reported in the *Times* of September 14 that he had left Eastport in a private car. This reporter was not much more confused than the doctor had been when he wrote that "pneumonia was feared but did not develop. Dr. Bennett said today that his patient was convalescing."[57] Ill as he had been, Eleanor and Howe signed him up for future public service activities almost before his trouble was completely and properly diagnosed. In such activities they had a pliant patient. As the central figure, Roosevelt himself, save in rare moments of depression or irritation, showed a gallantry almost debonair.

Conflict about the physically inert man came, however, when the handsome, dominant Sara came home from her European holiday expecting to be met at the pier by her son. This time she was met by the news of the illness of the beloved boy she had never quite willingly relinquished.

Sara, said her grandson James, "never quite forgave mother for marrying her boy, Franklin, right out of college at a time when Granny was looking forward to enjoying a few years with Franklin all to herself."[58] Across their married lives she made many gifts in order to dominate them. Sara, as James put it, was "an aggressively bountiful provider."[59] Early in her married life Eleanor had had a minor attack of hysterics when they moved into the 65th Street house, given them by Sara and about which Eleanor had scarcely been consulted.[60] Now, though Eleanor stated it gently in her memoirs, the mother-in-law was prepared to dominate again.

"His mother," she wrote, "was really very remarkable about this entire illness. It must have been a terrific strain for her, and I am sure that, out of sight, she wept many hours, but with all of us she was very cheerful. She had, however, made up her mind that Franklin was going to be an invalid for the rest of his life and that he would retire to Hyde Park and live there. Her anxiety over his general health was so great that she dreaded his making any effort whatsoever."[61]

The differences between the two women were not always as gentle as Eleanor's prose. And neither Sara nor Eleanor, who, with Howe, was determined upon the continuation of Franklin's active career in business and politics, always concealed their feelings from the perceptive Franklin. Sara, who James said had a "capacity for magnificent martyrdom"[62] wrote her son during his convalescence in "an almost intangible but unmistakably patronizing attitude toward Mother."[63] On the other hand Eleanor later wrote him of her feeling about his mother, "I'm trying to be decent but I'm so conscious of being nasty that I'm uncomfortable every minute!"[64]

Clearly, though generally marked by Rooseveltian decorum, it was a nasty situation. Sara, as Freidel said, moved "with her usual dogged vigor."[65] She made an oblique attack on Eleanor's position through Howe. She had never liked the sallow unkempt little man. She regarded him, Howe's biographer wrote, as a "disreputable outlander underfoot all the time."[66] Eleanor, however, increasingly dependent upon him in her plans, had brought him to live in the tense and unhappy Roosevelt household. In the process, as Sara sharply pointed out to her adolescent granddaughter, Anna, she had been moved to a small fourth-floor room while Howe was given her old room on the third floor with a private bath.

Anna was ready for the old lady's petty prod. Earlier she had been hurt by her father in the irritations of his illness. This happened when, as James wrote, his father's "nerves were raw from his first experiment with the terrible imprisonment of the wheel chair plus the pressures of his own inner conflicts." He asked Anna to help him put away some books. She dropped them. In "a sudden, unreasonable fury," her father berated her.[67] There were other such incidents between the annoyed father and the sobbing girl.[68] These were only painful incidents compared to the explosive episode of Anna and Howe and the rooms.

"Someone," wrote Eleanor in evasive euphemism of her mother-in-law, "had suggested to her that it was unfair that she should have a little fourth-floor room and Mr. Howe should have the large room on the third floor front."[69]

Anna exploded to her mother as an unloved, mistreated child. The façade of determined cheerfulness by all in the crowded adjoining 65th Street houses was cracking. Eleanor, as she wrote, "always had a very bad tendency to shut up like a clam, particularly when things are going badly."[70] Yet in the face of the sick husband, the maneuvering mother-in-law, and the unhappy, adolescent daughter, suddenly one afternoon in the spring she went to pieces. As she was reading to her two youngest boys, she suddenly found herself sobbing and unable to stop. The little boys were amazed. Young Elliott came in from school and fled from the spectacle. Howe unsuccessfully tried to find out what was the matter. She wept through dinner, then found a vacant room in the adjoining house of her mother-in-law. At last she pulled herself together. There is no suggestion in her story as to where the immobile Franklin was in a house of tears, adult and juvenile.

The certainty is that he rose above the affliction of polio and the depression incident to it. Also he escaped from the violent tugs and pulls of emotion about him as a possibly defenseless center. In sickness as in health, Franklin Roosevelt was a complicated man despite his apparent extrovert exuberance (such a superior soap opera as *Sunrise at Campobello* notwithstanding). The perceptive Tugwell believed that "Franklin was never intimate in the ultimate sense with anyone, including Eleanor. . . . The place she made for herself in American life may have been a kind of substitute for the place in Franklin's life she never had. . . . Eleanor shared everything with Franklin that she was allowed to share and opened her faithful heart completely to his desires and needs. But Franklin himself did not possess the key to his own unconscious reticences, and there was very imperfect reciprocation."[71] So far as desires were concerned, there is reason to believe there was no reciprocation at all.[72] Francis Biddle, member of his class and his Cabinet, was even sharper in his analysis of Roosevelt's apartness. He wrote of "his capacity to wound those who loved him."[73]

Roosevelt went, as he wanted to go, the active way Eleanor and Howe urged upon him. Yet he never disdained his mother's wishes. Despite her supposed plan to immobilize him genteelly at Hyde Park, he was not resentful. Instead he kept his love for and relationship to this familiar place she provided for him to such an extent that as President one of his critics dubbed him the Country Squire in the White House. He declined with stubborn urbanity to be possessed by contestants. Twice on the same page of the second volume of her autobiography, Eleanor mentioned almost as excuse for what seemed to some to be his deviousness, his "dislike of being disagreeable."[74]

He disliked disagreeable surroundings. He had many reasons for recovery to full, active life. The gallantry with which he sought it deserves all the honor it has received. Yet sometimes the praise slipped beyond realism into an almost mystical legend-making. Frances Perkins, who as his Secretary of Labor more and more enjoyed the social pleasures of Washington, perhaps best stated the doctrine of the metamorphosis of the man.

"Franklin Roosevelt," she declared in her memoirs about him, "underwent a spiritual transformation during the years of his illness. I noticed when he came back that the years of pain and suffering had purged the slightly arrogant attitude he had displayed on occasion before he was stricken. The man emerged completely warm-hearted, with humility of spirit and with a deeper philosophy."[75] Such a legend may now be unalterable. Yet his son James, a sensitive fourteen-year-old boy at the time of his father's illness, rejected this revelation. He could not, he said, "accept the theory that Father would not have been a great man and a great public figure had he not gone through his personal Gethsemane. Indeed, I believe it was not polio that forged Father's character but that it was Father's character that enabled him to rise above the affliction."[76]

Some others believed that one incentive always in his mind but hid in reticence was Lucy Mercer, now married in Aiken. The

Henderson sisters, Elizabeth and Mary, believed that his affection for her was never interrupted, not even by what James called his Gethsemane. They also believed, however, that if Franklin and Lucy could have freely fulfilled their affection, he would have been happy but would never have become President of the United States: "She would not have pushed like Eleanor."[77]

Eleanor and Howe, of course (though only as aides to his own determination), saved him from the plan of his mother to make him and keep him the invalided country squire. He went back to the job Van Lear Black had saved for him and only a little more than casually to the practice of the law. With Howe's help he took on jobs which would keep his name in the papers and himself in political remembrance. He and Howe also dallied—sometimes dangerously—in a variety of moneymaking schemes. Meantime Eleanor expanded her political, business and charitable interests and activities apart from his. Franklin's vocation, however—by no means an avocation—was his activity in determination to learn to walk again. He got diverse treatment and plenty of advice. William G. McAdoo, who would marry his third wife after he was seventy, wrote him, "I cannot help but feel that you would be benefited by the gland treatment."[78] Franklin required no such esoteric cure, popular with aging men at the time. By late 1922, as Eleanor said, as a man only forty years old, he "was entirely well again and lived a normal life in every way, restricted only by his inability to walk."[79] Ten years later in a campaign biography Earle Looker reported the results of an examination of the cooperating Franklin by three eminent physicians. They summed up their findings: "We believe his powers of endurance are such as to allow him to meet all demands of private or public life."[80]

Certainly in 1922, unwilling to accept forever such inability, he turned often to the South and to serenity in the company of new friends and old ones—including later many children, victims as he was of polio. Eleanor did not care for the South. As a child her expectations about it had been built high by her great aunt, Mrs. James King Gracie, who, like her sister Mrs. Theodore Roosevelt the elder, had been a Bulloch of Georgia. The old lady had made her feel that life in the South must be gracious and easy and charming. It was a disappointment to Eleanor, she wrote, "to find that for many, many people life in the South was hard and poor and ugly, just as it is in parts of the North."[81] On Franklin's visits to the South she joined him briefly during these winter holidays which she regarded "as a necessity and not a pleasure." On the houseboat which he first tried in his quest for muscular development, she had a sinister feeling: "When we anchored at night and the wind blew, it all seemed eerie and menacing to me. The beauty of the moon and the stars only added to the strangeness of the dark waters and the tropic vegetation. . . ."[82]

Also while he fished and swam, she had begun to do a fairly regular job for the women's division of the Democratic State Committee, and was finding the work very satisfying. She had little time to spare on visits to the eerie and menacing land.

TEN

The Sheltered Life

(1)

"Mr. and Mrs. Rutherfurd will leave immediately for the former's home at Allamuchy, N.J.," had said the *New York Times* in reporting Lucy's wedding.[1] This took her from the dull Decatur Apartments where she had lived with her mother to an historic and princely estate, The great Rutherfurd House in this secluded area in the Allamuchy Mountains had been built by a member of the family generations before. . . .[2] In the thousand acres about it were lake and deer parks, mountain slopes. It was no mere retreat, however. The big place's name, Tranquility Farms, was justified not only by its rich serenity but also by productive fields. Some notion of its agricultural proportions was given later when five fire companies from nearby places like Hackettstown fought a fire all night in sixty-five tons of hay stored in one concrete barn. They dammed one of the brooks which ran across the estate to provide water for their fire fighting.[3]

Remote as Tranquility was, it was not always secure from dangers other than fire. Some years before Lucy came to mother Winthrop's athletic brood, sensation had been stirred by a reported threat by kidnapers, aware of the Morton and Rutherfurd fortunes, to abduct his two infant sons from the isolated estate.[4] No such crime occurred. Perhaps now the name Tranquility was justified for the house, its owner and his new wife in the terms of a statement from a book called *The Countryman's Year* which Eleanor Roosevelt applied to herself about this time: "Back of tranquillity lies always conquered unhappiness."[5]

Despite the sorrows that had come into his life before his marriage to Lucy, Winthrop Rutherfurd had in general spent a serene, if undramatic, career. Indeed, except for such inevitables as death and taxes, the troubles he had faced were only occasional irritating details involving his dogs. Just a year before he married Lucy, as a member of the Westminster Kennel Club he had been in some sort of quarrel with the American Kennel Club. A writer about society, not dogs, reported that he was involved in what might be a "serious crossing of swords" between the two organizations since the A.K.C., now had the control of judges and was in a position to be "actual dictator to the only real runners of a first class dog show in all America."

"Winthrop Rutherfurd," this report said, "does not relish being made to eat the leek, forced upon him by the A.K.C. officials entirely below his status both in knowledge of high bred dogs and general sportsmanship."[6]

Apparently in the interest of tranquillity, Rutherfurd who belonged to the class of breeders who sometimes paid $1500 for a fox terrier, consented to apply for an A.K.C. license. No better judge was available for the fox and Irish terriers.

Rutherfurd definitely did not keep Lucy by the kennels at Allamuchy. He maintained a residence in New York. Also in 1921, *The Preferred List Washington and Vicinity* gave his address as "Graystone" on Klingle Road.[7] Republican that she was, the fastidious Mrs. Larz Anderson moaned that in Harding's Washington "the capital had got into the hands of real-estate men, calling themselves 'realtors,' and booming the city as if it were some new Western town. All the beauty and dignity were gone. Huge tenements, cheaply built and ungainly, were rising in every direction, even in the residential portion."[8] Not all change was jerry-built. In the oldest residential portion about Lafayette Square conservative citizens, backing the then hardly needed pres-

THE SHELTERED LIFE 211

sures of business on government, were already constructing on the
old Eustis-Corcoran House site the temple-like structure of the
Chamber of Commerce of the United States. It was designed by
Cass Gilbert, pompous, good salesman architect, who also designed the monumental Supreme Court Building which seemed
too gaudy to an old Justice like Brandeis. Perhaps, though quietly,
change was also marked in old Washington when, as the U. S.
Chamber building was constructed, W. C. Eustis, horseman, Cave
Dweller and Pershing aide, died in New York on November 25,
1921, on his way to visit his family at the Morton estate in Dutchess County. His death came, it was stated, from a recurrence of
pneumonia contracted in France during the recent war. Certainly
his ties with the recent past in Washington were marked by the
presence by his deathbed of the handsome physician, Admiral
Grayson.

Behind Indiana limestone and Vermont marble façades, however, Washington and its society were grossly altering. This was
not yet true of Klingle Road, which ran briefly wooded and protected by a few large estates, such as The Causeway of the rich
James Parmelees of Cleveland, from Woodley Road into Rock
Creek Park. Certainly this almost rural lane in a city was secluded
from the new capital which the young Dean Acheson, then private
secretary to Justice Brandeis, saw as one in which "the gilded
broom had swept the White House clean of any lingering taint
of professional intellectuality."

Graystone was far from the rumors Acheson heard "of a scene
at the house on McPherson Square of the publisher of the *Washington Post*, Ned McLean, when Secretary Hughes found that a
party for the Cabinet was to be entertained by movies of a Demp-
sey championship fight, illegally transported in interstate commerce." Klingle Road remained apart from the world in which, as
the future Secretary of State reported "A young woman of doubtful reputation had her skull bashed in—it was said by a bottle—in
an equally doubtful hotel, after a riotous party allegedly attended
by some who might more profitably have spent the night gathering strength for official duties."[9]

Alice Longworth, who heard similar rumors, reported that "no rumor could have exceeded the reality." At a White House reception she went, in response to an invitation and out of curiosity, upstairs to the President's study. She found "the air heavy with tobacco smoke, trays with bottles containing every imaginable brand of whisky stood about, cards and poker chips ready at hand —a general atmosphere of waistcoat unbuttoned, feet on the desk, and the spittoon alongside."[10]

The Rutherfurds on Klingle Road were hardly aware of such official society in 1921, or when in 1922, according to the Washington social directory, they had a place at 4445 Massachusetts Avenue. Oddly, the not always infallible *Social Register* in the same year also listed this as the residence of the Prince and Princess Antoine Bibesco. The Prince, as long-time Roumanian minister in London, had married Elizabeth Asquith, daughter of the former British Prime Minister. The Bibescos were acquaintances of the Franklin Roosevelts "from Washington's diplomatic circle," as their son reported later.[11] In 1921 Franklin, calling the Princess "Elizabeth," possibly described her well. When the Bibescos were visiting at Campobello in July that fated year, one of the children's nurses, Mademoiselle Thiel, fell overboard while sailing. Franklin commented: "I wish Elizabeth had fallen off the *Vireo* instead of Mlle. I think she would float quite high out of the water!"[12] The Princess did float quite high in letters and society. She dedicated not only her books but individual short stories in them to important personages, one notably to Alice Longworth.

Such persons in such a society did not keep the Rutherfurds much in Washington. Violetta now had a place for her mother, and Minnie, though not ready for the chimney corner, could be useful in helping with the little Marbury boy born in the year of Lucy's marriage. In Aiken the Rutherfurds found the activities, the atmosphere and the society they required.

Change was coming also in that old center of the quiet but physically strenuous rich—but slowly, almost imperceptibly beside its riding paths, polo fields, golf course. There young Tommy Hitchcock was only beginning to become the world's most famous polo player, though already at the war's end, as a veteran aviator of eighteen, debutantes had begged his aunt Edith Eustis to have him visit her in Washington during the holidays as a "picturesque figure." The winter community in South Carolina kept its traditions and its barriers. Ladies and gentlemen spending their energies in the outdoors wanted no night clubs or night club society. Drinking in the great houses and some ostentatiously modest ones out along Whiskey Road was restricted to decorous cocktail parties. Many of the householders came from such similar summertime centers of rich men's sport as Westbury, Long Island, near which the Hitchcocks had kennels and stables, and Pride's Crossing, Massachusetts. Pride's Crossing, with its Myopia Hunt Club, was a scene almost set for the study of the sociology of the overprivileged. "Gussie" Gardner had had his principal estate there. Such overendowed wise men as Henry Adams and Justice Holmes had places nearby. Franklin Roosevelt on a number of occasions played golf there, at the Essex County Country Club, with Livy Davis.[13]

Wealth at Aiken was by no means the only criterion, though plenty of it was indicated by such names as Harry Payne Whitney, John Jacob Astor, James J. Hill, W. K. Vanderbilt and others who came early to enjoy its playing fields and bridle paths.[14] Yet skill and sportsmanship, good manners and good taste counted more. The wealth which nevertheless marked the place came from as wide a range as banking, manufacturing and a fortune derived from the Pinkerton detective agency. A map of the exclusive colony gave space to only ninety-five homes.[15] Opulent people gave their places cute names: Mouse Trap, Prickly Pear, Scanty Shanty, Sunny Corner, Calico Cottage, Horsehaven, Cocktail Cottage, Tea Tray, the Black Stables. The presiding place, more sedately named Mon Repose, was the home of Mrs. Thomas Hitchcock, Sr., who as a Eustis was a founder and guardian of the sporting community. Naturally as the sister-in-law of Rutherfurd's first wife she welcomed him to Aiken. She welcomed him also as a fellow breeder of thoroughbred dogs. She had her beagles; her husband fox hounds. Lucy was welcomed not only as Rutherfurd's young wife but for her loveliness and charm.

The property and the town seemed made for the Rutherfurd household. Apparently the house which he originally bought from the Gardner estate was not the stately, fireproof mansion he later constructed on the site. Fire was a hazard at Aiken as at Allamuchy. Not long after the Rutherfurds were settled there, the Hitchcock house, Mon Repose, burned. It was rebuilt and blessed by the priest of the Catholic Church the Rutherfurds attended.

Constance Lodge Gardner, widow of the rich belligerent Republican Congressman and polo player, had wanted the place no longer. Like Alice Longworth, apparently she preferred the society of Washington. Both had become early figures of the new, free women, supposedly developed only in the gay twenties. Both despised what they regarded as middle class pruderies. Alice discarded corsets long before that became a general custom shocking to some elders. Constance was a steady cigarette smoker when many disapproved.[16] Still Alice in particular kept friends in Aiken. In a sense it was a Rooseveltian as well as a Eustis sort of place. Not only was Franklin's half brother one of the first visitors to its exclusive though unostentatious hotel. Nick Longworth made annual visits to friends there. In the year in which the Rutherfurds planned their move, Theodore Roosevelt's daughter, Ethel, and her husband, Dr. Richard Derby, in ill health came to Aiken as the restorative resort it had originally been considered. One articulate native, a lady real estate agent named Eulalie Salley, long afterward said that in the years ahead Franklin Roosevelt often visited there. The rumor that he did was prevalent later. Mrs. Salley, as one Aiken resident put it, "used to brag that FDR came to Aiken in a private car." Despite his prominence no newspapers ever mentioned such visits. Local railroad employees and others were sure that he never came.[17]

What a place it was for the young Rutherfurds! There they became amateur golfers deserving national notice on sports pages. They rode, hunted, played polo. In addition to their Aiken acquired skills, young Winthrop and Hugo were to become "nationally known as oarsmen." Alice matched her brothers on the links. Hugo as a boy grew to the interests and skills which later made him the leader of an expedition to photograph African natives and wildlife for the American Museum of Natural History. Old Winthrop became member, director and historian of the Palmetto Golf Club. He contributed to the building of a steeplechase course. Lucy was the much loved lady of Ridgeley Hall, adjoining the big Dolan place, inadequately labeled as Calico Cottage. On the turf and under the pines the young Rutherfurds shared their father's interests and basked in their stepmother's graces. Lucy began her marriage as a mother. Then, on June 14, 1922, she bore her own child—a girl named Barbara.

Unlike her mother this daughter was born to the sheltered life.

(2)

In Franklin Roosevelt's "inability to run around," there were, wrote Ernest K. Lindley, "compensating advantages which in time became a really powerful asset." This perceptive first biographer of FDR explained, "He had an excellent excuse not to do what he did not wish to do."[18] Except for the use of his legs, however, he could do all that he had done or wished to do in the years before. He was at no one's beck and call. Others had to meet him on his own ground. In a sense he was not only immobilized but enthroned. Pity he could push aside. From demands he could retreat, if he wished, with excuses of health or, if he otherwise wished, demonstrate amazing vitality. He did not always need to be the captive that he seemed. Still he could count on acceptance of that notion when it served him.

He let the legends grow which pleased him. One which flourished—and flourishes still—was the myth that from his illness—a disease which, he noted, in 75 percent of the cases struck children[19]—he emerged transformed from the playboy to the philosopher. He had never been mere playboy; he never really assumed the solemnity of the patriarch. In his sickness he showed fortitude. In his recovery (generally a delusion so far as his legs were concerned), he demonstrated determination. In neither did he ever lose his gaiety, his zest for life and his liking for the companionship of congenial spirits, many of whom were not generally concerned with good works or great causes. One symbol of such lively folk was certainly Livy Davis.

Eleanor, as she had testily decided in Paris, did not like Davis, perhaps because he was her antithesis in practically everything. He has seemed to historians an inconsequential character in the Roosevelt story. Some intimate guardians of the Roosevelt legends described him as a vulgar person inclined to indecent exposure whom FDR was only too glad to dismiss from his companionship. Possibly FDR might have better liked a better man. But Livy cannot be disregarded. He was personally and psychologically important to FDR particularly in the days of his hope that he might become mobile again.

Permanent as was the injury to Franklin's legs, his acute illness was brief. Before he was brought, supposedly in as much secrecy as possible, from Campobello to New York, he was already corresponding about old interests and plans for the future. Freidel wrote that his mental rehabilitation came "by the end of the first week of his illness."[20] In the hospital in New York he was even more active in communications. When he came home from the hospital to the 65th Street house he was in effect well in all respects except his mobility. By April 1922, he had achieved crutches and braces, which despite his efforts were to be his essential aids for the rest of his life. He went to Boston in July to be fitted for better braces and there told Bertie Hamlin that "he was gaining very surely."[21] Without any intention of becoming Sara's invalid squire he went to Hyde Park for the summer, swimming regularly in the pool of his friend and neighbor Vincent Astor. A man, for months alive and alert in all but his legs, late in 1922 he arranged to lease a houseboat, the *Weona II*, for rest and relaxation, fishing

and swimming in what he hoped would be therapeutic Florida
waters. This cruise was to be followed by similar ones on a houseboat, the *Larooco*, which he bought in partnership with a Boston
friend, John S. Lawrence, who also had troubles with his legs.
These cruises continued in the winters of 1924, 1925 and 1926.
They served his morale; they brought him also into a life sheltered from family contentions. He was away from his mother's
domination, though his loving letters to her indicated no resentment of her plans to rusticate him. Similarly he was much away
from the energetic Eleanor who "came down only twice during
the three years."[22]

In Florida in the midst of its boom, he saw some political personages, notably James M. Cox and William Jennings Bryan. The
Larooco was big enough to accommodate a reception for William
Green, president of the American Federation of Labor, and thirty
labor movement companions. Roosevelt preferred the company of
Florida natives in Tavernier, a village named after a pirate, to
that of the wintering elite of Palm Beach where he found "the
growth of mushroom millionaires' houses luxuriant." He added of
that rich man's resort in the gay log he kept, on February 17,
1924: "The women we saw went well with the place—and we de-
sired to meet them no more than we wished to remain in the
harbor an hour more than necessary."[23]

Most of his own houseboat companions, however, were no ple-
beians. Some by birth and purse could afford to scorn Palm Beach.
Old Dutchess County and Harvard men and women friends, they
were agreeable companions disinclined to bring solemn problems
into what Roosevelt described as "this somewhat negligée existence." Possibly he shocked Sara a little by his report that "all wan-
der around in pajamas, nighties and bathing suits!"[24] Yet oddly
a picture of Roosevelt as the ultra respectable convalescent was
given by his son James and his collaborator Sidney Shallett. He—
or they—wrote that Livy Davis "offended Father's sense of pro-
priety"[25] on the second day of his visit in March and April 1924,
"and there is no indication in the log that, despite their long and
close friendship, he ever was invited back."[26] Livy had arrived,

apparently much to Franklin's joy, on March 16, 1924, "weighed down with sundry wet and dry goods" but looking like a sick child "and is recuperating from shingles, boils, bunions and cold in the head."[27] Evidently Franklin was exaggerating as he must have been on the following day when he made the entry in the log which James quoted:

> Mon. March 17th [1924]
>   Water too cold to swim & wind too high to go to reef—L.D. went to the R.R. bridge & came back minus trousers—to the disgust of the two ladies. Earlier he had exercised on the top deck á la nature. Why do people who must take off their clothes go anywhere where the other sex is present? Captain Morris remarked quietly that some men get shot for less.[28]

Certainly this was an austere entry. Also this was strange behavior by Livy whose modesty before native women in Haiti had seemed hilarious to Franklin and companions six years before. The certain thing is that James was wrong in his statement that a morally outraged Roosevelt dropped his old friend Livy from his companionship. The record suggests, indeed, that in Roosevelt's affliction Livy was often his good friend and gay aide as he had been back in their active war days. On this occasion he stayed over a week after the supposedly disgusting self-display. Indeed, three days later when a heavy storm involved the *Larooco* in difficulties ("Hell to pay"), FDR's log said with approval, "Davis got the awning off but had to disrobe to do it as it was raining."[29] When Davis departed on April 5, the wife of the recently outraged Captain Morris waved a towel at him in apparently fond farewell.[30]

Later that same year, in August, Mrs. Hamlin made a note of their seagoing companionship in Northern waters. A month earlier Bertie had noted the appearance of Franklin as he nominated Alfred E. Smith for the presidency as "the Happy Warrior." Happy and thrilled she wrote: "Franklin stood at the desk at the platform as if nothing was wrong with him—his fine height and superb head showing in silhouette from where we sat."[31] Pundits added their applause to Mrs. Hamlin's description. Mark Sullivan described his speech as "a noble utterance." Walter Lippmann, who was later to belittle him as presidential material, wrote him, "I am utterly hard-boiled about speeches, but yours seemed to be perfect in temper and manner and most eloquent in its effects." In retrospect Freidel thought the crippled Roosevelt's dramatic delivery of the speech inspired such warm admiration for him as to help make him the most popular figure at the convention.[32]

Now a month later he was in seagoing garb on the Massachusetts shore with Livy. Mrs. Woodrow Wilson and Edith Helm were visiting Mrs. Hamlin at her Mattapoisett house. She wrote, "When we returned (from our drive) we found Livingston Davis waiting for us—he & Franklin Roosevelt were anchored in the harbor in a small sail yacht with a gas launch. We had thought they might turn up as a lot of mail had come addressed to Franklin in our care. We all went out to see them and found Franklin looking finely—he had been in for a swim."[33]

How much the two old friends saw each other in the months following is not clear. On March 7, 1926, however, Franklin wrote his mother from "Near Long Key" a letter of condolence about the sudden death of Sara's sister, Annie Delano Hitch. "Her passing," he wrote, "[is] as I would have mine be." In the same letter he noted his anticipation of the probable arrival of Livy on the 15th. Obviously despite James' report Livy had been invited back. Obviously also FDR was disappointed on March 12 when he wrote, "Livy wires from Nassau he cannot come."[34]

The two friends had been in correspondence about Roosevelt's life and plans. A year before, on April 25, 1925, he wrote Livy about big investment, involving more than two thirds of his fortune, in his new enterprise for health and happiness for himself and other polio victims in Warm Springs, Georgia. Eleanor, who disliked the South and feared Franklin's inclination to speculation, had taken a dim view of this adventurous development of the old run-down Georgia resort with its pool of natural warm waters. Roosevelt's enthusiasm was not dampened by her fears.[35]

"You would howl with glee," he wrote Livy, "if you could see the clinic in operation at the side of the pool, and the patients doing various exercises in the water under my leadership—they are male and female of all ages and weights."

Clearly he knew while writing gaily that he could count on Davis' serious sympathy.

"In addition to all this I am consulting architect and landscape engineer for the Warm Springs Co.—am giving free advice on the moving of buildings, the building of roads, setting out of trees and remodelling the hotel. We, i.e., the Company plus F.D.R., are working out a new water system, new sewage plan, fishing pond, and tomorrow we hold an organization meeting to start the Pine Mountain Club which will run the dance hall, tea room, picnic grounds, golf course and other forms of indoor and outdoor sports. I sometimes wish I could find some spot on the globe where it was not essential and necessary for me to start something new—a sand bar in the ocean might answer, but I would probably start building a sea wall around it and digging for pirate treasure in the middle."[36]

Actually he had found the retreat he wanted where he could not only devote himself to the improvement of his legs but also for sufficient intervals escape—without losing touch—from the pressures of politics, business and multiple good causes seeking his labors and his name. It was his sand bar in an often troubled sea.

True, the busy Eleanor did not like the place. Her visits there, as her son wrote, were only "sporadic."[37] Howe, she said, paid only occasional visits to Warm Springs.[38] Of his New York entourage his most constant companion was his secretary Marguerite LeHand, called "Missy," who had been his secretary since the 1920 campaign. Young and pretty, though delicate from rheumatic fever as a child, she was permitted to take little exercise.[39] She managed, however, to look after many of Franklin's needs as well as his correspondence without ever giving Eleanor any sense of jealousy. Also she had a gaiety which Eleanor lacked and sometimes distrusted. Possibly aware that Missy later arranged for convivial parties for FDR away from austerities in Eleanor's household, the wife came to feel that the secretary who "liked a good time" occasionally let her social contacts get "mixed with her work and made it hard for her and others."[40] Warm Springs in its most primitive state did not disturb Missy's city sensibilities. Eleanor frankly preferred expanding activities in New York to long stays in Warm Springs. She and Franklin made a "joint decision" that she would "pursue her activities in the East" and he would "spend as much time as he could in Warm Springs."[41]

"I remember," Eleanor wrote of Warm Springs, "the first house we lived in and my surprise that I could look through the cracks and see daylight. I can also remember driving with Miss LeHand one day to a nearby town to buy some chickens and my perfect horror when I learned I had to take them home alive, instead of killed and dressed. At Hyde Park there were chickens in the farmyard, but that was a mile away from the house and I didn't hear them being killed. In Warm Springs they ran around in our yard, until the cook wrung their necks amid much squawking and put them in the pot. Somehow I didn't enjoy eating them!"[42]

The Warm Springs to which Franklin went in first hope certainly did not resemble Aiken, half a day's drive away. Yet he enjoyed the taste of the whole countryside. He liked the attentions paid him by Georgians. Among polio victims at Warm Springs, many of them far worse off than himself, his ebullience and confidence made him the one-eyed who was king in the land of the blind. Sometimes he spoke of the rural South in such praise as to seem to dangerously downgrade New York.[43] Still he welcomed attentions from New York politicians indicating their faith in his voter appeal. Sometimes the sheltered life seemed only a device to permit him to determine political timing for the fulfillment of his ultimate ambitions. In 1924, 1926, and 1928 he put his appealing image behind the fortunes of Al Smith and built his own appeal in the process.

Yet, confidential letters to him from Howe, who understood his predilections, indicated the ineradicable differences between Roosevelt of Hyde Park and Smith and other politicians from the sidewalks of New York. In the winter before the tumultuous convention of 1924 Howe reported: "I took lunch with some of the

Albany boys and they told me in one way at least Smith is much drier than he used to be. How long he has sworn off for this time, God knows. Let us trust until after the National Convention."[44] And the year after that convention Howe sent word: "Mrs. Smith is back from Europe and complains to your 'Missus' that there are too many ruins in Rome. She is talking too much for Al's good, describing with much gusto and detail their special audience with the Pope and how he referred to Al as his son and the great knowledge he displayed on the political campaign."[45] Later FDR realized that this feeling of snobbery down could be matched by snobbery up. When he reluctantly agreed to run for Governor in New York in 1928, to help Smith's national ticket with the upstate New York vote, he found that he was treated by top Smith aides "as though I was one of those pieces of window dressing that had to be borne with because of a certain political value in non-New York City areas."[46]

Irrelevant as he has seemed to historians, very possibly at this time Livy Davis appeared to FDR as a man more to be envied than Al Smith or any other politicians on the apparent rise.

A person then as before anxious to make money, Roosevelt found Livy, as Livy described himself, almost the model of the man who made money without really trying. Perhaps Davis exaggerated his easy rise to riches in a report to his fellows in the Harvard Class of '04. There must have been inherited money behind a young man who had made nine trips to Europe before entering Harvard.[47] But he told a lively tale of his acquisition of opulence.

"Upon graduation," he told his classmates, "I started as general utility office and errand boy in the office of George Mixter, note broker, in Boston. Became partner—he supplying the money and I the legs—in 1908, and upon his death in 1910, took over the business in my own name. By luck and good fortune the business and profits grew, so that in January 1917, it was merged with Bond and Griffin, with which firm I was identified until, on account of changing methods of financing corporations, note broking died, and left me like a driver of a horse car in the streets of New York in those days of modern locomotion.

"Not being able to sell bonds, I left Bond and Griffin . . . and since have had desk room with friends endeavoring to discover a line in the present disturbed condition of New England industry which would be attractive to pursue. While a main endeavor may be lacking, there are many of secondary import, being a director in the Boston & Albany, Chester & Becket, Norwich & Worcester, Vermont & Massachusetts and Ware River Railroads, Nashawena Mills, trustee of the Provident Institution for Saving and Trustee for several estates."

Such business activity seemed almost a side line. He was engaged in such intellectual activities as Roosevelt might still pursue as active member of the American Antiquarian Society, the American Meteorological Society, the Royal Meteorological Society of Great Britain and the Visiting Committee of the Harvard Board of Overseers. He kept up his interest in the Navy, the Island of Haiti, and Central Europe to which he had gone when he left Franklin's staff in Paris in 1919.

Yet to the man only hoping for the use of his legs in the warm water pool in Georgia, Livy's physical activities must have seemed treasures greater than his wealth. Franklin could still sail, hoisted in and hoisted out of a boat. But Livy—

"Besides my own boats I have raced in interclub matches, and through the courtesy of friends, have raced on every type of boat from large schooners to 'brutal beasts,' in many waters from the Great Lakes to the Bahamas; and have cruised every foot of the way, barring the few miles from Havre de Grace to Annapolis on the Chesapeake, from Halifax around Cape Sable through the Bay of Fundy southward along the coast, and through the canals to and around Cape Sable, Florida, and up the West Coast to the Chokaloskee River, and also the Bahamas—happy memories of all kinds of boats, boon companions, infinite variety of sea, scenery, and weather, and divers adventures."

The sea and sailing were not all:

"Took up riding to hounds, but after three years discovered that in order to attain adequate cooperative functioning between horse and rider all other activities would have to be subordinated.

"Golf, boat racing, and curling are marvellous sports when competing with one's cronies, but when the opponents are men of another nationality—to have the stars and stripes sewed on your mainsail and a foreign flag on the other fellow's—certainly quickens the zest. For several years I have been pitted annually against the Canadians in these sports—in Canada the alternative years—and hereby recommend international competitive sports for the agenda of any Peace society, and to any individual."

Livy mentioned no troubles. Instead he was looking ahead. "Am at present," he wrote, "struggling to get settled in a new house just built in Brookline with enough land around it to keep me fit for years to come in combatting weeds and pests, and in propagating plants, shrubs and flowering trees."[48]

Franklin seemed to have enough land to occupy him too. He had a car with special handles, instead of pedals, in which he could ride about it. Also he had servants and friends who could help him aboard the train when New York affairs required him. Such affairs did not always concern politics or business. In the winter of 1924–25 he had a ceremonial role to play as the father of a debutante. Anna was eighteen then. Franklin and Eleanor gave an elaborate dinner for her at their 65th Street house. Later a large dance was given for her by proud old Sara at the Colony Club. The social world Anna was entering seemed gay and charming, apparently little changed since the more formal time when Eleanor had been presented to select, certain society at a big party at Sherry's. At Anna's parties Franklin was the much-tanned captain of the *Larooco*, in the pale city for the occasion. Already then there were rumors, emanating from the South, that he was again seeing Lucy Mercer.[49] They were only vague whispers, but in a family in which whispers could be loud. Even in the jazz age, as was long before said of children, little pitchers had big ears. Young and old seemed undisturbed. All the Roosevelts made a decorous display of unaltered tradition as the young of the twenties danced at Anna's party and to old Sara's music.

(3)

"The traditions some of us love best" which Sara had stoutly defended in 1917 seemed guarded in no sheltered life in the twenties. The most respectable old brownstones had become speakeasies. Even old Washington now accepted Elinor Wylie as a poetess, not a pariah. Exhilaration, not exile, sent her to New York. Her divorce from frayed Horace Wylie seemed only an anticlimax involving leaving an old man as she had left a young one. Her marriage to William Rose Benét, a lesser poet than herself, made no music. There was sympathy when a stroke paralyzed her face and marred her beauty. There was no surprise when she died, as many thought, by flinging herself down a staircase. It took the reticence about that, the suggestion imposed on history that she suffered a second stroke,[50] to arouse the gossips at all.

Still there were households in which prevailed the splendid decencies, the stratified codes, of the society of which Edith Wharton was the historian. One, of course, was the Roosevelt family in which in none of its branches had divorce ever occurred. It was not immune. When Franklin was first recovering from the polio, in the autumn of 1921, Eleanor's sister-in-law, Hall's wife Margaret Richardson, bore her fourth child, a lively little girl named Eleanor, too, after her aunt. Then in the winter following, Hall appeared in New York and in a manner which his sister sensed was ominous asked her to go out to dinner with him.

Hall, then around thirty, was a mountain of a man but one about whom his family always said, "He's just a boy at heart."[51] His sister regarded him almost as a son and a son in whom she took great pride. She realized that he had never had to work very hard but had great powers of concentration. "He could," she wrote, "work in a room filled with people all talking and laughing, and apparently be oblivious to their presence."[52] Very often, however, he led the laughing and talking, sometimes with a glass in his hand. Yet he had done well as an engineer after his brilliant career at Harvard. He had worked for the Guggenheims in mines near Dawson City in the Yukon where, as Eleanor felt, far from civilization they had had a baby named Henry Parish Roosevelt.[53]

Now as the father of four, Hall took Eleanor to a small restaurant. There with other people crowded at tables about them, he told her he had decided to get a divorce. As she related the incident she told more about herself than about Hall and his wife. While she said she saw the sides of both, she made it clear that the trouble came, she thought, from Margaret's inability to keep up with Hall's brilliant mind.[54] However, her thoughts as he talked were sharply self-revealing. She recalled a remark long before by the much respected mother of one of her own bridesmaids: "If you love a person, you can forgive the big things. But if the little things of life are always wrong, if another person's mannerisms or some peculiar trait or characteristic irritates you, it becomes something which is beyond endurance. It is the little things that make life unbearable, not the big things."

More significantly she wrote: "I knew what this would mean to the family, all of whom believed that when you made your bed you had to lie in it."[55]

As Hall indicated, this was a view in process of revision not only in the family but around it. At almost this very same time it was common gossip in Boston that Mrs. Alice Gardiner Davis had left Livy and was staying at the Beacon Street home of her parents, the Robert H. Gardiners. The "exclusive set" was concluding that the separation was final. This seemed sad to some because Alice Davis in her marriage to Livy had found a husband "of a position as exceptional as her own and an acknowledged factor in smart clubs of New York and Washington as well as Boston."[56] Their divorce, however, did not long seem shocking in the Roosevelt family. When, in 1927, Livy married the former Mrs. Georgia Appleton of New York, FDR wrote casually to his mother about it,

"I wish much I could get on for Livy's wedding in Bar Harbor, but I am to lunch with them in New York on Friday."[57]

Far greater attention was paid in America to the annulment by the Sacred Rota of the Catholic Church of the marriage of Consuelo Vanderbilt and the Duke of Marlborough. The Duchess had secured her legal divorce from the diminutive Duke in 1921. The annulment was essential to her marriage to a French gentleman of a devout Catholic family. What aroused American attention in New York, Aiken, and other social scenes was the report from Rome that the Rota had acted because when seventeen, Consuelo had been forced to marry the Duke by her mother though she was in love with "an American named Rutherfurd." The *New York Times* at the time reported Lucy as saying that they had received many calls but they preferred "not to make any statement."[58] In its obituary of Rutherfurd later, however, it quoted Rutherfurd himself as saying when this news came "Yes, some thirty years ago I knew Miss Vanderbilt and I was one of her great admirers."[59] The incident at the time seemed more nostalgic than sensational. Momentarily at sixty-four, it made Winthrop seem a romantic figure once again, as the handsome lover set aside for the titled Englishman. Even among the austere (save the few always ready to see the Catholic Church as subservient to the rich), it was a matter to be regarded less with a grimace than a grin. That was evidently the case in the Catholic Rutherfurd household and among the Rutherfurd friends.

Much less routine were the romantic fortunes of Franklin's wartime friend, Nigel Law. From Washington he had been transferred to duty in the British Embassy in Paris. There the lady he met and loved was no lovely, unattached social secretary but the wife of the British Minister Plenipotentiary under whom he served. Apparently much younger than her husband, Sir Joshua Milne Cheetham, she was Anastasia, daughter of M. N. Mouranieff, Russian Ambassador to Rome in the first decade of the century. She and Cheetham were married in 1907. She bore him a son in 1910, when they were living in Cairo. During his service in Egypt, from 1910 to 1921, Anastasia attained a fame of her own.

When World War I engulfed the Middle East in 1914, she joined the Red Cross working in hospitals throughout the tragic Gallipoli campaign. A year or so later she was appointed Principal Red Cross Commandant in the East. This involved organizing all the varied Red Cross activities in Egypt and Palestine. She managed to do this without giving up work in hospitals as well. Several times she was mentioned in dispatches. She was decorated by the king when she was honored as a Commander of the Order of the British Empire by the British Government. The head of the ancient Order of St. John of Jerusalem made her a Dame of Grace of the Order "for service in the cause of humanity."[60] When her husband was transferred to Paris in January 1921, she was not only a woman of prestige in her own right but still a beautiful lady as well.

It is sad that the love story of Nigel Law and Anastasia was told only as the aging Sir Joshua brought it into court in terms of suspicions, discovered letters and the reports of chambermaids and inquiry agents. Still more romance than guilt marks the letters from his subordinate to his wife which Sir Joshua found and produced in court. In them Law addressed Anastasia Lady Cheetham as "Darling," "Dearest," "My Nastia." He told her how much he missed her while "minding the shop" and pretending to interest in South American loans and defaulting governments. "Oh! Nastia," he wrote of his longing for her.[61]

Sir Joshua got his divorce. Apparently despite his spreading of the story in the court and the papers, he made provision for his former wife. Perhaps he was ready for a change from the able, younger and passionate Anastasia. A year after his divorce he was married again to a lady with the less exotic name of Cynthia whose father was a knight commander of the Order of the Bath. Nigel, whose ardor was evidently embarrassing to the sedate Foreign Office, was listed as unemployed after October 1, 1922, which was before the divorce suit was tried. In May 1929, however, *The Times* reported: "A marriage between Mr. Nigel Law and Anastasia Lady Cheetham was celebrated quietly in London yesterday."[62] They lived quietly at "High Trees, Chalfont St. Peter, Bucks," and apparently happily ever after.

After he left America, Law had lost touch with Roosevelt "except for an occasional exchange of letters usually at Christmas."

"I always regretted," the Englishman wrote, "that I was never able to accept his invitation to stay with him at the White House when he was President."[63]

The presidency was only an incalculable possibility with Franklin in these years. His ambition, he often indicated, first involved his legs. As the twenties passed he wrote to the same classmates Livy had informed about his activities. Franklin was Governor of New York, however, when he wrote for the 25th anniversary report of his class. He was less exuberant than Livy though much more in the public eye. He wrote:

"During the past three years I have devoted much time to the establishment of the Georgia Warm Springs Foundation for the treatment of infantile paralysis, arthritis, etc., and the results obtained seem to be increasingly satisfactory.

"In 'home affairs' I have been very happily married since 1905 and the circle includes a daughter, four strapping sons and one granddaughter who must be very nearly if not quite the eldest grandchild of the Class. I find time at home to practice forestry, as I would rather plant trees than cut them down; also to collect books, manuscripts and prints and to delve into naval history and the local records of my home county. Outside of two slim volumes and various magazine articles, I have deferred serious writing until after the Class of 1904 has had its 50th reunion. I may have more leisure time then."[64]

Not even Franklin Roosevelt could count on that much time. Livy Davis had less. To "Dear Old Liv" Franklin turned jubilantly when he was chosen as Grand Marshal for the Harvard Commencement in 1929. "I assure you," he wrote, "that being Governor is nothing in comparison. I expect to call on you a million times before commencement. Come to Albany if you can, any time."[65]

A year later he was not so anxious for Livy's aid. Indeed, in an answer to a letter from Davis which he had delayed writing until he could find "a quiet moment," Franklin seemed to regard what Livy must have intended as help as an intrusion to be lightly dismissed. Livy had written that a friend of his would like to write a biography of the rising Roosevelt. But now on the sea of politics Franklin was moving with crowded sail.

There was no law against Livy's friend writing such a book, he said. Then he added: "However, there are some six or eight other scribes in the field at the present moment and from present appearances it looks as if sometime this summer there will appear simultaneously on all news stands and in all book shops a whole library of authentic, imaginative or apocryphal stories concerning my daily habits in the last forty-nine years.

"Of course, if this friend of yours insists, he may see me for fourteen and a half minutes and I will tell him the story of my life in that period. I doubt if I could give him the other half minute."[66]

It is doubtful that Livy asked for it. Another year went 'round. Then on January 12, 1932, the month in which FDR at the head of the field of candidates formally announced for the presidency, Livy went to "the woodshed" of the estate in Brookline where he had enough land to keep him "fit for years to come in combatting weeds and pests, and in propagating plants, shrubs and flowering trees." He shot himself there. His obituary spoke of him as "one of Brookline's wealthiest citizens." In his will he left $1000 to FDR "in grateful remembrance of joyful comradeship."[67]

ELEVEN

Meridian Hill

(1)

Like the booming nineteen twenties, 16th Street swept up in steep ascent to Meridian Hill to which so many embassies and legations had moved. There the mansion at 1624 Crescent Place looked like a fortress. It had been built in the pre-income tax days of 1911 by Henry White, rich, able, and personable diplomat, who had married Margaret, the eldest of the handsome Rutherfurd girls whom Edith Wharton had made her models. They enjoyed it briefly before Margaret's death in 1916. Then it had been available as guest house for such visiting wartime personages as Marshal Joffre and Premier Viviani.

Now in the late twenties it was the residence of Eugene Meyer who had come as wartime dollar-a-year man under Wilson. He had remained as man rich enough to indulge an inclination for public service and official society, rising on the government financial escalator, presided over by Secretary of the Treasury Andrew Mellon, to become under Hoover Governor of the Federal Reserve Board. Meyer and his pretty, earnest wife, Agnes, had no purpose to make the house a scene for a social battle. Certainly they did not mean to provide for Alice Longworth a stage which, in her sometimes magic seeming fashion, she could scorn and dominate at the same time.

Alice was at or near—possibly she feared beyond—her meridian at the beginning of the Hoover administration. Her hope of another Roosevelt administration under her brother, Theodore, Jr., in which she might be a less beneficent Auntie Bye, had been dashed when young Ted had been defeated for Governor of New York, in 1924, by Al Smith. She would not soon forget that her cousin Eleanor had helped in that business. Still new hopes rose. She and her Nick had come to joint triumph in 1925. Then he was elected Speaker of the House, and she, almost as one not to be outdone, produced at the age of forty-one and after two decades of marriage, their only child, a much loved little girl named Paulina.

The Longworth prospect seemed as bright as that of the soaring Stock Market. Nick encouraged no speculation, however. Soon after his election as Speaker he went abroad to visit his sister Clara, who had married the Comte de Chambrun, descendant of Lafayette. Leading French politicians enthusiastically entertained him. Premier Aristide Briand at a brilliant luncheon lifted a glass to Nick as future President of the United States. Diplomatically and wittily, Longworth turned the toast aside. With the linguistic aid of his sister, he used the word *marotte* in an idiomatic phrase instead of the word *abeille* in producing the French equivalent of a denial that he had a presidential bee in his bonnet. He was serious about that, he told Clara. Yet, after August 2, 1927, when Coolidge cryptically announced that he did not choose to run again, there was at least some buzzing in Nick's bonnet—and Alice's.[1]

There was a change in his tune to Clara. He wrote her that "under any circumstances in 1928, the field is open, and I cannot help realizing that I may be called upon to undertake the great adventure." He was, he said, among those generally listed as possibilities but "the whole thing is on the lap of the gods."[2] It did not stay there long. Hoover was nominated on the first ballot in 1928, though, as Alice wrote later, few of the "big-league politicians" really wanted him. His nomination, she said, resulted primarily from "the huge publicity organization he and his supporters had built up and kept on the job for him unceasingly."[3]

Certainly neither the glittering Alice nor Nick, the charming, able, bald Beau Brummell of the capital, seemed cast down as the first Hoover social season started. And Alice appeared to be acting more in familiar character than in unusual pique when, using a Meyer dinner party in their palace on Meridian Hill, she precipitated what the press gaily described as "the Alice Longworth-Dolly Gann feud." As Alice reported it, it mixed up prohibition and protocol. She and Nick shared strong prejudices against prohibition. They bought quantities of grapes and experimented in making wine. They produced a home brew which won the compliments of such a distinguished visiting Englishman as Arthur Balfour. They had, Alice reported later, a small still "with which our butler managed to concoct a very passable gin from oranges."[4] Also Nick, who enjoyed Bohemian company in his love of music, had strong notions of protocol, too. As for herself Alice said, ". . . anyone who knew me was aware that rank and conventionality were things I always fled from and shirked." Yet sometimes "the temptations to make trouble became too strong for me," she admitted.[5] That was the case when they were invited to an elaborate dinner by the Meyers.

The so-called Longworth-Gann feud, Alice wrote, was triggered by a conversation with Agnes Meyer. This feud or social rumpus was no Peggy Eaton affair which altered the fortunes of statesmen. It involved only the question as to whether Mrs. Dolly Gann, the sister hostess of part-Indian Vice-President Charles Curtis or Alice and other wives of officials, domestic and diplomatic, should take precedence at dinner parties. Mrs. Meyer "happened to mention" to Alice that at this elaborate party, to which the Longworths were invited, Mrs. Gann would sit highest at the feast. Alice told Mrs. Meyer she doubted that under such circumstances Nick would come. With "a little mischief," as she said, she made certain that he wouldn't.

"The Meyers, much to Nick's disapproval," she wrote, "had after years of serving things to drink, decided to have a dry house.

That aroused Nick's wrath. He had little sympathy with those who were dry from conviction, but if they went dry from what he considered political expediency, it exasperated him."[6] That provided basis for what she later labeled as mischief: "Instead of saying nothing and letting Nick go to the dinner, I told him the horrid news of the seating, whereat he promptly said he would not go, that he was very glad to get out of the despised dry dinner, using as an excuse 'the slight' to the foreign ladies. The next day he had a large lunch party in the Speaker's dining room of the House, and made a good story about how he had managed to dodge doing what he did not wish to do."[7]

The fat was in the fire or perhaps more accurately the crepes suzette were more than decoratively aflame. Alice, however, was almost demure about the whole matter. "Of course, obviously," she said, "there never was any row. . . ."[8] She and Dolly Gann, she insisted, remained good friends. She did not mention Mrs. Meyer's reaction. Actually, as such a long time Washington observer as Bess Furman wrote in her social history of the White House, the feud was no frolic. It was "a test of respective social prerogatives between the Vice-President and the Speaker."[9] To quiet it, Mrs. Hoover set up extra functions at the White House to smooth the ruffled feathers of Mrs. Gann and her part-Indian warrior brother. Maybe the victory was not clear but the readiness for decorative battle of Alice was displayed. Dolly Gann soon disappeared into the social obscurity from which she had briefly emerged. Mrs. Meyer became a very serious writer for the *Washington Post*, which her husband later acquired, and a traveling reporter, bent on good works, almost as peripatetic as Eleanor Roosevelt was to become. Alice continued to stride. If afterward she seemed a little apologetic about her mischief in the matter, she was certainly not abashed.

Nick, whose part in the whole furore Alice afterward minimized at her own expense, may have been as prejudiced as he seemed impulsive in his escape from the Meyer dinner. He was protective of the position of his wife and the prestige of the House over which he presided. Also, regularly he enjoyed withdrawal from the rigid patterns of Washington protocol and official jugglings and jealousies there. He sailed often with rich Percy Pyne, who in World War I days dispensed the liquid refreshment which led Franklin Roosevelt to list his house as "The Saloon." Annually, also to refresh himself after Congressional strain (which also involved rank, place, and contention), he went to share the Eustis-Hitchcock-Rutherfurd sort of society which prevailed in Aiken.

In that resort, of course, there was a sometimes imperceptible but always implacable protocol, though one unrelated to diplomacy and politics. He looked forward to it with relish in 1931. Then after the incredible Market crash, he and any other sensible man could be thankful that the presidential lightning had not hit them. Before that Alice, perhaps made more solemn by motherhood or more austere by the Republican's choice of Hoover, in 1928 felt that the country had become "all body and no soul." When Bulls on the Stock Market were acting as it might be feared that toddling Paulina might act among the bric-a-brac with which the Longworth house was always crowded, she recorded herself later as a sort of prophetess: "The golden calf was giving triple cream and no one seemed to care much about anything else."[10]

Yet when Nick headed for Aiken, care had begun to be clamor. There the golden calf in secure pastures in the resort was still producing cream even if too little milk got to mouths in the country. Some Congressmen, before Nick's gavel fell at the end of the session in March 1931, had been not only political but impolite in both Democratic opposition and Western Republican insurgency. He needed rest and relaxation after the adjournment of the 71st Congress. Aiken was the place for both. Paper losses on the Stock Market since its crash fifteen months before had not littered the immaculate lawns of quiet plutocrats there. It still seemed incredible in Aiken that so many Democrats, working with insurgent Republicans, had been elected that Nick's continuance as Speaker depended, so he said, "upon an all wise Providence."[11] Providence had other plans.

Certainly Providence seemed hardly to blame for all that was taking place in politics and finance. Busy in Albany, Franklin

Roosevelt could not go South then as Nick was doing. Though involved in governmental duties and mounting pre-announcement presidential manipulations, he had hoped this March to get down to Warm Springs by May 1, "if the legislature will adjourn."[12] He was still hoping in April.[13] He had, however, to make a hurried trip to Europe where his mother, on one of her regular sojourns there, had been stricken with pneumonia. In June he hoped to get South in September.[14] Actually, he did not make it until October, then for little more than two weeks.

This spring that Roosevelt missed in the South was especially beautiful. Aiken and, to a lesser degree, Warm Springs seemed serene places walled away from the more and more visible surrounding destitution. In the March and April of Nick's visit to the South Carolina resort, the camellias were lingering and the azaleas were exploding in almost pyrotechnic bloom in elaborately tended gardens along the pine-lined roads. Nick was as welcome as the azaleas. An admiring newspaperman there wrote that "he overcame the obstacle of wealth to reach a position of power in political circles."[15] He had not left the circle of wealth to do it.

Many servants provided better than make-shift beverages with a kick which the Longworths had produced in their basement. His and Alice's ideas of an unfettered elite coincided with Aiken's notions of the right of ladies and gentlemen to their juleps, properly frosted and served in decorous surroundings. Also in the resort, as in Washington, select parties were enlivened—and often prolonged—when the Speaker provided words and music for such ballads as his favorite, *Abdul A-Bul-Bul Amir*.[16]

One special Rooseveltian tie to Aiken which Nick may not have considered, was a coincidence involving the Franklin Roosevelts. Longworth's hosts were the James F. Curtises whose "Curtis Cottage" was a two-story house of fifteen to twenty rooms surrounding, on three sides, a lovely garden court. Curtis, wealthy lawyer with connections in Boston, New York, and Washington, was a natural member of the Aiken colony. He had been born in Manchester, Massachusetts, close to Pride's Crossing. At Harvard in 1898, he had been intercollegiate golf champion—an achievement which he never left out of *Who's Who* to the end of his days. He had married in Washington Laura Merriam, daughter of William Rush Merriam.

This gentleman, a retired director of the Census, was also banker and politician, and president of the Tabulation Machine Company, the corporate ancestor of the International Business Machines Corporation. In Washington the Merriams lived at 1728 N Street, N.W., in the same block as that in which Lucy Mercer had lived as a child and just across the street from the Roosevelt residence to which she went to become a social secretary. The Curtis position in America was not only nationally crowned by Nick's visits to them. It was indicated in Aiken by the marriage of their daughter Laura to George H. (Pete) Bostwick, polo player from Westbury, Long Island, where the playing field bore the Bostwick name.

In the South Carolina resort, Speaker Longworth found himself quickly remote from the "tumult and contention."[17] He came to Aiken, however, with a cold—or soon developed one there. It seemed a trivial ailment at the outset. At first no doctor was called. Then on April 7, the Associated Press reported him to be in a "serious although not a critical condition" after the development of pneumonia.[18] That day Alice, in this time of limited air travel, entrained for the resort.

Nick's condition seemed better. "The sunny beauty of a spring day," wrote one of the gathered reporters on April 8, contributed to a sense of reassurance.[19] Almost poetically, a correspondent told readers the country-over that the wind rustled the magnolias and billowed through evergreens planted among a profusion of Southern shrubbery. Spring, he reported, had brought a burst of blossoms to the pergola which closed the fourth side of the court of "Curtis Cottage." Then at nightfall a series of bulletins came almost in panic from the three doctors in attendance, headed by Dr. R. H. Wilds.

Wilds was not merely a small-town physician. A Massachusetts gentleman (from Oysterville), he was an ensconced member of the exclusive winter colony. He served with Winthrop Rutherfurd as a member of the board of the Palmetto Golf Club which included such sporting, financial, and *Social Register* figures as Eugene Grace, president of Bethlehem Steel, and the polo players, Thomas Hitchcock and Devereux Milburn. Also, the doctor seemed competent in handling a respectful press. One of its members reported: "By a prearranged signal, in order to disturb the family as little as possible, Dr. Wilds had the shade in the bedroom raised as the moment of death came and newspaper offices in the nation had the flash before servants in the household knew Mr. Longworth had died."[20]

Alice took disciplined command though now there were "blue shadowed hollows in her cheeks."[21] On streets left unpaved to protect the hoofs of horses, the cortege moved through the town in which all business was suspended to a special train provided by the government. To it was attached the private car of Charles Clark, son of the Montana mining magnate and U. S. Senator, William A. Clark, who had vigorously opposed the conservation policies of Alice's father. Aiken was the sort of place which muted such memories. The train moved northwestward across the Carolina mountains to Cincinnati. The funeral there was as unofficial as possible considering the presence of Herbert Hoover. The President hurried back to Washington and to his perplexities in the nation in which the month before the number of the unemployed had risen to 8,000,000.[22]

The widow Longworth came back to Washington, too. Soon to help pay the taxes on Nick's estate she began to write her memoirs for *The Saturday Evening Post* and for later book publication by Scribner's. For a while she was withdrawn from the society of Washington and even Cincinnati in which she spent much time at her typewriter. History was being made, however, even as she wrote it, and the society which was so much her subject did not lapse in her absences. Indeed, almost exactly two months after Nick died, a social event seemed to tie together the Cave Dwellers and the Mellonites of the Hoover administration, and both Washington and Aiken—possibly Democrats and Republicans. Also in a way it marked the continuing Dutchess County colony on the Potomac. This was the wedding of Edith Morton Eustis's daughter, Margaret, to David Edward Finley, on June 10, 1931.

Finley got on the same public service escalator on which Meyer had risen. He, at forty, was almost as fragile and wispy looking as Secretary Mellon and became closer to him than Meyer. Son of a Democratic Congressman from South Carolina, he had graduated from the University of that state. Then as did so many other sons and attachés of Congressmen, he took his law at George Washington University. Briefly he was a subordinate of Meyer's in the War Finance Corporation under Harding. By 1927, however, he had become special assistant to Mellon. Also (as Meyer still was not), he was listed in the *Social Register*. Nothing indicated his social place better than his marriage to a Eustis.

On the day after this event, the *Washington Star* gave more space to it than to two other items: (1) a dinner given by the Japanese Ambassador and Mme. Debuchi for Colonel and Mrs. Charles Augustus Lindbergh who were about to make a flight to the Orient; and (2) the presentation to the Court of St. James's of Mrs. Ernest Simpson, once Mrs. Winfield Spencer, Jr., of Washington, and before that Wallis Warfield, a Baltimore girl who danced in Washington, too.

The wedding was held at Oatlands House, near Leesburg, where Franklin Roosevelt had so happily visited. One of the ushers was Ronald Campbell, counselor of the British Embassy, whom Roosevelt had known as the house-mate of Nigel Law during the Wilson years. Another was Foxhall Daingerfield, now living in Washington with Henry Randall Webb, leading member of the Society of the Cincinnati who had been one of the pall-bearers at Carroll Mercer's funeral. Prominent in the group were Winthrop and John Rutherfurd, the bride's cousins and Lucy Mercer's handsome stepsons. A string band played the wedding march and at the reception for the few close friends in attendance. It was a happy occasion for a close-knit company. The Depression seemed far away from the Virginia hills. Morton Eustis, who gave the bride away, was then twenty-five, showing talent as a writer—such as his mother had hoped to be. Like his father he loved his horses and his dogs, but the theater appealed to his talents and brought him into a society in which statesmen and cave dwellers seemed less important than such theatrical companions as the famous acting couple, Lynn Fontanne and Alfred Lunt. On this wedding day, young Morton was handsome, gay, gifted. He was to bring to reporting the eyes of a poet and become a patriot without pompousness. In the nuptial music at stately Oatlands no one dreamed that he would fall in action in a war no one then feared. Certainly no such eventuality was foreseen as that in his bloody blouse there would be found an affectionately autographed picture of the Eustis family friend, Franklin Roosevelt. Roosevelt, in 1931, was only an aspiring politician who like other Democrats was critical of Mellon, the boss of the groom.

No unhappy omens marked the marriage. From it the Finleys hastened to New York where they boarded the glittering German liner *Bremen* which was setting standards for luxury and speed in Atlantic crossings. It moved in perfection in this month as in every other. Yet from Germany word had come to Washington from German President Paul von Hindenburg, senile and beset, that his land was suffering from "internal and external tensions caused by distress and despair."[23] They threatened, he said, the economic and social order of Europe. In the month of the Finley marriage, while they were at sea or had barely landed in Britain, President Hoover, on June 20, announced his moratorium for a year on international debt and reparations payments. Finley as a newly-wed, in July, became adviser to the American Delegation at a London Financial Conference. Small and fragile as he was, he seemed a boy with only a finger at the dike. So did greater men.

Alice Longworth's fingers, growing more accustomed to the keyboard which at least seemed stable in a confused world, typed out her recollections. She concluded them almost like a dowager at the final end of dancing years. Evidently, looking back it never occurred to her that there could be almost as many years before her as behind her. The good days were gone. Neither the members of the House nor the Senate were "as strong or as interesting" as they had been. The multiplying Washington correspondents each seemed more and more the type of newspaperman "who writes gossip and scandal, and deals in personalities and trivialities."[24] Alice evidently assumed herself beyond such things. Still possibly, she admitted, she had looked at Washington so long that she regarded it with a "scoffing eye." Certainly she so regarded the rising fortunes of her distant cousin Franklin bearing, she thought, a remarkable facial resemblance to Woodrow Wilson who she had hated with such vivacity and venom. She picked out her last lines on the typewriter: ". . . I have perhaps allowed myself to become a little too detached—to see it as 'a dream or mock show and all therein but Pantalones and Antics'—and not to take it too 'hard.' "[25]

Detached she never was. Great as was her loss and fiercely loyal as she always was, weeds she never wore on her spirit. Laughter, wit, hospitality she made into a multicolored cloak. In the protection, however, of what she regarded as her own—or what by some right she felt should be her own, even a place at table—she carried a sort of jeweled dagger beneath it. The White House she regarded as hers in much the same way in which as a child she thought that the terraces of the Capitol "belonged personally" to Uncle Cabot—Senator Lodge.[26] She had even resented the occupancy of the White House by the Tafts the day her father put them in it. She had been incensed when Mrs. Taft spoke of sending her a ticket to the White House for the Inaugural luncheon.

"Instead of taking it as routine," she wrote, "I flew shouting to friends and relatives with the news that I was going to be allowed to have a ticket to permit me to enter the White House—I—A very large capital I—who had wandered in and out for eight happy winters. Indeed, I gave myself over to a pretty fair imitation of mischief-making."[27]

Mischief with her was not always an imitation. Sometimes it was more than mischief. It often was her armament in defense of her traditions and her tribe. Certainly she regarded the name "Roosevelt" as an exclusive possession. Perhaps Alice and other Oyster Bay Roosevelts had a right to resentment, as Eleanor herself afterward thought, about a stunt which she and Howe had staged when Alice's brother, Ted, was running for Governor of New York. Though TR, Jr., as Franklin's successor as Assistant Secretary of the Navy had, so Eleanor kindly wrote, "nothing to do" with the recent Teapot Dome scandals, the tall Mrs. R. and the short, swarthy Howe did not let that deter them. They "had a framework resembling a teapot, which spouted steam, built on top of an automobile; and it led the procession of cars which toured the state, following the Republican candidate for governor wherever he went!"

This was, Eleanor wrote later, "a rough stunt and I never blamed my cousin when he retaliated in later campaigns against my husband."[28] Decline in the political fortunes of her brother, perhaps even the disappearance of Nick from the political field, however, seemed to Alice more to be tolerated than the meteoric and, as it appeared to some, menacing rise of the entirely collateral, upstart, recently crippled has-been, Franklin Roosevelt, of the decorative but expected-to-be-obscure Hyde Park branch of the family.

Alice wrote her memoirs and paid her taxes. There can be no doubt about how she voted in the election of 1932, little as she cared for the Hoovers personally. Perhaps there should be no mystery about her reaction when she received an invitation—complete undoubtedly with ticket—from Eleanor's social staff to a party for all Roosevelts of every branch, sort and kind to be held at the White House on Franklin's inauguration day. Certainly in the family and in the land now Eleanor's place was high at the table. A greater mystery may be whether the invitations to the likes of Alice were sent in magnanimity or triumph or accepted in courtesy or bitter levity. Neither Alice nor Eleanor mentioned this party in their recollections.

(2)

As President-elect Roosevelt had taken what he was sure would
be his "last holiday for many months."[29] Late in January he went
for ten days to his beloved Warm Springs. Then, early in February,
he sailed on the great yacht *Nourmahal* of his cousin and friend,
Vincent Astor, with a company of rich, social companions, with
none of whom, said his son James, did he have "any deep intellectual or political affinity."[30] Indeed, after the election campaign,
James thought he deliberately sought escape from the men of
ideas and politics. The company provided "an escape back to the
world of Groton, Harvard, Fly Club and other things far removed
from the pragmatic, vital arena"[31] of the presidency before him.
He fished, he had fun, he gained weight. The trip was a delight
even though it ended in an attempt to assassinate him by a de-
ranged man with a bad aim in Miami. In the crowd which eagerly
greeted him, others were hit, including Mayor Anton Cermak of
Chicago.

While Franklin was gone, Eleanor dutifully assumed the new
responsibilities before her. With her friend the Albany Associated
Press reporter, Lorena Hickok, she came to Washington to make
preliminary plans for moving into the White House. She and Miss
Hickok stayed at the big Mayflower Hotel at De Sales Street and
Connecticut Avenue. Its fashionable bulk altered the avenue down
which she had walked so many times when she and Franklin had
lived just above it on N Street. Now old landmarks, like the big
brick British Embassy, were gone. She and Lorena, who was to
become her intimate companion and dependent, went down the
avenue past the monumental Chamber of Commerce Building
where the old Corcoran House had stood. In Lafayette Square,
now changing too, she and Lorena parted. With "considerable

trepidation"[32] Eleanor hurried to the White House door, conscious of memories that in the old Navy days she had thought how marvelous it must be to live there.

"Now, I was about to go there to live," she wrote, "and I felt that it was anything but marvelous."[33]

The life she had earnestly and energetically made for herself was evidently over. Recently, almost with the fervor of last chance, she had crowded it with more activities. In addition to her teaching in the Todhunter School and activity in connection with the small Val-Kill furniture plant, she had increased her writing for publication. With her daughter, Anna Dall, as associate, she had assumed the editorship of one of the increasing number of magazines run by Bernard Macfadden, physical culture enthusiast who understood the marketability of sex. The publication Eleanor edited was pure enough, a journal of sweetness and guidance called *Babies: Just Babies*. Also, to help fill the life of her own, she conducted a radio program for a facial cream company.

With regret she contemplated, as one biographer put it, the "barrenness of smiling at White House receptions."[34] She sought some escape from that. With little hope she had suggested to Franklin that he might like for her to do a real job and "take over some of his mail." He looked at her "quizzically," she remembered. He told her that he did not think that would do, that Missy LeHand had been handling his mail for a long time and might feel that she was interfering.

"I knew he was right and that it would not work," she wrote, "but it was my last effort to keep in close touch and feel that I had a real job to do."[35]

Her feeling of frustration added to the awareness of adversity which attended what should have been the joyously triumphant movement of the new President's special train to Washington, on March 2. It ran to expectation and acclaim. Continuity was emphasized by the presence on board of old, gay Josephus Daniels under whom Franklin had sometimes restively served. Still the train moved through a corridor of industry now crowded with the unemployed. In towns beside it and continentally beyond it, banks were closed in all the forty-eight states. The nation which had recently seemed at its meridian was at its nadir. And to national paralysis was added personal tragedy.

In Miami, Florida, Mayor Cermak of Chicago, who had rushed in hope of aid for his city, was dying of the wound from the bullet intended for Roosevelt. This train would not have been moving to Washington if the bullet had reached its target. The moving train was heavily freighted with the news of the death that morning of Montana Senator Thomas J. Walsh, the nemesis of the Harding corruptionists, who was to have been the most prestigious member of the Roosevelt Cabinet. No bullet had removed Walsh just before he was to have become Attorney General. Instead the great old Westerner and Catholic liberal with the gray mop of hair and the drooping walrus mustache, had, in effect, died of presumption about his powers. As a seventy-three-year-old widower of fifteen years, Walsh had married barely a week before the inauguration a "vivacious and much younger"[36] lady, Señora Maria Nieves Perez Chaumont de Truffin, widow of a rich Cuban banker and sugar planter. After a brief honeymoon in Florida, the old Senator had died on a train moving through the Carolinas on the morning of March 2.

The party of the President-elect reached Washington at 9:20 P.M. Well wishers, office seekers, politicians and advisers were waiting. They crowded the corridors of the Mayflower. More were there next morning when the incoming President began in the capital his endless conferences about the problems of the nation pushing in upon him like the crowds in the halls. In this time of responsibility, his cigarette seemed most confidently tilted. Eleanor's morning plan was shaped by a different mood. Far down in an Associated Press story of the crowded day was a brief paragraph, probably written by Miss Hickok.

"She began the day before 9 A.M.," it said, "with a visit in a taxicab, without any escort, to Rock Creek Cemetery to see St. Gaudens' statue *Grief* which she said she considers the most beautiful thing in Washington."[37]

Many besides Mrs. Roosevelt were fascinated by the mysterious sphinx-like figure, erected long before over the grave of Clover Adams, in the District's oldest cemetery. Companies of tourists, whom Adams, before he joined Clover in the earth by the monument, affected to scorn, made their way to it. Before he died the little historian had had to take steps to protect it from cliché-copying by makers of "cemetery horrors."[38]

No special memories tied Eleanor to the monument. She had been an infant far away when Clover Adams killed herself. She had read with disappointment Adams' famous book, *The Education of Henry Adams*, during the leisure of the ocean trip to Paris with Franklin in 1919. Then she had written to her mother-in-law Sara, now in 1933 triumphantly in Washington with her son, ". . . very interesting but sad to have had so much and yet find it so little."[39]

Still as one who found her present great place less than basis for jubilation, the trip to the cemetery, which she did not mention in her memoirs, was a strange one. The ancient burying ground, containing costly monuments to others like the Leiters, lies out beyond the Soldiers' Home, about as far as it is possible to go from downtown Washington within the District of Columbia. Even the taxi drive must have taken much of the morning if Eleanor only sat briefly on the granite bench before the bronze figure.

Certainly she had to hurry back to the Mayflower. Some social events had been canceled due to the death of Walsh. Others crowded the day. She shook the hands of an interminable line of women at the Women's Democratic Club, more at another reception at the Congressional Club. She had to rush away from that to join her husband in his formal and, as it turned out, tense call on the Hoovers at the White House. Certainly this protocol call was not in historical fact, as reporters described it on the day, an occasion on which the Roosevelts and the Hoovers could "chat quietly for an hour about picnics and camping."[40]

Much disturbed Hoover, who regarded Roosevelt not so much as his successor but as a danger to the republic, tried in heavy handed desperation to use the occasion as a last chance to extract pledges from Roosevelt as to continuing policies. The call became as stiff as stone and bronze. The paralyzed Roosevelt deftly parried. Hoover blustered in almost paranoid pique. In dissembled distress Eleanor broke the impasse with polite farewells. Then as "tall, swiftly moving woman"[41] she swept on to other events marked by a sort of "picnic" surface. She did her duty in the life of her own to the last. She "ended her day between 9:30 and 10 P.M., with the last of her weekly radio speeches."[42] Her facial cream sponsorship at this hour suggested that there was still money for cosmetics in a nation which lacked bread.

As always there was a picnic or barbecue quality to the inauguration and the days before and after it. It brought to town some desperate for help and others who found it an occasion for elegant play. The Larz Andersons, the late Nick Longworth's cousins, attended as plutocrats who had voted for Roosevelt. Anderson paid more attention to the parties than the policies Roosevelt proclaimed. From their special seats they watched ceremony and parade. From their box he surveyed the milling masses on the floor at the inaugural ball. Anderson was impressed by the "well-behaved mass of people, well dressed and intelligent looking" who lined the streets. He was pleased but a little appalled by the swarm at the Inaugural Ball, so great that many women fainted. Also he noted that as a result of the crowding at the ball's end "thousands of dollars worth of wraps were left finally unclaimed." Still, "It was fun," he said, "to watch the milling masses" among whom Mrs. Roosevelt was "almost unobserved in the hazy hall." He and his friends shared a feeling of elation. The "pervading air of bone-dryness and holier-than-thouness fell off like a mantle."[43] That was a wrap which, he felt, could be well lost.

Anderson made little note in his report of the crowded day of the central event which still rings in history as that time when, in a chill breeze under gray skies, Roosevelt assured the nation that it had "nothing to fear but fear itself." Some, including Hoover, were not sure of that. Fear of physical violence to him, indeed, gripped his staff when the Secret Service left him unguarded at the Union Station.[44] Eleanor Roosevelt felt a different kind of timidity. The occasion, she said in an exclusive interview which she gave to Miss Hickok in the afternoon after the ceremonies, was "very, very solemn and a little terrifying."[45]

She talked to Miss Hickok in her new White House sitting room. There conversation was so often interrupted by enthusiastic friends and relatives that they had to retreat to the bathroom. She could talk confidently to the unprepossessing-looking woman reporter. Franklin and Howe, Eleanor wrote, had agreed to this exclusive story for Hickok "because she was the outstanding woman reporter for the Associated Press and they both had known her and recognized her ability in New York."[46]

Hickok meant more than this to Eleanor. To persons in the White House she seemed a symbol of some of the unexpected people to whom Mrs. Roosevelt paid special attention and from whom she received a needed adulation.[47] It seemed to mark an eagerness for affection which she bound to herself by her prestige. Sometimes this did injury to the recipients of her attentions. Hickok, who had great promise as a hard-boiled seeming newspaperwoman, became a sort of dependent of Eleanor's aid in governmental and party jobs. She lived for a time at the White House, sharing the prestige of that residence.[48] She accompanied the fast moving first lady on many of the trips she made to see the sad and seamy underside of America in the Depression. Eleanor got her a job with Harry Hopkins or Hopkins hired her because of her intimacy with Mrs. Roosevelt. In Hopkins' relief organization she became, with Martha Gellhorn (later for a time Mrs. Ernest Hemingway), one of the ablest of his "field investigators." Later she had a place with the Democratic National Committee. In some ways as a coughing woman with a weak heart who smoked too much, she seemed almost Mrs. Roosevelt's counterpart of Franklin's Louie Howe.

Others did not agree that Mrs. Roosevelt's possessiveness hurt her. Indeed, one who came into the Roosevelt family belatedly saw her as the special symbol of Eleanor's kindness to so many people. Elliott's fifth wife, Patricia, saw Hickok as a diabetic who eventually became an invalid. Then Mrs. Roosevelt found a place for her to live in Hyde Park and helped her to secure publication of writings for children.[49] There was hardly a job for her at the White House in 1933. Malvina Thompson, Eleanor's intensely practical secretary, was on hand. Also she found other experienced aid she needed as social secretary in now widowed Edith Benham Helm, who had been initiated into the craft by Eleanor's Auntie Bye and had had White House experience with Edith Wilson.

Certainly on Inauguration Day Miss Hickok was a qualified reporter who could be depended upon to produce the "friendly and discreet" story which she wrote after the sitting room and bathroom interview.[50] She wrote more vivid stuff about Eleanor and this day than Eleanor herself later put into her "My Day" columns.

"The crowds were so tremendous," Eleanor said, "and you felt that they would do anything—if only someone would tell them what to do."[51]

By this time in the afternoon, it was clear that Franklin would tell them what to do, too precipitately as some feared. But in the waning day Eleanor, as interviewed, took a self-effacing place.

No woman, she said, "can light-heartedly take up her residence here."[52] But she was sure of her duty. In the immediate future she would chiefly occupy herself "with housekeeping." She did not minimize that role: "We women must go about our daily task of homemaking, no matter what may happen, and we needn't feel that ours is an unimportant part, for our courage and our willingness to sacrifice may well be the springboard from which recovery may come."[53]

Eleanor and Lorena in this interview were more than discreet. They went together beyond the limit of facts both knew in describing the household over which Eleanor presided. Lorena quoted her as saying that she expected to be able to visit often Anna and her husband and her children. Lorena passed to the country Eleanor's statement about Elliott who was moving to

Texas: "His wife, Betty, and the baby will follow as soon as he finds a place. Until then they are going to stay with me."[54]

Eleanor herself was a more dependable reporter later when she wrote in 1949, "Soon after we moved into the White House, Anna and her two children came to live with us, for she was separated from her husband though not yet divorced. . . . Elliott was separated from his wife and left soon after the inauguration to look for a new job in the Southwest, stating firmly that he had no use for the East and never wanted to live there again. His first marriage had been a complete disillusionment. He had found no community of interests with his wife and realized rather soon that he had mistaken a feeling of sympathy for love. They were both too young to know that a successful marriage requires more than a desire to marry and a warm feeling for someone who has gone through experiences similar to one's own."[55]

As the following famous Hundred Days moved toward their end Elliott, off in Texas where Eleanor's brother Hall had some of his widely various connections, made history of a sort, too. News came of his divorce in Reno, the first in any family in the White House.

Not only did some things seem discreetly told. Some things were discreetly kept in long reticence. Among those Democrats rejoicing in the return to power of the party were the North Carolina sisters, Miss Mary Henderson and Mrs. Lyman Cotten. As a Congressman's daughters, both had been reared in party loyalty. Mary had long before been chairman of the committee in North Carolina working for woman suffrage. With its accomplishment she had become vice-chairman of the North Carolina Democratic Executive Committee. Elizabeth had shared her partisanship and her activity.

Now they had more to excite them than the arrival of a Democratic President after the party had been in exile for a dozen years. This new President was not merely an admired personage. He was also the dear friend of their dear cousin Lucy Mercer Rutherfurd, in Washington for the great occasion. They remembered that a White House car was placed at her disposal. Letters came from Roosevelt to Lucy. There were special tickets for the ceremonies. Even the young Rutherfurds, no longer children, the sisters said, heard of the President's affection for their stepmother.

One said, "Lucy, I have just heard that Franklin Roosevelt was in love with you. Was that true, Lucy?"[56]

Lucy brushed the question aside. But a member of the Roosevelt family did not doubt the story about the evidences of his affection FDR showed her at his inauguration. This person suggested, however, Roosevelt being Roosevelt, that the car provided for Lucy probably did not have White House insignia on its side.[57] Of course, Lucy needed no such attention. Cars suitable for such an occasion were commonplace to her. When she came to Washington she belonged naturally to the company of such people as the Larz Andersons, who among other things enjoyed the great banquet at the new Sulgrave Club which Evalyn Walsh McLean, so recently an intimate of the Republican Hardings, gave for visiting Democratic dignitaries. Her close friends the Eustises may have been torn on this occasion between old affection for Franklin and the termination of David Finley's service as Honorary Counselor of the American Embassy in London under Ambassador Mellon whom Democrats were soon to be charging used his Treasury post to dodge his taxes.

At the end of the day of the New Deal's inauguration, however, Roosevelt solidarity seemed as demonstrable as American unity appeared to be. While telegrams of support from all kinds of Americans were pouring in, this evening Franklin and Eleanor held their family party for seventy-five relatives. Alice, of course, was there. So were her brothers, Archibald, investment broker, and Kermit, shipping magnate, explorer, author. Most friendly of the Oyster Bay branch of the family, Kermit had been with Franklin on his cruise on the *Nourmahal*. Old Sara, as patrician who had not liked politics or politicians, was present and beaming. She had naturally taken Franklin's arm earlier in the day, letting Eleanor tag behind. Soon, in an age of miracles, she was to make a radio speech on Mother's Day urging aid to needy mothers. Alto-

gether it appeared to be a happy family time in a country confident that it could be happy again, too.

Quickly banks were closed, then safely opened again. Government costs were cut and increased, too. Employment improved
almost at the rate of mounting confidence. But no chance of
storm was risked in these golden days. The arrival of more shabby
war veterans in March stirred fears of a possible repetition of the
collision between bonus seeking service men and the military
which had occurred under Hoover. This new veterans' invasion
was more easily placated.

From her housekeeping, Louie Howe took Mrs. Roosevelt to
the comfortable camp which had been provided for the men.
There, in effect, he pushed her into a kindly mingling with the
veterans. Already a plan had been shaped to put the complaining men into Roosevelt's favorite employment device, the Civilian Conservation Corps. Some of them later were surprised to
find themselves, sans bonus, clearing fields and planting trees.
Mrs. Roosevelt's visit, however, oiled the plan. Newspapers
quoted the bonus marchers as saying, "Hoover sent the Army.
Roosevelt sent his wife."[58] Eleanor, too, found the experience,
which she had at first feared, exhilarating. Certainly her entry
into the bonus army situation dates best the beginning of a new
life for herself. It provided escape from the glittering capitivity of
life as a formal First Lady which she had feared. The woman
who went to the camp never again left the roads to American
problems—or her own energetic good works among them.

Not all felt so set free as the New Deal advanced. Some statesmen were confused in extemporized policies for recovery even as
the indices of national employment and production rose. Some
lesser persons felt frustrated long before any general conservative reaction began to show itself. One of them was Minna Mercer
(no longer Minnie). She was living then in an apartment house
in an excellent Washington neighborhood. The address on her
stationery, 2100 Massachusetts Avenue, was in the same block as
the palace of the Larz Andersons and almost across the street from
the Longworth house. From it she wrote directly to General

Frank T. Hines, administrator of Veterans' Affairs, who like her Carroll had come into the Army in the Spanish-American War.

"Regret having to trouble you," Minna wrote on October 2, 1933, "but on September 8th, I received from you as Administrator Veterans Bureau, notice that my appeal—in regard to my pension had been granted.

"This morning I received the check for fifteen dollars. I had been counting upon the larger sum—beginning July. This has been a severe disappointment, & I venture to ask, when I shall be in receipt of the thirty dollars per month and if the back issues of fifteen dollars—during July-Aug-Sept—will be reimbursed— Thanking you again and repeating my apologies and reason for troubling."[59]

Some others were grumbling, perhaps with less reason than Minna. Roosevelt wrote to his new ambassador in London in November: "All goes well here, though some of the inevitable sniping has commenced, led by what you and I would refer to as the Mellon-Mills influence in banking and certain controlling industries. The point is that employment continues on a much higher basis, and in spite of certain pessimists I think we shall get through the winter much better than I expected."[60]

At least one person was afraid he would. In Cincinnati, Alice Longworth had watched the improvement in the American mood under Franklin. She was not elated by it. From an old Longworth family house at 2412 Grandin Street, she wrote on the typewriter she had learned to use to the much-loved, one-time White House social secretary Belle Hagner, now Mrs. Norman L. James of Baltimore.

"Dear Belle," she wrote on December 6, in a letter in which she described the hard work she had done in completing her memoirs. At the end she added:

"I think Franklin is getting away with it—Whereat I say x#%&$x)%&$$$$xxx."[61]

Sometimes louder even than the cheers such cryptic grumbling seemed rising in the land.

TWELVE

Lonely Triumph

(1)

"Like a big wedding cake. The kind with the white mountain frosting."

So Henrietta Nesbitt described the White House as she looked at it through the iron fence before she went into it to work in March 1933.[1] Others more familiar with the great old mansion saw behind its unchanging façade, a new liveliness after the glum tenure of the Hoovers. Baruch, who had moved as confidant and counselor in its halls more than a decade before, found it, as he had expected knowing Franklin Roosevelt, a place full of children and dogs and of the clutter which always gave the new President's surroundings a "lived-in" quality.[2] Others were impressed by the youth of some of those who rushed in and out on important missions from endless conferences. Even the Washington spring seemed more luminous for the confidence exuded from the house beyond its fountain and green lawns.

Certainly in the excitement of recovery or the mounting hope of it, it was no place for mere quiet domesticity. Yet there was room and need for household demonstration of unity which the President was seeking—and getting. Alice Longworth, who was invited to dinners,[3] was then subdued and quiet after a pattern set in a letter under her mother's frank: "Pounds of butter would be as safe in my mouth as in an ice box."[4] Though a little older than Eleanor's grandchildren, Paulina Longworth, "a nice quiet girl," aged eight, "came often to play with her White House cousins."[5] Certainly at Eleanor's entry there seemed not the slightest basis for a recent outburst of the fastidious *New York Post* that "She's certain to wreck the new Administration."[6]

Those who were later to disapprove of her position in the administration could note that Eleanor remained the First Lady in the background for just two days. Then, persuaded as she said, by her shadow Hickok, whose colleagues among the ladies of the press undoubtedly resented the exclusive interview she had been given on Inauguration Day, Eleanor began to hold regular press conferences of her own. Her primary purpose, she wrote, was to help women reporters to hold their jobs at a time when many were losing them. Also she was anxious to put a stop to old abuses of which she was told, such as society reporters using "many devious means to get information, even bribing people in the house." This was a first step, however, in reseizing a life of her own. In meeting the women reporters she was determined never to trespass on her husband's prerogatives.[7] Yet, clearly the lady of the distaff side was, though only purring to begin, to become a dynamo.

She had already made arrangements about that housekeeping which she had told Hickok was to be her first concern. Louie Howe, who approved her press conferences, apparently lay the groundwork for this when, according to the long-time chief White House usher Ike Hoover, he made an early and "most unusual" call involving White House jobs.[8] The four principal ones allotted to Eleanor included her able, no-nonsense secretary Malvina Thompson, and the gentle, experienced Edith Benham Helm. Also, to tend to the housekeeping she brought Henrietta Nesbitt and her unemployed husband, Henry F. Nesbitt, to the Executive Mansion. Mrs. Nesbitt, who won no plaudits for the White House fare she served except from the stubbornly loyal Mrs. Roosevelt, was responsible for the details of living which surrounded FDR. He moved in debonair confidence to domestic and international problems. He seemed almost an impotent small boy, however, in the complaints he made across all his years in the White House about the food, which, under Eleanor's direction, Mrs. Nesbitt provided.

Others, though never Mrs. Roosevelt, considered this housekeeper an odd choice for the position. Eleanor had known her in Hyde Park when, as Mrs. Nesbitt herself wrote, she was the "stranded" wife of an unemployed man. Perhaps, as may have seemed pertinent to some later, he had been a "salesman for a whaling industry, but whale meat didn't go over." Almost accidentally she got into local politics. Also, as a fairly desperate means of support in which many women were engaged at this time, she made cakes and doughnuts for sale. Mrs. Roosevelt became a customer for her pastries both in Hyde Park and Albany. On such a basis she offered the job of White House housekeeper to Mrs. Nesbitt. As extra inducement she provided a job for the jobless Mr. Nesbitt who had helped shell nuts and roll dough. Mrs. Nesbitt did not exaggerate her own qualifications. She came to the White House, she said, to her "first job" at the age of fifty-nine.[9] She stayed there thirteen years. After that, with even less qualifications but with perhaps some help, she wrote a book which disclosed her as perceptive backstairs or downstairs historian of the life of the President whom she greatly admired but could seldom please.

Despite the cooking lessons Mrs. Roosevelt had taken a dozen years before, she had, as her son said, "no appreciation of fine food."

"Victuals to her," he wrote, "are something to inject into the body as fuel to keep it going, much as a motorist pours gasoline into an auto tank."[10]

Others agreed. Robert Sherwood, playwright and speech writer, wrote, "It ill becomes a guest to say so, but the White House cuisine did not enjoy a very high reputation."[11] Rexford Tugwell, who greatly admired Eleanor, admitted she was no housekeeper. Even the scrambled eggs which she prepared in a sort of symbol of her capacity, he said, "were very ordinary scrambled eggs."[12] At the White House, Grace Tully remembered, Roosevelt had to take the food served, "like it or not." She added, "Mostly he didn't like it. . . ."[13]

Until he became discouraged, Roosevelt, said James who shared the distaste for the Nesbitt fare, "fancied himself a gourmet."[14] As a release from strain, he enjoyed good, light company sharing good food and drink. And often with uninspiring food, after disapproved cocktail, Eleanor served her causes as conversation and brought to the table a wide variety of persons with diverse purposes who might not have gotten access through his office door. Once, indeed, Anna told her mother that her pressure on him about her public concerns at the dinner table was ruining her father's digestion.[15] She and her brothers did not share the opposition to Roosevelt's pre-dinner cocktail, which was one matter about which Eleanor and Sara agreed.

Back in the days when Franklin was first going South in his hope of walking again, Eleanor had succeeded in temporarily impressing her anti-alcoholic views on her adolescent children. James remembered writing—or had recalled to him by his mother —what he regarded later as the "stuffiest" letter to his father who was then enjoying his grog on the *Larooco* and at Hyde Park, too. At Groton, James had heard a lecture on the evils of drink which he passed on as a lecture of his own to his crippled but convivial father. Buying liquor, he solemnly told his sire, was encouraging bootleggers to "break the law and certainly that isn't living up to the standards of good Citizenship is it?"

He went on: "You know it's always been rather of a shock to me when I come home from School to find the closet next to my room so full of liquor and I know Elliott thinks also that if it must be around, it might be in smaller quantities. I suppose you think I'm an old ass but I really mean it. . . ."[16]

Later, sharing his father's pleasure, James recalled that while his father was "constantly bombarded"[17] on the subject he declined to be browbeaten though he sometimes retired with his cocktail to his own little study. As they grew up he and the children joined in sharing the convivial hour. They enjoyed watching their father making a ceremony as he told visitors how he "learned to make a *really* dry Martini."

"I used to mix my Martinis," James quoted him as saying on such occasions, "nice and gentle—one and one half parts of gin to one part of vermouth. Then Anna became old enough for a cocktail and said, 'Pa, this is awful—you've got to make them dryer—two-to-one.' So I made them two-to-one.

"Then Jimmy came along and said, 'These aren't fit to drink —you should make them three-to-one;' then Franklin, who called for five-to-one, and now Johnny, who insists that a really dry Martini should be six-to-one. So if you don't like what I'm serving you, don't blame me!"[18]

Roosevelt, who was a conservative drinker, liked to make a dramatic show at the cocktail hour, using a variety of measuring and mixing devices. Sometimes he put a dash of Pernod in his unorthodox martinis. But when Eleanor was in town, the rituals were not prolonged. She bustled in a hurry to announce that the dinner of unexciting Nesbitt character was waiting.

While national and international affairs continued pressing, a sort of gentle conflict grew between the Eleanor-Nesbitt axis in the White House and the more convivial company in the executive offices. "Quiet but lovely"[19] Missy LeHand, who lived as Howe did in the White House, and who Mrs. Roosevelt thought sometimes let her social contacts get mixed up with her work,[20] was a leader in the effort to give the President the relaxation over his food and drink that she thought he needed. Sometimes during Mrs. Roosevelt's increasingly frequent absences she invited people to the White House whom she thought the President would enjoy. Eleanor was sure, however, that Franklin "never gave this type of social gathering a thought."[21]

Missy sought allies. One who seemed strange was Secretary of the Interior Harold L. Ickes who, in his rough executive and political ways, rather liked being called a curmudgeon. Also he fancied himself a bon vivant. Furthermore, at the time he was much irritated by Eleanor's meddling, as he considered it, in the affairs of his department in connection with subsistence home-

stead projects for the poor and patronage for friends and relatives.
Some, like Raymond Moley, in the maze of New Deal jealousies
regarded the record left by Ickes as a hodge-podge of venomous
gossip.[22] The certainly not financially impractical Baruch, who
accompanied Eleanor on some of her journeys to these projects,
described her as "a great and gallant" woman.[23] Ickes, however,
though his admiration for her grew later, at this point regarded
her as a vexatious intruder. He was irked by reports that she had
listened attentively to a tale by Secretary of the Treasury Henry
Morgenthau that he had agents timing women employees in the
toilets. With regard to one instance of her supposed pernicious
activity in his department he mentioned her and her Dall grandchildren still visiting at the White House: "Soon I will expect
Sistie and Buzzie to be issuing orders to my staff. Fortunately
they can't write yet."[24]

He was an equally caustic critic of White House food and
beverages. Late in the second year of the New Deal, he noted in
his crusty diary that "White House dinners are neither inspiring
nor do they stand out as Lucullan repasts." However, what
shocked him most was the one glass each of two domestic wines
which Mrs. Roosevelt had announced she would serve. "The
sherry," he wrote, "was passable, but the champagne was undrink-
able."[25] This, he noted, was not his view alone.

"The President joked about the champagne," he wrote three
days later. "He asked me whether I had ever tasted worse champagne and I frankly told him that I never had. . . . The President
said that he had been apologizing ever since to dinner guests for
this champagne."[26]

Perhaps it was as such a gastronome and judge of wines that
Missy suggested the house of the recently widowed Ickes as a
place where the President might get away in "absolute secrecy"
for an "undisturbed evening" with a few drinks and dinner in gay
company. The company was not spectacular. The three ladies
present were Missy, her assistant Grace Tully, "a buxom and
cheery Irish girl,"[27] and Tully's sister Paula, who, as an actress
out of work in the Depression, had handled FDR's confidential

files before marrying Charles Rollin Larabee of Washington. The men invited were Larabee, who had a job under Ickes; Alfred T. Hobson, a minor official in the Reconstruction Finance Corporation who could sing; and Thomas G. Corcoran, also of the RFC, but roving now as a Roosevelt favorite and aide. Corcoran, of course, brought along his guitar which became famous in the Roosevelt story along with his role in his freewheeling manipulations for the President.

If the company was not especially distinguished, both Mrs. Roosevelt and Mrs. Nesbitt might have learned something about presidential tastes from the menu. Ickes described it lovingly in his *Secret Diary*. After cocktails, dinner was served at a table on the lawn.

"We started with honeydew melon, then had cold salmon with mayonnaise dressing, as well as cucumbers and tomatoes, bread and butter, then squab with peas and potatoes. Then followed a green salad with a choice of cream, Swiss, or Roquefort cheese. For dessert there was my own special ice cream, black raspberry, with cookies and coffee to finish with. For wines, I served Chateau Yquem, a good claret, and a good vintage champagne. We had liqueurs afterward and when the dining table had been removed, the butlers brought out and put on a table, with a supply of cracked ice, Scotch, rye and bourbon whisky, gin and Bacardi rum. . . . The President certainly carries his liquor well. He must have had five highballs after dinner."[28]

Evidently the President enjoyed himself. Still the group was composed of the off-duty companions in his serious concerns. They did not represent the kind of society to which he had turned when he chose his shipmates on Vincent Astor's yacht or those with whom he had sailed on the *Larooco*. Increasingly such old friends were among those who were saying that he was a traitor to his class. Sometimes as his predilections indicated, he felt that those whose capitalism and social order he had preserved had deserted him. He had been ready to let the line be drawn, however, just two weeks before this gay occasion at the Ickes' place, in a great speech accepting renomination at Franklin Field in Philadelphia. Then to a roaring crowd, the like of which Ickes had never seen, he had lashed out at the "economic royalists" in direct reference to the recently organized American Liberty League, composed of an impressive body of politicians and American plutocrats including his old acquaintances the du Ponts of Delaware.

Roosevelt had not been confident of his re-election at the beginning of the year. Certainly, however, then Eleanor was marching forward in a life of her own, related to, but not entirely dependent upon, her position as First Lady. Their lives in this first term had seemed increasingly interlocked with Eleanor as his itinerant reporter on aspects of American life calling for remedy which, as a man bound to his chair, he could not go himself to see. He referred often to things "My Missus" had told him. Yet certainly these missions, though they served him, meant a separation which neither seemed to mind.

Schlesinger, who, as he said, "thought a long time" about the Franklin-Lucy story, wrote in 1967 an enigmatic article about the Franklin-Eleanor relationship at this period. Franklin, he related, at an informal supper on May 12, 1935, told Fulton Oursler, editor of a popular weekly called *Liberty*, about a plot for a mystery story he had carried in "my mind for years." It was insoluble, the President said.

The story was about a rich man who wanted to disappear to a new life but carry his money with him, perhaps to try out a certain experiment in public health and recreation in some small city where, in his new identity, he would not be recognized. Schlesinger put down Roosevelt's words about his character as Oursler quoted him. "But he's tired, fed up with his surroundings and habits. Perhaps his wife, to whom he has been married for twenty years, now definitely bores him. Perhaps, too, the sameness of his middle-aged routine has begun to wear him down. Furthermore, he is disheartened at the hollowness of all the superficial friendship surrounding him." Oursler eagerly grasped at a feature he labeled "The President's Mystery Story." He got detective fiction pros to write their versions as to how the rich man could escape into another character. The editor paid the President, Schlesinger said, $9000 for the idea and the title—the money going to the Warm Springs Foundation. Oursler wrote an enthusiastic introduction to the series.

"Stephen Early, Roosevelt's press secretary," Schlesinger said, "made minor changes in Oursler's manuscript. Overprotective in the manner of press secretaries, he cut the reference to 'public health and recreation' as the object of the experiment. And he also cut the reference to the millionaire's boredom with marriage, fearing that 'it might be construed by some readers as the President's "personal feelings." ' "

The historian Schlesinger went on to relate that Oursler also recalled "that when he first met Mrs. Roosevelt, she told him she had in mind dramatizing a novel about a disillusioned wife called *All Passion Spent*." When later Oursler got Roosevelt's story of the disillusioned husband wanting escape, Schlesinger added, the editor could not help remembering Mrs. Roosevelt's dramatization idea. In erudite escape from this Ourslerian web about which he wrote, Schlesinger said for himself: "Recent assertions about Lucy Mercer Rutherfurd would make it tempting to draw drastic conclusions from this coincidence. Yet the linkage is not very impressive.[29] Still, Schlesinger's recital of it was valued sufficiently highly for *McCall's*, which bought the article, to give it a full page advertisement in *The Wall Street Journal*, perhaps other papers.

No such scholar-blessed fantasy built on belatedly reported coincidence is needed to point the frequent factual separations of the Roosevelts. Eleanor now was constantly in passage on the American scene. In the spring of 1934, "Franklin suggested"[30] that she make a visit to troubled Puerto Rico. Accompanying her on this trip were Tugwell and Hickok and a number of women correspondents who more and more expected her to make news. From Puerto Rico they went to the Virgin Islands. She came home with more reports of desperate need like those she had brought back from domestic trips. Also, soon after she returned, Franklin himself set out on a cruise which took him through the

Caribbean and the Panama Canal out to Hawaii. With many stops and speeches en route, Eleanor went West with Lorena to join Miss Thompson, Press Secretary Steve Early and the wheezing Howe to meet the returning Franklin.

Already then the conservative muttering against what seemed the more and more radical New Deal had grown. In Aiken such an old gentleman as Winthrop Rutherfurd was lamenting the fortunes of the nation under Roosevelt despite the soothing dissent of Lucy.[31] But if Franklin's political prospects seemed threatened from the right, Eleanor's position, despite some of her snorting old friends and new enemies, seemed reaching a popularity that was financially marketable.

Soon after she began to talk to the press ladies, she began to write more herself. She made a contract to write a monthly question and answer page for the *Woman's Home Companion*. In 1934, she wrote a child's guide to Washington. She resumed her radio broadcasting. The greatest evidence of her personal position came, in January 1936, when some then respectable prophets and pollsters were suggesting that Franklin's continuance as President after one term was gravely—or perhaps happily—to be doubted. Then, regardless of that hazard, the United Features Syndicate gave her a five-year contract for a daily newspaper column which became her famous "My Day." This diary of her life was filled with travel reports, names of a variety of persons met, items of good will and reports of good works. About this time, she told Mrs. Nesbitt that she was making $75,000 a year, the equivalent of the President's salary, and giving it all to charity. Certainly her voice on the air was heard. And her column was read, reverenced, and ridiculed.

Alice Longworth was delighting her select circle of friends with mimicry of Eleanor's oratory. Even in the White House offices, a loyal Roosevelt employee, Mary Eben, put on her "Mrs. Roosevelt act" for delighted fellow workers who found amusement in the satirization of the "Missus" on the podium. Grace Tully wrote that Mrs. Roosevelt herself unsuccessfully tried to get both Alice and Mary to perform for her.[32] No such reticence in ridicule was shown by the columnist Westbrook Pegler, who, as an early Roosevelt admirer, had become a savage Rooseveltian critic. In one of his milder assaults he wrote a parody of Eleanor's "My Day." Perhaps only those who remember the column can appreciate its priceless humor. He wrote in burlesque of Eleanor's reports:

> Yesterday morning I took a train to New York City and sat beside a gentleman who was reading the 1937 report of the International Recording Secretary of the World Home Economics and Children's Aptitude and Recreation Foundation of which my good friend, Dr. Mary McTwaddle, formerly of Vassar, is the American delegate. This aroused my interest and I ventured to remark that I had once had the pleasure of entertaining a group of young people who were deeply concerned with the neglected problem of the Unmarried Father. It turned out that the gentleman himself was an unmarried father so we had a very interesting chat until he got off at Metuchen.

If the United Features Syndicate had been betting on having its First Lady columnist writing from the White House after the 1936 election, it won in the greatest landslide in American history. Soon after his victory, Franklin set out on a long tour of South America. On it his plans took shape for mounting battle against the "economic royalists" and those who seemed to be their supporters in the Congress and on the U. S. Supreme Court. Still, even considering the unexpected guests he often found at the White House, there was something amazing about the presence as house guest there, early in 1937, of Ethel du Pont, pretty princess of economic royalty who was his son Franklin, Jr.'s fiancée. Ethel may have pointed the amazing engagement by going down with appendicitis while she was there.

The visit did not alter the Roosevelt ways. Franklin went on with what seemed to conservatives in Wilmington, Delaware, Aiken and many other places, his wildly radical program. Eleanor continued articulate, active, and after her fashion gay. Mrs. Nesbitt noted in her diary in May that she had had "another horrid nightmare of a day with meals for the President" who "has been so difficult to feed recently." Also she noted, as of the same date, that Eleanor's Press Party "was a huge success." Mrs. Nesbitt was not usually pleased by these parties for the press since sometimes after them as much as a bushel basket of cigarette butts was swept up from the floors and carpets she guarded. This one, however, she reported with evident pleasure.

"Mrs. Roosevelt and her brother Hall Roosevelt with six or eight couples started it off with a Virginia reel which was very much applauded. They were all in costume. . . . The whole thing went off very well and we were serving beer, rye bread, sausage, cheese and crackers, et cetera, in the lobby during the evening and until supper was served."[33]

She did not note the President's reaction. But two days later she did make an entry: "The President is cutting up an unusual tizzy-wizzy, as Mrs. R calls it. . . ."[34] He had plenty of other things on his mind to cause a tizzy-wizzy, but the presence of the dancing Hall may have had something to do with this particular one. He had treated Hall not only as a brother but a child. As late as 1932, when Hall was serving as city controller of Detroit, he had depended upon him in lining up Michigan delegates.

Hall had not only become more and more addicted to gin, but also to using the White House telephone. He had been involved in some strange deals down in Texas with Elliott who was engaged in great speculations related to radio, airplanes, real estate. Ickes made notes about Elliott's financial activities as President's son. Mrs. Roosevelt's biographer, Alfred Steinberg, reported that the President sent word to Jesse Jones, chairman of the Reconstruction Finance Corporation, to make even a doubtful loan to Hall—anything to get him out of town.[35]

Roosevelt's escape from things that nagged him was not easy. More like the society he sought was that offered by his greatly loved military aide, General Edwin Watson, and his wife Frances, a well-known concert pianist, who had built a beautiful house in Virginia at Charlottesville. Watson often played the role of court jester, ready to be the butt of his own jokes, but behind his warm grin he was a shrewd and resourceful man. Unfortunately on Roosevelt's first visit there, though the juleps were expertly made and the company excellent, he suffered a slight touch of food poisoning. Other visits were happier.

Strangely perhaps Roosevelt moved into the sort of society he enjoyed when he seemed to be entering the lion's den. Ostentatiously he took along such symbols of his radicalism as Harry Hopkins, Secretary of Labor Frances Perkins, and Secretary of the Treasury Henry Morgenthau (understood to be ready to aim at rich folks' taxes), when he went to Wilmington, Delaware, to attend the wedding of Franklin, Jr., and Ethel du Pont. James, who went along, reported that rarely had he seen his father to appear to have a better time at a social function than at this wedding in June.

"It richly appealed to his sense of humor," James said, "to be the center of attraction at the lavish affair, given by his new in-laws to whom, as Father well knew, his name was a dirty word. . . . Also, it was a good party; Pa enjoyed the rich food and champagne, and, as I remember it, kissed all the bridesmaids."[36]

It was "a good party" and as President and father-in-law he stayed to the last. Busy Eleanor, however, could not spare that much time. Henry Morgenthau, who in the same month listed Ethel's father as a tax dodger, had to leave early. So did Mrs. Roosevelt, whose tax deductions for charity were to be questioned by Republicans in retaliation. The editor of Morgenthau's diaries told of the wedding primarily from the point of view of the Secretary of the Treasury who was then involved in serious negotiations with regard to the stability of the French franc. He wrote: "The next day, June 30, Morgenthau, who was admittedly distracted, attended the wedding of Ethel du Pont and Franklin Roosevelt, Jr., in Wilmington. After the ceremony he joined Mrs. Roosevelt, who was racing to a radio broadcast in Washington. Squeezed into the front seat of a three-year-old Chevrolet between the driver and a state trooper, with the First Lady in the back, the Secretary feared that upon his return to his office he would find the 'currency club' disbanded."[37]

According to Mrs. Roosevelt's biographer, Steinberg, this was an erroneous account. He wrote, "Eleanor had to leave in the middle of the affair to hurry to a radio broadcast in Wilmington, where she strangely told the nation, 'I don't know whether to be happy or sad. I, for one, always am torn between the realization of the adventure that two young things are starting on and its possibilities for good or bad.' Then she rushed back to the reception."[38]

Presumably like Morgenthau's "currency club" it was still in session when she returned.

(2)

In gay, pretty Betsey Cushing Roosevelt, wife of his boy James, Franklin Roosevelt had the kind of companionship he enjoyed when he went to Warm Springs in March 1937. He needed respite from responsibilities then. Behind him in Washington were the repercussions of the sit-down strikes in the Middle West. Hardly less violent was the debate over his plan, as it was called, to "pack" the Supreme Court which had been setting aside New Deal legislation. He needed Warm Springs. His visits there had grown shorter. The problems of the presidency restricted his leisure. Also the Georgia village was now watched when he was there by reporters and politicians, too.

Just ten years before this visit he had spent three months on one sojourn there, swimming back to health. In that earlier time, he had not only time but privacy. He was, indeed, so little noticed then that when Rexford Tugwell, brain truster turned historian, undertook in 1958 to compile a chronology of his stays at Warm Springs, he found difficulty in tracing Roosevelt's arrivals, departures and activities.[39] Tugwell quoted Mrs. Roosevelt as saying that in these years "the newspapers paid little or no attention to him"[40] except on such a dramatic occasion as that when, on the arm of his son James, he moved bravely to the podium to nominate Al Smith for the presidency.

"People," Tugwell commented, "cannot remember the names of Vice-Presidents, let alone the personal details about unsuccessful vice-presidential candidates."[41]

He could only provide a "skeleton account"[42] of "Roosevelt's peregrinations"[43] in the years before Roosevelt ran for governor, the chronologist stated. As of the year of that candidacy, he wrote, "it is very possible that during this visit Roosevelt spent considerable time traveling around the South."[44] By 1937, however, though still much enjoyed, Warm Springs had become less and less a place in which Roosevelt could count on release, not to speak of rehabilitation. Still in March of this year, as always in the spring, the dogwood was blooming among the pine trees in the sweeping ravine below the sundeck of the house he had had a young Georgia architect, Henry Johnston Toombs, design for him. He looked forward to the two-week holiday he would have in that cottage, already called the Little White House, and the company there of his son and secretary James and his wife Betsey.

Long before this, as James emphasized in the subtitle of his book about his father, Roosevelt had been "a lonely man." Now that loneliness had deepened. Louie Howe, querulous, jealous but loyal to the last, had died just the spring before. Roosevelt needed James—and Betsey. Just before he reached Warm Springs on this trip, Mrs. Roosevelt had passed as close by as Atlanta, where she inspected a slum clearance project on one of her lengthening lecture tours. She had opposed his recent appointment of James as one of his secretaries. She could foresee, she wrote later, that this would result in attacks on both her husband and her son. She could not dissuade James from accepting.

"I protested vehemently to Franklin," she said, "and told him he was selfish to bring James down."

Perhaps once again he looked at her "quizzically."

"Why should I be deprived of my eldest son's help and of the pleasure of having him with me just because I am the President?"[45]

He "had a point," Eleanor admitted, but she was unhappy about it and, as she felt later, her fears were justified. Certainly James had been one to lean on at political conventions and else-where. Despite a spate of criticism about his White House place and his remarkable insurance earnings as the President's son ear-lier, James was helpful to his father. On at least one occasion, how-ever, Eleanor and Franklin agreed on a veto to a suggestion he made. James himself recalled that he suggested that they "might appease" Alice Longworth, whose tongue was sharper than ever, by appointing her to a vacancy on a harmless commission. He got back a memo from his father: "I don't want anything to do with that woman!"[46]

Certainly, however, the 1937 trip to Warm Springs charmingly emphasized that Roosevelt got more than James' help and com-pany. He also got the blond, lovely Betsey, who, the observant Grace Tully felt, was probably FDR's "favorite of those who mar-ried into the family."[47] James himself later said that his father was fond of her—"more so, in fact, than Mother was."[48] Eleanor, however, had given Franklin the first news of James' and Betsey's engagement on November 22, 1928, soon after he had won elec-tion as Governor of New York. Eleanor's letter then began on the familiar theme of troubled family finances in a household in which, beyond private incomes, Roosevelt was earning at least $35,000 a year. She expressed approval of this daughter of Dr. Harvey Cushing, famous Boston brain surgeon: "She is a nice child, family excellent. . . ." She only pointed, though with less vehemence, the too-young theme of which Sara had made so much in their case a quarter of a century before.[49]

Still, as James put it then, they were "terribly in love of course." Soon the father-in-law's affection for this girl almost equaled—and outlasted—the son's. Two years after the marriage, Betsey rode the presidential campaign train and with Anna was introduced to roaring crowds by FDR as his "two blond glamour girls."[50] In a sense, these two, daughter and daughter-in-law, were to become beloved figures in Roosevelt's life.

There was, of course, room in the presidential mansion for

James and Betsey and their little girls, Sara Delano and Kate. Their elders "made it as homey as possible," said James. They were encouraged to have their own friends in for cocktails and dinner. But the son in the White House made a clear parental distinction: "Father always was delighted to greet them. Still, it wasn't the most relaxing place in the world, and one of the hazards of being around there in the evening was that you might get roped in on one of the musicales or Virginia Reels which Mother always was arranging."[51]

Other arrangements were made which evidently pleased Father: "When we moved into our own place in the old Georgetown section of Washington, I had a ramp built from our garage to the first floor so that Father could visit us with the least possible inconvenience. He enjoyed coming over to spend an evening with us, and we would have a dinner of the type of food he liked—steak, roast beef, or game—quite different from the uninspired White House fare against which he lodged so many futile protests. Sometimes he would come with some of the White House staff, and occasionally we would invite a friend who would be good company and eschew weighty conversation, for we knew that Pa did not want to remake the world every evening."[52] With the plus of family affection they gave him the kind of hospitality which he also sought at the home of his aide and secretary, "Pa" Watson, at the house of Ambassador Joseph P. Kennedy, "who had a big family and a place in the country," and later at the residence of Princess Martha of Norway.[53]

Despite the pilgrimages thither of politicians and the presence of reporters, he did not always want to remake the world all the time at Warm Springs. Betsey and James understood that, too. Some visitors left records of the role Betsey played there. Apparently she even on occasion shifted Roosevelt from his customary martinis to old-fashioneds. Even such a professed curmudgeon as Ickes watched her with admiration (even with carelessness about his losses) in a poker game which included such presidential companions as himself, Hopkins, Morgenthau, Tugwell, and Frank C. Walker (later Postmaster General). Betsey, he reported, was "the heavy winner."[54] Not only at the cocktail hour did she help free presidential talk and presidential laughter.

At Christmas in this year 1937, James told his father that in his company "Bets and I have been happier than ever before."[55] Certainly there were no signs then, even in a fuming country and an angry world, that Betsey would not continue to be a sort of glittering Christmas tree ornament in the Rooseveltian establishment. Yet possibly the criticism his mother had solemnly foreseen caused James to develop, in 1938, the ulcers which sent him to the Mayos in Rochester, Minnesota, in July and again for a serious operation in September. There was loss in the occasional sparkle Roosevelt needed when, despite newspaper clamor, James and Betsey were divorced, in 1940, in the most approved pattern of reticence. This meant not only the relinquishment by FDR of a daughter-in-law in whom he delighted. Somehow it marked, too, his further separation from a society whose approval he did not ask but whose company he enjoyed. Betsey would later become a charming representative for America as the wife of John Hay Whitney, Ambassador to Britain. Dutchess County would be graced when her sister, Mary, whom Ickes thought "more beautiful, but not so sweet,"[56] married Franklin's neighbor and *Nourmahal* shipmate, Vincent Astor, who had soured on the New Deal.

No one expected that the 1937 spring visit of the President to Warm Springs would be his longest from this point on. He came back three times in 1938, once for almost as long a stay at a time when he was engaged in a futile effort to "purge" members of his party in Congress who did not support the party's—or his—programs. Yet even when he spoke sharply then in Georgia of those who "still believe in the feudal system,"[57] his concerns were pulled to the menacing march abroad of dictators who openly scorned any systems but their own. Possibly this shift pulled him, as a man closer to international problems, from backcountry Warm Springs to more frequent stays in cosmopolitan Dutchess County.

Certainly, in 1938, he called upon Toombs, the Georgia architect, to design a sanctuary for his escape in Hyde Park. It placed his retreat nearer to old friends to whom he was more and more turning. Variously called "Hilltop Cottage," "Top Cottage," and "Dutchess Hill Cottage," the house for which he had Toombs draw plans was a place for the President, in his own words, "to escape the mob."[58] Even in wartime it was to have no telephone. The hill to it was so steep that in icy weather ascent to it was dangerous. But in spring there were dogwoods among the trees below it as at Warm Springs. He could take people there but only upon specific invitation could people come there to him. In this cottage he had had taken the photograph of himself which he affectionately inscribed to a well-loved young man about to go overseas: "To Morton Eustis from his mother's and his old friend— Franklin D. Roosevelt."[59] They were such old friends as described FDR's own spirit. At the time this picture was taken at Hilltop, Morton had just been commissioned in the Army he had entered long before Pearl Harbor—and then by faking his eye examination. Like Roosevelt he was a village vestryman. Morton both played the organ in the church at Oatlands and in the Army wrote the words and music for bawdy soldier songs. His mother, who shared and cherished his unstilted grace, later published one of his rollicking ballads, "The Orders of the Day," containing the lines:

> Our slogan is pure
> It is toujours manure
> On the Orders of the Day.[60]

That was the sort of flippancy in the midst of the most serious concerns, rejection of stuffiness even on the road to glory, which Roosevelt hoped to find in the cottage of this photograph. He was infuriated when the wordy press described it as his "dream house."[61] It received, however, plenty of press attention when, after much protocol in Washington, Eleanor served hot dogs to the British King and Queen there in the summer of 1939. Despite such occasions, the cottage in an even more secluded sense was Warm Springs without the warm pool in which he no longer put hope.

Yet the cottage provided not only seclusion; also in a revealing, almost brutally comic way, it brought him to a symbolism of change in his life and his world. When he was building the retreat on the hilltop, he remembered a bronze statue he had seen when, as young Assistant Secretary of the Navy in 1915, he had made an official visit to the Panama-Pacific Exposition in San Francisco. He was not recalling any such glittering work of artistry as the Tower of Jewels. He thought instead of a bronze statue set in the foreground of a colonnade at the fair. It "represented a young girl, beautiful in form and feature, petite and poised most impressively in a kneeling attitude, the hands of great delicacy, the curve of the neck and shoulders being exceedingly graceful." It was, Roosevelt said, "a conception of youthful feminine beauty and spirituality which had always lingered in his mind."[62]

He undertook to get a copy for the grounds of his cottage sanctuary. That required quest and time. But when a figure by the statue's artist arrived, he was shocked. It was not a blithe bronze of a fragile and delicate girl. Instead it was a stone mass of a woman, "big breasts, mammoth in all of her proportions—no curves, no grace, no delicacy." The figure was kneeling "but her head was square . . . sides straight . . . hands hanging down like great hams, to which were attached square fingers."[63]

Roosevelt's surprise did not disturb the artist, Robert Stackpole. A quarter of a century after he shaped the girl of Roosevelt's remembrance, he was sculptor for the Golden Gate-Pacific Exposition in 1939, which like the earlier fair marked the beginning of a great war. Calmly, almost as if instructing a dull child, he explained his new creation to the President.

"The changes . . . in the world, in you, and in me made the exact copying or reproduction of the first statue unattractive, so I did the job as I would do it now. Symbolism is elastic and the beholder is always free to see what he wants, but here are a few things I thought of when I was working. Big mass movements in thinking and labor naturally reflect in art. The slender and graceful belong less to us now. I've tried to make heavy and strong forms. She is more bent and the burden heavier. Too, I thought of the great building in your administration, especially of Boulder Dam."[64]

To others who were dismayed, Stackpole explained that the "bronze figure, which the President admired as a younger man, was the work of my youth—my immaturity. It was not my best; but it was the best I could do then. The President today represents strength and power, and those are the qualities which I wish to infuse in my gift to symbolize the President . . . to whom all the world looks for guidance."[65]

Possibly the artist was right in his artistic views. But Roosevelt was not seeking guidance in strength and power. As he did not want to remake the world all the time, he did not care for the remaking of a precious remembrance. At the suggestion of his correspondence secretary then, William D. Hassett, the gift, which certainly could not be declined, was placed not by the cottage but the library which he had already prepared to receive his papers. Also, as Hassett impishly suggested, much shrubbery was planted around it.

Roosevelt declined to dismiss his remembrance of the delicate girl in bronze. He searched further. And somehow later he secured a faithful reproduction of the original figure. It was only eight or nine inches high. He placed it on the mantel in his house high above "the mob" of people, pressures, duties. He had his triumph but he was lonely in it.

(3)

The ceremonial occasion in June 1939, when Britain's King and Queen came visiting, seemed afterward an event of exquisite irony. It paraded a decorative past, like one of Dresden figures on an iron stage. Circumstance seemed irrelevant by pomp. In the humid heat of the Washington summer, tall George VI in his early forties, and Elizabeth, looking young and beautiful, appeared only to the pessimistic like participants in a charade of which no one could guess the meaning. They came decoratively in the peace Mr. Chamberlain had assured at Munich. Hiding any royal fears under royal affability, they brought a large, ornamental company in which, as the White House found, royal servants were far more arrogant than royalty itself. In prelude to their appearance arrived voluminous documents about protocol, covering everything from majestic prerogatives to hot water bottles which Britons evidently required regardless of weather. The imperial directions worried greater personages than apprehensive Henrietta Nesbitt.

Yet, the visit of their majesties to the hot capital moved with the precision of a quadrille. Only such a character as Harold Ickes would have dodged the garden party at the British Embassy. There, as protocol required, he, like everybody else, would have had to go in heavy morning coat and high silk hat. He decided not to mill about with a lot of "uninteresting, climbing and supercilious people." He preferred that afternoon a cocktail party, where "practically everyone was in his shirt sleeves," given by a young Texas Congressman named Lyndon Johnson.[66]

Ickes had not been invited to the great state dinner at the White House, which in part won for Mrs. Nesbitt an appreciative present from the King and Queen.[67] The curmudgeon diarist, however, and his pregnant young wife did attend the musicale afterward arranged by Mrs. Roosevelt. It went off well, too. Marian Anderson had to be delicately persuaded to sing Negro spirituals instead of operatic arias. A folk singer of Eleanor's selection was frisked by the Secret Service. The presidential guards had received, from "someone who wanted to be disagreeable," the First Lady said, a tip that he was "a communist or a bolshevik and likely to do something dangerous."[68]

Yet the musicale pleased even Ickes, though he kept wondering in the crowded, sweltering East Room why the President had not let him air-condition the White House as a works project. Also, he seemed to be at least as interested in the members of the company present as in the music and the singers. He noted various people among the guests, especially the variety of Roosevelts, including Eleanor's tall brother Hall.[69]

Hall sat as far below the salt or the King and Queen as he could possibly be placed at the big horseshoe table.[70] His presence, however, pointed problems besides protocol with which Eleanor was this summer also concerned. James and Betsey Roosevelt were at the table though their separation was already imminent. Two months later the President, indicating that he realized that it would be news to his son, wrote James, "Bets was here for two days. . . ."[71] (The words following that statement were deleted by the editors of the *Personal Letters*.)

The royal visitation, of course, extended to Hyde Park where, in addition to the picnic in the cottage on the hilltop, the matriarch Sara gave a dinner so elaborate that she had to borrow china from neighbors all around Dutchess County. Its fate seemed almost symbolic in a decorous world. During dinner a serving table collapsed, scattering and smashing dishes. And after dinner a tray loaded with decanters, glasses, ice, clattered to the library floor. Eleanor, who duly reported then to readers of "My Day," the crashes which humiliated her mother-in-law, later expressed her own surprise. She would "never know" she wrote, what had happened to her well-trained White House Negro butlers who had been brought up for the occasion.[72] Anyone else might have wondered if the butlers had not gotten to the decanters before they passed them.

Something of the manner in which she passed lightly over these incidents of Sara's shame marked her published attitude toward her brother Hall. After the White House dinner, as an advanced alcoholic he had gone back to coastal Dare County, North Carolina. There he was much of the time voluntarily sequestered, as his father had been years before in the little western Virginia town of Abington. And to the North Carolina coast, scarcely two weeks after the departure of their majesties, Eleanor went to his fiftieth birthday party. There then, in addition to a group of Hall's diverse and unidentified friends, were gathered some almost as distinguished personages as many who had assembled for the royal visitors.

Hall had become well-known on this shore though there was no mention of his presence when Franklin had come two years before to celebrate the 350th anniversary of Sir Walter Raleigh's efforts to establish a first English colony there. The President had used the occasion as one for a first attack on those who had defeated his court reorganization bill. Now Hall was holed up down the shore from the county seat of Manteo in the Goosewing Club. This was a hunting and fishing place owned by Nicholas (or Nickoli) Miller, a diamond merchant said to be from South Africa, whom Hall had met in some of his various business transactions. Natives remembered that with two marriages behind him, Hall was accompanied there by a woman, locally reported to be a Russian much given to sun-bathing in the nude.

Among those who knew Hall there was Paul Green, author of the open-air drama *The Lost Colony*, which annually celebrates Sir Walter's settlement that mysteriously disappeared. Hall was, Green recalled, "a genial, expansive fellow in keeping with his size." He remembered their meeting. The playwright wrote: "'My name is Hall Roosevelt,' he said, and he took off in wordage from there. He let us know that he'd been driving down from Norfolk at 90 m.p.h. 'Yes, I pushed the old accelerator down through the floor,' he said, and so had outrun the cops both real and imaginary."[73]

Green described a visit to Hall's quarters "across a trackless waste of sparsely grassed dune."

"I got there late," he related, "and Hall had some other visitors present. I don't remember who they were. (This maybe was not his birthday party.) Hall was standing in the middle of the floor with a half-gallon jar of orange juice in one hand and a fifth of gin in the other. Then he got to reciting *Hamlet*, and an argument broke out about the prince's attitude toward his step-daddy, the usurping king, or some fool thing. Hall hollered for a copy of the play. And believe it or not, someone fished up a copy from somewhere—a little teeny book with fine print. And though the light in the room was very dim, he stood and read extensively from it and without glasses."[74]

Because of Mrs. Roosevelt's visit, the birthday party was covered —though at a distance from the Goosewing Club—at great length. Also much attention was attracted to the occasion because, to see the play, if not to join the party, came an amazing array of military brass. Little more than two months before Hitler invaded Poland it included General George C. Marshall, just appointed U. S. Chief of Staff, and General H. H. Arnold, Chief of the Army Air Corps. They and their wives and other prominent persons occupied honored places in the open-air theater at Fort Raleigh.

Hall had left Dare County at five o'clock in the morning, driven to Washington and got back at 3 P.M. with Eleanor and her imperturbable Miss Thompson. "Within an hour," newspaper reports said of Eleanor, "she was sunning herself on the beach of the Outer Banks," though certainly not in the fashion reported of Hall's lady companion.

The newspaper of Franklin's old boss, now Ambassador Daniels, reported the occasion in democratic detail. The least formal thing about it, the paper said, "was Mrs. Roosevelt's arrival in Fort Raleigh. She came, perched like the queen that everybody in Dare County discovered when they glimpsed her, high in a CCC truck, with two stalwart CCC lads, serving as sort of anchors for her." At the end of the rough ride through the sands, she climbed down from the truck and, "almost unnoticed," entered the theater as the lights went out.

"Mrs. Roosevelt wore," said the reporter who was not letting her go unnoticed, "the pink or maybe some sort of lavender dress that has been pictured in every country weekly in the republic. The dress was a part of her wardrobe when the King and Queen were in America. Hall Roosevelt wore white cotton pants and a cotton sweat shirt. The whole evening was as informal as that, and as Mrs. Roosevelt's pretty striking entrance into the historic enclosure at the north end of Roanoke Island, scene of England's first gesture toward empire, three and a half centuries ago."

One detail of her visit, however, was kept private. The disappointed reporter wrote, "No list of the guests at the week end house party was given out by Hall Roosevelt whose birthday was being celebrated. It numbers about twenty. Request for a list was declined."[75]

Mrs. Roosevelt told little more about the occasion in "My Day." She informed her readers that she and Miss Thompson had just gotten back from one trip when they set out for Dare County where Hall had gathered "a number of friends." They arrived there on Saturday, July 1, and "stern duty" called them away Sunday for Richmond where, at the meeting of the National Association for the Advancement of Colored People, she presented Marian Anderson the Spingarn Medal "in recognition of her achievement as one of the great artists of this time."[76] Of Hall's birthday celebration she only said, "It was a very jolly party and I enjoyed it very much."

"Stern duty" seemed an increasing reality in the world, though many at home once again felt that Europe's dangers were Europe's business. When Roosevelt had visited Warm Springs in April 1939, he had left with the ominous words, "I will be back in the fall if we do not have a war."[77] Yet despite the outbreak in Europe, he was back briefly in November, but as a man who less and less could leave the mounting problems of the world behind him in Washington. Nineteen forty ushered in a year, in which as the cause of the Allies grew more desperate in Europe and isolationism stiffened at home around Roosevelt's concern for the world, Eleanor made the most dramatic demonstrations as to how, in sharp contrast, she could both hurt and help him—involve him in harassment and deserve his admiration.

The hurt came first. For a long time, despite disapproval in the staff around Roosevelt, Eleanor had given time, aid, and money to the American Youth Congress.[78] She had attended as a sort of audience for the defense an investigation of the organization by the House Committee on Un-American Activities and apparently approved when young Joseph Lash, who was to be her great friend and "stand-by,"[79] ridiculed the committee to its face.[80] With Russia in alliance against the Allies, however, she had asked its leaders if they were communists. Solemnly they told her "No" and she "decided to accept their word, realizing that sooner or later the truth would come out."[81] Some were not supporters of the cause of the Soviets, then violently anti-Ally. Arthur Schlesinger, Jr., in his story of the Roosevelt years, wrote that her friend Lash was a Socialist who "resisted the communist embrace."[82]

Eleanor, however, not only accepted the protestations of loyalty of all the leaders of the group. Also, when the organization met in Washington in February 1940, she spent hours on the phone arranging sleeping space for many of the delegates in such government facilities as the riding hall and guardhouse at Fort Myer. She paid the transportation to Washington of some of the young people.[83] Mrs. Nesbitt wrote, "February brought a deluge of rain and the Youth Congress. Cots were lined up in every available room, and we were going at top speed, trying to keep up, and shorthanded, because so many of the help were sick."[84] Also, Eleanor "thought it advisable to ask Franklin to speak to them." He was not pleased when, standing in the rain, he saw among the five thousand youths gathered on the White House lawn such banners as "The Yanks Are NOT Coming" and "Keep America Out of War."[85] Instead of patting them on the back, as Eleanor thought they expected, he "felt obliged to say some pretty harsh things about their responsibilities and attitudes toward life." On his own grounds, they loudly booed him. Eleanor wrote that she was indignant at the bad manners and the lack of respect of the group she had assembled. However, she reported that Franklin only "smiled at me genially and said, 'Our youngsters are always unpredictable, aren't they?' "[86]

Eleanor appeared in a very different fashion when reluctantly she went at the call of Jim Farley, Hickok and others to the Democratic National Convention in Chicago in July. Though some reactionaries were also reluctant, the convention was ready and willing to nominate for a third term Franklin, who had stayed away. But it grew rambunctious at his wish that dreamy-eyed, mop-haired Henry Wallace be named as his running mate. Even the President's son, Elliott, had come from Texas with the announced intention of nominating Jesse Jones for the second place on the ticket. Eleanor flew to Chicago and in a speech of great dignity and force quieted the tumult and brought the convention to acceptance of Wallace. As she prepared to depart for home, a call from Franklin on the West Coast stopped her plane. He had listened to her speech. She had done a very good job.

Franklin never ran against a man for whom he had greater respect then and later than Wendell Willkie. Both saw eye to eye on the responsibility of America in the world crisis, though the pressures of the campaign forced both to give reassurances they regretted later to strong anti-war sentiments. Willkie's appeal pulled Franklin from his planned above-the-battle attitude in the campaign. But even his political animosity was directed at others. He and Eleanor both resented the sharper and sharper things Alice Longworth was saying about their personal lives in the campaign. Unfairly, perhaps he thought of her in connection with Nick's kin, René de Chambrun, now the son-in-law of Pierre Laval, leading collaborationist with the Germans in the occupation of France. In Washington, though no collaborationist, Alice was an isolationist now.

"I was panting after my parent, longing to go into the First World War," she declared. "Then along came the Second World War, and I said, 'We've tried that thing; let's see if we can keep out this time.' We all swing back and forth."[87]

The swing or shift irritated Roosevelt.

Others stirred his ire, notably three reactionary and isolationist Congressmen: Joseph Martin, Bruce Barton, and Franklin's Dutchess County neighbor, Hamilton Fish. In October, Candidate Roosevelt moved in full fighting spirit to the great forum of Madison Square Garden in New York. There with his family and friends arrayed on the platform behind him and a cheering multitude before him, he put these Congressmen's names in ridicule into a lilting phrase, "Martin, Barton, and Fish." It was as easily chanted as Wynken, Blynken, and Nod. Then and afterward crowds cried it back to him like a cheer.

A delicate detail was missed in the applauding tumult. Harry

Golden, a young Jew with journalistic aspirations, had gotten a place in the press gallery. An older hand in presidential reporting pointed out to him the important people on the platform and in the audience. He identified Roosevelts and Roosevelt chieftains. Then, said Golden, later to become famous as an author, his friend nodded toward a very handsome woman on one of the first rows of the audience. She was accompanied, Golden said, by men whom he recognized as New York City detectives.

"That," said his informant, "is Mrs. Winthrop Rutherfurd."[88]

In such an exciting campaign, no significance needed to be attached to the presence of one lady among thousands of spectators. Certainly the role of other ladies in that campaign and after Roosevelt's victory is better documented. Eleanor herself testified to what obviously seemed to her to be the prehensility of Alice.

"Neither Franklin nor I," she wrote, "ever minded the disagreeable things my cousin Alice Longworth used to say during the various campaigns, though some of the people around Franklin resented them bitterly. When the social season started after the third campaign, in which she had been particularly outspoken, she was invited as usual to the diplomatic reception. General Watson, Franklin's aide, wondered if she would have the face to come; in fact, he was sure she would not. Franklin was equally sure that she would be there, so he and Pa Watson made a bet on it. On the night of the reception, when Alice was announced, Franklin looked at Pa with a grin, and said in a loud voice: 'Pa, you lose!' "[89]

If the year started with such a joke, it ushered in a sad time for both Franklin and Eleanor and in personal affairs as well as war worries. Harry Hopkins, who was to become Franklin's great war aide, seemed dangerously ill. Then, in mid-June, Roosevelt suffered a very special loss. Every year a hospitable Washington hotel manager had given a gay party for the White House staff. This year it was held in the mansion so the President could attend. At it, after the President had retired, Missy LeHand suddenly wavered and crumpled to the floor unconscious.[90] The stroke which she suffered could not have been entirely a surprise.

Always frail, more than a dozen years before she had been seriously ill at Warm Springs.[91] While her mind remained sharp and her temperament genial, in the White House she had been delicate. Now, however, the gentle guidance in many small things and some large ones, too, was gone.

Other personal tragedies came in the dismal summer, a year after Hitler had overrun Europe. In August 1941, old Sara was fading. Hall, who had seemed so bibulously vigorous at the Goosewing Club, could no longer be left on a remote shore. Still clinging to his gin, he was moved to a little house not far from Eleanor's Val-Kill cottage at Hyde Park.

In August, with elaborate deviousness, Franklin set off on a "fishing trip" which carried him to his historic meeting with Winston Churchill on shipboard at Argentia. The prospect gave him release. Also, the Atlantic Charter which they shaped was a banner in his cause to carry America to the aid of the Allies. He came home to his mounting responsibilities. "Fortunately," however, as Eleanor said, he decided to go to Hyde Park for the weekend of September 4. He was there when patrician old Sara died on September 7.

This was a doubly tragic day for Eleanor. As Sara was dying, Hall became very ill. On the day of her mother-in-law's funeral he was moved to the Vassar Hospital in Poughkeepsie, then to Walter Reed Hospital in Washington. Eleanor spent much time, night and day, by his bedside. In "My Day" she wrote that as she watched she kept thinking of William Ernest Henley's *Invictus* with its phrase about an "unconquerable soul."[92] Also when he died, on September 27, 1941, she wrote that there was much for his children "to be proud of in their inheritance."[93] Long afterward she wrote even more eulogistically and more frankly, too, about him in her memoirs.[94] After his funeral in the East Room of the White House, she carried him home to Tivoli for burial.

Characteristically, however, while she was watching at the bedside of her dying brother, on September 22, she agreed to take on the non-defense activities of the new Office of Civilian Defense "necessary for the protection of the civilian population as a whole."[95] This brought her, she said, to the most unfavorable press she had ever had. Much unfavorable—and as she thought unfair—criticism came with her appointment of a young dancer, Mayris Chaney, "to develop a recreational program to be used for children in shelters in case of bombing." From the clamor that arose, she wrote, "one might have thought Congress considered dancing immoral."[96] Certainly she worked by night and by day. If her companionship was needed in the White House, there was little time for it.

Damned for his aims and much baffled in his purposes to arm America and aid the Allies, Franklin in the White House this autumn seemed withdrawn into himself. Earlier in the year, when she watched beside him, Missy LeHand had said that a persistent cold from which he suffered was "a case of sheer exasperation."[97] Now he seemed to turn from oppressive news and violent isolationist opposition to retreat within himself in escape from tensions. He worked much with his stamp albums. He sent items to be saved in the Library at Hyde Park. His appetite was bad, which Mrs. Nesbitt felt was a kind of contagion related to the diet to which the active but skeleton-like Hopkins was restricted. He began, while "babying" Japan along to keep the peace, to take time to dictate to Missy's successor, Tully, anecdotes and amusing recollections from happier days: experiences in the Wilson years, boyhood memories of his father's yacht, the first *Half Moon*. Sherwood, who was standing by as a speech writer and eager helper, wrote: "In the midst of the uncertainty and hair trigger danger of the months before Pearl Harbor, Roosevelt expended a great deal of time on a project for a fishing retreat for Hopkins and himself."[98] The record about his interest in this plan for a secure place on a storm-swept Florida key relates to mid-November 1941. Roosevelt took time to draw an elaborate plan for a house which he believed would be hurricaneproof.

He sent a memo about the plan to the hospitalized Hopkins, among whose travels as a skeleton in armor had been a trip to Russia, now flung by Hitler to the Allied side. "Perhaps," the President wrote, "if we go down to Warm Springs within a

week, you could run down and stay . . . in Key West for a week
and look it over."[99]

Roosevelt did set out for Warm Springs on November 28,
expecting to stay two full weeks.[100] The annual Thanksgiving
dinner which he enjoyed with the polio patients and other
friends had been postponed for his arrival on November 29. That
was to be his only day and night there. Secretary Cordell Hull,
in the midst of his long dialogue with Japanese emissaries, phoned
him. The time of talk was coming to its end. Roosevelt was back
in Washington on Monday, December 1. Then the dialogue had
only become a Japanese mechanism for delay and deception.

A week later the bombs fell at Pearl Harbor. Mrs. Nesbitt
finally got every window in the White House "either painted
black or covered with black sateen."[101] Also, as Mrs. Roosevelt
flew off on a civilian defense mission to rumors of a bombed West
Coast, all White House affairs were canceled. This, Mrs. Nesbitt
noted, "gave me a chance to finish the Christmas baking in
peace."[102] The house was not to be peaceful long. On December
22, Winston Churchill and his staff suddenly appeared after secret
passage. Other war guests, including Molotov of Russia and
refugee royalty, came. With rationing and the like Mrs. Nesbitt,
now pushing seventy, had enough on her mind. It was not her
business that some of the guests "didn't seem to fit together, like
asking Queen Wilhelmina along with Joe Lash of the Youth
movement, and having Mr. Churchill and Mayris Chaney at the
same time. She was the dancing one, Miss Chaney."[103]

Life was not entirely altered behind the painted windows and
the black sateen.

THIRTEEN

Call Home the Heart

(1)

Missy LeHand heard the news of the attack on Pearl Harbor in her cottage at Warm Springs where she was hoping to regain her mobility after the stroke she had suffered the summer before. Despite the defect in her speech, instinctively she tried to reach the President by telephone. Of course, she could not reach him on this day of shock and reaction. The phone to his desk in his oval study was occupied with reports and commands. Others in the room, crowded with top civilian and military officials, took the dictation Missy would have received when he shaped his "day of infamy" report to the Congress and the nation. There was not room on Roosevelt's phone or in his mind for the lonely Missy so recently become crippled and uncertain in speech by an attack almost as sudden as the Japanese assault.

"I could not put it through to the President," said Grace Tully of the call from her old superior whom she loved very much.[1]

The desperate call was only a sad little detail in the tumultuous day which extended far into the night. History noticed the more important thing that Roosevelt, in the turtleneck sweater he had had on when the news cracked his Sunday apart, looked more than ever like the confident commander. The frustration, which Missy had noted before she fell stricken at the party the summer before, was gone. His fatigue seemed to fall from him like a discarded cloak. Perhaps he never learned that Missy in Warm Springs had tried to reach him. Yet her inability to get to his voice through the essential barriers about the presidency emphasized the inability he would face in his need to reach one whose quiet voice and easy company he would need more than ever in the pressures and tensions of war. Possibly in her efficient congeniality Missy had in peacetime made less imperative his need for the companionship of Lucy Mercer Rutherfurd.

Now as his responsibilities and tensions multiplied he would have less time and more need for her company. The difficulty of communication with her was one he declined to face. Rationing gave greater excuse for his dull White House fare. But the greater security measures thrown around the presidency gave him a privacy he had been denied before. As plans for operations in the distance were put into effect, on hand soldiers suddenly appeared to close and guard the White House gates. Friends, often his own family, as well as the enemy were denied knowledge about his movements. That served personal as well as global stratagems. Also, sometimes disregarding strategy and security, he moved to the company he required with an insouciant disregard of concealment which was a more perfect dissemblance.

The war for him had not waited for the bombs. Its imminence became clear and final in Warm Springs a week before the news came from Hawaii. He had gone there for expected rest. There would be time in it for contemplation of that place safe from all the winds which he discussed with Harry Hopkins. He arrived on Saturday, November 28, and went straight to see Missy in her cottage. He stopped there again on the following day when the visit had become only a turn around back to Washington and the certainty of war. Missy had been on the verge of tears when she saw him go.[2] Evidently both understood the darkness ahead. Missy would not lithely walk or easily speak again. She came to the White House briefly in the next year, then in steadily failing health she lived in her home north of Boston.[3] Almost incidentally Mrs. Roosevelt saw her there when she went to Boston to visit the Chelsea Naval Hospital.⁴ Naval operations under Roosevelt moved island to island and continent to continent. Missy died in the summer in which he went as Commander-in-Chief to the Pacific from a country in which as party chief he faced a campaign for a fourth presidential term with a strange combination of determination and distaste.

Obviously a certain disregard for domestic consequences made his mood as the first traces of approaching autumn came this year. On August 17, 1944, he returned to the White House after an absence of thirty-five days.⁵ That had been after the journey which took him to Hawaii and the Aleutian Islands in the not yet subdued Pacific—a voyage to war councils which Thomas E. Dewey, his opponent in the campaign ahead, smirkingly described as "Mr. Roosevelt's holiday."⁶ It had hardly been a vacation from the great vexations which attended his responsibilities. Hardly anyone knew then that in San Diego, before he sailed, he had had what his son James had feared was a heart attack. Suddenly seized with pain, he had had his son help him stretch full length on "the deck" of his railroad car. He lay there gasping. Then, mustering his strength, he went out to review waiting troops. In a letter to Mrs. Roosevelt he lightly described the excruciating experience as "the collywobbles."⁷

There was rough weather on his voyage. His speech from the West Coast on his return had not sounded good. His photographs were worse. Certainly on his return to his office in Washington he looked weary and worn. An August weekend at Hyde Park, where Eleanor was maintaining the summer base for her wide-ranging operations, had not rested him. His correspondence secretary, Bill Hassett, who accompanied him there, described Mrs. Roosevelt as giving "elaborate directions" and noted: "many visitors at mealtime—all ages, sexes and previous conditions of servitude—hardly relaxing for a tired man."⁸

Back in the White House he was "still a little tired and nervous."⁹ Yet there, on August 29, in a news conference definitely "on the record," he surprised reporters with the announcement that the old warrior, whom his bitter rival Willkie had called "the champ," was going back into political action with a speech in September to his old, tough friends, the unionized Teamsters. There was a flash in his eyes which only faded after reporters had rushed to file their stories. He entrained again for the Labor Day weekend at Hyde Park. Then those who had expected to wake up in Highland, across the Hudson from Hyde Park, found the train moving to a stop in northwestern New Jersey.[10]

Roosevelt in his wheel chair descended on the small elevator built into the rear platform of his observation car. With the aid of Secret Service men, he moved to an automobile. Then he was off to the big Rutherfurd House on Tranquility Farms, near Allamuchy. Some members of his entourage looked up from their magazines or card games with surprise. Yet not even the three press service reporters, allowed under wartime "volunteer censorship" to accompany him but not write about him, showed much interest. Roosevelt had all sorts of acquaintances in big houses. The word went around that he had stopped to see an old friend, Mrs. Winthrop Rutherfurd, whose husband had died a few months before. Even in the stress of war and particularly in the freedom which absences from Washington gave him, Roosevelt was constantly making visits of kindness, condolence, or conviviality. They marked his grace—and his loneliness, too.

Those on the train, including supposedly vigilant and impartial newsmen, wished him any relaxation he could get. Apparently only Hassett made any written note of the incident at Allamuchy. A gray gentleman, devoted to the President, who called him "deacon" before he promoted him to "bishop," Hassett was an erudite Vermont Yankee and devout Roman Catholic. Generally he looked solemn until, beneath twinkling eyes, he snickered at an amusing world or snorted at pretensions in it. At the beginning of the "black out" time, during which he traveled much with the President, he bought himself a little journal.[11] In it in affectionate fashion he wrote for himself—and only possibly for history—as much of the story as he saw of Roosevelt's "off the record" movements which could not be reported in wartime.

Of the stop at Allamuchy, he scribbled two pages.[12] But

when the time came, as it later did, for his diary's publication, he obliterated them. His published story of the trip via Allamuchy only noted the train's departure from Washington and its arrival in Highland late in the afternoon, not as usual in the morning. Mrs. Roosevelt, he noted, met the train.[13] The President was taken to her Val-Kill Cottage which was her own separate one, like his on the hilltop—both independent of the main Roosevelt family house, seldom referred to by its name Springwood.

Obviously Roosevelt, stopping a train full of witnesses, indicated that there was nothing he wished to hide from history about this visit. Hassett himself, after he had meticulously (as he thought) edited his diary to cut out this incident and some other details, never seemed quite sure why this visit of Franklin to Lucy should be regarded as unmentionable. Yet only reluctantly he agreed to put in a footnote, elsewhere in his book, where he had deleted another passage.[14] It is inconceivable that he had been presidentially so instructed in secrecy. Some sort of instinct in Hassett and others seemed to shape a kind of spontaneous concert of silence about all things pertaining to Lucy Mercer Rutherfurd.

Certainly Roosevelt, in his different roles as candidate and commander, treated the "volunteer censorship" by press and radio as something to be put on and taken off like the old Navy cape he wore in the portraits made of him by Elizabeth Shoumatoff, whose friend and patron Lucy was. Sometimes restless newsmen did not feel that he handled censorship with the meticulous care with which Madame Shoumatoff arranged his cape for her compositions. He flung it aside when he required audiences as politician. Yet he recognized the need for protection and wanted privacy, too. Indeed, it was not so much privacy he wanted as unscrutinized opportunity for release from the loneliness which more and more oppressed him.

His was more than the loneliness all Presidents endure. It did not begin with the war. His children and his friends recognized that. So did some who seemed associated with him only or largely as great aides in great enterprises. Much has been written about it by Tugwell who not only knew him in life but as historian devoted years to research about him after his death. This early Brain Truster, as a great admirer of Eleanor Roosevelt, saw soon and late a separation between the Roosevelts behind the elaborate façade of a more-than-marriage partnership which they maintained. Much of it Tugwell blamed on the reticence of Franklin who seemed to the majority of his countrymen an almost extravagantly articulate man.

"Even Eleanor, most of the time," this official and friend said, "had little idea of his real feelings. And by the time he was President she knew very little more what he was thinking than did any of the rest of those around him."[15] By 1940, when in addition to her earnings from "My Day" she was getting $3000 for radio broadcasts, Tugwell thought that "it was plain that the lives of Franklin and Eleanor ran together less as the years passed."[16] Soon, he said, "She was not only the President's wife any more. She was beginning to be the great lady that still another generation knew so well."[17]

Within the family, James Roosevelt, in his book about his father, elaborated the theme of his subtitle, "the story of a lonely man."[18] He certainly told no household secret when he wrote that as the White House years lengthened, "Mother's travels and activities had become global."[19] And even those who most approved Eleanor's good works and peripatetic concerns generally understood before James wrote it that the one thing which his mother could not bring to his father "was that touch of triviality he needed to lighten his burdens."[20] James expressed that better when he wrote of the times when he and his first wife in their house tried to surround him with company which understood that the President "did not want to remake the world every evening."[21] Certainly a better expression than a "touch of triviality" was needed for the kind of gaiety and charm with which Bets had blessed her father-in-law.

Eleanor, who readily agreed that she was not Franklin's confidante, had an explanation satisfying to herself about his frequent withdrawal into himself.

"His was an innate kind of reticence," she declared, "that may have been developed by the fact that he had an older father and a very strong willed mother, who constantly tried to exercise control over him in the early years. Consequently, he may have fallen into the habit of keeping his own counsel, and it became part of his nature not to talk to anyone of intimate matters."[22]

Sometimes she understood or suspected that he cloaked himself with mock solemnity and fantastic jokes in a serious world. On occasion she chided him for his "careless levity."[23] As she defended Mrs. Nesbitt, however, often she failed to understand his weariness with conversation that was all zeal and little zest. Others besides James and Bets sought company for him which perhaps seemed merely amusing but was terribly important to him. Far from trivial it was sustenance for the spirit of a man hungry for the balm of those who brought him in the little leisure he could grasp not more problems but peace.

From no one could he get that in greater measure than from Lucy. Yet Lucy remained after all the years to Eleanor the never forgotten threat to her marriage, her love and her pride. Because of Lucy she had made a life of her own. She had grown expansive in it, found it satisfying. In the White House it made her appear almost as first minister without portfolio but with the readiest access to power. But even in duty there was an aspect of substitution. Her own eminence had grown almost as a mask perpetually worn in a marriage which had survived in every quality except romantic love.

An awareness of a relationship of convenience, respect, and affection where love had once been grew imperceptibly among many who knew the Roosevelts best. It was suspected even by some whose place close to them was more official than personal. So even among those who had great admiration for both Eleanor and Franklin, there grew, as Hassett best documented, a sort of rule of reticence about the happiness which Franklin found in the woman who seemed only a sort of fragrance from the past. Some closest to both Franklin and Eleanor, not regarding themselves as conspirators, were ready in reticence to welcome Lucy while protecting Eleanor. The chief conspirator was Franklin himself.

Roosevelt was a man who understood that secrecy could never be merely a negative thing. He enjoyed the building of pretenses as when he went off "fishing" and brought back the Atlantic Charter. There had to be a substitute scene and not merely a blank wall. In the midst of wartime security in addition to his ordinary addiction to royalty, he paid special attentions to a charming foreign Princess. He enjoyed the pictorial company which the lovely princess, her children and her occasional husband provided. Yet he must have enjoyed, too, even encouraged, the completely false, romantic rumors which spread about his interest in the royal lady. The lady of his affection now as long ago was Lucy Mercer. Their tenderness for one another in the war years warmed and lit a dark time.

The resumption of their relationship, if indeed resumption is the word, certainly began before the White House windows were darkened with paint or black sateen curtains and before Hassett bought his little book. Roosevelt turned to Lucy and those close to her at least as early as the summer of 1941. On June 26, White House files show that he saw Winthrop Rutherfurd at noon.[24] This was undoubtedly Lucy's stepson as the older Winthrop, then 79, had already suffered a stroke and was confined to his house in Aiken. This younger Rutherfurd was no longer a boy; a man of thirty-seven he had graduated from Princeton in the class of 1928. After the war began, Roosevelt had an "off the record" meeting with Lieutenant W. Rutherfurd on May 18, 1943, at 2:30 P.M., and similar "off the record" meetings with Captain Rutherfurd on both July 8, at 4:45 P.M., and September 8, 1943 at 5 P.M.[25] During this period also, the White House staff recalled visits for lunch with the President at his desk by young Barbara Rutherfurd, Lucy's daughter who had known the President since her early childhood. In all "off the record" engagements persons coming to see the President entered by the East Entrance or "by the White House proper."[26] Visits of some intimates were not recorded in any manner.

With much greater precision, however, Grace Tully documented another instance of Franklin's affection for the children of Lucy's household in May 1943. Then Churchill had come again for a fortnight's visit to the White House. Hassett noted of the visit that "Churchill is a trying guest—drinks like a fish and smokes like a chimney, irregular routine, works nights, sleeps days, turns the clock upside down."[27] Still he was Winston Churchill. And there was much clamor for tickets when on this visit he agreed to speak to a joint session of Congress. "Mrs. Roosevelt," said Tully, "usually distributed the tickets but for this particular occasion the President requested that some of the tickets be turned over to him."[28]

This was not his first such request for tickets for some not on Eleanor's list. In January 1941, he had asked her for such tickets rather suggesting that in distribution she had gone rather heavily on tickets for Roosevelt family and relations. He wanted tickets for some White House helpers, and some Warm Springs folk, other "really personal friends who rate invitations."

"Also," he added, "it is possible that people may come in whom I personally have overlooked and I would like to have six tickets in my pocket to be used if necessary. This is a reduction from the twelve I suggested before. Can do?"[29]

Now before the Churchill speech in 1943, he got seven tickets. He asked Grace to deliver them: to the visiting Duke and Duchess of Windsor, to Myron Taylor Ambassador to the Vatican and his wife, to the British Minister of Transport Lord Leathers, "who is a dear," and to Mr. and Mrs. John Rutherfurd.[30]

In 1943, also he "agreed"—or arranged—for a portrait of himself by Elizabeth Shoumatoff to go from him as a gift to young Barbara Rutherfurd. In May, Tully reminded him that he had agreed to see and presumably sit for the artist who was then living at Hidden Hollow, Locust Valley, Long Island.[31] She arrived in Washington on May 12. In July, with her brother, Dr. Audrey Avinoff director of the Carnegie Museum in Pittsburgh, she came to lunch at Hyde Park, bringing the water color of Roosevelt with her. Hassett, who later expressed some impatience with Shoumatoff referred to her in his "off the record" journal as "the Russian lady."[32] The description was correct as far as it went. Madame Shoumatoff was of a family from Tulchin, Russia, members of which had come to the United States before the Communist revolution. In America Elizabeth Shoumatoff was in demand for portraits from wealthy members of the social world. After the July visit, Roosevelt wrote to Avinoff in typical Rooseveltian language that "it was grand to see you and Madame Shoumatoff at Hyde Park." He thanked him for a very fine etching of Our Lady of Kazen which "I am delighted to add to my collection."[33] Obviously, however, Franklin was more interested in the sponsor of their visits to him, the lady of Aiken.

He had begun seeing her often in a rather pathetically sly fashion before this time. Lucy had concerns which brought her to Washington. Her mother, the still voluble Minna, was becoming more and more obsessed about her need for her pension as she grew older. Obviously she had no necessity to be. With two such well-to-do sons-in-law as Rutherfurd and successful Dr. Marbury, she had been well cared for. In the late thirties some of her letters came from a pleasant hotel in Atlantic City where she was attended by a nurse, and from the fashionable Chamberlain at Old Point Comfort. By 1941, however, her daughters had found it necessary to place her in the Waverly Sanitarium, in Rockville, Maryland, near Washington. But Minna, at seventy-eight, found "this place," twelve miles from the capital, a disturbing distance from her old haunts. Her pension, she noted had been raised from $40 to $45 a month but "I am alone—in this sanitarium—my children and grandchildren are away from me. . . ."[34]

As resident in Washington Violetta was closer to the responsibility for their mother. Violetta herself, however, was already troubled in her marriage to a physician who sometimes showed a roving eye for the ladies. She needed Lucy's love and support. And Lucy, worn by the devoted care she gave to her elderly paralyzed husband,[35] needed relaxation and release, too. She and Roosevelt began to meet regularly in Washington for long drives together shortly after Pearl Harbor. Accompanied by Secret

Service agents whose duty was only to protect him, the President rode out to a meeting place on a road beyond Georgetown. Lucy would be waiting there in what Secret Service men remembered as an old car. They would drive and talk for two hours and the President would return to the White House a man refreshed by the lady whom his protectors remembered as a charming and beautiful woman.[36]

They met elsewhere. Late in 1943, Roosevelt had come back from conferences in Cairo and Teheran showing definite signs of strain. And as 1944 advanced, he came down with a bronchial infection which he could not shake off. Early in April, for rest and recovery he went to Baruch's estate, Hobcaw Barony, in South Carolina. Hassett did not make this trip. Perhaps that may account for his statement that "The Boss paid a heavy penalty in accepting Bernie Baruch's hospitality. Bernie added himself to the household and so was there most of the month F.D.R. spent in South Carolina."[37] Mrs. Roosevelt, who only flew down one day for lunch while Roosevelt was there, came home feeling that his visit to Hobcaw "was the very best move Franklin could have made."[38] Evidently she had not heard the report that Lucy also came to Hobcaw while the President rested there. Secret Service men made arrangements for her trip. Baruch remembered ruefully in his old age that he had had to let her have some of his gasoline ration tickets which were more difficult than money for him to secure.[39]

Lucy had much on her heart at this time. Trouble had come to her in the month before, while Franklin was suffering from the cold which took much out of him. In Aiken, Winthrop Rutherfurd, to whom she had given devotion and care during the five years following his stroke, died at the age of eighty-two. As a sad woman, not quite fifty-three, Lucy had taken his body to Tranquility for burial.[40] The Russians were then sweeping into Bessarabia. The Nazis were striking back on Cassino's rim. Private losses seemed small as the world bled. Yet at the end of a quarter of a century as the wife of a great gentleman, though one old enough to have been her father, Lucy as widow needed such strength as she could derive from the lasting affection of Franklin Roosevelt. They shared loneliness as they had not been able to share the union of their lives.

When Roosevelt returned to the White House, supposedly much rested, Mrs. Roosevelt was in New York. But Anna, in Washington, was concerned about him. No one thought it odd that, along with the Secretary of State, Franklin's companion in the car which rolled into the White House grounds was his distant cousin Margaret Suckley who was to be on hand on other occasions when Lucy Mercer visited him.[41]

There is, Hassett's diary notwithstanding, no real record of these years when security covered the President's movements. Hassett was present on significant occasions, left in Washington on others. One of the places to which Roosevelt went in this period was a guarded hide-away provided for him in a state park in the Catoctin Mountains in western Maryland. FDR named it Shangri-La after the idyllic retreat pictured by James Hilton in his novel *Lost Horizon*. Sometimes Franklin took "a circuitous route" to it.[42] Perhaps symbolically as the place for a sometimes underprivileged President, his quarters there, now much remodeled, had been a shelter for underprivileged boys from Baltimore.

One of its virtues in wartime was that it was only sixty miles from Washington. A greater virtue was the guarded privacy the President could have there. Also, nearer than Washington was Leesburg, where old friends of his and Lucy's lived. By a slip in James' book, in mention of a visit FDR made to the hospitable home of "Pa" Watson and his wife shortly before the Normandy invasion, the Watson place was described as near "Leesville." Actually it was near Charlottesville. There is no Leesville in Virginia lest it be some inconsiderable village unmentioned in gazetteers. Leesburg, in a country of great houses and wide meadows for blooded horses, was a place then where a President could have found surcease and serenity—as he had found it in visits to the Eustis place, "Oatlands," years before. In these later days, as Alice Longworth heard, Edith Eustis on occasions called the President to say, "There is someone here you want to see."[43] He understood whom she meant.

During this period, also, there may have been other visits than those regularly counted to Warm Springs. Turnley Walker, in *Roosevelt and the Warm Springs Story*,[44] rather suggests that there were. But wherever he was, there were those ready to help him have the visits with Lucy which lifted his spirits. Some inadvertently were drawn into the process. One among these last was his daughter, Anna, then Mrs. John Boettiger. Once as a child, perhaps because he loved her much, she was, during his first convalescence from illness in 1921, the spark of his irritations. Now with her husband in service she lived, with short absences, at the White House during the last seventeen months of his life—a time when Eleanor's sense of duty carried her more and more and farther and farther away. Anna loved her father as he adored her.

"It was immaterial to me," Anna said later, "whether my job was helping plan the 1944 campaign, pouring tea for General de Gaulle or filling Father's empty cigarette case. All that mattered was relieving a greatly overburdened man to make his life as pleasant as possible when a few moments opened up for relaxation."[45]

With Boettiger and all the Roosevelt sons off at war (in capacities of danger and patriotism in which Roosevelt had a right to pride), and with Mrs. Roosevelt adding to her American concerns travels to England, the Pacific and the Caribbean, Roosevelt was often in the big house with his daughter and her small son, Johnny. During this period Lucy came to the White House for dinner more than once. Ushers and others made no records of many who came informally through the White House's great front door. They remembered that Lucy came several times and helped to make life as pleasant as possible for the overburdened President.[46]

She had been coming there as happily welcomed guest before, in a sense, he returned her calls at Allamuchy. Certainly it is possible that at Allamuchy Franklin and Lucy planned later meeting at the close of the political campaign before him which he was to describe, using all capital letters, as "THE DIRTIEST CAMPAIGN IN ALL HISTORY."[47]

It had begun in that speech to the Teamsters in which, adding old humor to old fire, he brought ridicule upon those Republicans who had spread a story that on his trip to the Pacific by accident his little dog Fala had been left on one of the Aleutian Islands and Roosevelt had dispatched a destroyer to retrieve him. To the Teamsters, Roosevelt said that he and his family had borne personal attacks. But, he said with stinging solemnity that "unlike the members of my family, Fala resents this. . . . He has not been the same dog since. I am accustomed to hearing malicious falsehoods about myself but I think I have a right to object to libelous statements about my dog."[48]

This speech turned out to be devastating ridicule. Still Roosevelt, taking no chances in Dutch-up determination to beat Dewey whom Ickes—or was it Alice Longworth?—described as looking like the little man on a wedding cake, added a demonstration of endurance to his thrust of derision. He answered the concern about his health, which his photographs had aroused and "wicked"[49] whispers had amplified, by a strenuous pre-election tour of New York City in the pouring rain. Perhaps, as some felt who heard him speak later in the evening to the Foreign Policy Association, he had been fortified after this experience with more than enough martinis. But without stimulants his spirits were high. This was one election he was more than ordinarily determined to win. Dewey was the only opponent he ever hated. As he went to bed with victory on election night, with more grim satisfaction than elation he spoke to Hassett of his defeated opponent in terms of an old, earthy American epithet.[50]

So Roosevelt extended his presidency far beyond that of any other man and longer, as was made the law later, than any other man could hope to do. And Fala romped on the White House grounds as a fixed figure in the folklore of American politics. The little Scottie had become a symbol in cartoons, the subject of articles, even books. Certainly he was more publicly prominent than Margaret Suckley who had given him, under his registered name Murray the Outlaw of Fala Hill, to Roosevelt. Though it is not to be expected Miss Suckley, or Daisy as her intimates called her, deserves to be better remembered in the Roosevelt story than many others who have cluttered its scenes. So does that other Roosevelt cousin, Laura Delano. Miss Delano happened to have (politically quite irrelevantly) kennels of fine long-haired dachshunds and Irish setters. These two maiden ladies played similar roles as the companions of Roosevelt and Lucy on at least two significant occasions. Though they alike gave Roosevelt devotion and received great affection from him, the two women could hardly have been more dissimilar.

Of the two, Laura (or "Polly") came into the Roosevelt picture earlier and was closer kin to him. Franklin had long been amused by her patrician ways and love of jewelry. His affection for her endured. Durable, too, was her effusiveness and love of decorative appearances. Deducting a decade and a half from her age, she must have appeared in 1944 much as she was when her godson's wife, Patricia Peabody, the fifth Mrs. Elliott Roosevelt, described her at a family dinner in Eleanor's apartment in the early 1960s.

"She had bright purple hair with a deep widow's peak painted on with eye shadow, and a complexion paper-white," Patricia Roosevelt wrote of the tiny Polly. ". . . Her thin arms and hands were alive with bracelets and rings of diamond, sapphire and jade. One dinner ring on her right hand had a diamond the size of an egg. . . . Pushed into her hair to complete the ensemble, like a crown, was a large diamond bar pin. . . . Laura Delano was, after all, the grand dame of the clan, heiress to part of the Atlantic Coast Line fortune and owner of a fabulous home overlooking the East River in New York, on Sutton Place. She also had a splendid 200-acre country estate at Rhinebeck, New York, . . . and one of the finest collections of jade in America."[51] Possibly when in wartime she traveled on the guarded presidential train she made no such display. She must even then, however, have made vivid contrast with Daisy Suckley.

As Franklin's frequent traveling companion, Miss Suckley was described as almost kitten quiet in personality and appearance. Obviously such an impression was incorrect. The picture of her, somehow always drawn in subdued colors, is of a small woman sitting quietly crocheting in the presidential presence. Actually, Hassett's diary indicated that no one, outside the routine White House staff, rode more often on the President's train by his invitation in the war years. Few people more completely shared his interests in his books, papers and the Hudson River countryside which he loved so much.

There was nothing merely mousy about a woman who joined a presidential party of male bird lovers who accompanied Roosevelt on a bird call count in the deep darkness beyond midnight. Roosevelt regarded her as an adequate hostess for him when, Eleanor being absent, he entertained the ex-Empress Zita at luncheon in Hyde Park. Hassett presented little vignettes of Daisy not merely as a woman going over papers with the President in his library but as a companion convivially sharing sherry with him at Hyde Park and drinks with him on his train. Perhaps the best picture of her is one she drew herself in an article she wrote after his death about a happy ride with him and Fala around Dutchess County in the car so equipped with hand levers that he could drive it himself—and often at a dizzy pace. In it she did not even mention her own name but her quality was mirrored in her appreciation of the man beside her, exuberant in release from care. Somehow in that reflection Daisy Suckley could be as clearly and as appreciatively seen as the blue heron she and Roosevelt together watched standing knee-deep in the Val-Kill pond at twilight.[52]

Certainly Polly and Daisy were alike as companions for the President who did not crowd the conversation with problem questions and political ideas. They were also alike as women whose reticence and cordiality could be counted on when Lucy joined them, as at least twice she did, in the Little White House at Warm Springs.

Polly and Daisy rode with him late in November 1944 when

he went beyond the bitter political campaign for rest once more in the Georgia town. Hassett, also along, raised the curtain by his berth as the train roared South in the early morning of November 28. A glorious sunrise of pink and violet seemed to give a promise of a happy time before, first, Roosevelt's fourth inauguration and then the already planned trip to Yalta to meet Churchill and Stalin in shaping the meaning of the victory which already seemed assured. At Warm Springs citizens and patients gathered to greet him. School children marched to welcome him. At a big Thanksgiving Dinner of the Foundation, "Roosevelt spoke long and informally to the patients."[53]

But work followed the weary. On November 29, Wednesday, Hassett wrote, "The biggest batch of mail I ever laid before the President came in the overnight pouch from the White House."[54] More mail came. The weather turned cold and rainy. But if the President lacked sun, there was warmth and serenity in the Little White House.

No published record or diary or remembrance has reported that Lucy helped make this pleasant period in an overburdened life. Hassett, as he had of the Allamuchy visit, edited her presence out of his diary before publication. She had, however, been there for the first days of FDR's visit. On Sunday, December 3, the President disposed of his mail quickly and early. He said that he would have an early lunch so as to motor with his guest as far as the little town of Talbotton on her way to her home in Aiken.[55]

It is twenty-five miles from Warm Springs to Talbotton and the junction there with the main highway via Macon and Augusta to Aiken. The day was decidedly cold but clear. And in the bright day in the little town Franklin, at the end of the last full year of his life, told Lucy good-by. They looked forward, beyond the great duties which still lay before him, to their next meeting.

(2)

As afterwards was more and more evident, Roosevelt had desperately needed that interlude of relative relaxation at Warm Springs following his re-election in 1944. On the day after his victory he had indicated his readiness for release when a member of his staff asked about his plans for the afternoon.

"Nothing," he said, "but go for a ride with Harry Hooker—just two tired quarrelsome old men."[56]

Hooker had more qualifications as company than his own age and fatigue. As a man who had long ago been one of Franklin's law partners, he was one of those old friends to whom he more and more turned. Hooker, however, did not merely emerge from a pleasant past. His friendship for Franklin—and Eleanor—had extended across the years. He had gone with Eleanor on some of her early forays from the White House against poverty. He had been guest staying in the White House on that first crowded Christmas of the war when there was room at a dinner for sixty for such diverse characters as Churchill and Mayris Chaney.[57] He had sat at the same table amused by the pretensions of ancient aristocracy of the kin and aides of Madame Chiang Kai-shek who looked like a flower set on a steel stem.[58] Now, however, perhaps his age, maybe tensions which made him subject to the joke that he was quarrelsome, also created a perceptiveness about his old friend the President.

Hooker, as it turned out, was more than a tired man on this day of victory in which he rejoiced. Soon afterward, he was ill. So Franklin and Eleanor "bundled him up and took him to Washington."[59] There they discovered that he had a really serious heart attack and should not have been moved. They put him to bed in the White House where he remained a long time guest and, on occasion, one free to speak warnings and fears.

He was there in January when Franklin, guarding his own strength and not merely the public purse, dispensed in wartime with the great city-wide ceremony of a presidential inauguration. He decided to be sworn in on the South Portico of the White House with a strictly limited group around him there and with spectators standing in the South Grounds. "No fuss, feathers or peacock parades," Hassett described the plans.[60]

Even so it was a strenuous occasion for a tired President. There was push for place not only on the portico but on the grounds before it. The largest luncheon during the Roosevelt tenure was arranged. Hundreds more were invited for tea in the afternoon. "Pa" Watson, in general charge, maintained his joviality against all pressures. Edith Helm, after nearly two decades of White House experience, was "calm, poised, and practical."[61] Even Henrietta Nesbitt was at seventy adequate to the occasion. Eleanor was serene, though the presence of thirteen grandchildren plus other house guests crowded her out of her room and her bed. Hassett at the brief ceremony wrote of his worries about Roosevelt standing bare-headed and without cloak or cape in the cold raw weather as he spoke to the crowds standing in the grounds covered with snow.[62] James was alarmed when, after the ceremonies, he and his father were briefly alone in the Green Room before the great luncheon began. The President was thoroughly chilled. The same type of pain which he had suffered in San Diego, though less acute, was stabbing him again.

"Jimmy, I can't take this unless you get me a stiff drink," he said. "You better make it straight."

James brought him half a tumbler of whisky. He watched his father, as if he had never handled a drink before, toss it down.[63] Even to Eleanor it was clear that Franklin was far from well. Yet, two days later, taking Anna along, he boarded the cruiser *Quincy* at Norfolk for the journey to Yalta. The sea voyage did seem the kind of restorative relaxation he always enjoyed. He looked forward to his meeting with the other two of his only equals then on earth. Though they loom larger in history, his dealings with Churchill and particularly Stalin seemed to put him under less strain than emotional tensions in his own staff. They particularly involved James F. Byrnes, who, though now almost assistant President as Director of War Mobilization and Conversion, still smarted from the fact that he had been put aside as Vice-President and now bristled in resentment that he was not Secretary of State.

Anna, keeping her glass filled with ginger ale instead of vodka, joined heartily in the ceremonial toasts exchanged. Still above smiling lips she watched with increasing concern her father's sagging strength. It was becoming world evident. The photographs of FDR with the plump Churchill and the steel-like Stalin came back to the White House to shock his staff. These were no grisly caricatures made by a partisan press. U. S. Army Signal Corps photographers, serving the Commander-in-Chief, had alone been permitted at Yalta. Only the most carefully selected ones they made—still showing him haggard—were released to the press.

All things considered, the conference seemed a success. Yet the trip home was no happy return. Frail Harry Hopkins had to go for a sort of skeleton's holiday to the resort of Marrakesh in North Africa. Then, as the *Quincy* turned homeward, General Watson, much more to the President than a man of infinite jests, suffered a stroke. He died before the ship passed out of the Mediterranean. In the spirits of those who sailed on her, the cruiser became his catafalque. Oddly Hassett, who later wrote in his journal of his long fears about Roosevelt's health, was one who rejoiced in the appearance of the returning President.

"The President has come home in the pink of condition—hasn't looked better in a year," he wrote.[64]

The tall devoted Anna did not think so. She had become more than ever concerned about her father at the Crimean conference. His doctor did not reassure her. Now in desperate fear she saw the possible necessity of such protective procedures as had surrounded the stricken Woodrow Wilson more than two decades before. Behind a presidential secretary who would serve as much as possible as a front, she and her husband were prepared to help bear the burdens, deal with some of the decisions of the presidency. It was a plan which could never have worked in terms of the personality of the President or the pressures of those whose prestige much depended on demonstration that they had access to him. It was more a symptom of a daughter's fear than a design for hope.

Eleanor Roosevelt was evidently not so disturbed. She realized that when Franklin made his report to Congress on Yalta, sitting down and publicly referring to the weight of his braces, he "had accepted a certain degree of invalidism."[65] She found him less and less willing to see people for any length of time and more dependent upon a midday rest. Evidently, however, she did not modify her role as incessant adviser. She was surprised to discover that the problem conversation which she regularly brought to their meals was a burden he could no longer tolerate.

"For the first time," she said, she began to realize "that he could no longer bear to have a real discussion, such as we had always had."[66]

Her discovery came between his return from Yalta on February 28, and his departure for Warm Springs a month later—a time during which they quietly celebrated their 40th wedding anniversary on St. Patrick's Day. Not long afterward, at dinner with Franklin and the still not fully recovered Hooker, she let her voice and her strong opinions rise in opposition to compulsory military service for all young men in peacetime which Hooker favored. Later she herself blandly described the incident and her friend Hooker's outrage at her insensitiveness. Possibly Hooker then barely recovering from his heart attack was a tired, quarrelsome old man. He was an indignant one.

"I disliked the idea thoroughly," she wrote, "and argued against it heatedly, probably because I felt Harry was so much in favor of it that Franklin seemed to be getting only one side of the picture. In the end I evidently made Franklin feel I was really arguing against him and I suddenly realized he was upset. I stopped at once, but afterward Harry Hooker took me to task and said that I must not do that to Franklin again."[67]

She accepted the rebuke: "I knew only too well that in discussing the issue I had forgotten that Franklin was no longer the calm and imperturbable person who, in the past, had always goaded me on to vehement arguments when questions of policy came up. It was just another indication of the change which we were all so unwilling to acknowledge."[68]

Still such change in him did not impel her to leave her increasing "round of duties"[69] when on March 29, after a day of almost intolerable pressures, Franklin set out again for belated rest in Warm Springs. Anna could not go with him because her small Johnny was seriously ill with a gland infection which necessitated his treatment with the new drug, penicillin, at the Naval Hospital.[70] Eleanor was happy that Franklin had invited to accompany him his cousins Laura and Daisy, whom she knew "would not bother him as I should have by discussing questions of state."[71]

As the President's train left Washington the wisteria was in full bloom on the South Portico. Already the second installment of cherry blossoms were out on the mall. The train rolled into Georgia on a "perfect day, warm and sunny."[72] Yet beyond such dependable reports as the weather much confusion attends this whole historically scrutinized visit of the President to the Southern village he loved. Some afterwards reported that he seemed "just like a setting up dead man"[73] as he arrived to the usual loud welcome. Michael F. Reilly, chief of the Secret Service detail, remembered that for the first time Roosevelt seemed like an absolutely dead weight as he helped transfer him to his car. He reported to the naval physician in attendance, Commander Howard Bruenn, that Roosevelt was "heavy."[74] Yet Hassett noted that the President "drove his own car to the Little White House atop the hill." Certainly he was no zombie driving.

Responsibilities followed him. Big pouches full of mail, bills, documents arrived. News came of rising debate about what the President had done at Yalta. Congress was restive in the evident approach of peace. To Warm Springs came what Roosevelt described as the "Primadonnaish" resignation of Jimmy Byrnes. Yet he knew that he had the faith of young men at the front as he had had that of Morton Eustis who had felt as soldier, though entitled to place among economic and social royalists, that the New Deal had laid the original base for victory. This gallant son of Edith's had written home early in the war that "all those complaining are doing so not because of New Deal bungling but because their own pocketbooks, their pleasures and their personal conveniences are being affected."[75] On the eve of D-Day Morton had written his mother, "I have great faith in Roosevelt's ability not only to win the war but, even more important, to win the peace."[76] Such faith often made the burden of responsibility greater than the criticisms of the faithless and the fault finders. In "security" Roosevelt's life often seemed not only blacked-out but blacked-in.

Yet the Georgia countryside all about him was alight with spring. It was scene for the relaxation which he required from the pressures upon him. In research for his book, *When F.D.R. Died*, Bernard Asbell undertook careful studies as to the central detail of the release Roosevelt sought and found.[77] Through dogwood-lined roads, Asbell wrote, he drove, in the two-car procession the Secret Service preferred, on Monday, April 9, to a rendezvous at "a crossroads," perhaps at Talbotton, where he met an expected Cadillac convertible. It contained Madame Shoumatoff, a color photographer named Nicholas Robbins, and Lucy. The two ladies moved into the President's car, Lucy sitting in the middle next to the President. The photographer followed in the Cadillac. Lucy and the painter were conducted to the Little White House. The photographer, a Russian with a marked accent, was guided to the Warm Springs Hotel.[78] Asbell in his book reported that Lucy had commissioned Shoumatoff to do the painting in 1943 and that now Roosevelt "was returning the compliment,"[79] with a painting for Barbara. Actually the reverse was the fact.

On Tuesday morning, April 10, Robbins, who appears as an obscure and self-effacing artistic character, was summoned to the Little White House. There with Roosevelt's company of ladies looking on, he made pictures of the President in various poses, so that the artist might refer to them in completing her portrait.

Then, so he told Asbell, Roosevelt asked if he would take a picture of Mrs. Rutherfurd. The photographer waited until her blue eyes were lit "by a certain quality of reserved warmth he had come to admire." Asbell quoted him as making what seems a sort of cliché compliment.

"I have seen two smiles like that in my life. One was on Leonardo da Vinci's Mona Lisa; the other was Mrs. Rutherfurd."[80]

Not all this visit to Warm Springs was consumed with technical artistic procedures, though on the day of picture making Madame Shoumatoff, as Grace Tully wrote, was "very excited at her concept" of the new portrait.[81] There was conviviality in the sitting room overlooking the pines. They listened as Roosevelt called Anna to ask about little Johnny Boettiger. On April 11, as James learned, his "voice was strong and he was wonderful—full of fun and quips."[82] He was enthusiastic about the barbecue planned for the next day. On the phone, without mentioning Lucy's name, he indicated that an old friend was there and that all at the Little White House were having a delightful time.

On Wednesday afternoon, as Tully wrote, Roosevelt "went for a ride through the mountains with some of his guests." She did not name them. In the care in which recollections were handled at the time she wrote, there might have been four guests—or one. Since the President was, as Hassett reported, on this trip still driving his own little car he could have taken Lucy on such a ride as that upon which Daisy Suckley accompanied him at Hyde Park. Certainly the President's mood was described by Tully when she said, "Mike told me later that he sat for a long time at one of his favorite spots, as if he were looking onward and onward to some world of victory and peace."[83]

Thursday morning, April 12, began like all others. As almost routine, the mail was late. That seemed chiefly significant because a crowded day was planned. Out of affection for Roosevelt and to some extent at the prodding of the three "stand by" members of the press, Mayor Frank Allcorn of Warm Springs and Ruth Stevens, manager of the Warm Springs Hotel, were preparing a special old-fashioned Georgia barbecue—complete with the Brunswick stew which Roosevelt particularly liked. Afterward a show by the patients was to be presented. The President planned to come to the party at 4:30. Certainly his lack of any effort to treat Lucy as a sort of secret visitor was indicated by his placing her name on the guest list.[84]

Considering time out for the President's lunch and rest that was going to leave little time for attention to "the heavy batch of mail" which Hassett lugged to the White House soon after noon. Perhaps this as well as his afterward reported shock at the President's appearance accounted for Hassett's recorded irritation with the portrait procedures. The President began his work of study and signing "with his usual wisecracks," the secretary wrote. But in the room Daisy Suckley went on with her apparently interminable crocheting. The restless Laura moved about fixing vases of flowers. Lucy sat facing the President in content. Hassett, anxious to get his work done, gave the impression that Shoumatoff added clatter to confusion. She set up her easel and began sketching, talking to the President, measuring his nose, asking him to turn his head this way and that. Hassett, who thought the earlier portrait of FDR which she had done lacking in strength and only "pretty," regarded the artist as "altogether too aggressive." In such evident irritation he departed, leaving documents for the President to study. The President read as the woman painted. The servants began to set the table for lunch. Lizzie McDuffie saw Roosevelt raise his eyes to Lucy.

"The last I remember," she said, "he was looking into the smiling face of a beautiful woman."[85]

The President looked at his watch and spoke to the artist. "We've got just fifteen minutes more," he said.[86]

He lit a cigarette and turned back to his papers. He raised his left hand to his temple. He rubbed his forehead. Then the hand fell awkwardly down to the arm of his chair.

"Did you drop something?" Daisy Suckley asked.

"I have a terrible headache," said the President. Suddenly his body sagged in his chair. He slipped into unconsciousness.[87]

In the elaborate and sometimes conflicting reconstructions of this scene there was confusion in report and recollection. Turnley Walker, historian of Roosevelt's Warm Springs years, wrote that "the quiet of the cottage was shattered by the woman painter's scream."[88] Roles in the drama of the President's collapse were assigned by reports to all in the house, on the White House staff, among the newspapermen—to all save Lucy who was most concerned. When later he called the newspapermen, Hassett, whose skill was in handling detail, even omitted the fact that Lucy was among those present when the President was stricken. In the interlude of shock after Roosevelt's collapse, he talked on the phone in Washington with his former associate and old boss, Steve Early, who had been the President's press secretary until he resigned before Yalta. Nothing is so clear now, emphasized by Hassett's editing of the entry for the day in his diary, as that the omission of Lucy's name was not an oversight but a decision.

In this startled early afternoon, however, it was only evident that the President was a very ill man—though even that was apparently not entirely clear in Washington. The facts about Lucy's departure at this time have been confused. One story was that the Secret Service, for whatever its reasons may have been, had difficulty in getting her away. Another was that Grace Tully—or Laura Delano—in gentle firmness suggested that she and her artist friend leave promptly as the rooms in the guest house would be needed by members of the family. No other "members of the family" came when hours later Eleanor arrived. The certain thing is that Lucy was not a lady who would have had to be ejected. She required no suggestion from Tully as to the course she should take. Evidently, however, there was hasty departure. The desperate illness of Franklin, whose stentorian breathing could be heard throughout the house, removed him as the master of his household. Those whose place in it was private or official understood that. So did Lucy Mercer. In these hours, even more than when he was stricken long before at Campobello, he was Eleanor's—and Eleanor's alone. Even before Lucy had departed Laura Delano called Eleanor on the phone.[89]

April 12, like so many others, was a crowded day for Eleanor.

Her appointment book for the day listed seven appointments, including a press conference at eleven in the morning.[90] Mrs. Roosevelt told the assembled women reporters that she would be leaving in a couple of days for speaking engagements in New York. Then, of course, the important trip ahead would be that with her husband to the opening of the United Nations conference in San Francisco. She parried questions about the future of conquered Germany. She spoke of the world unity, in which all nations would have a voice, in the United Nations. The press girls filed out, other callers came.

Early in the afternoon she received the call from Laura Delano. Mrs. Roosevelt wrote that Franklin's cousin had called to tell her that he had fainted. Certainly the voluble Laura gave her more than that laconic message. She mentioned that he had been sitting for his portrait. Mrs. Roosevelt asked terse questions, Asbell said, "calculated to elicit all Miss Delano could tell her."[91] Then another call came from Admiral Ross T. McIntire, Naval Surgeon General and Roosevelt's regular personal physician. He had not regarded Roosevelt's condition as such that his presence was required on the Warm Springs trip. Indeed, shortly before it he had given reassuring interviews about the President's health to the press.

Now he told Mrs. Roosevelt that he had talked to Dr. Bruenn at Warm Springs. He was, Mrs. Roosevelt wrote later, "not alarmed." He thought it would be well, however, for them to go to Warm Springs that evening. He told her also, she remembered, "that he thought I had better go on with my afternoon engagements, since it would cause great comment if I canceled them at the last minute to go to Warm Springs."[92] So she went, as planned, to the annual tea of the Thrift Shop at the exclusive Sulgrave Club on Dupont Circle. She sat next to Mrs. Woodrow Wilson. A society reporter described Eleanor as "looking unusually smart and in soaring spirits."[93]

Mrs. Roosevelt made a short talk praising the work of the Thrift Shop and its leaders. Then entertainment began. In the midst of a piano solo, the master of ceremonies whispered to Mrs.

Roosevelt that she was wanted on the phone. Quietly she left her seat.

"Steve Early, very much upset, asked me to come home at once. I did not even ask why. I knew down in my heart that something dreadful had happened. Nevertheless the amenities had to be observed, so I went back to the party and said good-by, expressing my regrets that I could not stay longer because something had come up at home which called me away."[94]

She knew what awaited her. Early and McIntire told her that Franklin had died at 3:35 P.M., while dutifully she was listening to the music at the tea. Early told the press later that the first words she said were, "I am more sorry for the people of this country and this world than I am for ourselves." Later Eleanor could not remember making any such statement at all.[95] Vice-President Truman was called. She did remember telling him, "how much we would all want to help him in any way we could, and how sorry I was for the people of the country, to have lost their leader and friend before the war was really won."[96] She radioed her sons. Then quickly with Early and McIntire she was on a plane which flew through the night.[97]

Lucy learned of the death only as millions of other persons did. As soon as the photographer Robbins could be summoned by the Secret Service, she and her companions had driven off. At the wheel, once she slowed at the "crossroad" where Roosevelt had met them four days before.

"Isn't this the place?"[98]

The others nodded. They drove on. Lucy turned on the radio. Then as the clock on the dashboard stood at a few minutes before six the news she had been expecting came. Lucy was told as the world was: Franklin Roosevelt was dead. Darkness began to fall on the road ahead of her. The news and the pious, patriotic comment clattered into the night.

The lights burned in the Little White House Lucy and her companions had left behind them. Toward midnight Eleanor Roosevelt came into it. She was calm and composed.[99] She kissed the waiting women, Daisy, Laura, and Grace. She sat down and let them tell her the details of the dreadful afternoon. Then she went into the room where her dead husband lay. She closed the door and remained alone there for about five minutes. She came out drawn but dry eyed.

Elsewhere in the village the emotional Early poured out his news to Hassett who had written the story of the day in his journal as a very religious man. "In the quiet beauty of the Georgia spring," he wrote, "like a thief in the night, came the day of the Lord. The immortal spirit no longer supported the failing flesh. . . ."[100]

But Early blurted to him: "There's hell to pay, Bill. Mrs. Roosevelt knows that Lucy Rutherfurd was here."[101]

By no sign there did Eleanor show anger or hurt. When in the morning she went out of the cottage she spoke graciously to all the military and naval company which had converged upon the little town. Down the hillside in a procession of soldiers following a band which had been brought from Fort Benning, she rode in a car behind the hearse. With her were Grace Tully, and the two so different spinsters, Laura and Daisy, and the little Scottie Fala. Muffled drums added to the solemnity of the slow-moving cortege. It paused by weeping patients, many of them children, gathered before the Foundation's Georgia Hall. There the bands were muted while a Negro musician, one who had amused Roosevelt often and had come to amuse him at the interrupted entertainment the day before, played "Going Home" on his accordion.[102] The train moved slowly northward through sad multitudes in cities and towns, in little groups at crossroads, too. Eleanor Roosevelt moved in dignity in the procession through those who made lanes of mourning of the avenues in Washington, to the East Room ceremony, erect even at the last moving rites in the rose garden at Hyde Park where a lilac bush was unfolding its blossoms on this anniversary of Abraham Lincoln's death. Only once, almost secretly in the White House, she asked that the coffin in the East Room be opened so that she could go in alone to put a few flowers in it before it was closed forever. Also, in the rose garden at Hyde Park, as few realized, she wore the small fleur-de-lis pin

Franklin had given her as a bride. She saw that special care was taken of Josephus Daniels as a "precious person" who so long, long ago had brought her and Franklin to Washington as young people on an adventure together.

Evidently even in the midst of the solemn obsequies there was on her heart a secret something she had to face. She made direct inquiries. Had Lucy Mercer come to the White House in the times when she had been away? The truth could not be denied. Eleanor's resentment could not be dissembled. She announced that she was getting out of the White House immediately. She would not be persuaded that the Trumans were in no hurry for occupancy and that little Johnny Boettiger was still very ill.[103] On the train, which was now Truman's, she got back to the White House at 8:40 Sunday evening, already preparing directions "to leave it just as soon as possible."

"I had already started," she remembered long after, "to prepare directions so that the accumulation of twelve years could be quickly packed and shipped. As always happens in life, something was coming to an end and something new was beginning. I went over many things in my mind as we traveled the familiar road back to Washington."[104]

Edith Helm "marveled at the speed with which she worked." She watched the packing boxes being filled in the halls.[105] Such a long time house guest as Harry Hooker must have been surprised.

"I'll be out by Friday," she told Mrs. Nesbitt.[106]

The old housekeeper doubted it. But even on Monday morning she saw that Mrs. Roosevelt had "all her clothes out of the wardrobes and over chairs, and was sorting them."

"We worked like beavers," Mrs. Nesbitt recalled. "There were thirteen years of accumulation to sort out. She wanted to give mementoes of him to so many people, and we had to dig all these things out, and sort them and send them. She wanted everyone who had known him to have some little thing to remember him by."[107]

She was finished by Friday. The Associated Press reported her departure late that afternoon on the 6 P.M. train for New York. Accompanying her to the station in two black limousines were James and Elliott and their wives, Anna, Mrs. John Roosevelt, and Malvina Thompson. A station wagon filled with luggage and paper brief cases followed the limousines. Already in the morning twenty army trucks loaded with the personal belongings of the Roosevelt family had rolled out of the gates. One guard at the gate reported, "There wasn't enough room left in any of them for even a teaspoon."[108]

The press service reporter who watched Eleanor depart wrote: "She did not glance back at the stately White House, which had been her home for so many years. No lights gleamed within, and silence engulfed the scene where before there had been great activity."[109]

The *New York Times* sent a man down to see her on her arrival at her apartment at 29 Washington Square West. Her train had reached Penn Station at 10:10 P.M. She came to the apartment apparently alone in a taxicab. In the dark the waiting *Times* man sought a detail of addition to the news. She had nothing to say she told him. Then she spoke tersely.

"The story," she said, "is over."[110]

AFTERNOON BY ALLAMUCHY

As always in April at Aiken the camellias seemed waiting, in 1945, to be replaced by the azaleas. Generally only old men puttered on the course of the Palmetto Golf Club. The polo fields did not resound now to the cry of players or crack of stick on ball. Most of the young men like Lucy's handsome stepsons were still in uniform and at war. Some, who gave the resort its élan would never come back to play. The greatest polo player of them all, Tommy Hitchcock, Jr., had been killed in an air crash in England in April 1944—an aviator still unable to stay out of the game of war at forty-four. Morton Eustis, cousin of Hitchcock and of Lucy's stepchildren, had been killed near the village of Domfront by an anti-tank missile while standing in the turret of his own tank leading the way at high speed down the hedgerows of Normandy.[1]

Yet, when Lucy, grieving alone, came back to the genteel little town from Warm Springs, violence seemed far away. No one dreamed that beyond the tended woods great plants would soon rise for the production of the bombs Roosevelt had ordered. They would make puny the appalling power Henry Adams had seen in the dynamos half a century before. If then the dynamos in the Gallery of Machines in Paris, in 1900, seemed to Adams to express a mysterious force like that of the Virgin of the twelfth century,[2] the bomb, kept as secret as Lucy's place in Franklin Roosevelt's life, promised a force satanic in all the centuries. America, "saying in its turn the last word of civilisation," as Adams predicted, did not as he foresaw it include ability to threaten civilization itself.

No such things directly concerned Lucy. She was only brought as witness into history again when Elizabeth Shoumatoff submitted to her the "Finished Portrait" she made from the incompleted picture she had been painting of Roosevelt when he was stricken. The artist asked "several people who knew him well to give me their reaction."

"Mrs. Winthrop Rutherfurd was one and her approval, after a few minor changes including the blue tie, was complete."[3]

Such details in remembrance seemed all the duty which remained to Lucy. These last made pictures were for display. She had, though it belonged to her daughter Barbara, the first Shoumatoff portrait made in 1943, on April 9 (the same day of the year on which she arrived in Warm Springs, in April 1945, Madame Shoumatoff wrote).[4] It recalled happier times. Lucy did not envy the greater and growing prominence of Mrs. Roosevelt.

When the story was "over," as Eleanor said, she was once again prepared for a relatively private life of widowhood. Still, two days before the Friday on which she left the White House, in the midst of her packing she wrote in her column, "My Day," spreading though dismissing rumors which she said already surrounded her. She had to "beg," she wrote Congresswoman Mary Norton of New Jersey, not to make a speech proposing that she be sent as a special delegate to the San Francisco conference.

"Then I heard a rumor," she related on Thursday, April 19, "that I was going to run for a federal elective position and, finally, that I was a candidate for Secretary of Labor! I had to tell several people quite forcibly that nothing would induce me to run for public office or to accept an appointment to any office at the present time."[5]

She had two jobs, she insisted: her daily column which she "wanted to have considered on its merits" and her magazine page. She did not look ahead to the facts that she would also write six more books, deliver innumerable lectures, travel further and faster than ever. She did recognize, however, her new independence in widowhood.

"Because I was the wife of the President, certain restrictions were imposed upon me. Now I am on my own, and I hope to write as a newspaperwoman. I certainly should have the background to bring to the job, and if I have not developed powers of observation and correct reporting in the past years, that will soon be discovered."[6]

But her retreat merely to the typewriter or to dictation to always-ready Malvina Thompson was not prolonged. In November, President Truman, whose own wife left the concerns of mankind to him, appointed Mrs. Roosevelt as U. S. Representative to the United Nations General Assembly. She became chairman of the Committee on Human Rights of the UN Economic and Social Council. She served as a U.S. representative at the 4th through the 7th UN General Assemblies until 1952, when she was sixty-eight. Somehow to many the United Nations seemed most real as she reported it and her part in it in daily detail. Many felt a sense of outrage when she was not reappointed by the Republican administration in 1952. She had tasks a-plenty still. She gave to the unloved love she required herself—to the crippled and the imprisoned, the bitter and the threatened. Occasionally she seemed to some perfunctory, even rigidly time-rationing on her errands which were as likely to carry her to New Delhi as Detroit. Some in her presence noted that when she took off her glasses she also removed her hearing aid.

She moved everywhere carrying a small zipper-type case of blue canvas with red leather trim. In it, sufficing for all her needs and appearances, she carried three basic dresses, including a formal, one pair of shoes, a hat.[7] She traveled especially in the cause and service of the American Association for the United Nations. Her pace never slackened on her way to the eulogy she deserved, which one day would be delivered in a cathedral by Adlai Stevenson as an emotional man in a scarlet academic robe. Before he spoke it, it was kaleidoscopically clear that she was a woman who "would rather light a candle than curse the darkness."[8] With all this, as the last of the fifteen spouses brought to her in her lifetime by her five children reported, she earned $150,000 a year "but had to give most of it to charity because of taxes."[9]

No one was farther removed from such incessant concerns than Lucy Mercer Rutherfurd. Perhaps that was true by chance. It was certainly so by choice. She enjoyed her winter and summer gardens at Aiken and Allamuchy. She was a gay and pictorial grandmother to all the Rutherfurd tribe. Her pleasures and troubles were private as her life had been. Almost a year to the day after she had gone last to Warm Springs, her own daughter Barbara was married on April 8, 1946, in a quiet Catholic ceremony at The Pillars, home of old Aiken friends, the George Meads. Barbara's husband, Robert Winthrop Knowles, Jr., eight years her senior, was a great-grandson of the socially and poetically proper Henry Wadsworth Longfellow. Possibly more important in Aiken, Knowles was a golfer who had gained early prominence on the links when at eighteen, in 1934, he had won the Eastern Interscholastic Golf Championship in a tournament at the Greenwich Country Club in Connecticut.

Often during these years, Lucy, traveling between Aiken and Allamuchy, stopped by Chapel Hill, North Carolina, where her cousins the Hendersons lived. There her niece and namesake, Lucy Mercer Marbury, had graduated from the University of North Carolina in 1944. Lucy continued her visits in passage there after Roosevelt's death. In 1946, she came on such a trip. She walked the old, bulging village's paths with Lyman Cotten, Jr., who as a boy had held the ribbons at her wedding, waited eagerly for the cake. Now a professor of English, he strolled with Lucy, aware, as were those they passed, how lovely she was. They ambled to a locally famous overlook of the plains below the hilltop college town—"to the Battle Bench below Gimghoul Castle to look at the beautiful view."

"A student in one of my classes was at the Bench," Lyman wrote, "and he asked me if I had a match. As he left the Bench, Lucy laughed and said, 'That boy did not want a match he just wanted an opportunity to speak to you.' I replied, 'Maybe.' But I was sure that the boy did not want an opportunity to speak to his instructor—he wanted to look at Lucy Mercer."[10]

She kept loveliness to behold, but sometimes life—and death— turned to her a grisly face. Early in November 1947, her sister Violetta came to visit her in Aiken. This was no ordinary autumn stay with a well-loved sister in a no longer crowded house. Violetta needed a refuge she could only hope to find and Lucy, in big Ridgeley Hall, could only hope to provide. After a quarter of a century Violetta's marriage was threatened. Her husband wanted a divorce. Heartbroken Violetta was ready to free him with her own hand.[11]

She had, indeed, attempted suicide before she came to Ridgeley Hall this fall. Lucy had loved her, pled with her. She hoped she had eased Violetta's hurt and calmed her depression. On November 11, however, Dr. Thomas G. Brooks of Aiken, signed Violetta's death certificate giving the cause as "gun shot wound of the head." No autopsy was necessary. Violetta, at fifty-six, was out of her husband's way. Soon he was married again—to Marguerita Pennington who had been at the convent in Austria with the Mercer girls when all were young. However, Marbury found it best to move from Washington, where Violetta had been much loved, to Farmington, New Mexico.[12]

Death was becoming a familiar of Lucy's. Less than two months later, and ironically on Christmas Day, her mother died at the sanitarium in Rockville. She had had nearly sixty years of life since she had announced at the age of twenty-five that she was stopping counting birthdays. Three days later old Minna was buried in the Arlington National Cemetery to lie forever beside Carroll from whom she was separated so much while they were living. Since no inscription concerning her was placed on Carroll's stone, she seemed more than ever only his.[13]

From Aiken, Lucy wrote about the last details. She informed the Veterans Administration of her mother's death.

"Will you let me know," she wrote, "if there is anything further to be done about this. . . . Her last check was received by me and not cashed—but at the moment I have mislaid it—I think it was dated Dec. 31st, 1947, but do not remember. Will communicate with you when I find it."[14]

Much in life seemed to be mislaid now. Others felt out of communication with Lucy. She failed to come by Chapel Hill that spring. Her cousins began to worry about her and inquired. She

had been taken to Memorial Hospital in New York doomed with
leukemia. There seemed no need to make a noise even in the family about it. In the hospital on Saturday, July 31, 1948, she died.
The world little noticed. The *New York Times* obituary gave
much of its attention to her dead husband and the rich Alice
Morton who had been his first wife long before Lucy took his
name and eased his life.

More people, of course, were reading then about what Eleanor
Roosevelt did and what Eleanor Roosevelt said. Even surly Russian diplomats had found it difficult to sneer at her now well-
modulated, righteous voice. She wrote about censorship, wild
flowers, domestic red-baiters and filibustering in the Senate as an
insult to intelligence. She was reading Henrietta Nesbitt's book
about her years as White House housekeeper to the Roosevelts.
Mrs. Roosevelt was prepared to defend to the last the housekeeper
she had chosen.

"Mrs. Nesbitt is truly kind to all of us," she wrote in her column.
"It is true she didn't always like all of our friends and some of the
visitors seem to have been a real trial, but so far as my husband
and myself and the children are concerned she was certainly a very
charitable and generous friend. . . . I always got along well with
Mrs. Nesbitt. My husband became difficult about his food in the
last few years, and with rationing troubles it became more difficult
to give him the things he really wanted."[15]

In similar casual vein she wrote her column about her day on
Saturday, July 31. This day she drove westward across New York
and northern New Jersey to Wilkes-Barre, Pennsylvania, where, in
Sugar Notch at the coal mining center, she shared honors paid
her husband in the unveiling of a monument to the war dead.
Three thousand people applauded her as she appealed for peace.
The Anthracite Men's Choir sang "The Battle Hymn of the Republic." She seemed to represent still the republic which her husband had served—and to represent it well. "Dressed in a 'new
look' black and white print dress, together with a pearl necklace,
beautiful corsage and Navy-style box hat with a ring of flowers set
off with a black bow," said the *Times-Leader and Evening News*

of Wilkes-Barre, "Mrs. Roosevelt was charming and graceful." It added that she exchanged words with many persons and shook their hands.[16]

She was, however, still a busy woman. Duties awaited her back in New York. The afternoon was growing late. The road she followed between Wilkes-Barre and Hyde Park lay via Stroudsburg, Pennsylvania, and the Delaware Water Gap on the Pennsylvania-New Jersey line. So it ran, as twilight came on that afternoon, a little north of Allamuchy.

There the word had come to prepare Lucy's place in the Rutherfurd family cemetery at Tranquility under the little mountains and not far from the pond where occasionally a blue heron stood as at Val-Kill. Big, old Rutherfurd House loomed, solid and heavy in the dark. It had given Lucy shelter. She had given it grace, affection, a warm heart and a blithe spirit. She was welcome to its earth. Her story was over as Mrs. Roosevelt on her lengthening journeys rode by, hurrying home—and to the world.

SOURCES AND ACKNOWLEDGMENTS

A long story is over in the writing of this book. In no sense is it based upon my own recollections, though as man and boy, uniquely placed as witness, I lived in Washington during many of the years in which these events took place. I never met Lucy Mercer. I never heard her name until after she was dead. Though I had briefly become Roosevelt's press secretary at the time of his death, no word or whisper came to me about her presence with him when he was stricken. Certainly her place in his life was unknown to me. I came upon her story first when, nearly ten years after Roosevelt's death, I wrote *The End of Innocence* a book involving his life in the days when he was Assistant Secretary of the Navy. Already then the Roosevelt family in the publication of the *Personal Letters* had revealed that Lucy was more to him than a part-time secretary keeping the routine records of his wife's calls. There was an explosion among Roosevelt haters, hardly to be unexpected, when Grace Tully's book, *F.D.R.—My Boss*, gave most people the first inkling that Lucy Mercer Rutherfurd had been among those with Franklin Roosevelt when he was stricken. Not even newspapermen who covered the story of his death had known this before. The now incredible misstep in presidential public relations, which suppression of this fact involved, invited the conversion of a beautiful story into a scandalous tale. Perhaps that was intended—as it failed to do—to protect the feelings of the proud Eleanor Roosevelt at the time. It succeeded in putting Eleanor, Franklin and Lucy into a triangle unfair to the grace which attended the tangle of their lives.

Possibly the protectors of the proprieties at Warm Springs acted in shock from impulse. Yet the secrecy there was a part of a pattern of reticence rigidly maintained. Grace Tully, loyally devoted to Roosevelt and his memory, somehow seemed almost traitor to the decision of silence when she mentioned Lucy's presence in print. But some of those who maintained it were puzzled. One such was Bill Hassett. He talked about it cryptically when he visited at my house during his escapes from Vermont winters. He wanted me to keep a copy which he sent me of his diary in a form not divested of all references to Lucy. He talked sometimes troubled about the decision of silence. Yet only reluctantly at my suggestion did he put in a footnote in his deleted diary as published stating the then obvious fact that Lucy was on the tragic Warm Springs scene.

Others, not involved in the protection of Mrs. Roosevelt, were less reluctant. Lucy's cousins, the Hendersons, felt that a beautiful story should not be hidden. Some closer to the principals involved were ready to talk about the story for which they felt no shame but were doubtful that they should speak now as witnesses. Some such are those listed in my notes as "confidential sources." The story, however, does not depend upon hearsay or remembrance. In researches across twenty years I have come upon much documentation even in an affair and a time in which the phone call, as in so many things today, had taken the place of the letter. There is, I am sure, more to be discovered. There is much that needs revision, too, in the Roosevelt record. Amazingly his first biographies, both evidently authorized and written with his assistance, can be misleading. Ernest Lindley and Earle Looker, still regarded as prime sources,[1] both date the crucial polio attack Roosevelt suffered as coming later than the time now accepted as established. I have tried to avoid such pitfalls in chronology. The trail is still not always clearly blazed. The goldfish bowl is sometimes opaque.

History needs the full, clear, intimate story. This need with regard to Roosevelt and other great Americans was perhaps best stated by Raymond B. Fosdick in his introduction to the publication of the papers of Woodrow Wilson, an enterprise to which in a very slight way I was related. In a foreword to the first volume of this monumental collection Mr. Fosdick wrote:

"The overriding claims of history to the inspiration and recuperative values of the past cannot wisely be denied. It is the vision of the past that makes the present livable, and no era should be prevented from learning its secrets.

"This is a point of view that had already been widely accepted and the growing collections of personal letters and papers in the Library of Congress are an eloquent testimonial to this new attitude toward privacy. With the passage of years privacy becomes at best a relative term. There is a kind of statute of limitations which, after a reasonable period, allows us to unlock the secrecies and intimacies of a given generation without embarrassment or lack of taste. We are not shut off from the richness of the past because of modesty or a sense of inappropriateness which, however valid at the time, has probably outlived its relevance and meaning."[2]

In such a feeling this book has been written based on researches which began more than a score of years ago. Roosevelt has been dead nearly a quarter of a century. Lucy died two decades ago. Eleanor died in 1962. Their witnesses, relatives, friends and legatees are passing. It is time for this story to be told and told against the background of a Washington which is multitudinous in its reports but amazing often in its reticences.

In the names of those who have helped me in the shaping of this story I must put Hassett first. He was as lovely a soul as the camellias he planted at my door. Long ago Dr. Herman Kahn, then director of the Franklin D. Roosevelt Library at Hyde Park, helped me collect much of the material used here. In the years since I have been particularly aided by Mrs. Elizabeth Henderson Cotten and her son, Lyman A. Cotten, Jr., who felt that their cousin's story should be told. Admiral E. M. Eller, director of the Division of Naval History, gave me assistance above and beyond the call of duty. David Mearns, to whom this book is gratefully dedicated, brought to me not only the resources under his care as the chief of the manuscripts division of the Library of Congress, but also his knowledge of Washington in which he is perhaps the most erudite of the Cave Dwellers. He and my wife Lucy collaborated as my first aides and guides. Dr. Lodwick Hartley, head of the English Department at North Carolina State University, gave valuable critical reading to my manuscript.

I thank too few and those inadequately when I mention as ones to whom I am in much debt: Frank Allcorn, Bernard Asbell, John Ashwin, Tennant H. Bagley, Robert H. Bahmer, Roberta Barrows, Bugs Barringer, Bernard M. Baruch, Dr. Julian Boyd, William J. Bray, Philip C. Brooks, Brice McAdoo Clagett, Mrs. Turner Collins, Cloyce Creef, Moncie Daniels, A. T. Dill, Dr. Elizabeth Drewry, Peggy Duke, Lloyd A. Dunlap, Mark G. Eckhoff, Frank Freidel, Harry Golden, Mary A. Green, Paul Green, Mrs. Charles Sumner Hamlin, Ambrose Hampton, George Healy, Edith Benham Helm, Gerald Johnson, Mrs. Zebulon Judd, Fred C. Kelly, Carroll Kilpatrick, Mrs. Ruth Knutsen, S. L. Latimer, Jr., Nigel Law, Arthur S. Link, Robert A. Lively, Alice Longworth, Robert Mason, Robert J. McCloskey, Mrs. Charles McKenzie, George McMillan, E. W. Mullins, Jr., Charles A. Munn, Edgar B. Nixon, Legare H. B. Obear, Roy Parker, Dr. James Patton, Charles Palmer, Drew Pearson, Melvin A. Petit, Margaret Price, Michael F. Reilly, Mrs. Edwin R. Slaughter, Mrs. Bryant Smith, Clyde Smith, Mrs. Ruth Stevens, Bascom Timmons, Grace Tully, Frank Waldrop, Thomas Waring, Sir Arthur Willert.

NOTES

PROLOGUE

1. Catherine Drinker Bowen, *Yankee From Olympus, Justice Holmes and His Family* (Boston 1944), 362.

2. *New York Herald,* Dec. 11, 1861; Nicolay Papers, John George Nicolay to Therena Bates, Dec. 12, 1861.

3. *Leslie's Illustrated Weekly,* Feb. 22, 1862.

4. Carl Sandburg, *Abraham Lincoln—The Prairie Years and The War Years,* in one vol. (New York 1954), 290.

5. *Ibid.*

6. Alfred Steinberg, *Mrs. R.—The Life of Eleanor Roosevelt* (New York 1958), 22.

7. Carl Sandburg and Paul M. Angle, *Mary Lincoln—Wife and Widow* (New York 1932), 91.

8. Papers of Abraham Lincoln, Vols. 116 and 117. Sallie Carroll Griffin to Abraham Lincoln, July 1, 1863 and July 18, 1863.

9. Papers of Abraham Lincoln, Vol. 117. Telegram General Charles Griffin to Mrs. Charles Eames, July 18, 1863.

10. *Evening Star,* Washington, D.C. May 1, 1890.

11. Papers of Abraham Lincoln, Vol. 117. Fannie Eames to Abraham Lincoln, July 19, 1863.

12. Adam Badeau, *Grant in Peace* (Hartford 1887), 356–62.

13. *Abraham Lincoln—The Prairie Years and The War Years, supra,* 673.

14. Thomas M. Spaulding, *Dictionary of American Biography,* article on Charles Griffin.

15. Gothaisches Genealogisches Taschenbuch Der Graflichen Hauser, Gotha, Justus Perthe (publisher), 1942 edition.

16. Edith Benham Helm, *The Captains and the Kings* (New York 1954), 38.

17. Statement by Mrs. Lyman Cotten, Chapel Hill, N.C.; *New York Social Register* 1908.

18. *Town Topics,* Aug. 15, 1912.

19. Edgar Lee Masters, *Spoon River Anthology* (New York 1915), 194.

CHAPTER ONE

1. Edited by Worthington Chauncey Ford, *Letters of Henry Adams—1858–1891* (Boston 1930), 302.

2. *Ibid.*, 302.

3. Edited by Ward Thoron, *The Letters of Mrs. Henry Adams—1865–1883*, (Boston 1936), Jan. 26, 1882, 333–34.

4. *Ibid.*, 333–34.

5. Tyler Dennett, *John Hay, From Poetry to Politics* (New York 1934), 164.

6. Henry Adams, *The Education of Henry Adams* (Boston 1918), 45.

7. *The Letters of Mrs. Henry Adams, supra*, May 1865, 1–10.

8. *Ibid.*, 1–10.

9. Mrs. Burton Harrison, *Recollections Grave and Gay* (New York 1911), 358.

10. *Letters of Mrs. Henry Adams, supra*, Feb. 19, 1882, 349–53.

11. *Ibid.*, 349–53.

12. Marian Gouverneur, *As I Remember—Recollections of American Society During the Nineteenth Century* (New York 1911), 217–18.

13. Verne Lockwood Samson, *Dictionary of American Biography*, article on James Wormley.

14. Elizabeth Stevenson, *Henry Adams, A Biography* (New York 1955), 148.

15. *The Letters of Mrs. Henry Adams, supra*, Nov. 5, 1882, 395–96.

16. Edited by Isabel Anderson, *The Letters and Journals of General Nicholas Longworth Anderson* (New York 1942), 250.

17. *Letters of Henry Adams—1858–1891, supra*, 363.

18. *John Hay, From Poetry to Politics, supra*, 163.

19. Katharine Simonds, "The Tragedy of Mrs. Henry Adams," *New England Quarterly*, vol. IX, Dec. 1936, 564–82.

20. *The Letters and Journals of General Nicholas Longworth Anderson, supra*, 252.

21. William Roscoe Thayer, *The Life and Letters of John Hay*, 2 vols. in one (Boston 1929), Vol. II, 59.

22. James Truslow Adams, *The Adams Family* (New York 1930), 329.

23. Harold Dean Cater, *Henry Adams and His Friends* (Boston 1947) lxviii.

24. "The Tragedy of Mrs. Henry Adams," *supra*.

25. *Philadelphia Photographer*, vol. 19, Nov. 1882, 327.

26. *Henry Adams and His Friends, supra*, cxiv note 108.

27. "The Tragedy of Mrs. Henry Adams," *supra*.

28. *The Letters and Journals of General Nicholas Longworth Anderson, supra*, 250.

29. *Henry Adams and His Friends, supra,* L.

30. Edited by Mark DeWolfe Howe, *Holmes-Pollock Letters—The Correspondence of Mr. Justice Holmes and Sir Frederick Pollock, 1874–1932* (Cambridge 1941), vol. II, 18.

31. *The Education of Henry Adams, supra,* 329.

32. Edited by Worthington Chauncey Ford, *Letters of Henry Adams—1892–1918* (Boston 1938), 637.

33. Abigail Adams Homan, *Education by Uncles* (Boston 1966), 92.

34. *Letters of Henry Adams 1892–1918, supra,* 603.

35. Edited by Isabel Anderson, *Larz Anderson—Letters and Journals of a Diplomat* (New York 1940), 58.

36. *The Life and Letters of John Hay, supra,* vol. II, 73.

37. Frederick Logan Paxton, *Dictionary of American Biography,* article on William C. Whitney.

38. Information from the Division of Naval History, Navy Department.

39. *Army and Navy Journal,* June 26, 1886, Vol. XXIII, No. 48, 994.

40. Minnie Mercer Pension File, with the Veterans Bureau.

41. Joseph M. Toner Collection, Library of Congress.

42. Joseph M. Toner Collection, *supra,* undated and uncredited clipping.

43. Division of Naval History, *supra.*

44. Minnie Mercer Pension File, *supra.*

45. *Virginia Magazine of History and Biography,* October 1909, vol. 17, no. 4, 428; and family records of Mrs. Lyman Cotten.

46. Minnie Mercer Pension File, *supra,* Norfolk court records.

47. C. C. Pearson, *Dictionary of American Biography,* article on Robert F. Hoke.

48. William Alexander Hoke Papers in Southern Historical Collection, U.N.C., Chapel Hill, N.C.

49. *Ibid.*

50. *Ibid.*

51. Marshal DeLancey Haywood, *The Bishops of North Carolina* (Raleigh, N.C. 1910) 236.

52. Hoke Papers, *supra.*

53. Minnie Mercer Pension File, *supra,* Certified report of marriage from General Register Office, London; the *Army and Navy Journal,* June 26, July 3, and Sept. 15, 1888.

54. *Army and Navy Journal,* Sept. 8, 1888, 562.

55. Hoke Papers, *supra.*

56. *Ibid.*

57. Dr. Paul Barringer and D. M. Barringer, Jr., *Biography of Victor Clay Barringer,* in *Biographical History of North Carolina,* edited by Samuel A. Ashe, Vol. I (Greensboro 1905), 125.

58. Barringer tradition in North Carolina given by Osmond Long Barringer, Jr.

59. Hoke Papers, *supra.*

60. Death certificate of Violetta Mercer Marbury, "Informant Lucy M. Rutherfurd."

61. Hoke Papers, *supra.*

62. Marietta Minnegerode Andrews, *My Studio Window* (New York 1928), 33–34.

63. The *Philadelphia Record*, Feb. 28, 1917.

64. Confidential sources.

65. Allan Nevins, *Henry White, Thirty Years of American Diplomacy* (New York 1930), 105.

66. Elizabeth Eliot, *Heiresses and Coronets* (New York 1959), 188.

67. Henry F. Pringle, *Theodore Roosevelt, a Biography* (New York 1931), 117.

68. *The Clubfellow and Washington Mirror*, May 22, 1912.

69. Carl Charlick, *The Metropolitan Club of Washington* (D.C. 1964), 171.

70. John M. Lynman, *The Chevy Chase Club a History—1885–1957* (Chevy Chase, Md. 1958), 17, 18, 19.

71. WPA Guide Series, *Washington, D.C.—A Guide to the Nation's Capital* (New York 1942), 408.

72. Letter to author from Mrs. Lyman Cotten.

73. Minnie Mercer Pension File, *supra.*

74. William McKinley Papers, vol. 181–fo 143; and Elihu Root Papers, Letterbook No. 11, p. 49, 331, Box 174.

75. Josephus Daniels, *The Wilson Era—Years of Peace* (Chapel Hill 1944), 171.

76. *Letters of Henry Adams—1892–1918, supra,* 313.

77. *Ibid.,* 313.

78. William Allen White, *The Autobiography of William Allen White,* (New York 1946), 338.

79. *Ibid.,* 339.

CHAPTER TWO

1. *Letters of Henry Adams 1892–1918, supra,* Henry Adams to E. Cameron, Jan. 1904, 418.

2. *Ibid.,* Jan. 24, 1904, 422.

3. Edited by Elliott Roosevelt, *F.D.R. His Personal Letters—Early Years* (New York 1947), to Mama Oct. 26, 1902, 48.

4. *Letters of Henry Adams 1892–1918, supra,* to E. Cameron Jan. 10, 1904, 419.

5. Alice Roosevelt Longworth, *Crowded Hours* (New York 1933), 44.

6. *Letters of Henry Adams 1892–1918, supra,* to E. Cameron Apr. 20, 1902, 388.

7. *Recollections Grave and Gay, supra,* 278–79.

8. Eleanor Roosevelt, *This Is My Story* (New York 1938), 57.

9. *Crowded Hours, supra,* 17–18.

10. *Mrs. R.—The Life of Eleanor Roosevelt, supra,* 18.

11. *Crowded Hours, supra,* 17–18.

12. *Mrs. R.—The Life of Eleanor Roosevelt, supra,* 12.

13. *Crowded Hours, supra,* 2.

14. *Ibid.,* 13.

15. *F.D.R. His Personal Letters—Early Years, supra,* 224.

16. *Mrs. R.—The Life of Eleanor Roosevelt, supra,* 87.

17. *The Captains and the Kings, supra,* 45.

18. *Ibid.,* 45.

19. Ellen Maury Slayden, *Washington Wife* (New York 1962), 90.

20. *Ibid.,* 156.

21. *Ibid.,* 137.

22. *Crowded Hours, supra,* 46.

23. *Ibid.,* 61.

24. *Ibid.,* 29–30.

25. *Ibid.,* 26.

26. Paul F. Healy, *Cissy—A Biography of Eleanor M. "Cissy" Patterson* (New York 1966), 7.

27. *Mrs. R.—The Life of Eleanor Roosevelt, supra,* 37–38.

28. *This Is My Story, supra,* 113.

29. Rita Hale Kleeman, *Gracious Lady* (New York 1935), 233.

30. *F.D.R. His Personal Letters—Early Years, supra,* 518.

31. *Ibid.,* 517.

32. *Crowded Hours, supra,* 65.

33. Edited by Henry Cabot Lodge, *Selections from the Correspondence of Theodore Roosevelt and Henry Cabot Lodge 1884–1918* (New York 1925), Vol. I, 46.

34. Frank Freidel, *Franklin D. Roosevelt—The Apprenticeship* (New York 1952), 68.

35. *This Is My Story, supra,* 99.

36. *Ibid.,* 122.

37. *F.D.R. His Personal Letters—Early Years, supra,* 531.

38. *This Is My Story, supra,* 114.

39. *Franklin D. Roosevelt—The Apprenticeship, supra,* 71.

40. Eleanor Roosevelt, *This I Remember* (New York 1940), 14.

41. Irvin S. Cobb, *Exit Laughing* (Indianapolis 1941), 544.

42. *Letters of Henry Adams 1892–1918, supra,* to Charles Milnes Gaskell, Apr. 11, 1905, 446.

43. *Ibid.,* to Charles Milnes Gaskell, Dec. 17, 1908, 514.

44. *Ibid.,* to E. Cameron, Jan. 11, 1912, 577.

45. *Ibid.,* to E. Cameron, Jan. 11, 1912, 577.

46. Evalyn Walsh McLean with Boyden Sparkes, *Father Struck It Rich* (Boston 1936), 127.

47. *Ibid.,* 190–91.

48. *Letters of Henry Adams 1892–1918, supra,* to E. Cameron Feb. 18, 1912, 585.

49. *Ibid.,* to E. Cameron Mar. 18, 1912, 589.

50. *Ibid.,* to E. Cameron Mar. 3, 1912, 587–88.

51. *Henry Adams and His Friends, supra,* 728.

52. *Letters of Henry Adams 1892–1918, supra,* to E. Cameron Apr. 16, 1912, 595.

53. *Ibid.,* to E. Cameron Apr. 16, 1912, 594.

54. *Ibid.,* to E. Cameron Apr. 21, 1912, 595.

55. *Franklin D. Roosevelt—The Apprenticeship, supra,* 109.

56. Edited by Elliott Roosevelt, *F.D.R. His Personal Letters 1905–1928* (New York 1948), 187.

57. *Letters of Henry Adams 1892–1918, supra,* to E. Cameron Apr. 21, 1912, 595.

58. *Washington Wife, supra,* 199.

59. *My Studio Window, supra,* 352.

60. WPA Guide Series, *Connecticut* (Boston 1938), 148–49.

61. *This Is My Story, supra,* 196.

62. *Franklin D. Roosevelt—The Apprenticeship, supra,* 157.

63. *F.D.R. His Personal Letters—1905–1928, supra,* 200.

64. *Franklin D. Roosevelt—The Apprenticeship, supra,* note 157.

65. *This Is My Story, supra,* 197.

66. *Ibid.,* 209.

67. *Ibid.,* 207.

68. *Ibid.,* 203.

69. James Roosevelt and Sidney Shalett, *Affectionately F.D.R.* (New York 1959), 317.

70. *Ibid.,* 317.

71. *The Daily Picayune*, New Orleans, Nov. 15, 1913.

72. *This Is My Story*, *supra*, 199.

73. *Ibid.*, 200.

74. *Ibid.*, 203.

75. *Ibid.*, 213.

76. *Ibid.*, 206.

77. *Ibid.*, 196.

78. *Letters of Henry Adams 1892–1918*, *supra*, to E. Cameron Mar. 10, 1913, 610.

79. *The Clubfellow and Washington Mirror*, Jan. 29, 1913.

80. *Ibid.*, Mar. 5, 1913.

81. *Washington Wife*, *supra*, 199–200.

82. Eleanor Wilson McAdoo, *The Woodrow Wilsons* (New York 1937), 201–2.

83. *Ibid.*, 203.

84. *Ibid.*, 203.

85. *Ibid.*, 208.

86. *Town Topics*, Jan. 22, 1914.

87. *The Clubfellow and Washington Mirror*, Apr. 2, 1913.

88. *This Is My Story*, *supra*, 199.

CHAPTER THREE

1. Nathalie Sedgwick Colby, *Remembering* (Boston 1938), 197.

2. *The Captains and the Kings*, *supra*, 124.

3. Nancy Hoyt, *Elinor Wylie—The Portrait of an Unknown Lady* (Indianapolis 1935), 23–25.

4. *Ibid.*, 25.

5. *Ibid.*, 25.

6. Jonathan Daniels, *The End of Innocence* (New York 1954), 79.

7. *Town Topics*, Sept. 20, 1917.

8. *New York Social Register*, 1908; *Dau's New York Social Blue Book*.

9. *Letters of Henry Adams 1892–1918*, *supra*, to E. Cameron from Paris June 16, 1908, 501.

10. *Ibid.*, 501.

11. Elizabeth Drexel Lehr, *"King Lehr" and The Gilded Age* (Philadelphia 1935), 23–24.

12. Mrs. Lyman Cotten, *supra*.

13. *Town Topics*, Aug. 15, 1912.

14. *Ibid.*

15. *Ibid.*

16. *Ibid.*

17. *Ibid.*, Nov. 28, 1912.

18. Letter to author from Edith Benham Helm.

19. *Clubfellow and Washington Mirror*, May 22, 1912.

20. *Town Topics*, Sept. 20, 1917.

21. Letter to author from Edith Benham Helm.

22. *F.D.R. His Personal Letters 1905–1928, supra*, 219.

23. *Ibid.*, 220.

24. *Town Topics*, Jan. 29, 1914.

25. *The End of Innocence, supra*, 115–17.

26. *Town Topics*, Jan. 29, 1914.

27. *Letters of Henry Adams 1892–1918, supra*, to E. Cameron Mar. 2, 1902, 377.

28. *Town Topics*, Jan. 29, 1914.

29. *Ibid.*, Jan. 29, 1914.

30. *Ibid.*, Jan. 29, 1914.

31. *Washington Wife, supra*, 232.

32. *Ibid.*, 236.

33. *Letters of Henry Adams 1892–1918, supra*, 623.

34. *Ibid.*, 624

35. Bradley A. Fiske, *From Midshipman to Rear Admiral* (New York 1919), 534.

36. Herbert Hoover, *The Memoirs of Herbert Hoover—Years of Adventure 1874–1920* (New York 1951), 135.

37. *Town Topics*, Jan. 19, 1914.

38. *Washington Wife, supra*, 233.

39. *The Woodrow Wilsons, supra*, 211.

40. *Town Topics*, May 21, 1914.

41. *This Is My Story, supra*, 163.

42. *Washington Wife, supra*, 246.

43. *Town Topics*, Aug. 17, 1916.

44. *Letters of Henry Adams 1892–1918, supra*, 614.

45. *Education by Uncles, supra*, 92.

46. *Crowded Hours, supra*, 231–35.

47. *Ibid.*

48. *Ibid.*

49. *Ibid.*

50. *F.D.R. His Personal Letters 1905–1928, supra*, 229.

336   WASHINGTON QUADRILLE

51. *The Wilson Era—Years of Peace, supra,* 131.

52. *F.D.R. His Personal Letters 1905–1928, supra,* 237.

53. *Ibid.,* 238.

54. *Ibid.,* 229.

55. *Ibid.,* 243.

56. *Washington Wife, supra,* 245.

57. *F.D.R. His Personal Letters 1905–1928, supra,* 245–46.

58. *Ibid.,* 246.

59. *Washington Wife, supra,* 245.

60. *F.D.R. His Personal Letters 1905–1928, supra,* 243.

61. *Ibid.,* 238.

62. *Ibid.,* 238.

63. *Letters of Henry Adams 1892–1918, supra,* 626–27.

64. *F.D.R. His Personal Letters 1905–1928, supra,* 239.

65. F.D.R. statement August 14, 1914, quoted by Frank Freidel.

66. *Franklin D. Roosevelt—The Apprenticeship, supra,* 90.

67. *The End of Innocence, supra,* 143.

68. *Franklin D. Roosevelt—The Apprenticeship, supra,* 182.

69. *F.D.R. His Personal Letters 1905–1928, supra,* 251.

70. *The End of Innocence, supra,* 144.

71. *Town Topics,* Oct. 14, 1915.

72. Clara Longworth de Chambrun, *The Making of Nicholas Longworth* (New York 1933), 233.

73. *Franklin D. Roosevelt—The Apprenticeship, supra,* footnote 241.

74. *F.D.R. His Personal Letters 1905–1928, supra,* 258.

75. *Ibid.,* 256–57.

76. *Henry White—Thirty Years of American Diplomacy, supra,* 225–26 footnote.

77. Taft and Roosevelt, *The Intimate Letters of Archie Butt, Military Aide,* (Garden City, N.Y. 1930), 267.

78. *Town Topics,* Dec. 17, 1914.

79. *Ibid.,* Dec. 19, 1918.

80. Charles William Janson, *The Stranger in America* (London 1807), 156–57.

81. William Faux, *Memorable Day in America: Being a Journal of a Tour to the United States* (London 1823), 109, 113, 390; and Paraphrase of this in anonymous review in *The Quarterly Review* of John Murray, Albermarle Street, London, vol. 39, no. LVIII, July 1823, 338–70.

82. Pamphlet entitled "A Reply to Certain Insinuations," Published in an Article in the Sixty-eighth (sic) Number of the *Quarterly Review,* Washington, 1824, 3–4.

83. *Memorable Day in America, supra.*

84. *Ibid.*

85. George Rothwell Brown, *Washington: A Not Too Serious Study* (Baltimore 1930), 107.

86. Letter to author from Nigel Law.

CHAPTER FOUR

1. Edited by Anne W. Lane and Louise H. Hall, *The Letters of Franklin K. Lane* (Boston 1922), 165.

2. R. L. Duffus, *The Tower of Jewels* (New York 1960), 104–5.

3. Arthur Walworth, *Woodrow Wilson: American Prophet* (New York 1958), Vol. II, 16.

4. *F.D.R. His Personal Letters 1905–1928, supra,* 270.

5. *Woodrow Wilson: American Prophet, supra,* Vol. I, 247.

6. *Washington Wife, supra,* 247.

7. *The Intimate Letters of Archie Butt, supra,* Vol. II, 577.

8. Quoted by William D. Hassett.

9. Statement by Mrs. Zebulon Judd.

10. Alpheus Thomas Mason, *Brandeis: A Free Man's Life* (New York 1946), 494.

11. *Town Topics,* Feb. 11, 1915.

12. *Washington Wife, supra,* 229.

13. Mrs. J. Borden Harriman, *From Pinafores to Politics* (New York 1923).

14. The House Collection, the Diary of Edward M. House, Yale University Library.

15. Thomas Surgrue and Edmund W. Starling, *Starling of the White House* (New York 1946), 49.

16. Edith Bolling Wilson, *My Memoir* (Indianapolis 1938), 68–88.

17. *Woodrow Wilson: American Prophet, supra,* Vol. I, 419.

18. *My Memoir, supra,* 68–88.

19. *Town Topics,* Apr. 6, 1916.

20. Irwin Hood (Ike) Hoover, *42 Years in the White House* (Boston 1934), 72.

21. *My Memoir, supra,* 80.

22. *Ibid.,* 64.

23. *Ibid.,* 38.

24. *Town Topics,* Sept. 9, 1915.

25. *My Memoir, supra,* 13–14.

26. *Town Topics,* Oct. 14, 1915.

27. *My Memoir, supra,* 23.

28. *Ibid.,* 55.

29. *Ibid.,* 31–32.

30. *Ibid.,* 53.

31. Mrs. Lyman Cotten, family papers.

32. Washington, D.C. City Directory.

33. *Ibid.;* and Washington, D.C. *Social Register.*

34. *Town Topics,* Sept. 20, 1917.

35. *Letters of Henry Adams 1892–1918, supra,* 586.

36. James Ryder Randall, *Maryland, My Maryland.*

37. *Washington Post,* Sept. 14, 1917; *Washington Star,* Sept. 13, 1917; *Town Topics,* Sept. 20, 1917.

38. Minnie Mercer Pension File, *supra.*

39. *F.D.R. His Personal Letters 1905–1928, supra,* 280.

40. Francis Russell, *The Great Interlude* (New York 1964), 7–20.

41. *F.D.R. His Personal Letters 1905–1928, supra,* 291.

42. *Ibid.,* 291.

43. Carroll Kilpatrick, *Roosevelt and Daniels, a Friendship in Politics* (Chapel Hill 1952), 25.

44. *F.D.R. His Personal Letters 1905–1928, supra,* 317.

45. *Franklin D. Roosevelt—The Apprenticeship, supra,* 257.

46. *Town Topics,* June 10, 1915.

47. *Franklin D. Roosevelt—The Apprenticeship, supra,* 256–57.

48. Letter to author from Nigel Law.

49. *Ibid.*

50. *Ibid.*

51. *Letters of Henry Adams 1892–1918, supra,* 628.

52. *Washington Wife, supra,* 255–56.

53. *Ibid.,* 276–77.

54. *F.D.R. His Personal Letters 1905–1928, supra,* 338–39.

CHAPTER FIVE

1. *Roosevelt and Daniels—A Friendship in Politics, supra,* 23.

2. *F.D.R. His Personal Letters 1905–1928, supra,* 343.

3. *Affectionately, F.D.R., supra,* 95–96.

4. *F.D.R. His Personal Letters 1905–1928, supra,* 343; *Franklin D. Roosevelt—The Apprenticeship, supra,* 286.

5. *Franklin D. Roosevelt—The Apprenticeship, supra,* 287 and note 287.

6. *Franklin D. Roosevelt—The Apprenticeship, supra,* 129, 312, 323; and Frank Freidel, *The Ordeal* (Boston 1954), 322.

7. F.D.R. Diary, Mar. 5, 1917, Hyde Park Library.

8. The House Collection, *supra,* Jan. 12, Mar. 4, 6, 10, 11, 1917.

9. F.D.R. Diary, *supra,* Mar. 11, 1917.

10. Diary of Mrs. Charles Sumner Hamlin, 1916. Library of Congress.

11. F.D.R. Diary, *supra,* Mar. 11, 1917.

12. *Crowded Hours, supra,* 246.

13. *This Is My Story, supra,* 249.

14. *Crowded Hours, supra,* 245–47; *This Is My Story, supra,* 249–50; *The End of Innocence, supra,* 221–22.

15. E. David Cronon, editor, *The Cabinet Diaries of Josephus Daniels, 1913–1921* (Univ. Nebraska 1963), Aug. 21, 1917, 194.

16. *Franklin D. Roosevelt—The Apprenticeship, supra,* 301.

17. *Ibid.,* 301 and 421.

18. *Ibid.,* 302.

19. *Crowded Hours, supra,* 259.

20. The House Collection, *supra,* May 27, 1917.

21. *Washington Wife, supra,* 340, 344.

22. Mrs. Henry F. Butler, *I Was a Yeoman (F),* Naval Historical Foundation pamphlet, undated, 5 and 6.

23. *Larz Anderson—Letters and Journals of a Diplomat, supra,* 419.

24. Minnie Mercer Pension File, *supra.*

25. Letter to author from Nigel Law.

26. *I Was a Yeoman (F), supra,* 3.

27. Lucy Mercer Naval Record.

28. F.D.R. *His Personal Letters 1905–1928, supra,* July 16, 1917, 347.

29. *Ibid.,* July 17, 1917, 348.

30. *The New York Times,* July 17, 1917.

31. F.D.R. *His Personal Letters 1905–1928, supra,* July 18, 1917, 349.

32. *Ibid.,* 350.

33. *The Wilson Era—Years of Peace, supra,* 513; *The Cabinet Diaries of Josephus Daniels, supra,* 114.

34. Letter to author from Charles A. Munn.

35. F.D.R. *His Personal Letters 1905–1928, supra,* July 23, 1917, 351.

36. *Ibid.,* July 25, 1917, 352.

37. Letter to author from Nigel Law.

38. *Ibid.*

39. F.D.R. *His Personal Letters 1905–1928, supra,* 352.

40. *Ibid.,* 352.

41. Admiral William Sheffield Cowles to FDR, Aug. 17, 1917.

42. F.D.R. His Personal Letters 1905–1928, supra, 354.

43. Larz Anderson—Letters and Journals of a Diplomat, supra, 441.

44. Walter Camp to FDR, July 25, 1917.

45. Wire F.D.R. to Sara, Aug. 6, 1917, Hyde Park Files.

46. F.D.R. His Personal Letters 1905–1928, supra, Aug. 20, 1917, 358.

47. Social Register 1914; The Washington Post, May 25, 1916.

48. American Guide Series, Maryland (New York 1940), 348.

49. F.D.R. His Personal Letters 1905–1928, supra, Sept. 9, 1917, 360.

50. Ibid., Aug. 20, 1917, 358.

51. The Wilson Era—Years of Peace, supra, 340.

52. F.D.R. His Personal Letters 1905–1928, supra, Sept. 9, 1917, 361.

53. The Clubfellow and Washington Mirror, Sept. 25, 1912.

54. Ibid., Jan. 22, 1913.

55. F.D.R. His Personal Letters 1905–1928, supra, 359.

56. Ibid., Sept. 9, 1917, 361.

57. Carroll Mercer's death certificate.

58. The Washington Post, Sept. 14, 1917.

59. Town Topics, Sept. 20, 1917.

60. The Washington Star, Sept. 13, 1917.

61. Lucy Mercer Naval Record.

62. The Cabinet Diaries of Josephus Daniels, 1913–1921, supra, 253.

63. F.D.R. His Personal Letters 1905–1928, supra, Oct. 29, 1917, 363.

64. Ibid., 366.

65. Ibid., 361, 368.

66. Town Topics, Oct. 18, 1917.

67. This Is My Story, supra, 254.

68. Ibid., 259, 260.

69. Affectionately, F.D.R., supra, 159.

70. F.D.R. His Personal Letters 1905–1928, supra, 274–75.

71. Town Topics, Nov. 22, 1917.

72. Crowded Hours, supra, 263.

73. Ibid., 263.

74. TR to FDR, Nov. 17, 1917, Hyde Park Library.

75. Letter to author from Nigel Law.

76. Town Topics, Dec. 11, 1917.

CHAPTER SIX

1. Letter to author from Mrs. Charles Sumner Hamlin, Feb. 19, 1955.
2. *Crowded Hours, supra,* 258–59.
3. Letter to author from Nigel Law.
4. Jonathan Daniels, *Frontier on the Potomac* (New York 1946), 178.
5. *Crowded Hours, supra,* 259.
6. *Ibid.,* 271.
7. Isabel Anderson, *Presidents and Pies* (Boston 1920), 173.
8. The House Collection, *supra.*
9. *Town Topics,* Feb. 1, 1917.
10. Bernard M. Baruch, *The Public Years—My Own Story* (New York 1960), 30–31.
11. Margaret Coit, *Mr. Baruch* (Boston 1957), 180.
12. John Dos Passos, *Mr. Wilson's War* (New York 1962), 285.
13. British *Who's Who,* 1926.
14. Diary of Mrs. Charles Sumner Hamlin, *supra,* May 17, 1918.
15. *Ibid.*
16. *Ibid.*
17. Letter to author from Mrs. Charles Sumner Hamlin.
18. *Ibid.*
19. John Chamberlain, *Farewell to Reform* (New York 1932), 280.
20. *Crowded Hours, supra,* 271.
21. Diary of Mrs. Charles Sumner Hamlin, *supra.*
22. Letter to author from Sir Arthur Willert, Jan. 1967.
23. *Ibid.*
24. State Department Archives.
25. *Washington Wife, supra,* 222, 323, 356.
26. Joseph L. Morrison, *Josephus Daniels—The Small-d Democrat* (Chapel Hill 1966), 72.
27. Diary of Mrs. Charles Sumner Hamlin, *supra,* Jan. 18, 1918.
28. *Crowded Hours, supra,* 269.
29. Letter to author of Mrs. Charles Sumner Hamlin, *supra.*
30. Olive Clapper, *Washington Tapestry* (New York 1946), 238.
31. *Affectionately, F.D.R., supra,* 63.
32. *Franklin D. Roosevelt—The Apprenticeship, supra,* 320.
33. Arthur Schlesinger, Jr., *The Ladies Home Journal,* Nov. 1966.
34. Letters and conversations with Mrs. Lyman Cotten and Miss Mary Henderson.

35. Letters and conversations with Mrs. Lyman Cotten and Miss Mary Henderson, *supra*.

36. *Franklin D. Roosevelt—The Apprenticeship*, *supra*, 321; *New York Tribune*, July 4, 1918.

37. Woman's National Democratic Club, *Party Diary* (Washington, D.C., 1966).

38. Possession of author.

39. *New York Times Magazine*, tape recorded interview with Alice Longworth by Henry Brandon, Aug. 6, 1967.

40. *F.D.R. His Personal Letters 1905–1928*, *supra*, 373.

41. Diary of Livingston Davis, Hyde Park Library.

42. *F.D.R. His Personal Letters 1905–1928*, *supra*, 383.

43. *Ibid.*, 383–94; *Franklin D. Roosevelt—The Apprenticeship*, *supra*, 354 and footnote.

44. *Ibid.*, 467. Eleanor to Mrs. James R. Feb. 8, 1919, Paris.

45. *This Is My Story*, *supra*, 287.

46. *Franklin D. Roosevelt—The Apprenticeship*, *supra*, 322.

47. Diary of Livingston Davis, *supra*.

48. *Ibid.*

49. *Ibid.*

50. *Ibid.*

51. *Ibid.*

52. *This Is My Story*, *supra*, 267–68.

53. TR to FDR, Sept. 23, 1917.

54. *The Cabinet Diaries of Josephus Daniels, 1913–1921*, *supra*, 358.

CHAPTER SEVEN

1. Minnie Mercer Pension File, *supra*.

2. *Ibid.*

3. *Ibid.*

4. Carroll Mercer's wills.

5. *Ibid.*

6. *As I Remember*, *supra*, 214, 215.

7. *Town Topics*, Aug. 15, 1912.

8. Minnie Mercer Pension File, *supra*.

9. Hermann Hagedorn, *The Roosevelt Family of Sagamore Hill* (New York 1954), 406.

10. *Town Topics*, Feb. 13, 1919.

11. Minnie Mercer Pension File, *supra*.

12. Letter to author from Lyman Cotten, Jr., Jan. 29, 1967.

13. Letter to author from Mrs. Lyman Cotten.

14. Letter to author from Mrs. Charles Sumner Hamlin.

15. *This Is My Story, supra,* 270.

16. *Washington Wife, supra,* 344.

17. *This Is My Story, supra,* 271.

18. Diary of Livingston Davis, *supra.*

19. *F.D.R. His Personal Letters 1905–1928, supra,* 450.

20. Diary of Livingston Davis, *supra.*

21. *This Is My Story, supra,* 148–49.

22. *F.D.R. His Personal Letters 1905–1928, supra,* 466–67.

23. *Ibid.,* 453.

24. Letter to author from Nigel Law.

25. *This Is My Story, supra,* 295.

26. *Ibid.,* 299.

27. Edward G. Lowry, *Washington Close-Ups* (Boston 1921), 14.

28. *Town Topics,* July 10, 1919.

29. *Ibid.,* July 10, 1919.

30. *F.D.R. His Personal Letters 1905–1928, supra,* 277.

31. *Letters of Henry Adams 1892–1918, supra,* 96.

32. Leon Edel, *Dictionary of American Biography,* supplement 2, article on Edith Wharton.

33. Edith Wharton, *A Backward Glance* (New York 1934), 77–78.

34. Elizabeth Eliot, *Heiresses and Coronets* (New York 1959), 256.

35. The *New York Times,* Sept. 7, 1952.

36. *The Washington Capital,* vol. 16, no. 16, June 2, 1900, 7.

37. *Letters of Henry Adams 1892–1918, supra,* 313.

38. Edited by Edith Morton Eustis, *War Letters of Morton Eustis to His Mother—February 6, 1941 to August 10, 1944* (Washington, D.C. 1945), iii.

39. *F.D.R. His Personal Letters 1905–1928, supra,* 285.

40. American Guide Series, *Virginia—A Guide to the Old Dominion* (New York 1940), 390.

41. *F.D.R. His Personal Letters 1905–1928, supra,* 285.

42. Harry Worcester Smith, *Life and Sport in Aiken* (New York 1935), 63.

43. *Ibid.,* 197.

44. Albert W. Atwood, *Dictionary of American Biography,* article on John Pierpont Morgan.

45. *Life and Sport in Aiken, supra,* 197.

46. *Recollections Grave and Gay, supra,* 281.

47. A Backward Glance, supra, 47.

48. Charities, vol. 14, no. 25, Sept. 16, 1905, p. 1083–86.

49. Letters of Henry Adams 1892–1918, supra, 489.

50. Town Topics, Dec. 26, 1912.

51. Ibid., Feb. 26, 1920.

52. Ibid., Feb. 26, 1920.

53. Ibid., July 7, 1921.

54. The Bookman, vol. 15, no. 5, July 1902, 422.

55. A Backward Glance, supra, 143–44.

56. Edith Eustis, Marian Manning (New York 1902), 211–13.

57. Ibid., 211–13

58. F.D.R. His Personal Letters 1905–1928, supra, 412.

59. Letter to author from Mrs. Charles Sumner Hamlin.

CHAPTER EIGHT

1. Affectionately, F.D.R., supra, 93.

2. F.D.R. His Personal Letters 1905–1928, supra, 475–76.

3. Crowded Hours, supra, 282–83.

4. Ibid., 285.

5. Washington Wife, supra, 349.

6. My Memoir, supra, 270.

7. Ibid., 272.

8. F.D.R. His Personal Letters 1905–1928, supra, 479.

9. Ibid., 480.

10. The House Collection, supra.

11. J. A. Spender, Life Journalism and Politics (London 1927), Vol. II, 14.

12. Diary of Mrs. Charles Sumner Hamlin, supra, Oct. 29, 1919.

13. This Is My Story, supra, 305–6.

14. Woodrow Wilson: American Prophet, supra, II, 34.

15. Diary of Mrs. Charles Sumner Hamlin, supra, Nov. 3, 1919.

16. Washington Close-Ups, supra, 14.

17. Crowded Hours, supra, 288.

18. The Public Years—My Own Story, supra, 140.

19. My Memoir, supra, 111.

20. The Public Years—My Own Story, supra, 146.

21. Bernard M. Baruch, My Own Story (New York 1957), 285.

22. The House Collection, supra.

23. Ibid.

24. *Ibid.*

25. *Crowded Hours, supra,* 292.

26. *The Cabinet Diaries of Josephus Daniels, 1913–1921, supra,* 462.

27. David F. Houston, *Eight Years with Wilson's Cabinet 1913–1920,* (Garden City, N.Y. 1926), Vol. II, 49.

28. George Macauley Trevelyan, *Grey of Fallodon* (Boston 1937), 398–400

29. *This Is My Story, supra,* 305.

30. *Crowded Hours, supra,* 294.

31. *This Is My Story, supra,* 306.

32. *Ibid.,* 306.

33. *Ibid.,* 306.

34. *Woodrow Wilson: American Prophet, supra,* II, 381.

35. *Grey of Fallodon, supra,* 398–400.

36. Letter to author from Fred C. Kelly, May 1, 1955.

37. Letter to author from Bernard M. Baruch, July 1, 1953.

38. Letter to author from Fred C. Kelly, *supra.*

CHAPTER NINE

1. Diary of Mrs. Charles Sumner Hamlin, *supra,* Jan. 10, 1920.

2. *This Is My Story, supra,* 165.

3. *Ibid.,* 113.

4. *Ibid.,* 307–9.

5. *Ibid.,* 114.

6. *Ibid.,* 300.

7. *Franklin D. Roosevelt: The Ordeal, supra,* 36.

8. *The News and Observer,* Raleigh, N.C., Feb. 2, 1920.

9. The *Washington Post,* Feb. 3, 1920.

10. *The Cabinet Diaries of Josephus Daniels, 1913–1921, supra,* 492.

11. *Franklin D. Roosevelt: The Ordeal, supra,* 36–50.

12. *Ibid.,* 36.

13. The *Washington Post,* Feb. 13, 1920.

14. *Town Topics,* May 27, 1920.

15. Interview with Lyman A. Cotten, Jr., Mar. 12, 1966.

16. Letter to author from Mrs. Lyman Cotten, Jan. 29, 1967.

17. *The Cabinet Diaries of Josephus Daniels, 1913–1921, supra,* 497.

18. *Ibid.,* 542.

19. *Ibid.,* 494.

20. *F.D.R. His Personal Letters 1905–1928, supra,* 486.

21. *The Cabinet Diaries of Josephus Daniels, 1913–1921, supra,* 544.

22. F.D.R. to Wendell P. Blagdon, Dec. 17, 1919, Group X, FDR Library.

23. Minnie Mercer Pension File, *supra.*

24. Diary of Mrs. Charles Sumner Hamlin, *supra.*

25. *The Cabinet Diaries of Josephus Daniels, 1913–1921, supra,* 591.

26. *F.D.R. His Personal Letters 1905–1928, supra,* 489.

27. *The Cabinet Diaries of Josephus Daniels, 1913–1921, supra,* 91.

28. *F.D.R. His Personal Letters 1905–1928, supra,* 490–91.

29. *This Is My Story, supra,* 311.

30. *Ibid.,* 312.

31. Lodge to Charles S. Groves, July 26, 1920. Mss of Henry Cabot Lodge.

32. *Ibid.,* July 26, 1920.

33. The *Chicago Tribune,* Aug. 13, 1920.

34. *Franklin D. Roosevelt: The Ordeal, supra,* 85.

35. *Ibid.,* 72.

36. *This Is My Story, supra,* 319.

37. *F.D.R. His Personal Letters 1905–1928, supra,* 513.

38. Rexford G. Tugwell, *The Democratic Roosevelt* (Garden City, N.Y. 1957), 137.

39. *This Is My Story, supra,* 323.

40. *Ibid.,* 328.

41. *Franklin D. Roosevelt: The Ordeal, supra,* 97.

42. The *New York Times,* July 20, 1921.

43. *F.D.R. His Personal Letters 1905–1928, supra,* 517.

44. *Franklin D. Roosevelt: The Ordeal, supra,* 97.

45. Alfred B. Rollins, Jr., *Roosevelt and Howe* (New York 1962), 179.

46. Letter to author from Dr. Elizabeth Drewry.

47. Ernest K. Lindley, *Franklin D. Roosevelt—A Career in Progressive Democracy* (Indianapolis, 1931), 201.

48. The *New York Times,* Aug. 6, 1921.

49. *Maryland, supra,* 331.

50. *Town Topics,* Dec. 1, 1921.

51. *Franklin D. Roosevelt—A Career in Progressive Democracy, supra,* 201.

52. Ross T. McIntire in collaboration with George Creel, *White House Physician* (New York 1946), 35.

53. *Roosevelt and Howe, supra,* 183.

54. *Affectionately, F.D.R., supra,* 32.

55. *This Is My Story, supra,* 333.

56. *Roosevelt and Howe, supra,* 177.

57. The New York Times, Aug. 26 and September 14, 1921.
58. Affectionately, F.D.R., supra, 29.
59. Ibid., 37.
60. This Is My Story, supra, 162.
61. Ibid., 335.
62. Affectionately, F.D.R., supra, 35.
63. Ibid., 151.
64. Ibid., 151.
65. Franklin D. Roosevelt—The Ordeal, supra, 104.
66. Roosevelt and Howe, supra, 185.
67. Affectionately, F.D.R., supra, 86.
68. This Is My Story, supra, 338.
69. Ibid., 338.
70. Ibid., 338.
71. The Democratic Roosevelt, supra, 65.
72. Confidential sources.
73. Arthur Schlesinger, Jr., The Age of Roosevelt—The Coming of the New Deal (Boston 1959), quote 537.
74. This I Remember, supra, 2.
75. Frances Perkins, The Roosevelt I Knew (New York 1946), 29.
76. Affectionately, F.D.R., supra, 158.
77. Interview with Mrs. Lyman Cotten and Miss Mary Henderson.
78. William G. McAdoo to FDR, Dec. 15, 1922, Hyde Park Library.
79. This Is My Story, supra, 353.
80. Earle Looker, This Man Roosevelt (New York 1932), 155–56.
81. This I Remember, supra, 27.
82. This Is My Story, supra, 345.

CHAPTER TEN

1. The New York Times, Feb. 11, 1920.
2. Frank Shampanore, History and Directory of Warren County, New Jersey (Washington, N.J. 1931), I, 28.
3. The New York Times, June 8, 1939.
4. The New York Times, Mar. 21, 1944.
5. This Is My Story, supra, 363.
6. Town Topics, Jan. 16, 1919.
7. The Preferred List Washington and Vicinity, 1921.
8. Larz Anderson—Letters and Journals of a Diplomat, supra, 441.
9. Dean Acheson, Morning and Noon (Boston 1965), 46.

10. *Crowded Hours, supra,* 324.

11. *F.D.R. His Personal Letters 1905–1928, supra,* 518.

12. *Ibid.,* 516.

13. *Ibid.,* 223.

14. *Aiken Standard and Review,* May 29, 1964.

15. *Centennial Celebration Commemorating the Founding of Aiken, South Carolina—April 4th to 6th 1935,* pamphlet (Aiken 1935).

16. Jonathan Daniels, *The Time Between the Wars* (New York 1966), 37–38.

17. Letter to author from George McMillan, Apr. 25, 1967.

18. *Franklin D. Roosevelt—A Career in Progressive Democracy, supra,* 207.

19. *Ibid.,* 213–14.

20. *Franklin D. Roosevelt: The Ordeal, supra,* 106.

21. Diary of Mrs. Charles Sumner Hamlin, *supra,* after June 10, 1922.

22. *Affectionately, F.D.R., supra,* 164.

23. *F.D.R. His Personal Letters 1905–1928, supra,* 541–42.

24. *Ibid.,* 535.

25. *Affectionately, F.D.R., supra,* 164.

26. *Ibid.,* 164.

27. *F.D.R. His Personal Letters 1905–1928, supra,* 556.

28. *Ibid.,* 556.

29. *Ibid.,* 557.

30. *Ibid.,* 558.

31. Diary of Mrs. Charles Sumner Hamlin, *supra,* July 1924.

32. *Franklin D. Roosevelt: The Ordeal, supra,* 176.

33. Diary of Mrs. Charles Sumner Hamlin, *supra,* Aug. 1924.

34. *F.D.R. His Personal Papers 1905–1928, supra,* 600, 603.

35. *Franklin D. Roosevelt: The Ordeal, supra,* 199.

36. FDR to Livingston Davis, Apr. 25, 1925.

37. *Affectionately, F.D.R., supra,* 186.

38. *This I Remember, supra,* 29.

39. *Ibid.,* 28.

40. *Ibid.,* 114.

41. *Affectionately, F.D.R., supra,* 186.

42. *This I Remember, supra,* 27.

43. *Affectionately, F.D.R., supra,* 223.

44. Howe to FDR, 2/25/24, Hyde Park Library.

45. Howe to FDR, *supra,* Apr. 15, 1925.

46. Edited by Elliott Roosevelt assisted by Joseph P. Lash, *F.D.R. His Personal Papers 1928–1945* (New York 1950), Vol. I, 272; *The Time Between the Wars, supra,* 207.

47. The *New York Times,* Jan. 14, 1932.

48. *Harvard Class of 1904, Twenty-fifth Anniversary Report, June 1929,* Printed for the Class by the Plympton Press, Norwood, Mass.

49. Confidential sources.

50. Carl Van Doren, *Dictionary of American Biography,* article on Elinor Morton Hoyt Wylie.

51. *Affectionately, F.D.R., supra,* 258.

52. *This Is My Story, supra,* 179.

53. *Ibid.,* 219.

54. *Ibid.,* 350.

55. *Ibid.,* 350.

56. *Town Topics,* Dec. 22, 1921.

57. *F.D.R. His Personal Letters 1905–1928, supra,* 626.

58. The *New York Times,* Nov. 26, 1926.

59. The *New York Times,* Mar. 21, 1944.

60. Letter from Anastasia Law, Mar. 9, 1953.

61. The *Times,* London, Oct. 24, 1922.

62. *Ibid.,* May 17, 1929.

63. Letter to author from Nigel Law.

64. *Harvard Class of 1904, Twenty-fifth Anniversary Report, supra.*

65. *F.D.R. His Personal Letters 1928–1945, supra,* Vol. I, 24.

66. *Ibid.,* Vol. I, 175.

67. The *New York Times,* Jan. 12 & 14, 1932.

CHAPTER ELEVEN

1. *The Making of Nicholas Longworth, supra,* 288.

2. *Ibid.,* 309.

3. *Crowded Hours, supra,* 327.

4. *Ibid.,* 315.

5. *Ibid.,* 332.

6. *Ibid.,* 331.

7. *Ibid.,* 332.

8. *Ibid.,* 332.

9. Bess Furman, *White House Profile* (Indianapolis 1951), 314.

10. *Crowded Hours, supra,* 328.

11. *The Making of Nicholas Longworth, supra,* 317.

12. F.D.R. to John S. Cohen, Mar. 9, 1931; F.D.R. to Clark Howell, Mar. 31, 1931.

13. F.D.R. to Norman Mack, Apr. 22, 1931.

14. F.D.R. to William T. Anderson, June 22, 1931.

15. *The News and Observer*, AP report, Apr. 10, 1931.

16. Mark Sullivan, *Our Times—The Twenties* (New York 1935), 503.

17. *The News and Observer*, AP report, Mar. 4, 1931.

18. *Ibid.*, Apr. 7, 1931.

19. *Ibid.*, Apr. 9, 1931.

20. *Ibid.*, Apr. 10, 1931.

21. *Ibid.*, Apr. 10, 1931.

22. Arthur Schlesinger, Jr., *The Age of Roosevelt—The Crisis of the Old Order 1919–1933* (Boston 1957), 171.

23. *The Time Between the Wars, supra*, 189.

24. *Crowded Hours, supra*, 340.

25. *Ibid.*, 340–41.

26. *Ibid.*, 2.

27. *Ibid.*, 159.

28. *This I Remember, supra*, 31–32.

29. *F.D.R. His Personal Letters 1928–1945, supra*, Vol. I, 328.

30. *Affectionately, F.D.R., supra*, 277.

31. *Ibid.*, 277.

32. *This I Remember, supra*, 76.

33. *Ibid.*, 76.

34. *Mrs. R.—The Life of Eleanor Roosevelt, supra*, 186.

35. *This I Remember, supra*, 76.

36. Grace Tully, *F.D.R.—My Boss* (New York 1949), 178–79.

37. *The News and Observer*, AP report, Mar. 4, 1933.

38. *The Letters of Henry Adams 1892–1918, supra*, 613.

39. *F.D.R. His Personal Letters 1905–1928, supra*, 445.

40. *The News and Observer*, AP report, Mar. 4, 1933.

41. *Ibid.*

42. *Ibid.*

43. *Larz Anderson—Letters and Journals of a Diplomat, supra*, 645.

44. *Starling of the White House, supra*, 306.

45. *The News and Observer*, AP report, Mar. 5, 1933.

46. *This I Remember, supra*, 78.

47. Confidential sources.

48. *F.D.R.—My Boss, supra*, 146.

49. Patricia Peabody Roosevelt, *I Love a Roosevelt* (New York 1967), 215.

50. *This I Remember, supra,* 78.

51. *The News and Observer,* AP report, Mar. 5, 1933.

52. *Ibid.*

53. *Ibid.*

54. *Ibid.*

55. *This I Remember, supra,* 82.

56. Letter to author from Mrs. Lyman Cotten, June 20, 1958.

57. Confidential source.

58. *Roosevelt and Howe, supra,* 388.

59. Minnie Mercer Pension File, *supra.*

60. *F.D.R. His Personal Letters 1928–1945, supra,* Vol. I, 369.

61. Peter Hagner Papers in Southern Historical Collection, U.N.C., Chapel Hill, N.C.

CHAPTER TWELVE

1. Henrietta Nesbitt, *White House Diary* (Garden City, N.Y. 1948), 1.

2. *The Public Years—My Own Story, supra,* 242.

3. *White House Diary, supra,* 112.

4. Hagner Papers, *supra.*

5. *White House Diary, supra,* 172.

6. *Mrs. R.—The Life of Eleanor Roosevelt, supra,* 191.

7. *This I Remember, supra,* 102.

8. *42 Years in the White House, supra,* 225.

9. *White House Diary, supra,* 3–7.

10. *Affectionately, F.D.R., supra,* 238.

11. *Roosevelt and Hopkins, supra,* 214.

12. *The Democratic Roosevelt, supra,* 65.

13. *F.D.R.—My Boss, supra,* 115.

14. *Affectionately, F.D.R., supra,* 238.

15. *F.D.R.—My Boss, supra,* 110.

16. *Affectionately, F.D.R., supra,* 94.

17. *Ibid.,* 93.

18. *Ibid.,* 94–95.

19. *The Democratic Roosevelt, supra,* 193.

20. *This I Remember, supra,* 114.

21. *Ibid,* 108.

22. Raymond Moley, *The First New Deal* (New York 1966), 95.

23. *The Public Years—My Own Story*, supra, 254.

24. Harold L. Ickes, *The Secret Diary of Harold L. Ickes—The First Thousand Days 1933–1936* (New York 1953), 442.

25. *Ibid.*, 249–50.

26. *Ibid.*, 250.

27. *The Democratic Roosevelt*, supra, 193.

28. *The Secret Diary of Harold L. Ickes—The First Thousand Days 1933–1936*, supra, 634.

29. Arthur M. Schlesinger, Jr., *McCall's Magazine*, "The Mystery of the 'President's Mystery,' " Aug. 1967.

30. *This I Remember*, supra, 138.

31. Interview with Miss Mary Henderson and Mrs. Lyman Cotten.

32. *F.D.R.—My Boss*, supra, 119.

33. *White House Diary*, supra, 196.

34. *Ibid.*, 196.

35. *Mrs. R.—The Life of Eleanor Roosevelt*, supra, 224.

36. *Affectionately, F.D.R.*, supra, 304–5.

37. John Morton Blum, *From The Morgenthau Diaries—Years of Crisis, 1928–1938* (Boston 1959), 476.

38. *Mrs. R.—The Life of Eleanor Roosevelt*, supra, 258.

39. Rexford Tugwell and James E. Curry, *Franklin Roosevelt at Warm Springs, Georgia—Some Chronological Land Marks* (mimeographed study 1958), 1.

40. *Ibid.*, 1–2.

41. *Ibid.*, 1.

42. *Ibid.*, 2.

43. *Ibid.*, 31.

44. *Ibid.*, 33.

45. *This I Remember*, supra, 165.

46. *Affectionately, F.D.R.*, supra, 293–94.

47. *F.D.R.—My Boss*, supra, 123.

48. *Affectionately, F.D.R.*, supra, 310.

49. *Ibid.*, 210.

50. *Ibid.*, 230.

51. *Ibid.*, 307.

52. *Ibid.*, 307–8.

53. *White House Diary*, supra, 68.

54. *The Secret Diary of Harold L. Ickes—The First Thousand Days 1933–1936*, supra, 238–40.

55. *Affectionately, F.D.R., supra*, 308.

56. *The Secret Diary of Harold L. Ickes—The First Thousand Days 1933–1936, supra*, 554.

57. *Franklin Roosevelt at Warm Springs, Georgia—Some Chronological Land Marks, supra*, 59.

58. William D. Hassett, *Off the Record with FDR—1942–1945* (Rutgers University Press 1958), 22 note.

59. *War Letters of Morton Eustis, supra*, facing 92.

60. *Ibid.*, 13.

61. *Off the Record with FDR—1942–1945, supra*, 22.

62. *Ibid.*, 30.

63. *Ibid.*, 31.

64. *Ibid.*, 31 and 32 note.

65. *Ibid.*, 31.

66. Harold L. Ickes, *The Secret Diary of Harold L. Ickes—The Inside Struggle* (New York 1954), 643.

67. *White House Diary, supra*, 242.

68. *This I Remember, supra*, 191.

69. *The Secret Diary of Harold L. Ickes—The Inside Struggle, supra*, 642–48.

70. *The Captains and the Kings, supra*, end paper diagram.

71. *F.D.R. His Personal Letters 1928–1945, supra*, Vol. II, 912.

72. *This I Remember, supra*, 196–97.

73. Letter to author from Paul Green, May 22, 1967.

74. *Ibid.*

75. *The News and Observer*, July 2, 1939.

76. "My Day," July 4, 1939.

77. *Franklin Roosevelt at Warm Springs, Georgia—Some Chronological Land Marks, supra*, 62.

78. *This I Remember, supra*, 200.

79. *Ibid.*, 201.

80. *Mrs. R.—The Life of Eleanor Roosevelt, supra*, 269.

81. *This I Remember, supra*, 200.

82. Arthur Schlesinger, Jr., *The Age of Roosevelt—The Politics of Upheaval* (Boston 1960), 199.

83. *Mrs. R.—The Life of Eleanor Roosevelt, supra*, 269.

84. *White House Diary, supra*, 248.

85. *Mrs. R.—The Life of Eleanor Roosevelt, supra*, 269.

86. *This I Remember, supra*, 201.

87. *The New York Times Magazine*, article by Henry Brandon, Aug. 6, 1967.

88. Letter to author from Harry Golden, Nov. 9, 1966; *Carolina Israelite*, Sept.–Oct. Issue 1966.

89. *This I Remember, supra*, 219–20.

90. *F.D.R.–My Boss, supra*, 246.

91. *Franklin Roosevelt at Warm Springs, Georgia–Some Chronological Land Marks, supra*, 26.

92. "My Day," Sept. 7, 1941.

93. "My Day," Sept. 27, 1941.

94. *This I Remember, supra*, 228–29.

95. *Ibid.*, 230.

96. *Ibid.*, 232.

97. *Roosevelt and Hopkins, supra*, 293.

98. *Ibid.*, 377.

99. *F.D.R. His Personal Letters 1928–1945, supra*, Vol. II, 1239.

100. *Franklin Roosevelt at Warm Springs, Georgia–Some Chronological Land Marks, supra*, 64.

101. *White House Diary, supra*, 272.

102. *Ibid.*, 271.

103. *Ibid.*, 194.

CHAPTER THIRTEEN

1. *F.D.R.–My Boss, supra*, 249, 242, 257.

2. *Ibid.*, 249.

3. *Ibid.*, 342–43.

4. *This I Remember, supra*, 330.

5. *Off the Record with FDR–1942–1945, supra*, 264.

6. *Ibid.*, 265.

7. *Affectionately, F.D.R., supra*, 352.

8. *Off the Record with FDR–1942–1945, supra*, 267.

9. *Ibid.*, 267.

10. Interviews with William D. Hassett, Grace Tully, Roberta Barrows and others.

11. *Off the Record with FDR–1942–1945, supra*, 1.

12. Manuscript of William D. Hassett, 111, 112.

13. *Off the Record with FDR–1942–1945, supra*, 268.

14. Interviews with William D. Hassett.

15. *The Democratic Roosevelt, supra*, 66.

16. *Ibid.*, 529.

17. *Ibid.*, 529.

18. *Affectionately, F.D.R., supra,* subtitle.

19. *Ibid.*, 312.

20. *Ibid.*, 317.

21. *Ibid.*, 307.

22. *Ibid.*, 236.

23. *Ibid.*, 236.

24. Hyde Park Library files.

25. *Ibid.*

26. *F.D.R.—My Boss, supra,* 326.

27. *Off the Record with FDR—1942–1945, supra,* 196.

28. *F.D.R.—My Boss, supra,* 328.

29. *F.D.R. His Personal Letters 1928–1945, supra,* Vol. II, 1101–2.

30. *F.D.R.—My Boss, supra,* 328.

31. Hyde Park Library, Memo to F.D.R., White House files 5/12/43.

32. *Off the Record with FDR—1942–1945, supra,* 194.

33. F.D.R. to Avinoff, July 29, 1943.

34. Minnie Mercer Pension File, *supra.*

35. Wesley Pruden, Jr., in *The National Observer,* Aug. 22, 1966.

36. Interviews with Michael F. Reilly and other Secret Service men.

37. *Off the Record with FDR—1942–1945, supra,* 241.

38. *This I Remember, supra,* 328.

39. Interview with Bernard M. Baruch.

40. *The New York Times,* obituary, Mar. 21, 1944.

41. *Off the Record with FDR—1942–1945, supra,* 241.

42. *Ibid.*, 111.

43. Interview with Alice Longworth.

44. Turnley Walker, *Roosevelt and the Warm Springs Story* (New York 1953), 266.

45. *Affectionately, F.D.R., supra,* 348–49.

46. Confidential sources.

47. F.D.R. to Mrs. Rupert C. King, Dec. 21, 1944.

48. *Off the Record with FDR—1942–1945, supra,* 273 n.

49. *Ibid.*, 294.

50. *Ibid.*, 294.

51. *I Love a Roosevelt, supra,* 106–7.

52. Joseph N. Rosenau, editor, *The Roosevelt Treasury* (Garden City, N.Y. 1951), 166–69.

53. *Off the Record with FDR—1942–1945, supra,* 300.

54. *Ibid.,* 302.

55. Manuscript of William D. Hassett, 257.

56. *Off the Record with FDR—1942–1945, supra,* 295.

57. *This I Remember, supra,* 244.

58. *Ibid.,* 283, 285.

59. *Ibid.,* 338.

60. *Off the Record with FDR—1942–1945, supra,* 312.

61. *Ibid.,* 310.

62. *Ibid.,* 312.

63. *Affectionately, F.D.R., supra,* 354–55.

64. *Off the Record with FDR—1942–1945, supra,* 318.

65. *This I Remember, supra,* 342.

66. *Ibid.,* 343.

67. *Ibid.,* 343.

68. *Ibid.,* 343.

69. *Ibid.,* 343.

70. *Ibid.,* 343.

71. *Ibid.,* 343.

72. *Off the Record with FDR—1942–1945, supra,* 327.

73. Bernard Asbell, *When F.D.R. Died* (New York 1961), 15.

74. *Ibid.,* 22.

75. *War Letters of Morton Eustis, supra,* 27.

76. *Ibid.,* 202.

77. *When F.D.R. Died, supra,* 31; Manuscript of Bernard Asbell.

78. Report in research by Bernard Asbell.

79. *When F.D.R. Died, supra,* 31.

80. Report in research by Bernard Asbell.

81. *F.D.R.—My Boss, supra,* 360.

82. *Affectionately, F.D.R., supra,* 360.

83. *F.D.R.—My Boss, supra,* 360.

84. Frank Allcorn's papers, including this list, have been destroyed by fire.

85. *When F.D.R. Died, supra,* 36.

86. *Ibid.,* 36.

87. *Ibid.,* 37.

88. *Roosevelt and the Warm Springs Story, supra,* 291.

89. *This I Remember, supra,* 343.

90. *Mrs. R.—The Life of Eleanor Roosevelt, supra,* 309.

91. When F.D.R. Died, supra, 50.
92. This I Remember, supra, 343.
93. When F.D.R. Died, supra, 50.
94. This I Remember, supra, 344.
95. When F.D.R. Died, supra, 53.
96. This I Remember, supra, 344.
97. Ibid., 344.
98. Report in research by Bernard Asbell.
99. Off the Record with FDR—1942–1945, supra, 338.
100. Ibid., 333.
101. Interview with William D. Hassett.
102. Mrs. R.—The Life of Eleanor Roosevelt, supra, 310.
103. Confidential sources.
104. This I Remember, supra, 346.
105. The Captains and the Kings, supra, 248.
106. White House Diary, supra, 312.
107. Ibid., 311.
108. The New York Times, Apr. 21, 1945.
109. Ibid.
110. Ibid.

AFTERNOON BY ALLAMUCHY

1. William J. Miller, Henry Cabot Lodge, A Biography (New York 1967), 409.
2. Letters of Henry Adams 1892–1918, supra, 313.
3. Franklin D. Roosevelt's Little White House and Museum, a pamphlet, 22–23.
4. Ibid., 22–23.
5. "My Day," Apr. 19, 1945.
6. Ibid.
7. I Love a Roosevelt, supra, 153–54.
8. Eulogy delivered by Adlai Stevenson, Cathedral of St. John the Divine, Nov. 17, 1962.
9. I Love a Roosevelt, supra, 189.
10. Letter to author from Lyman Cotten, Jr., Jan. 29, 1967.
11. Letter to author from Mrs. Lyman Cotten, Oct. 25, 1958.
12. American Medical Directory, 1956 edition.
13. Letter to author from J. Metzler, supt. Arlington National Cemetery.
14. Minnie Mercer Pension File, supra.

15. "My Day," Aug. 12, 1948.
16. *Times-Leader and Evening News*, Wilkes-Barre, Pa., Aug. 2, 1948.

SOURCES AND ACKNOWLEDGMENTS

1. Letter to author from Dr. Elizabeth Drewry, Aug. 1, 1967.
2. Arthur S. Link, editor, *The Papers of Woodrow Wilson*, Vol. I—1856–1880 (Princeton, N.J. 1966), Foreword, vii–viii.

INDEX